1

**Original story by
Akira Kurosawa**

**Art by
Mizutaka Suhou**

**Translated and adapted by
Yoko Kubo**

**Lettered by
North Market Street Graphics**

Ballantine Books ★ New York

A Del Rey Manga/Kodansha Trade Paperback Original

Samurai 7 volume 1 copyright © 2004 by Akira Kurosawa/Shinobu Hashimoto/ Hideo Oguni/MICO · GDH · GONZO / © 2006 by Mizutaka Suhou
English translation copyright © 2009 by Akira Kurosawa

Published in the United States by Del Rey, an imprint of The Random House Publishing Group, a division of Random House, Inc., New York.

DEL REY is a registered trademark and the Del Rey colophon is a trademark of Random House, Inc.

Publication rights arranged through Kodansha Ltd.

First published in Japan in 2006 by Kodansha Ltd., Tokyo

ISBN 978-0-345-50183-7

Printed in the United States of America

www.delreymanga.com

9 8 7 6 5 4 3 2 1

Translator/adapter: Yoko Kubo
Lettering: North Market Street Graphics

CONTENTS

HONORIFICS EXPLAINED

Throughout the Del Rey Manga books, you will find Japanese honorifics left intact in the translations. For those not familiar with how the Japanese use honorifics and, more important, how they differ from American honorifics, we present this brief overview..

Politeness has always been a critical facet of Japanese culture. Ever since the feudal era, when Japan was a highly stratified society, use of honorifics—which can be defined as polite speech that indicates relationship or status—has played an essential role in the Japanese language. When addressing someone in Japanese, an honorific usually takes the form of a suffix attached to one's name (example: "Asuna-san"), is used as a title at the end of one's name, or appears in place of the name itself (example: "Negi-sensei," or simply "Sensei!").

Honorifics can be expressions of respect or endearment. In the context of manga and anime, honorifics give insight into the nature of the relationship between characters. Many English translations leave out these important honorifics and therefore distort the feel of the original Japanese. Because Japanese honorifics contain nuances that English honorifics lack, it is our policy at Del Rey not to translate them. Here, instead, is a guide to some of the honorifics you may encounter in Del Rey Manga.

-san: This is the most common honorific and is equivalent to Mr., Miss, Ms., or Mrs. It is the all-purpose honorific and can be used in any situation where politeness is required.

-sama: This is one level higher than "-san" and is used to confer great respect.

-dono: This comes from the word "tono," which means "lord." It is an even higher level than "-sama" and confers utmost respect.

-kun: This suffix is used at the end of boys' names to express familiarity or endearment. It is also sometimes used by men among friends, or when addressing someone younger or of a lower station.

-chan: This is used to express endearment, mostly toward girls. It is also used for little boys, pets, and even among lovers. It gives a sense of childish cuteness.

Bozu: This is an informal way to refer to a boy, similar to the English terms "kid" and "squirt."

Sempai/
Senpai: This title suggests that the addressee is one's senior in a group or organization. It is most often used in a school setting, where underclassmen refer to their upperclassmen as "sempai." It can also be used in the workplace, such as when a newer employee addresses an employee who has seniority in the company.

Kohai: This is the opposite of "sempai" and is used toward underclassmen in school or newcomers in the workplace. It connotes that the addressee is of a lower station.

Sensei: Literally meaning "one who has come before," this title is used for teachers, doctors, or masters of any profession or art.

-[blank]: This is usually forgotten in these lists, but it is perhaps the most significant difference between Japanese and English. The lack of honorific means that the speaker has permission to address the person in a very intimate way. Usually, only family, spouses, or very close friends have this kind of permission. Known as *yobisute*, it can be gratifying when someone who has earned the intimacy starts to call one by one's name without an honorific. But when that intimacy hasn't been earned, it can be very insulting.

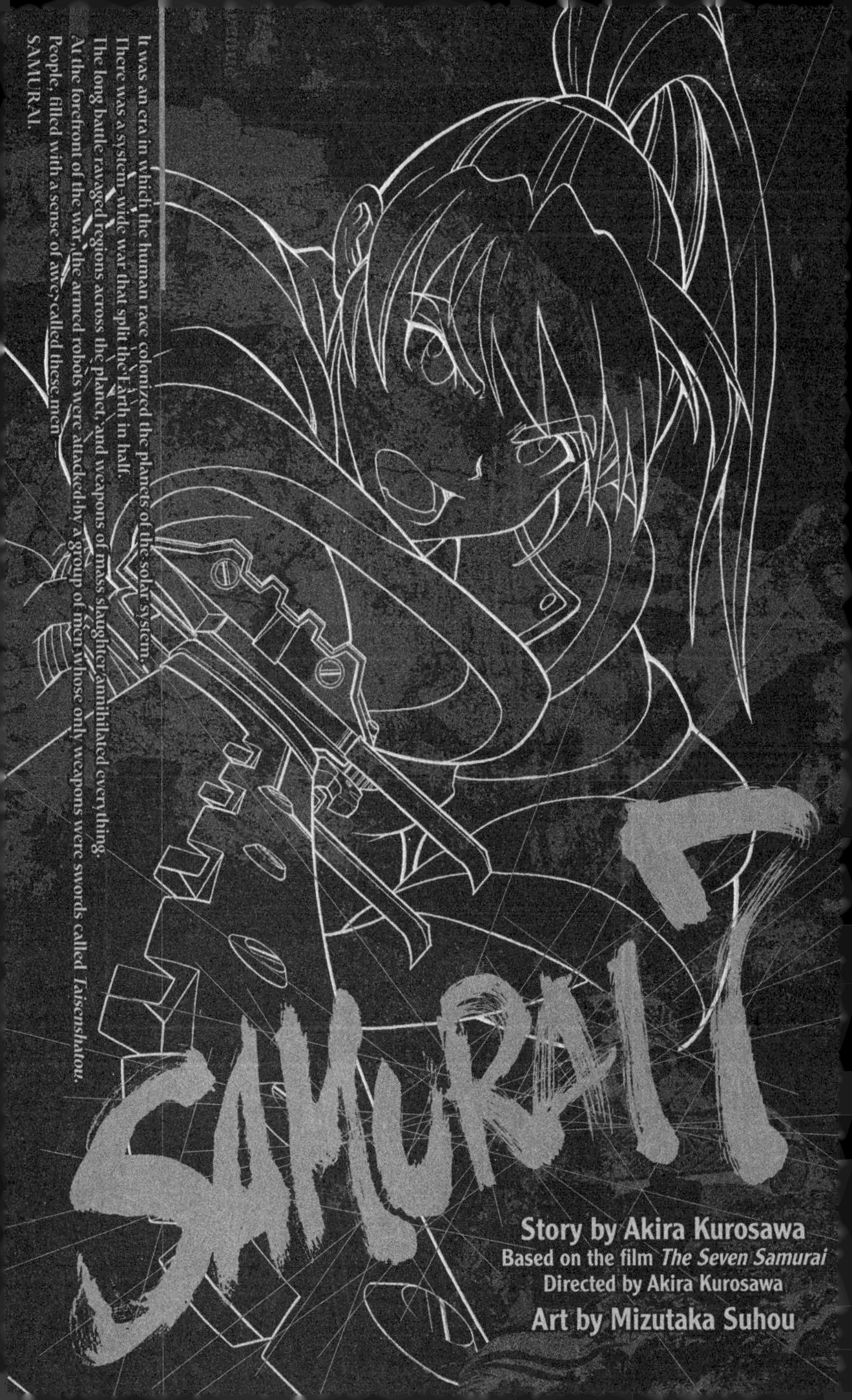

It was an era in which the human race colonized the planets of the solar system.
There was a system-wide war that split the Earth in half.
The long battle ravaged regions across the planet, and weapons of mass slaughter annihilated everything.
At the forefront of the war, the armed robots were attacked by a group of men whose only weapons were swords called *Taisenshatou*.
People, filled with a sense of awe, called these men
SAMURAI.

SAMURAI 7

Story by Akira Kurosawa
Based on the film *The Seven Samurai*
Directed by Akira Kurosawa
Art by Mizutaka Suhou

SAMURAI 7

Shichiroji   Katsushiro   Kyuzo
Rambei   Kikuchiyo   Gorobei
                Heihachi

The long-ago war left all humanity's colonized lands in ruins. The only weapon drawn to and against the surviving cyborgs of that war were the legendary warriors of the sword who feared nothing. These immortalized protectors of the weak were called SAMURAI.

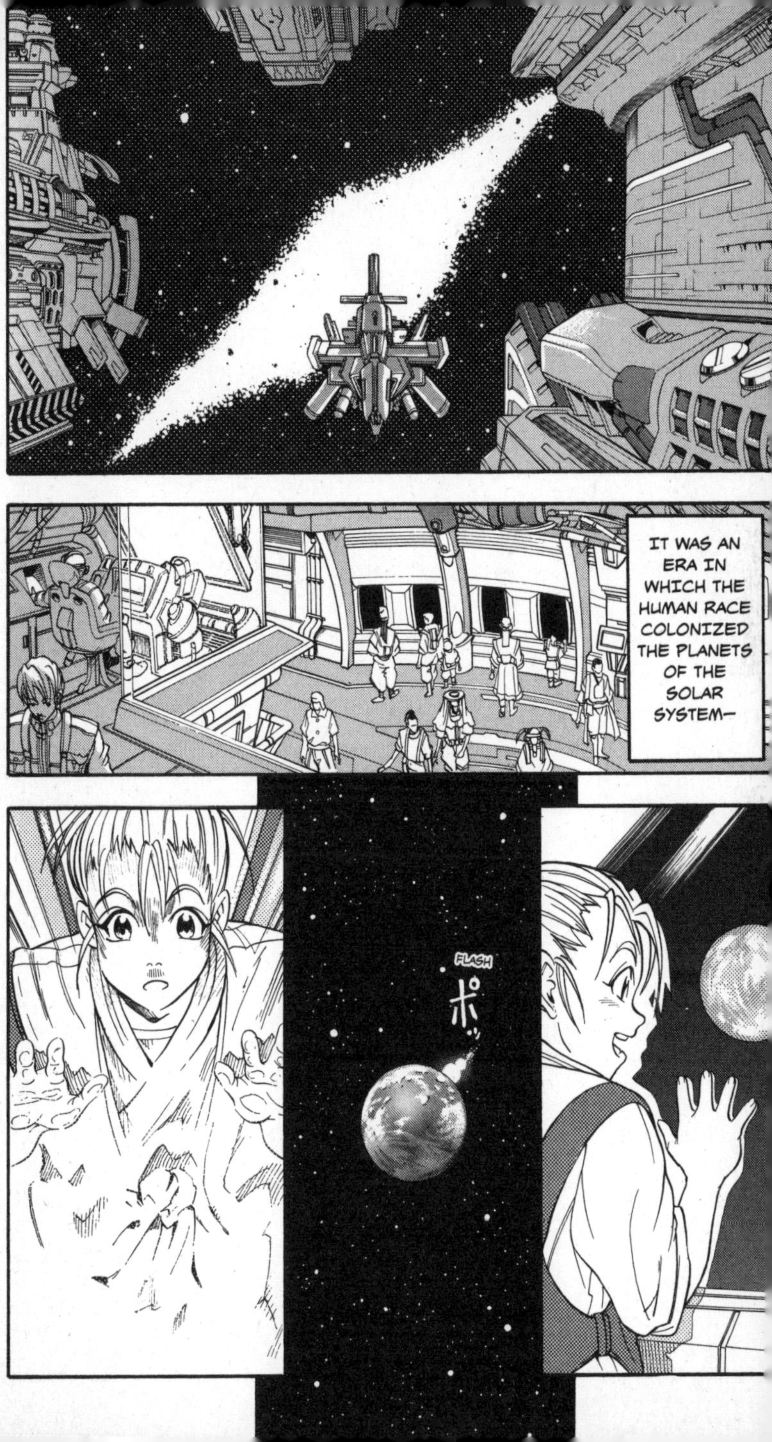
IT WAS AN ERA IN WHICH THE HUMAN RACE COLONIZED THE PLANETS OF THE SOLAR SYSTEM—
FLASH
ポッ

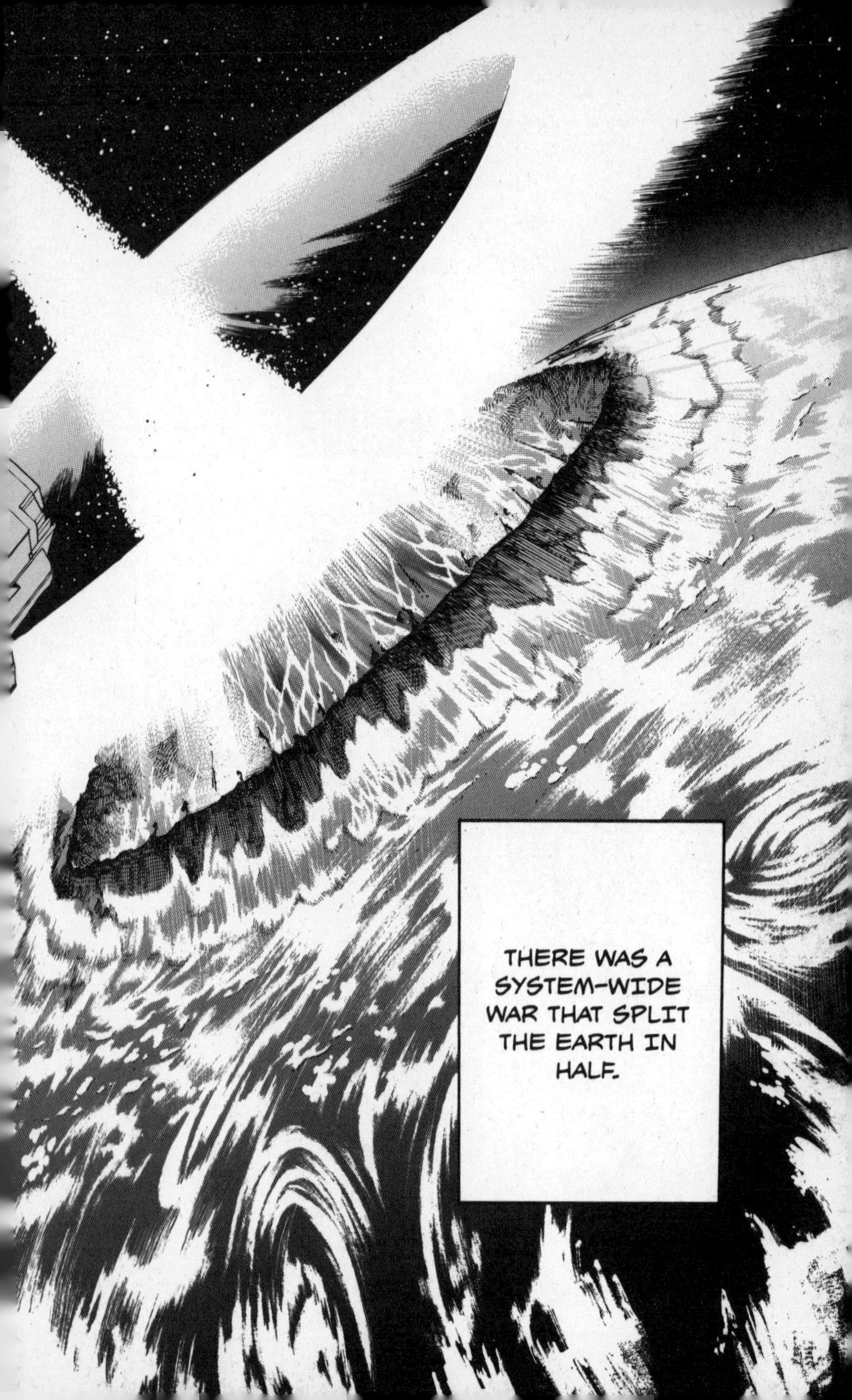
THERE WAS A SYSTEM-WIDE WAR THAT SPLIT THE EARTH IN HALF.

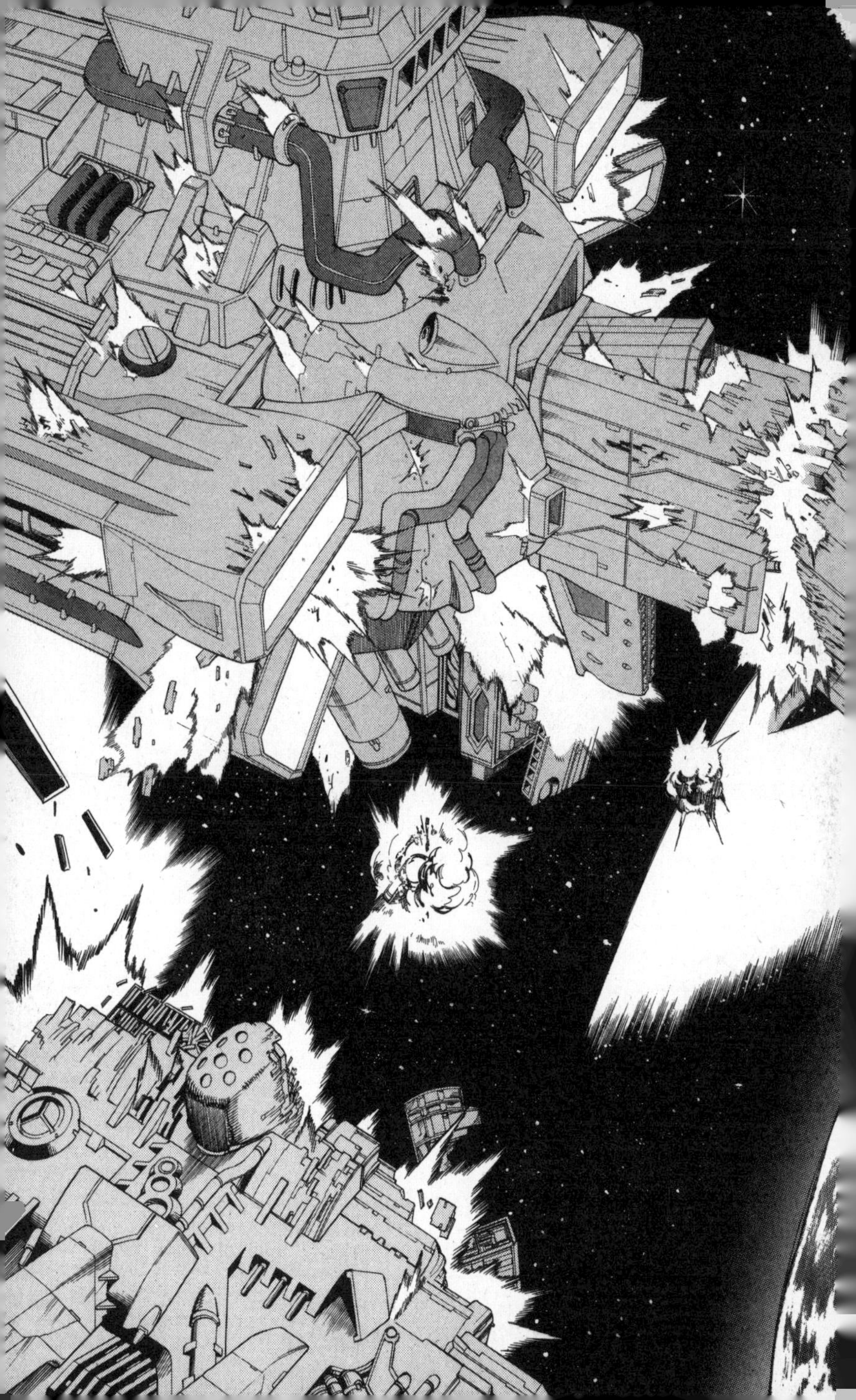

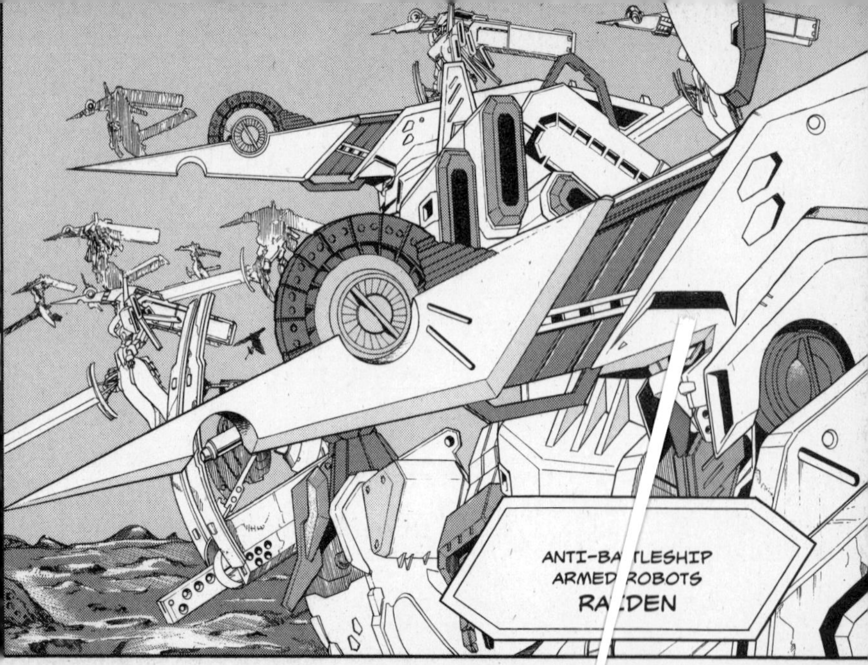
ANTI-BATTLESHIP ARMED ROBOTS RAIDEN

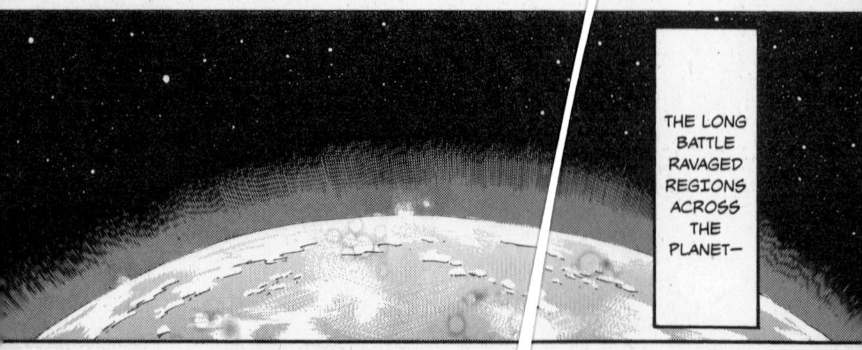
THE LONG BATTLE RAVAGED REGIONS ACROSS THE PLANET—

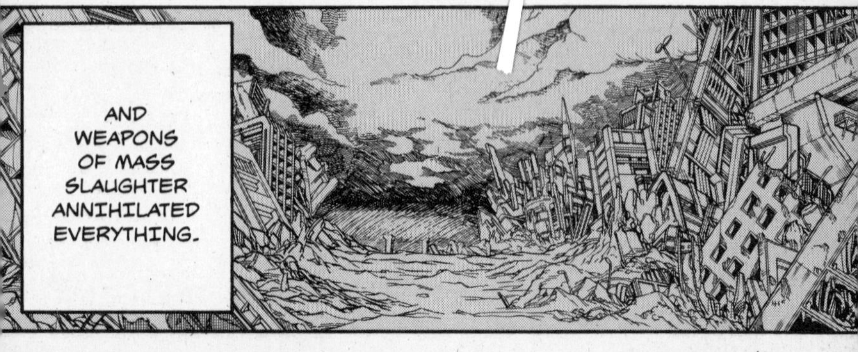
AND WEAPONS OF MASS SLAUGHTER ANNIHILATED EVERYTHING.

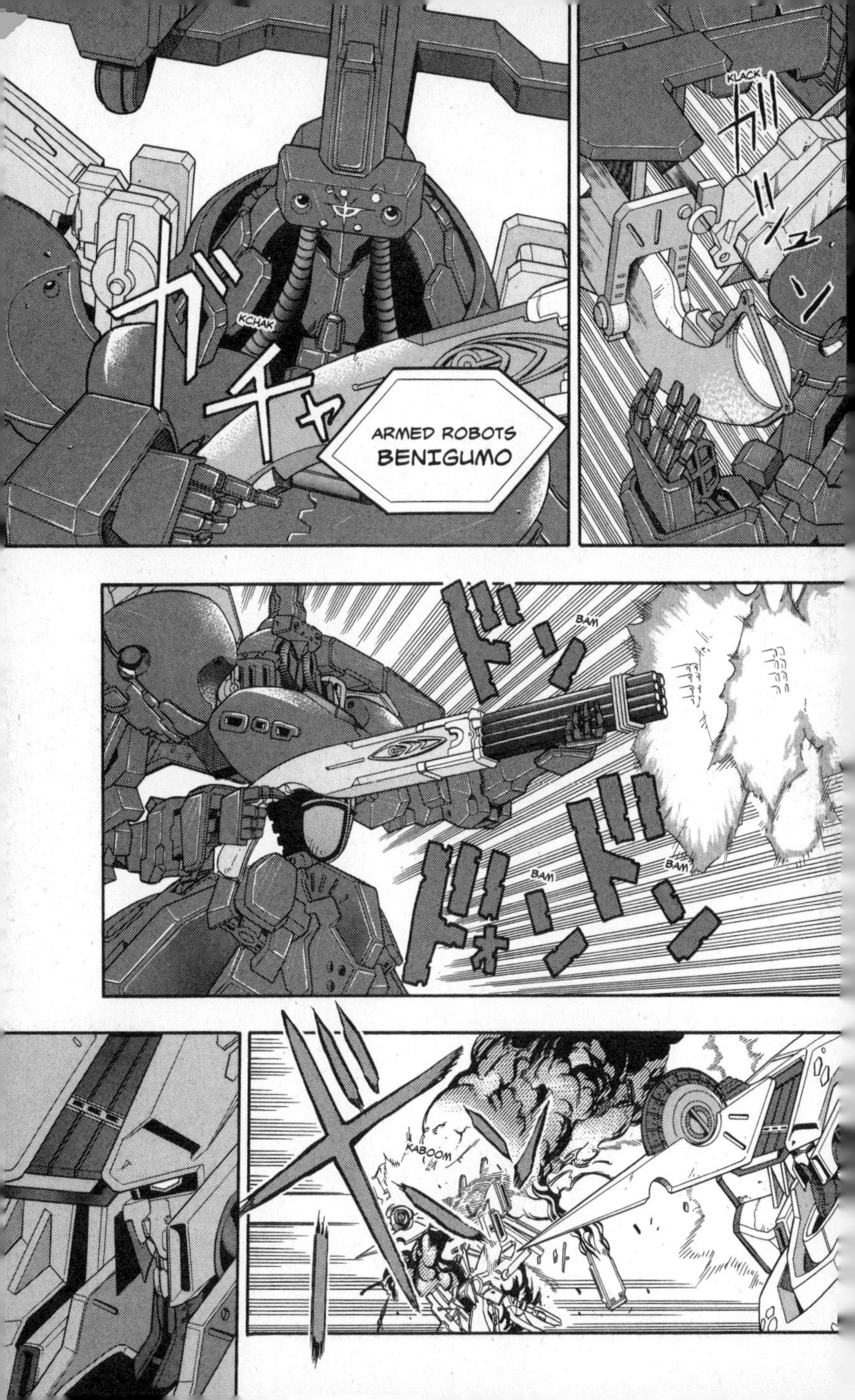
KLACK
KCHAK
ARMED ROBOTS BENIGUMO
BAM
BAM
BAM
KABOOM

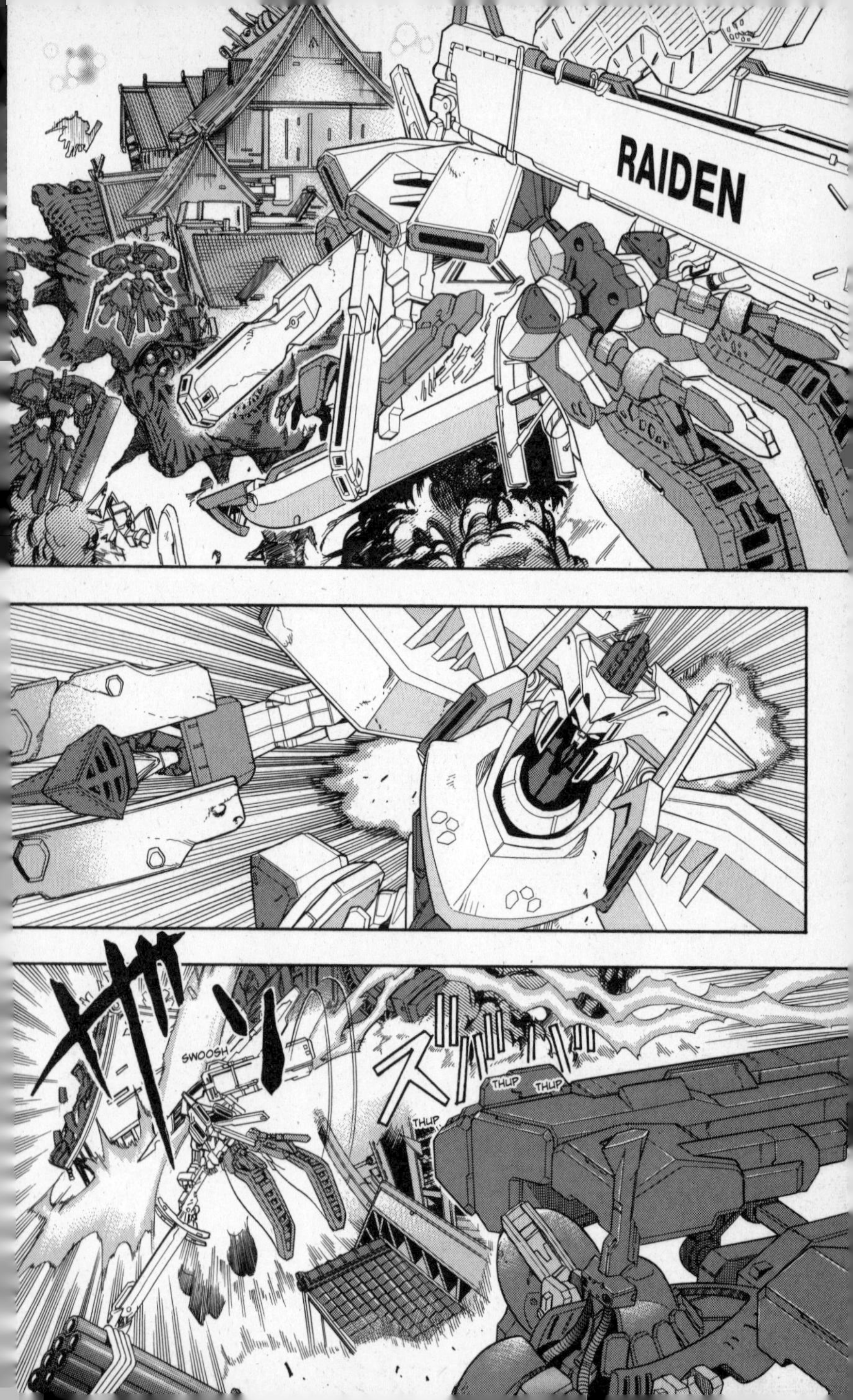
RAIDEN
THUP
THUP
THUP
SWOOSH

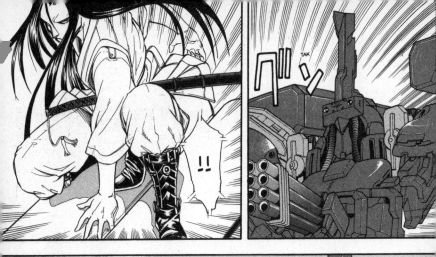

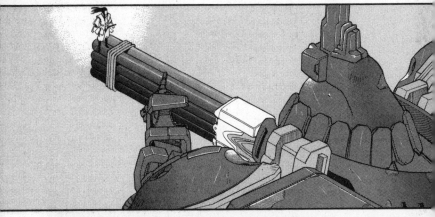

AT THE FOREFRONT OF THE WAR,
THE ARMED ROBOTS WERE ATTACKED BY
A GROUP OF MEN...

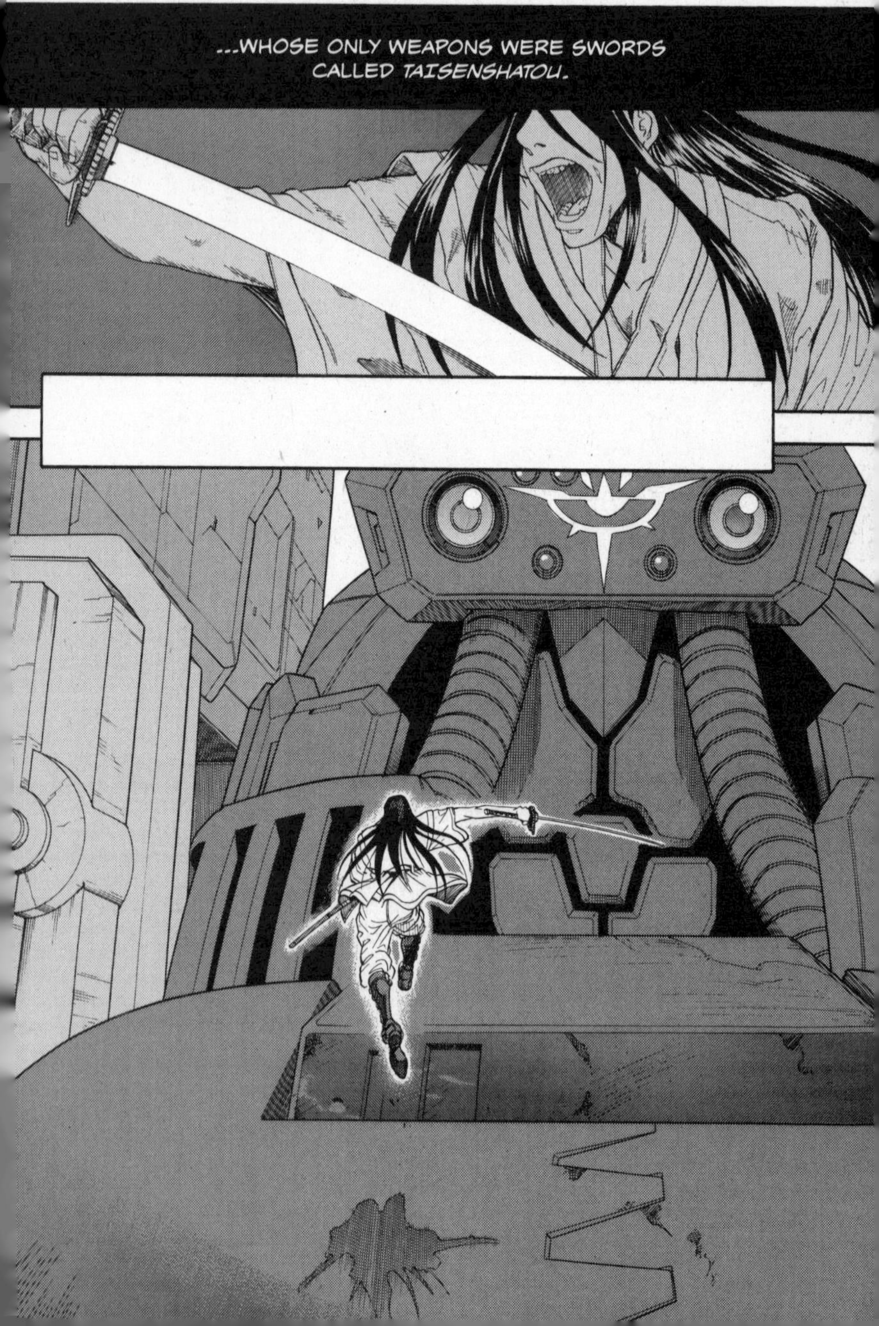
...WHOSE ONLY WEAPONS WERE SWORDS CALLED TAISENSHATOU.

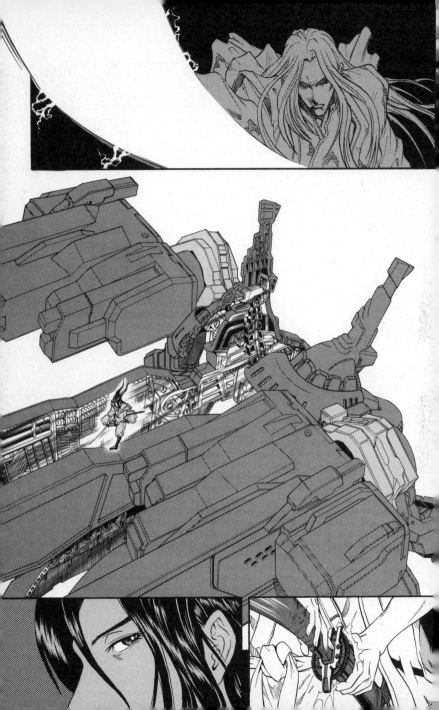

"SAMURAI"...

Art/ MIZUTAKA SUHOU

PEOPLE, FILLED WITH A SENSE
OF AWE, CALLED THESE MEN—

Chapter 1 – Katsushiro Trembles!

Story/ AKIRA KUROSAWA
(Based on the film *The Seven Samurai*)

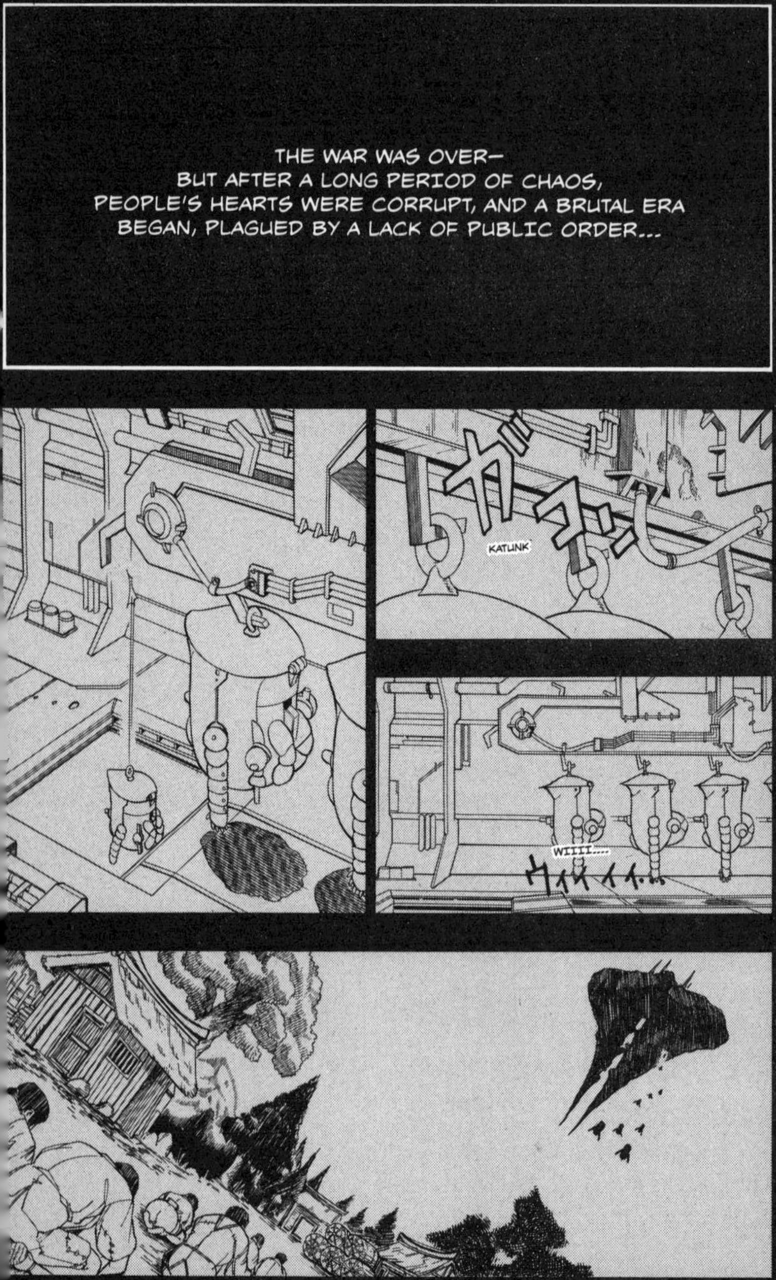
THE WAR WAS OVER—
BUT AFTER A LONG PERIOD OF CHAOS,
PEOPLE'S HEARTS WERE CORRUPT, AND A BRUTAL ERA
BEGAN, PLAGUED BY A LACK OF PUBLIC ORDER...
KATUNK
WIIII....

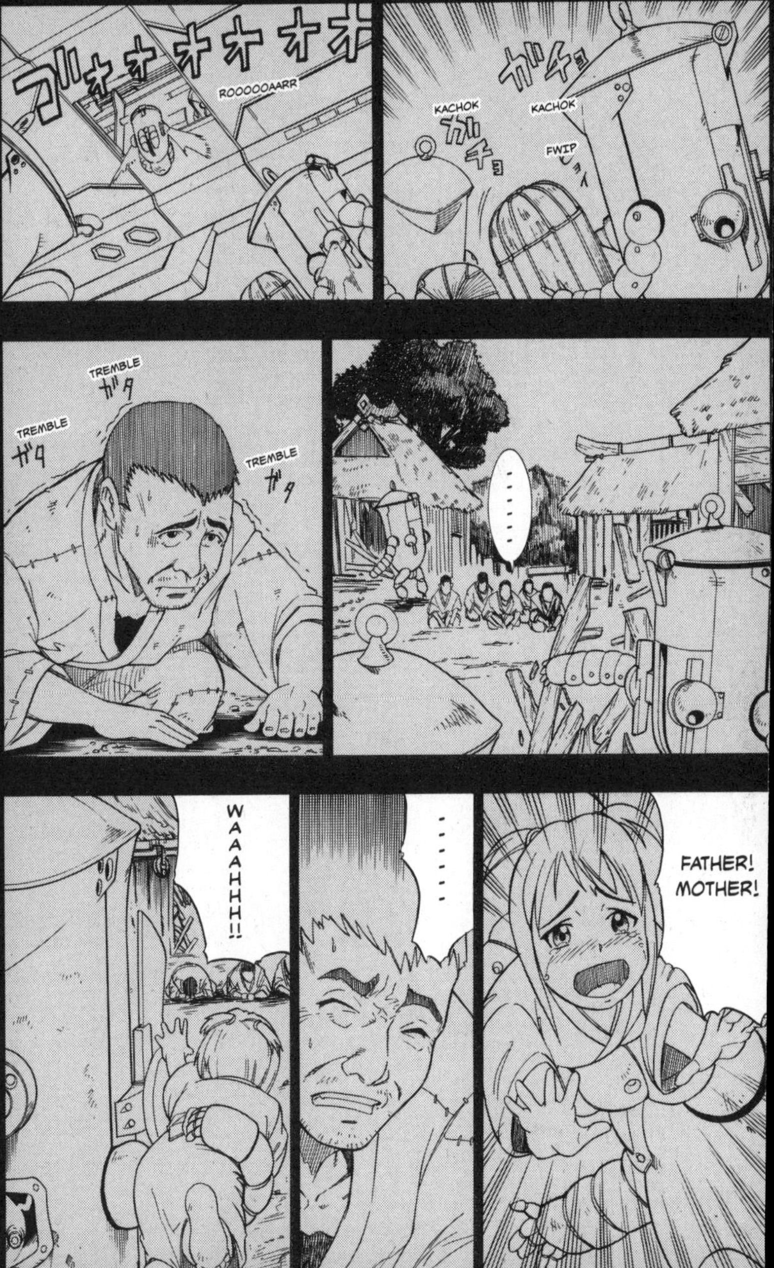

KACHOK
KACHOK
FWIP
ROOOOOAARR
......
TREMBLE
TREMBLE
TREMBLE
FATHER! MOTHER!
......
WAAAAHHH!!

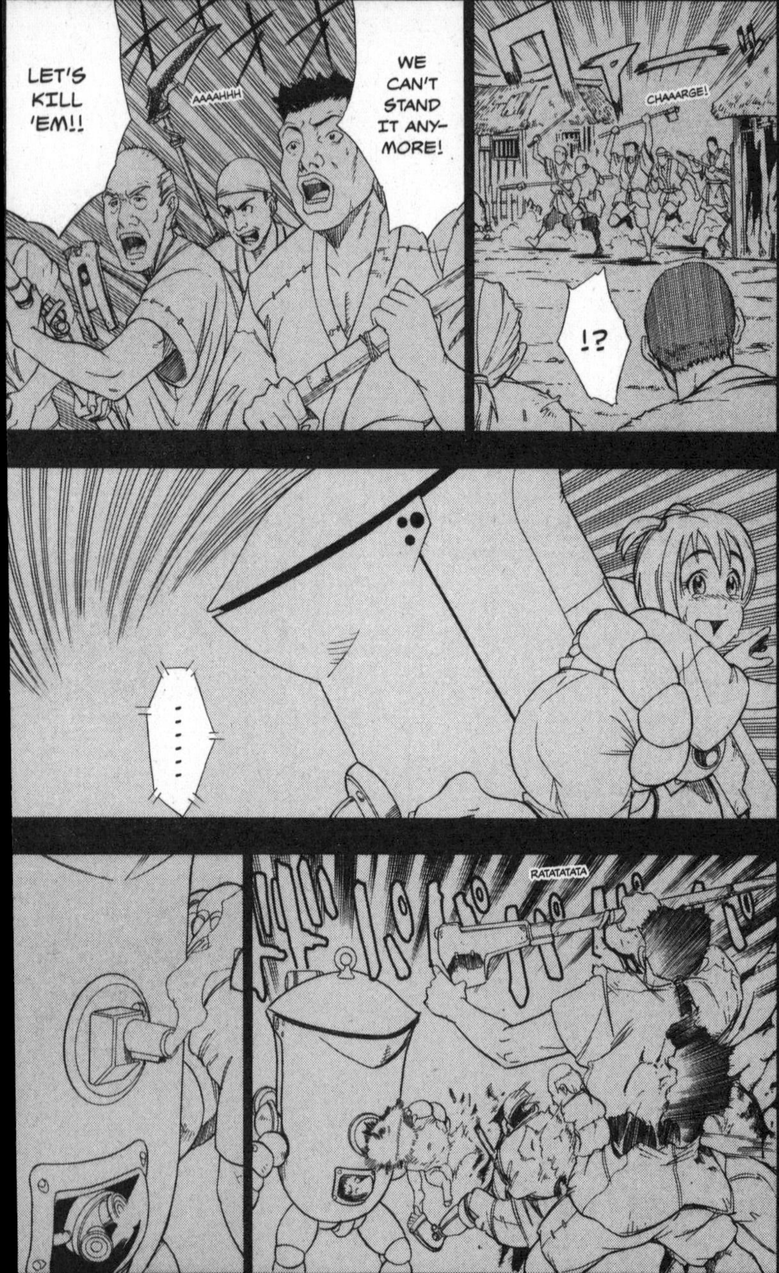
CHAAARGE!
!?
WE CAN'T STAND IT ANY-MORE!
AAAAHHH
LET'S KILL 'EM!!
......
RATATATATA

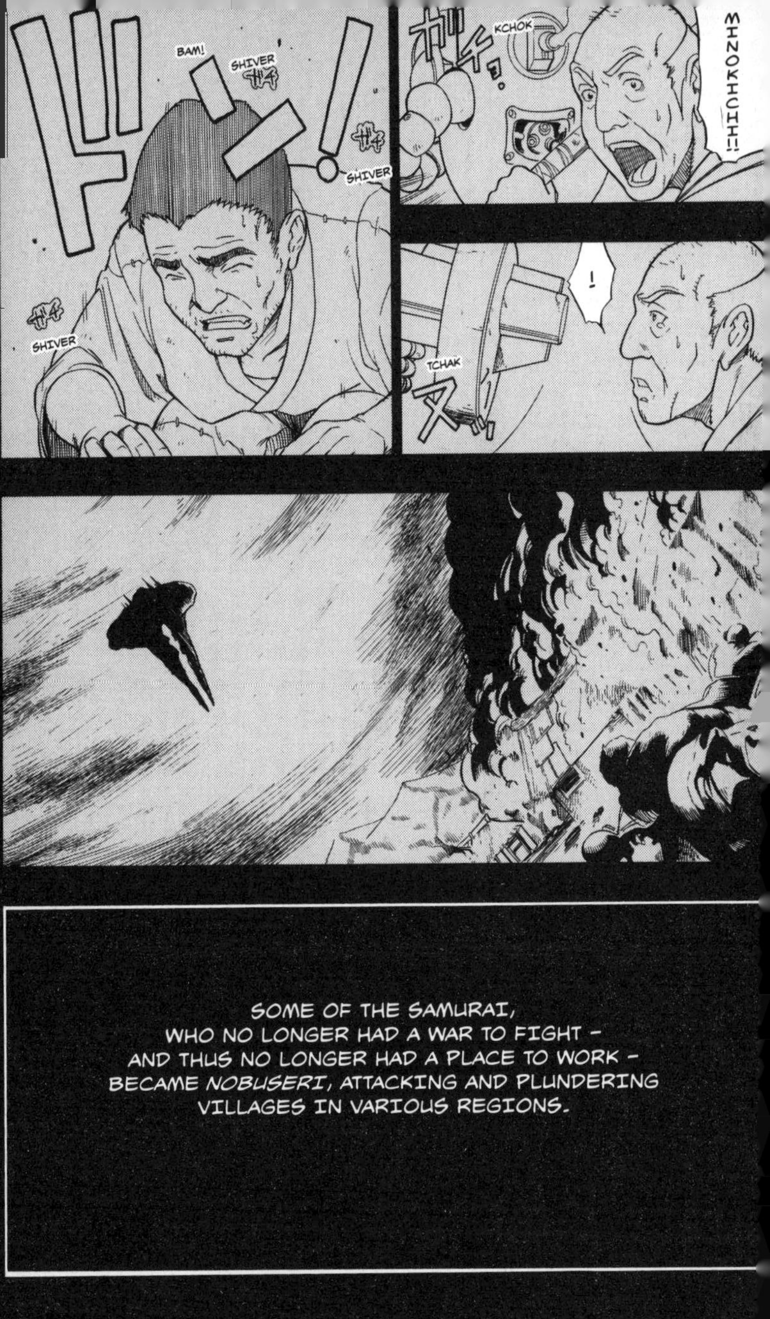
KCHOK
!
TCHAK
BAM!
SHIVER
SHIVER
SHIVER
SOME OF THE SAMURAI,
WHO NO LONGER HAD A WAR TO FIGHT -
AND THUS NO LONGER HAD A PLACE TO WORK -
BECAME *NOBUSERI*, ATTACKING AND PLUNDERING
VILLAGES IN VARIOUS REGIONS.

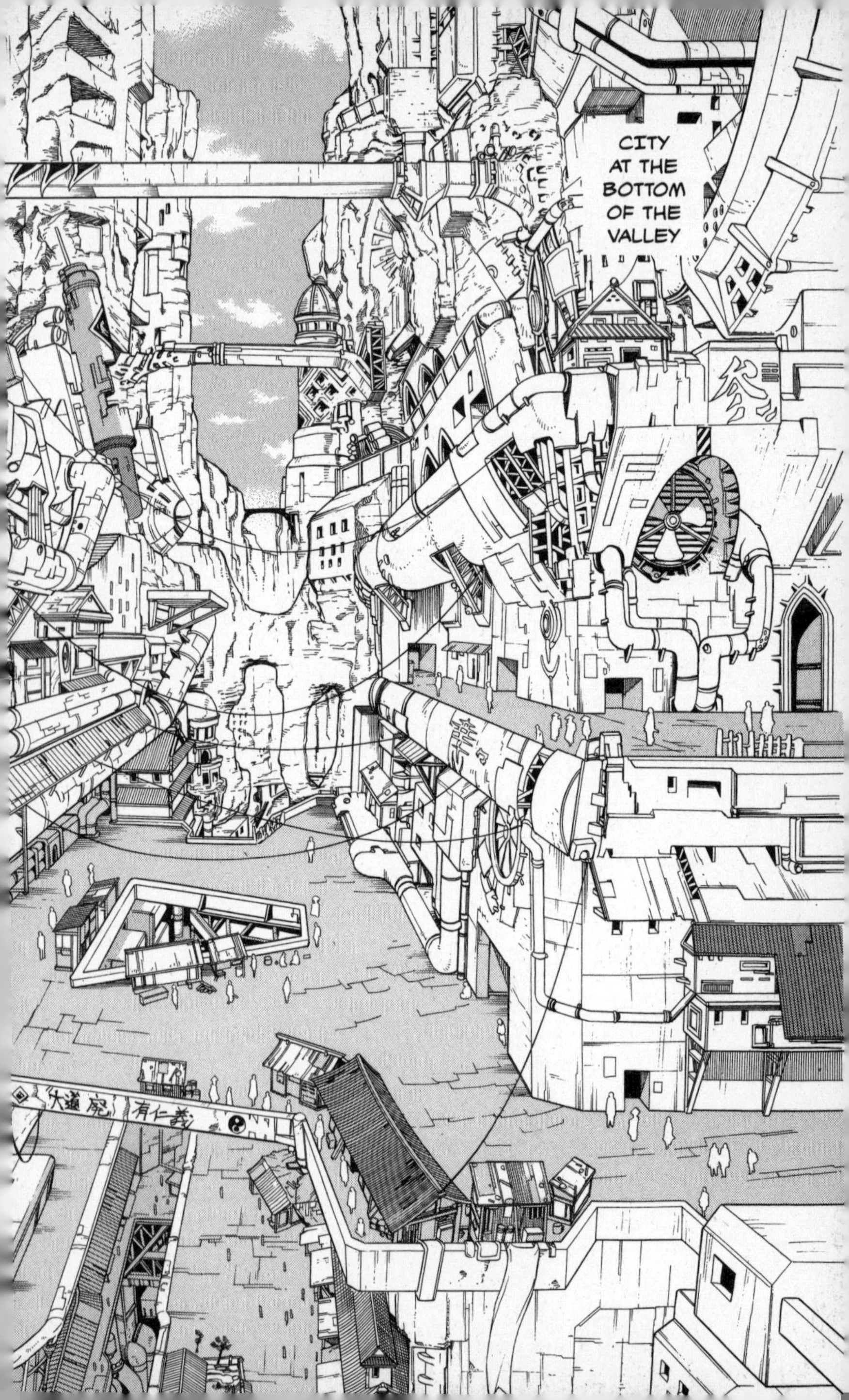
CITY AT THE BOTTOM OF THE VALLEY

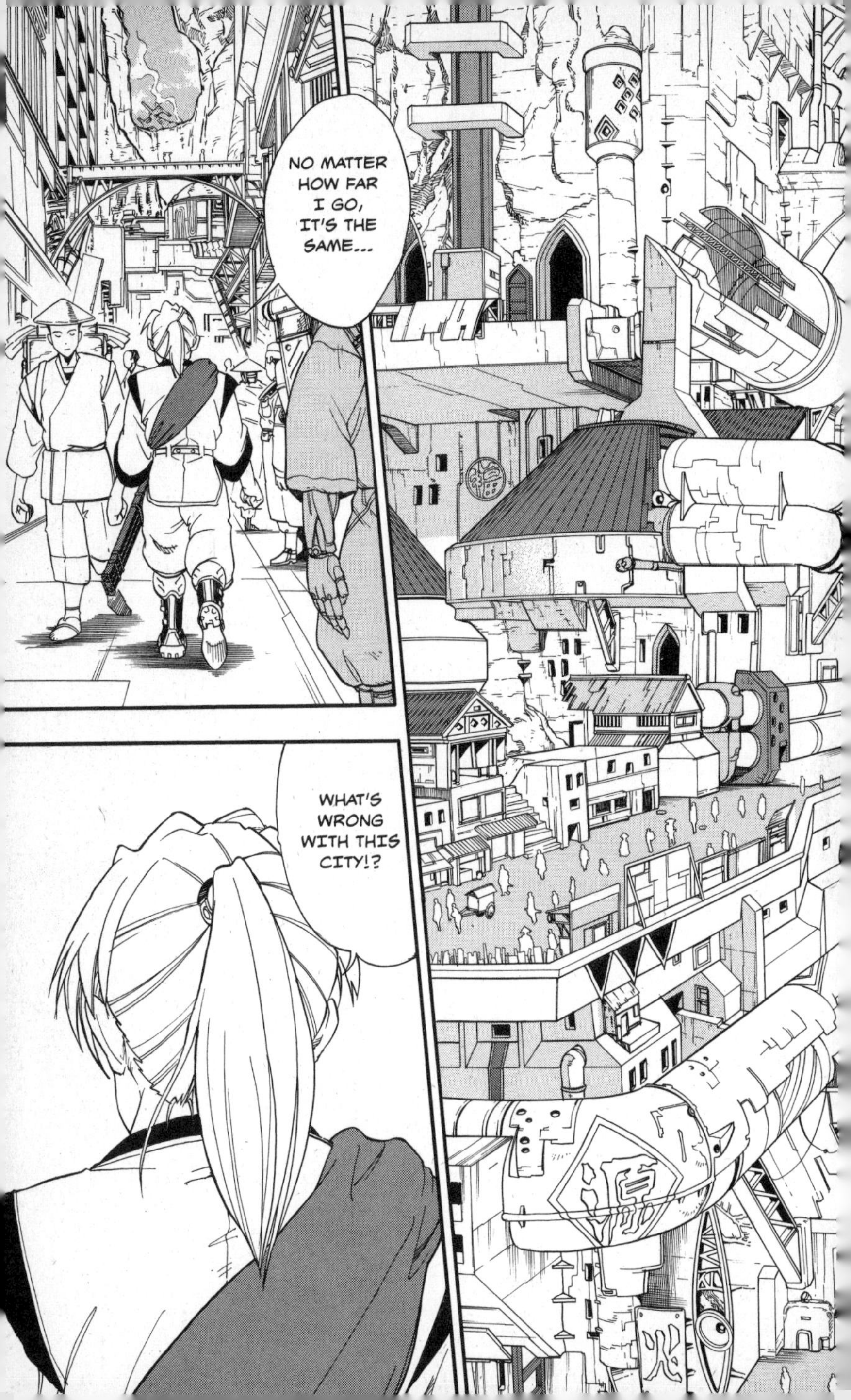
NO MATTER HOW FAR I GO, IT'S THE SAME...
WHAT'S WRONG WITH THIS CITY!?

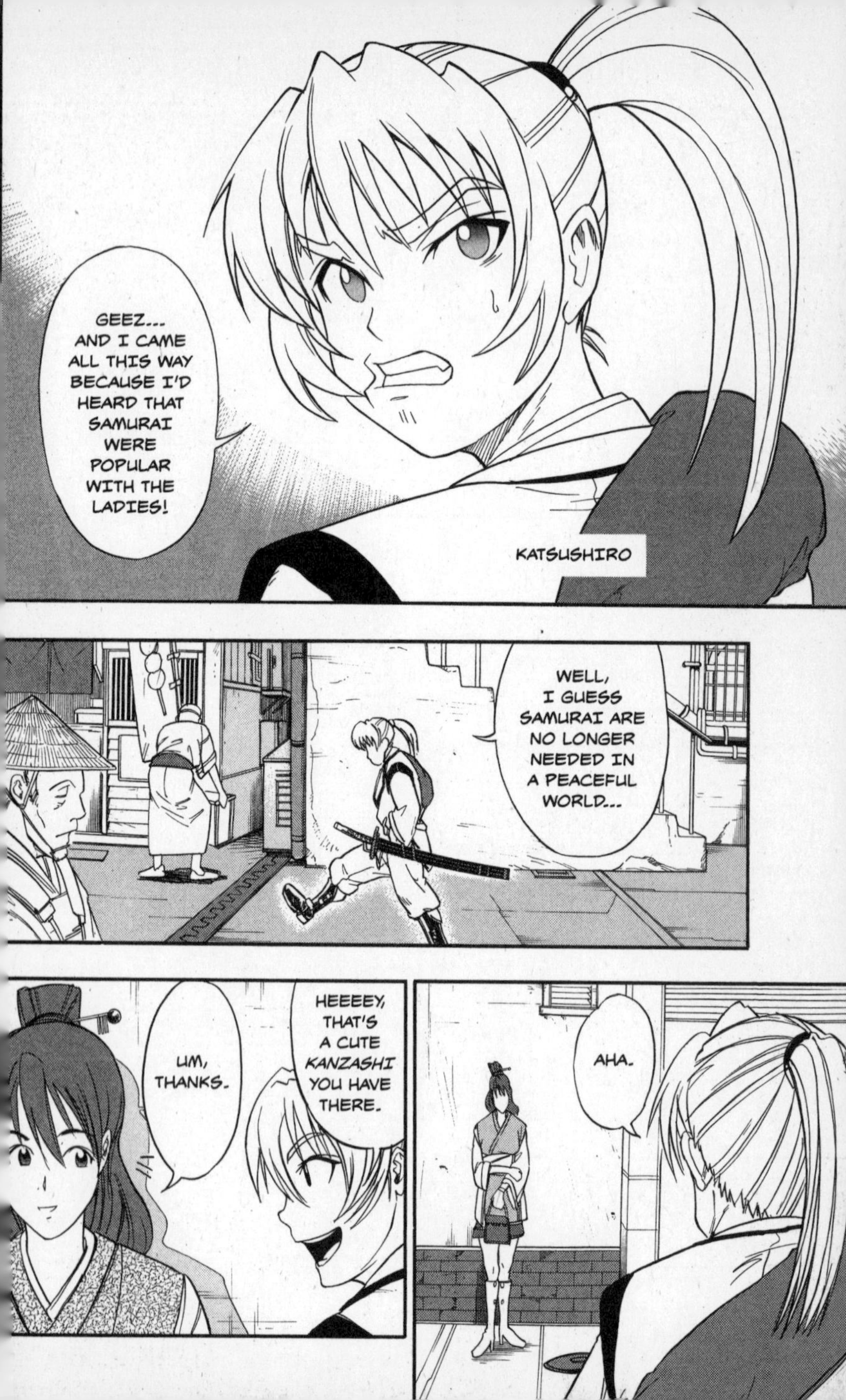
GEEZ... AND I CAME ALL THIS WAY BECAUSE I'D HEARD THAT SAMURAI WERE POPULAR WITH THE LADIES!
KATSUSHIRO
WELL, I GUESS SAMURAI ARE NO LONGER NEEDED IN A PEACEFUL WORLD...
AHA.
HEEEEY, THAT'S A CUTE KANZASHI YOU HAVE THERE.
UM, THANKS.

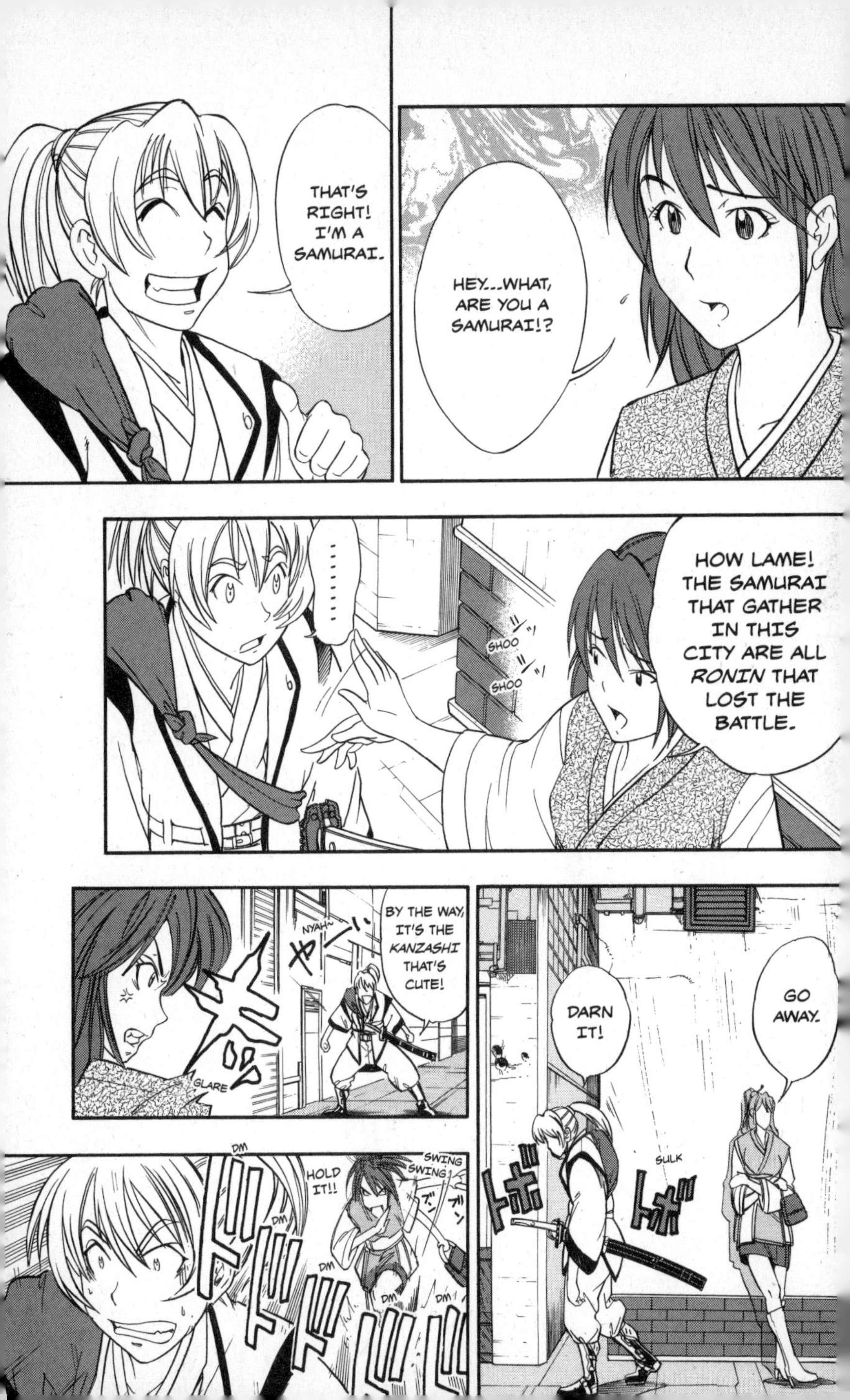
HEY...WHAT, ARE YOU A SAMURAI!?
THAT'S RIGHT! I'M A SAMURAI.
HOW LAME! THE SAMURAI THAT GATHER IN THIS CITY ARE ALL RONIN THAT LOST THE BATTLE.
SHOO
SHOO
......
GO AWAY.
DARN IT!
SULK
BY THE WAY, IT'S THE KANZASHI THAT'S CUTE!
NYAH~
GLARE
SWING SWING
HOLD IT!!
DM
DM
DM
DM
DM

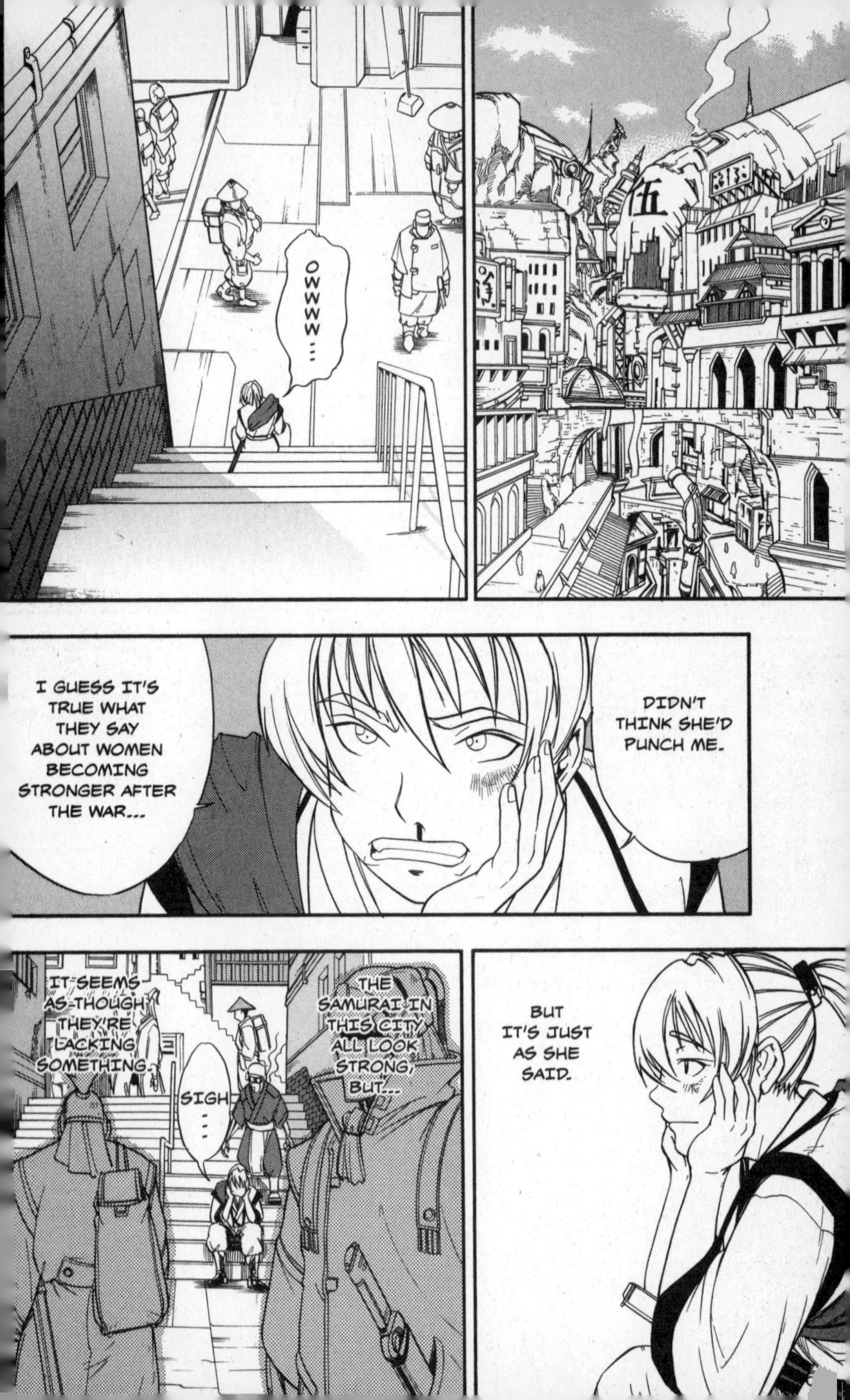
OWWWW...
DIDN'T THINK SHE'D PUNCH ME.
I GUESS IT'S TRUE WHAT THEY SAY ABOUT WOMEN BECOMING STRONGER AFTER THE WAR...
BUT IT'S JUST AS SHE SAID.
THE SAMURAI IN THIS CITY ALL LOOK STRONG, BUT...
IT SEEMS AS THOUGH THEY'RE LACKING SOMETHING.
SIGH...

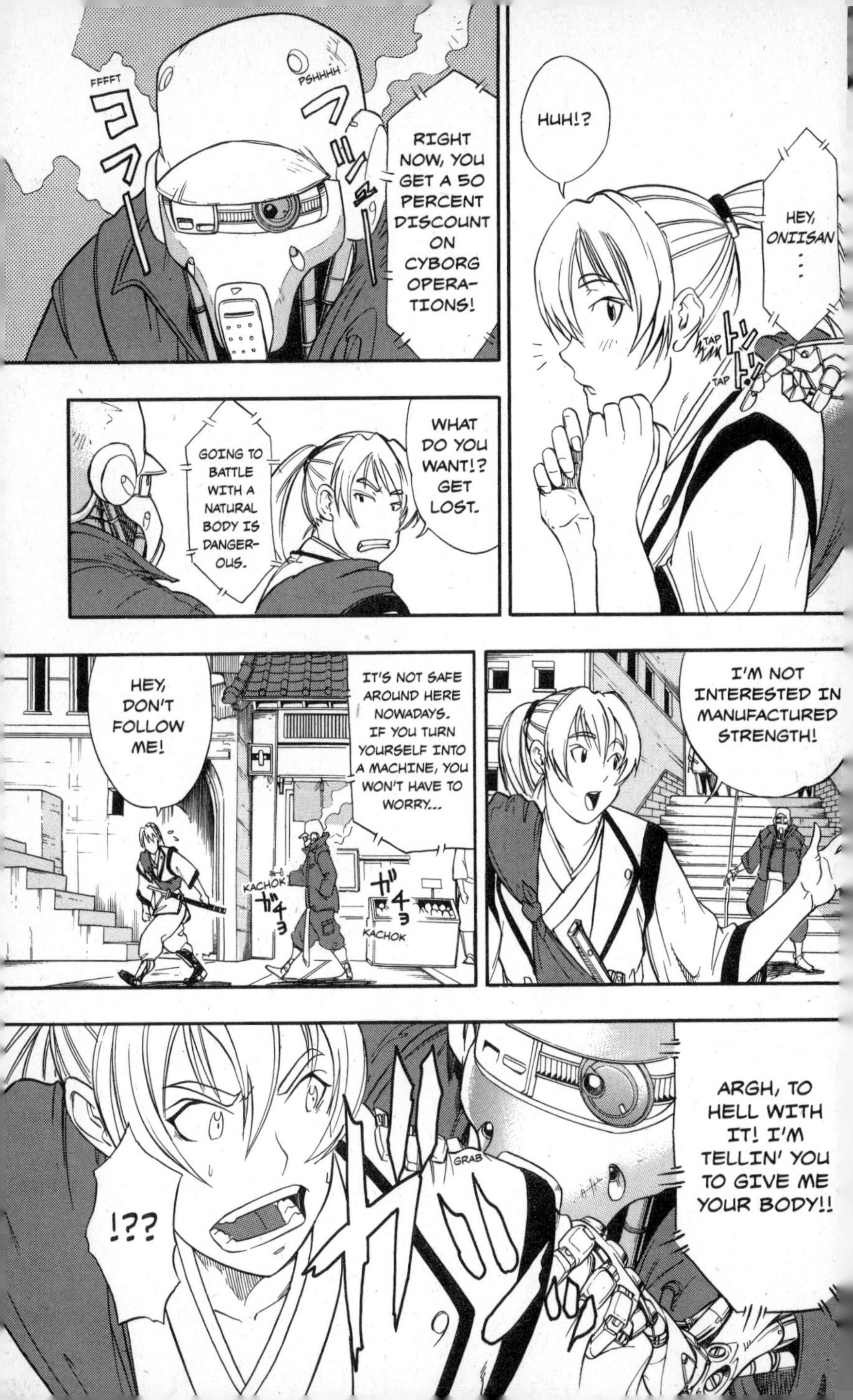
HUH!?
HEY, ONIISAN...
TAP
TAP
FFFFT
PSHHHH
RIGHT NOW, YOU GET A 50 PERCENT DISCOUNT ON CYBORG OPERATIONS!
WHAT DO YOU WANT!? GET LOST.
GOING TO BATTLE WITH A NATURAL BODY IS DANGEROUS.
I'M NOT INTERESTED IN MANUFACTURED STRENGTH!
IT'S NOT SAFE AROUND HERE NOWADAYS. IF YOU TURN YOURSELF INTO A MACHINE, YOU WON'T HAVE TO WORRY...
HEY, DON'T FOLLOW ME!
KACHOK
KACHOK
ARGH, TO HELL WITH IT! I'M TELLIN' YOU TO GIVE ME YOUR BODY!!
GRAB
!??

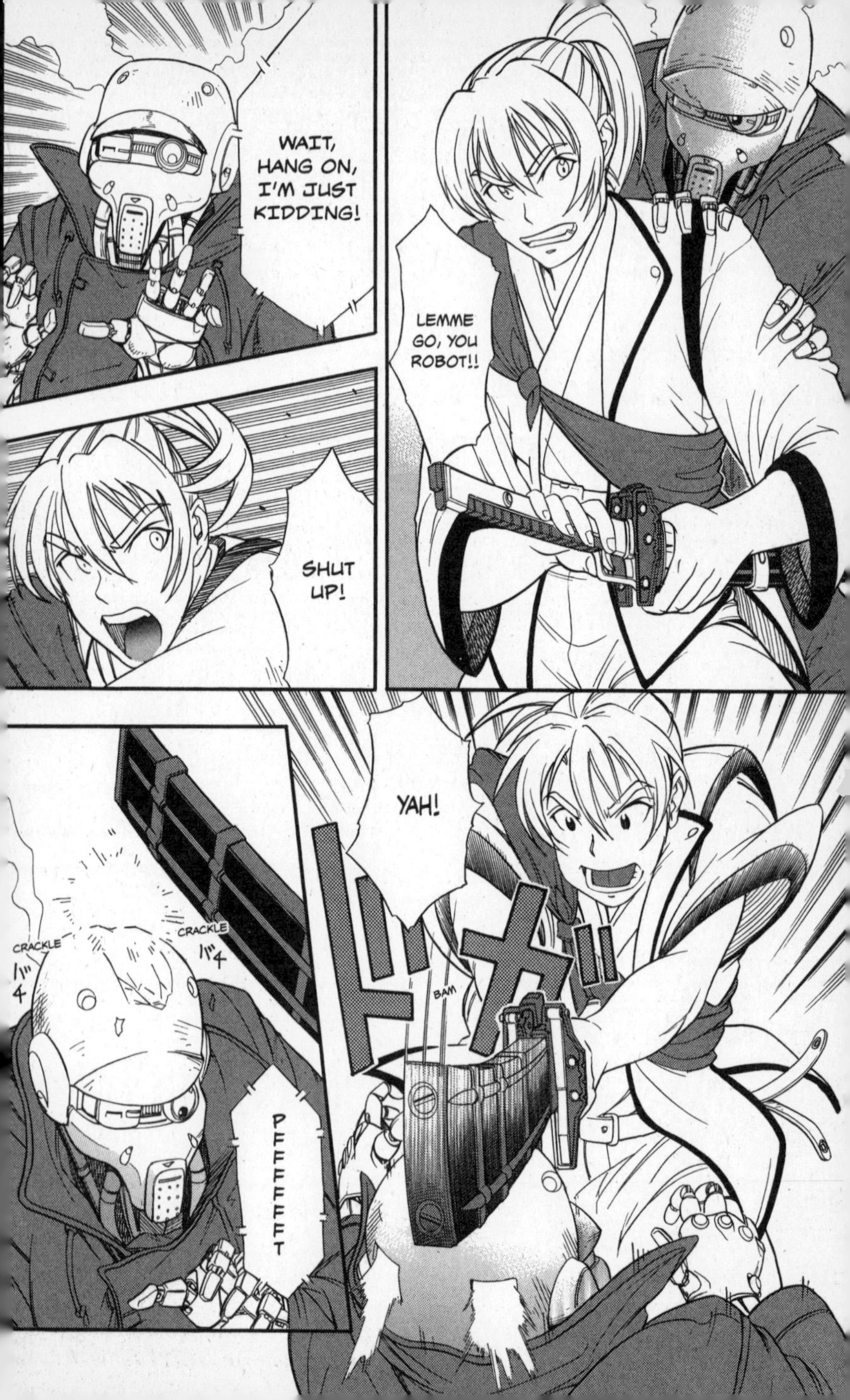
LEMME GO, YOU ROBOT!!
WAIT, HANG ON, I'M JUST KIDDING!
SHUT UP!
YAH!
BAM
CRACKLE
CRACKLE
PFFFFFFT

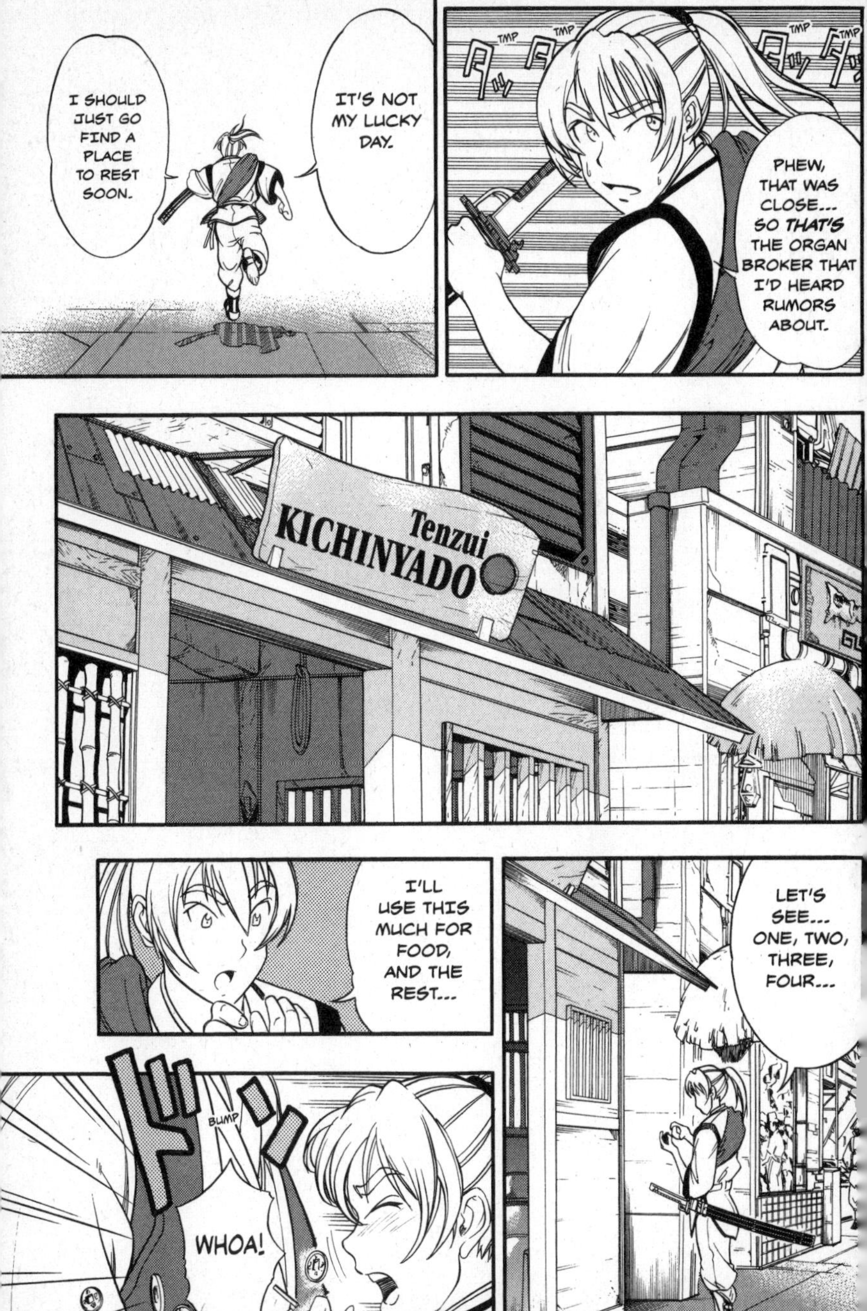
TMP
TMP
TMP
TMP
PHEW, THAT WAS CLOSE... SO THAT'S THE ORGAN BROKER THAT I'D HEARD RUMORS ABOUT.
IT'S NOT MY LUCKY DAY.
I SHOULD JUST GO FIND A PLACE TO REST SOON.
Tenzui
KICHINYADO
LET'S SEE... ONE, TWO, THREE, FOUR...
I'LL USE THIS MUCH FOR FOOD, AND THE REST...
BUMP
WHOA!

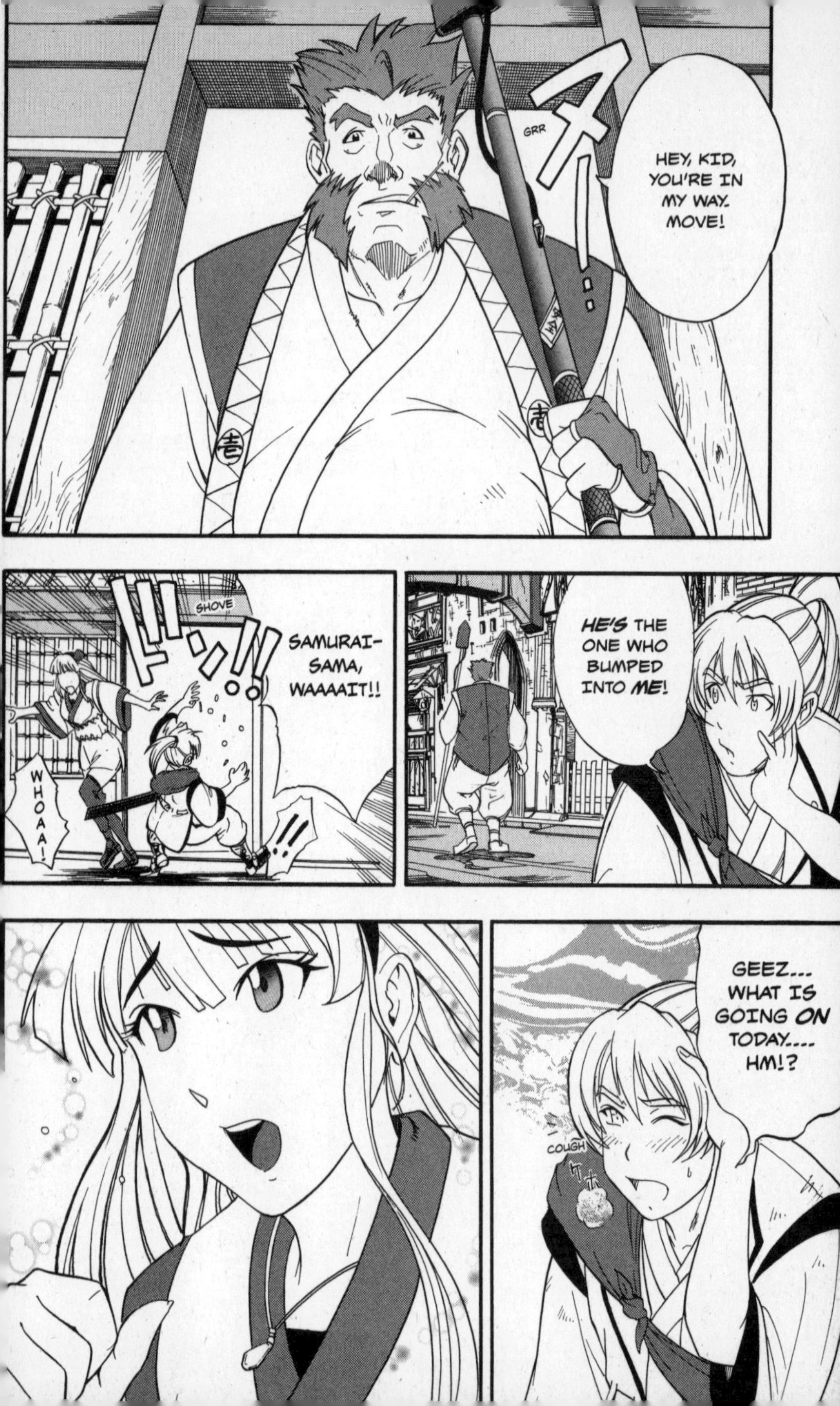
GRR
HEY, KID, YOU'RE IN MY WAY. MOVE!
HE'S THE ONE WHO BUMPED INTO ME!
SHOVE
SAMURAI-SAMA, WAAAAIT!!
WHOAAA!
GEEZ... WHAT IS GOING ON TODAY.... HM!?
COUGH

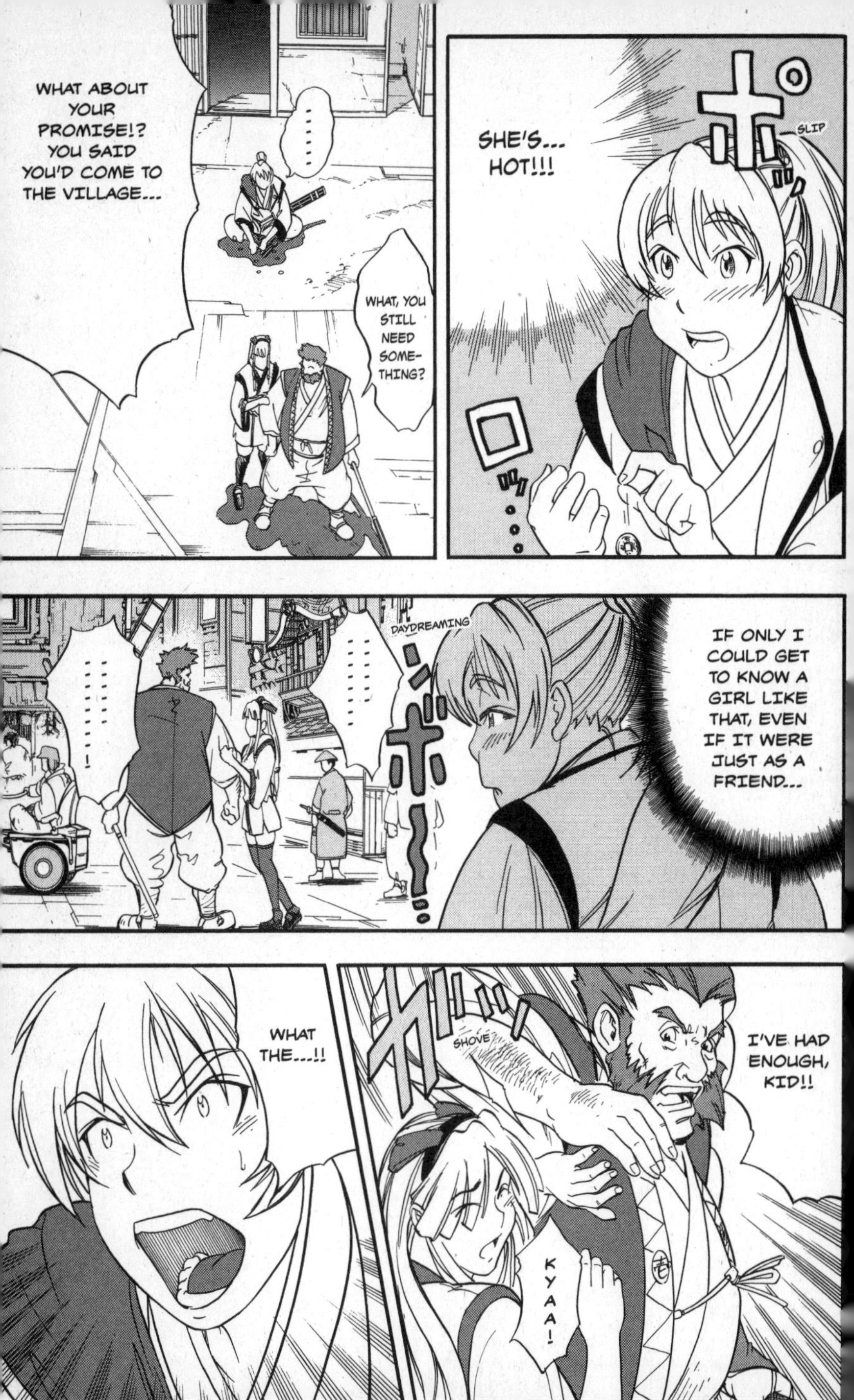
SLIP
SHE'S... HOT!!!
......
WHAT ABOUT YOUR PROMISE!? YOU SAID YOU'D COME TO THE VILLAGE...
WHAT, YOU STILL NEED SOMETHING?
IF ONLY I COULD GET TO KNOW A GIRL LIKE THAT, EVEN IF IT WERE JUST AS A FRIEND...
DAYDREAMING
......
......!
I'VE HAD ENOUGH, KID!!
SHOVE
KYAA!
WHAT THE...!!

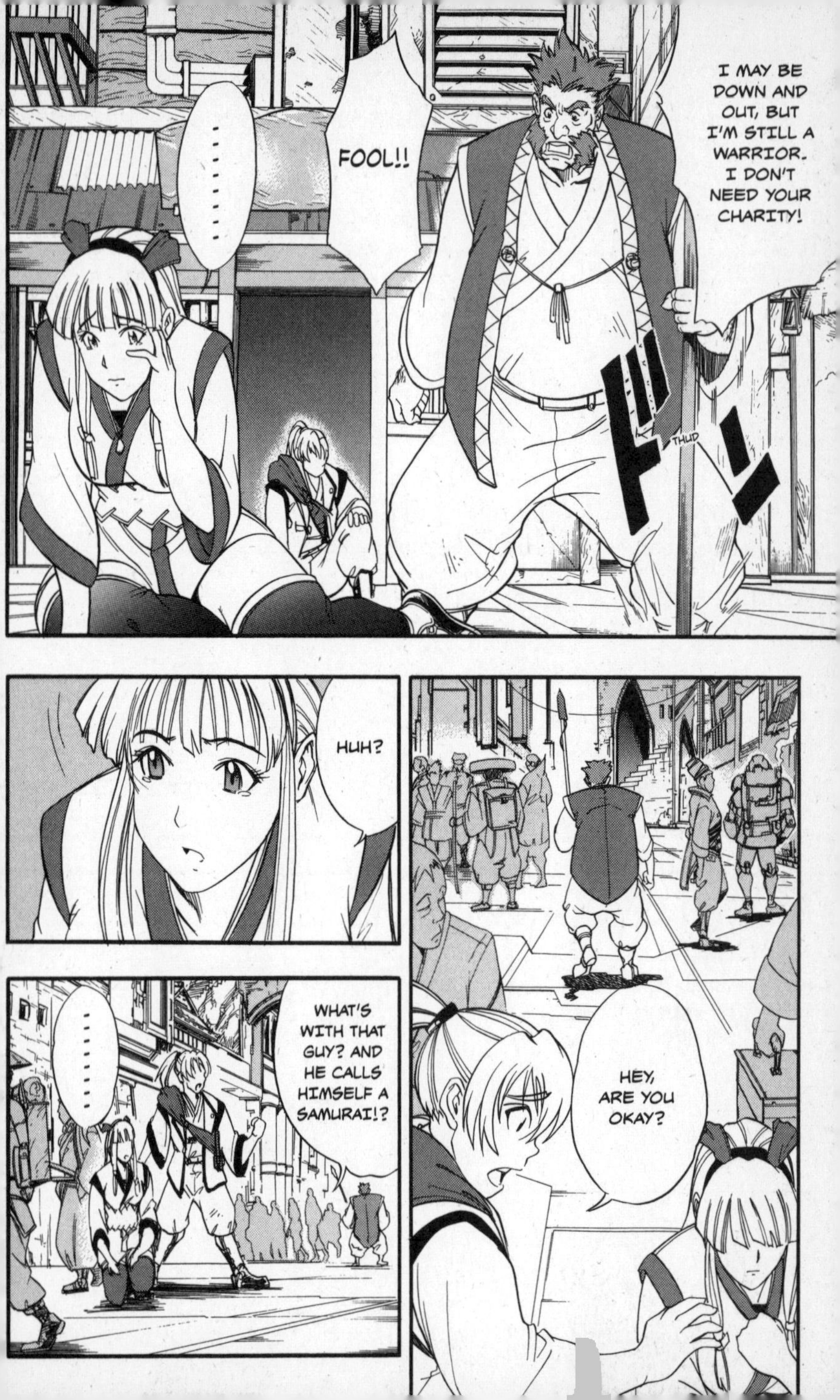
I MAY BE DOWN AND OUT, BUT I'M STILL A WARRIOR. I DON'T NEED YOUR CHARITY!
FOOL!!
THUD
......
HEY, ARE YOU OKAY?
HUH?
WHAT'S WITH THAT GUY? AND HE CALLS HIMSELF A SAMURAI!?
......

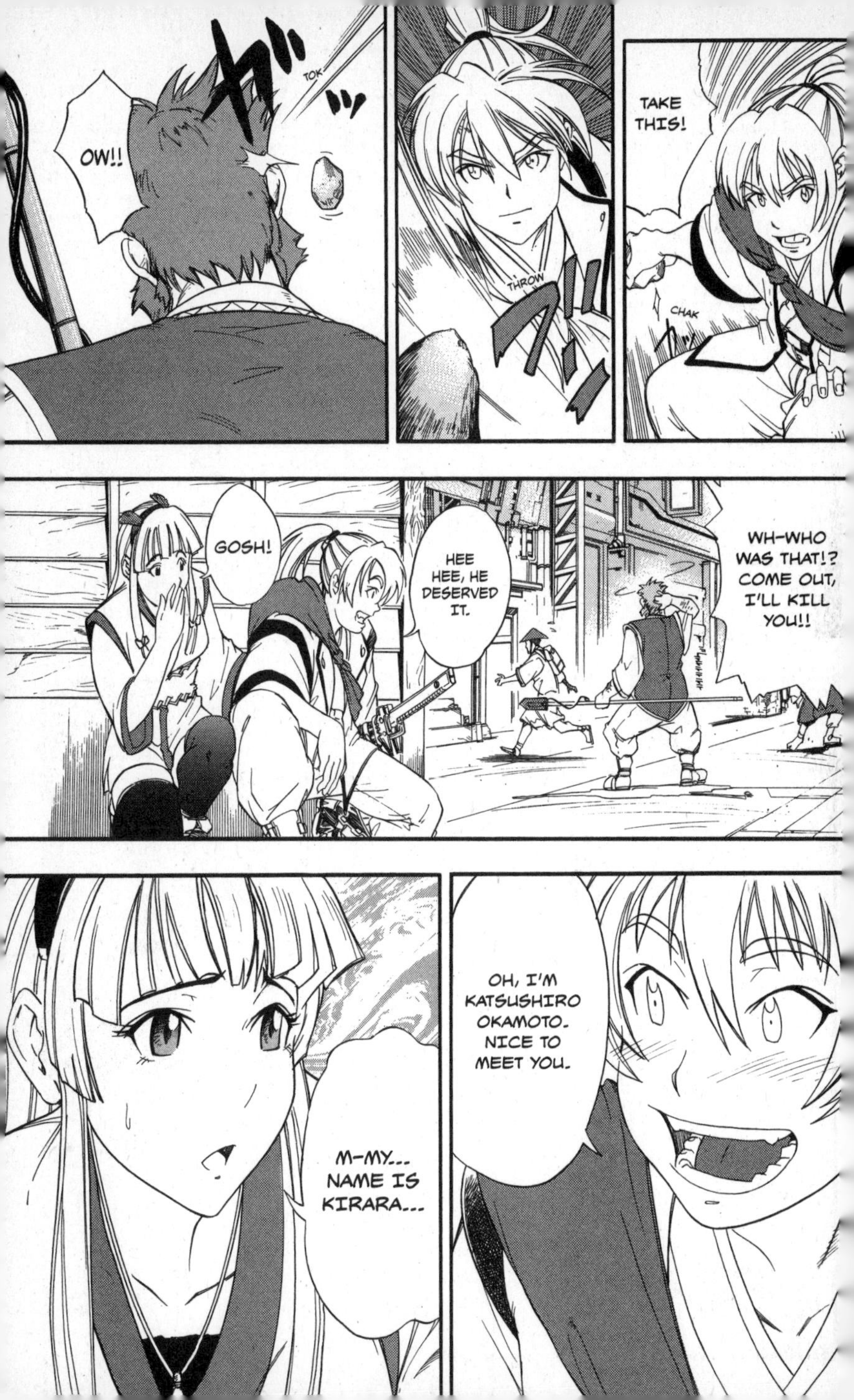
TAKE THIS!
CHAK
THROW
TOK
OW!!
WH-WHO WAS THAT!? COME OUT, I'LL KILL YOU!!
HEE HEE, HE DESERVED IT.
GOSH!
OH, I'M KATSUSHIRO OKAMOTO. NICE TO MEET YOU.
M-MY... NAME IS KIRARA...

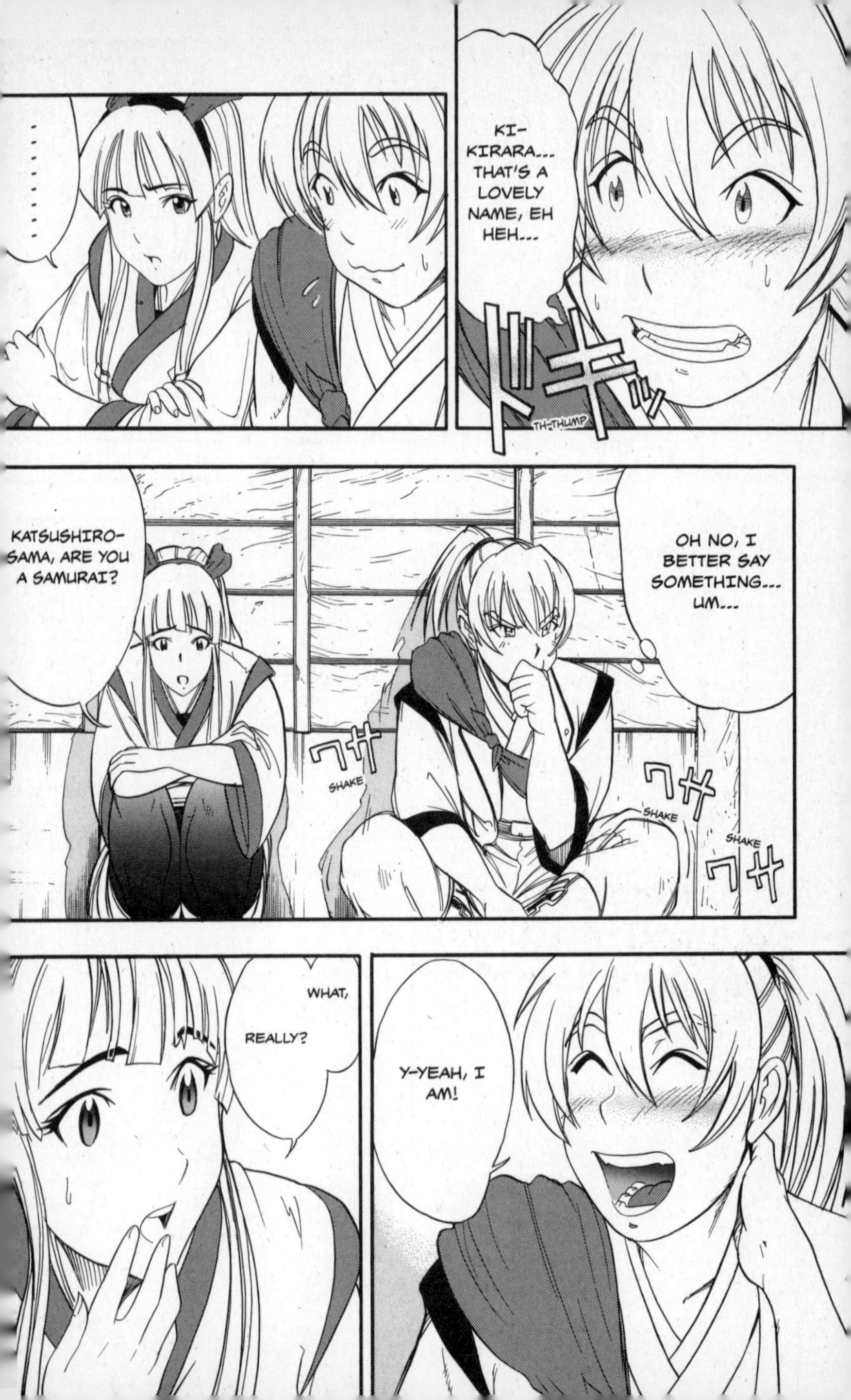

KI-KIRARA... THAT'S A LOVELY NAME, EH HEH...
TH-THUMP
......
OH NO, I BETTER SAY SOMETHING... UM...
KATSUSHIRO-SAMA, ARE YOU A SAMURAI?
SHAKE
SHAKE
SHAKE
Y-YEAH, I AM!
WHAT,
REALLY?

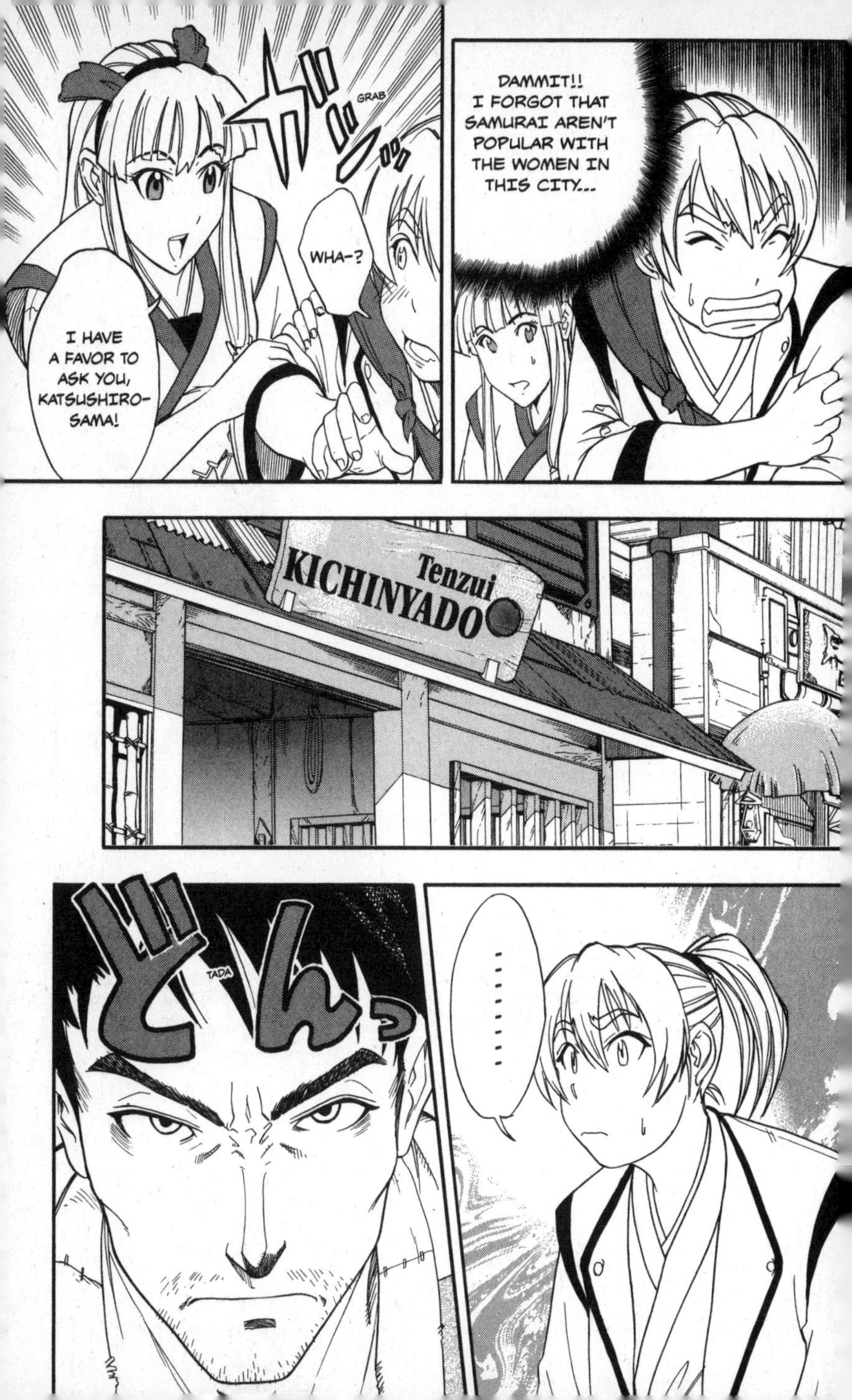

DAMMIT!! I FORGOT THAT SAMURAI AREN'T POPULAR WITH THE WOMEN IN THIS CITY...
GRAB
WHA-?
I HAVE A FAVOR TO ASK YOU, KATSUSHIRO-SAMA!
Tenzui KICHINYADO
......
TADA

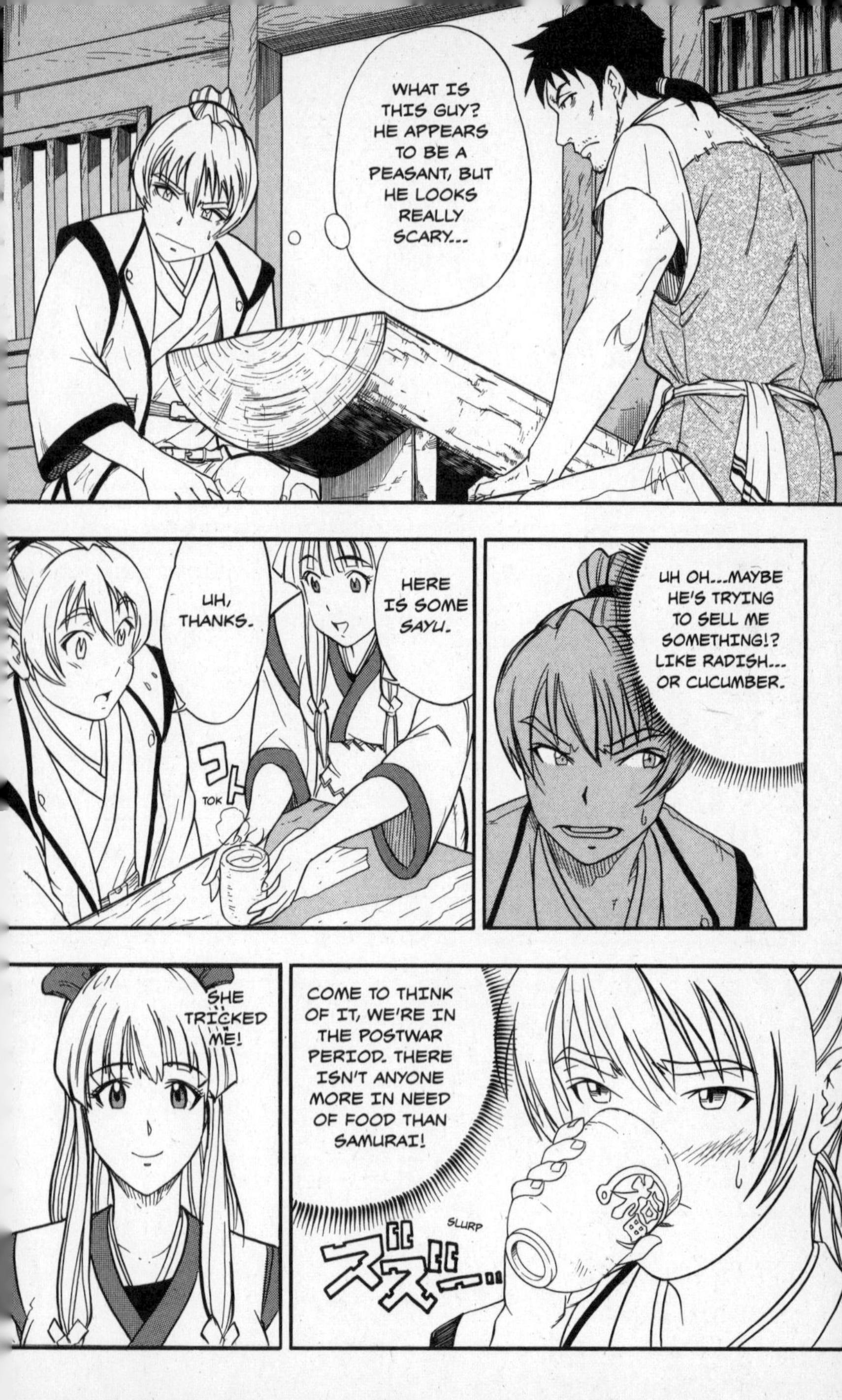
WHAT IS THIS GUY? HE APPEARS TO BE A PEASANT, BUT HE LOOKS REALLY SCARY...
UH OH...MAYBE HE'S TRYING TO SELL ME SOMETHING!? LIKE RADISH... OR CUCUMBER.
HERE IS SOME SAYU.
UH, THANKS.
TOK
COME TO THINK OF IT, WE'RE IN THE POSTWAR PERIOD. THERE ISN'T ANYONE MORE IN NEED OF FOOD THAN SAMURAI!
SLURP
SHE TRICKED ME!

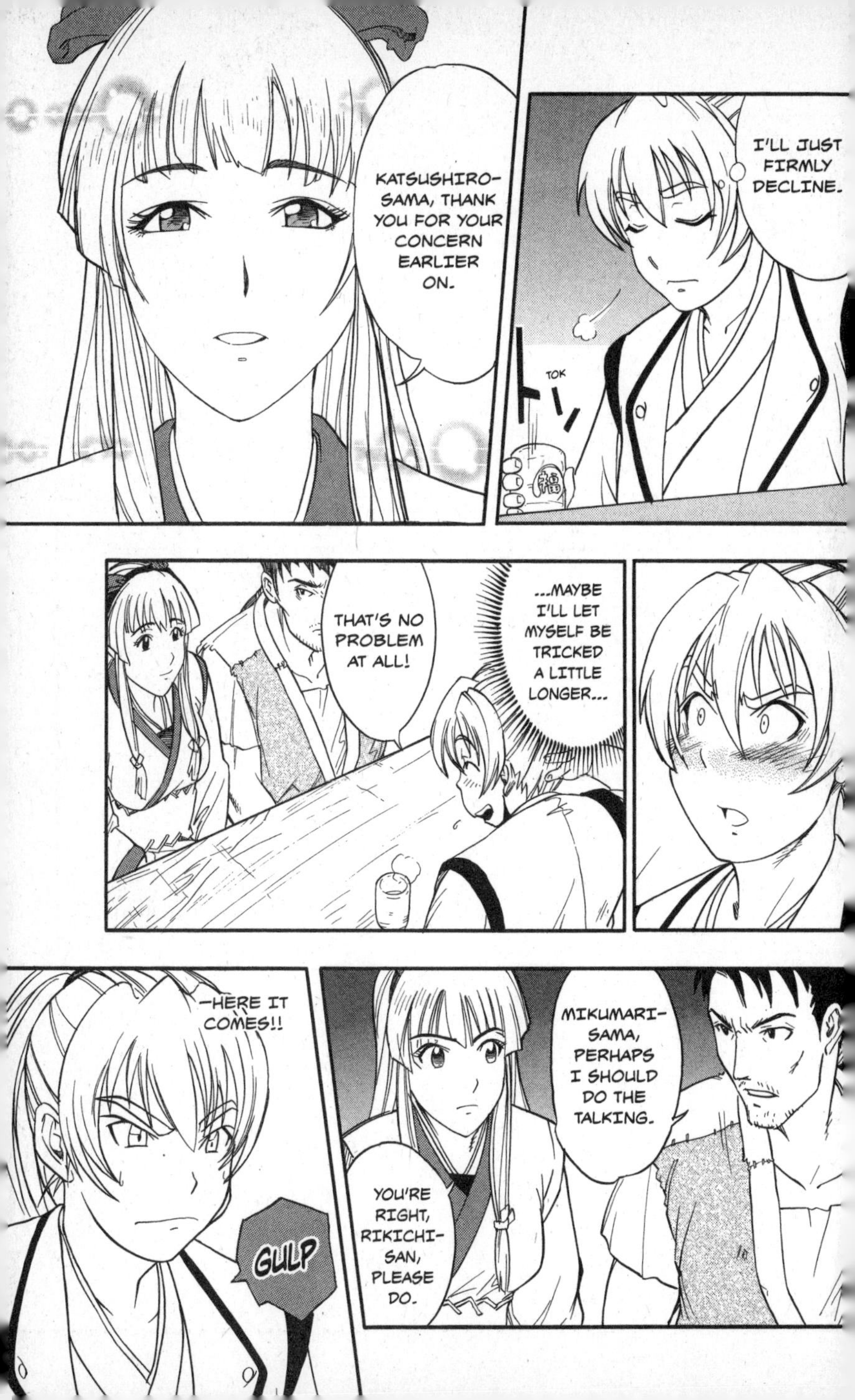
I'LL JUST FIRMLY DECLINE.
TOK
KATSUSHIRO-SAMA, THANK YOU FOR YOUR CONCERN EARLIER ON.
...MAYBE I'LL LET MYSELF BE TRICKED A LITTLE LONGER...
THAT'S NO PROBLEM AT ALL!
MIKUMARI-SAMA, PERHAPS I SHOULD DO THE TALKING.
YOU'RE RIGHT, RIKICHI-SAN, PLEASE DO.
—HERE IT COMES!!
GULP

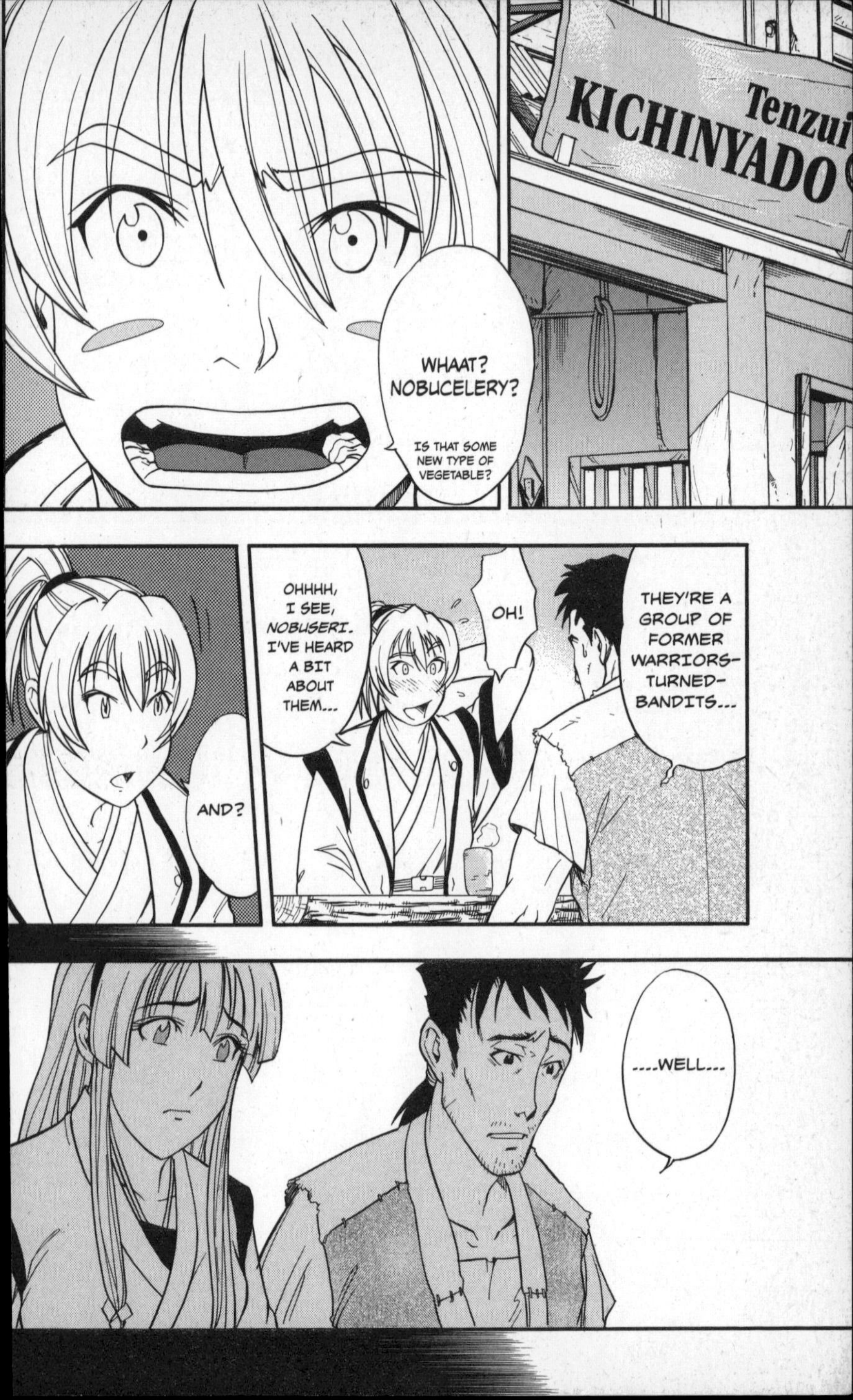
Tenzui
KICHINYADO
WHAAT? NOBUCELERY?
IS THAT SOME NEW TYPE OF VEGETABLE?
THEY'RE A GROUP OF FORMER WARRIORS-TURNED-BANDITS...
OH!
OHHHH, I SEE, *NOBUSERI*. I'VE HEARD A BIT ABOUT THEM...
AND?
....WELL...

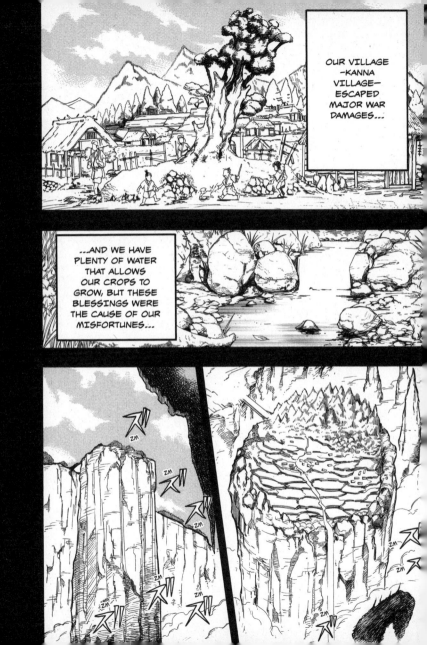

OUR VILLAGE —KANNA VILLAGE— ESCAPED MAJOR WAR DAMAGES...

...AND WE HAVE PLENTY OF WATER THAT ALLOWS OUR CROPS TO GROW, BUT THESE BLESSINGS WERE THE CAUSE OF OUR MISFORTUNES...

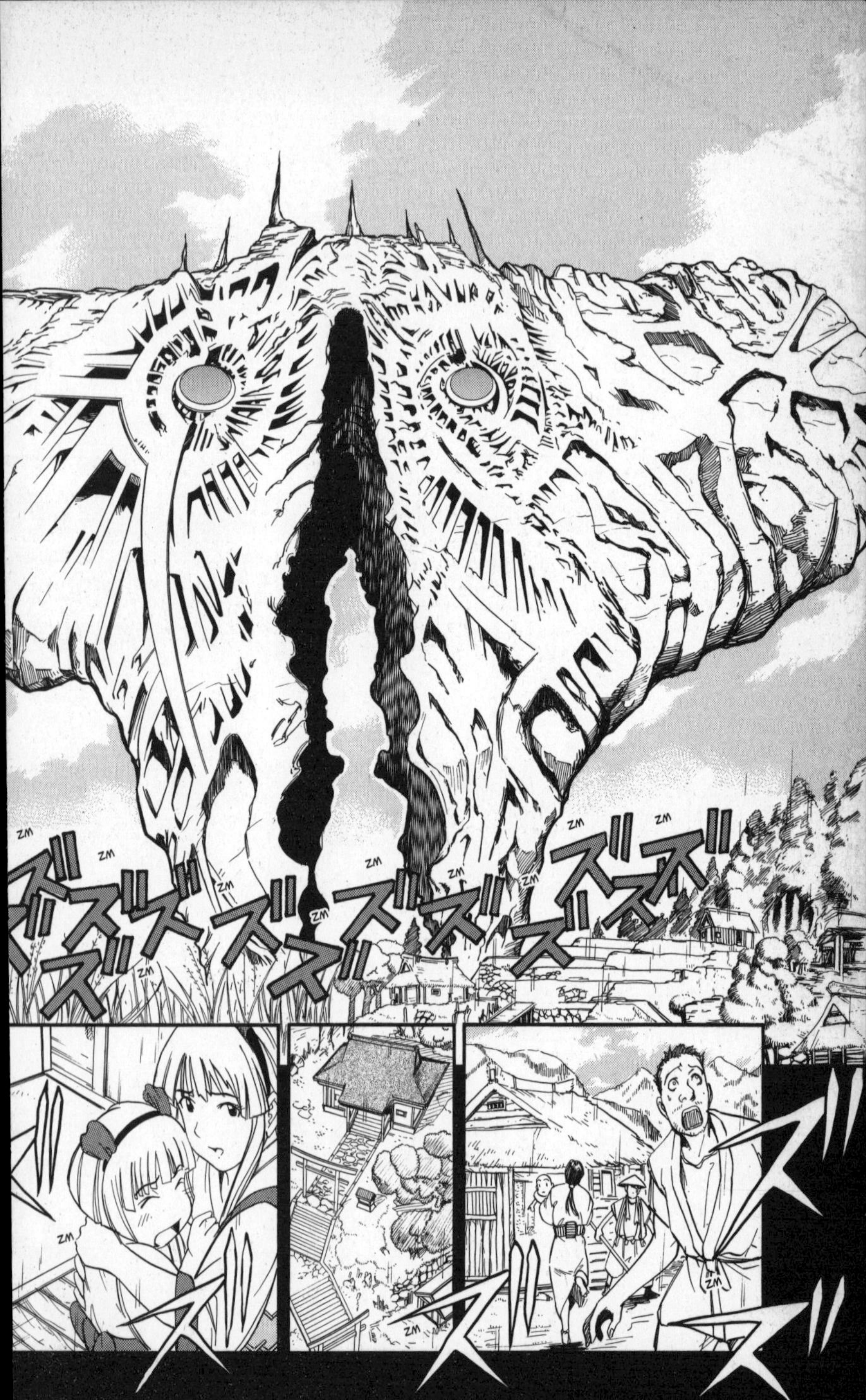
ズズズズズズズズズズズ
ZM ZM ZM ZM ZM ZM ZM ZM ZM
ズズ
ZM
ズズ
ZM
ズズ
ZM

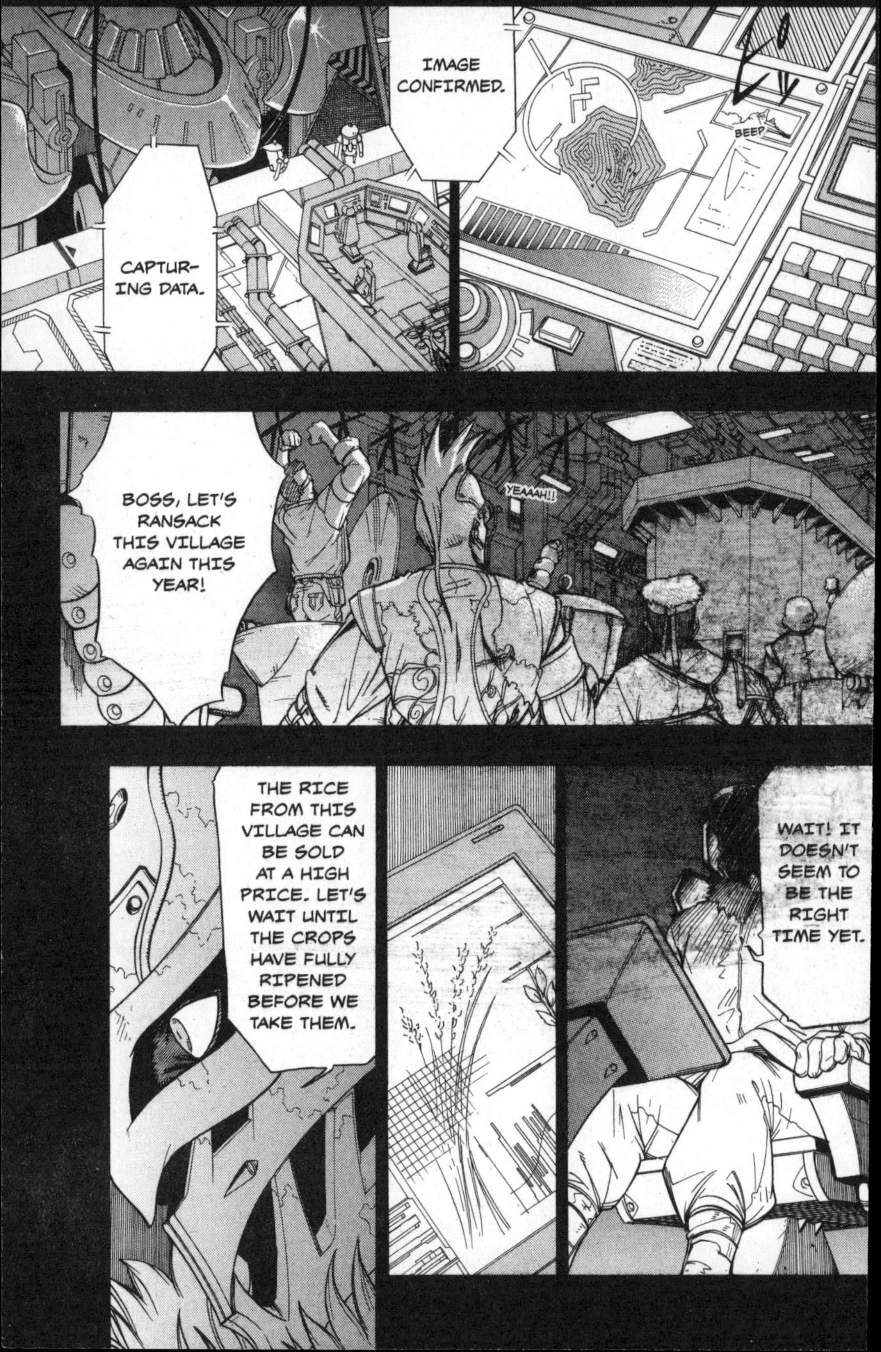
IMAGE CONFIRMED.
BEEP
CAPTURING DATA.
YEAAAH!!
BOSS, LET'S RANSACK THIS VILLAGE AGAIN THIS YEAR!
WAIT! IT DOESN'T SEEM TO BE THE RIGHT TIME YET.
THE RICE FROM THIS VILLAGE CAN BE SOLD AT A HIGH PRICE. LET'S WAIT UNTIL THE CROPS HAVE FULLY RIPENED BEFORE WE TAKE THEM.

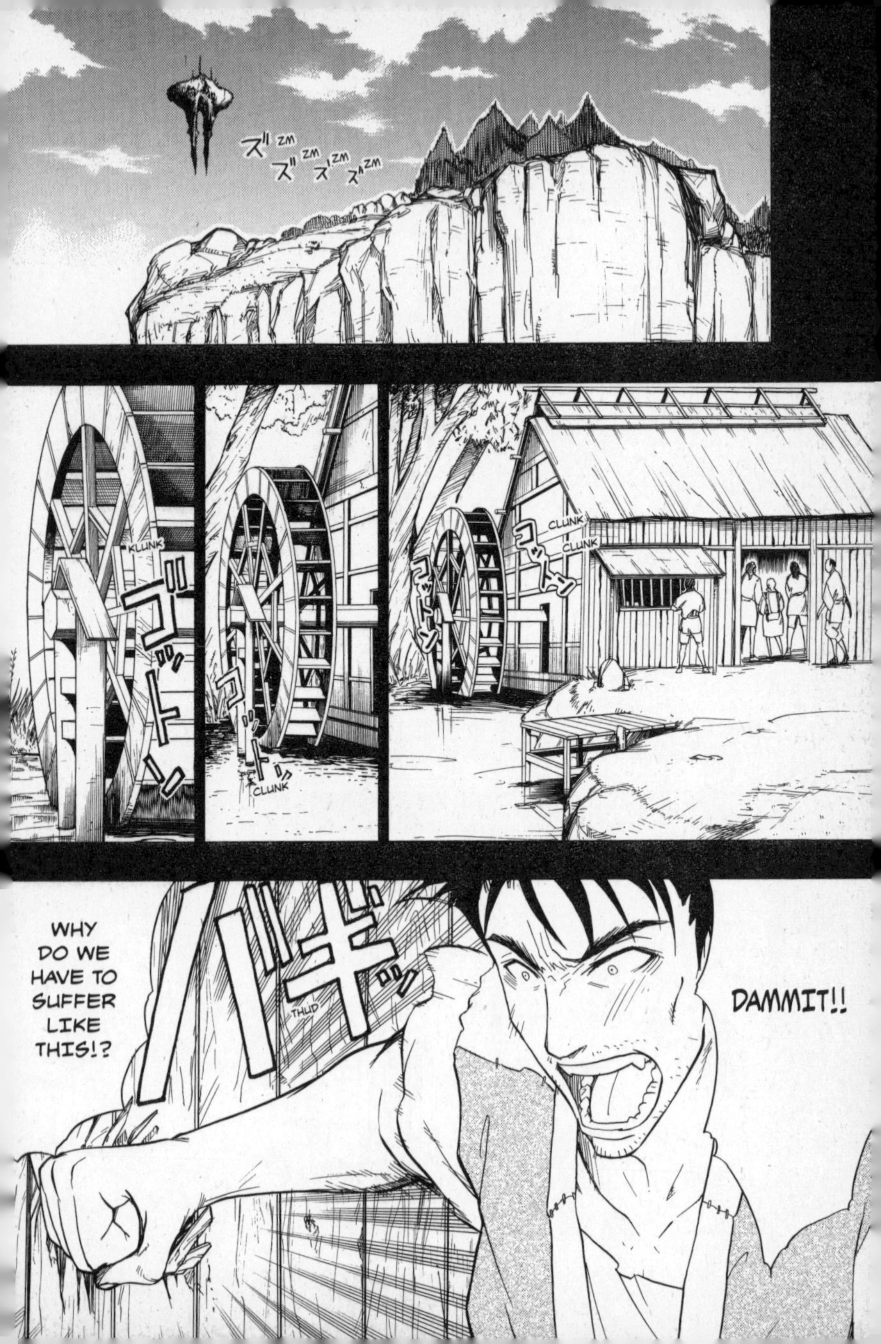
ZM ZM ZM ZM
CLUNK
CLUNK
CLUNK
KLUNK
DAMMIT!!
THUD
WHY DO WE HAVE TO SUFFER LIKE THIS!?

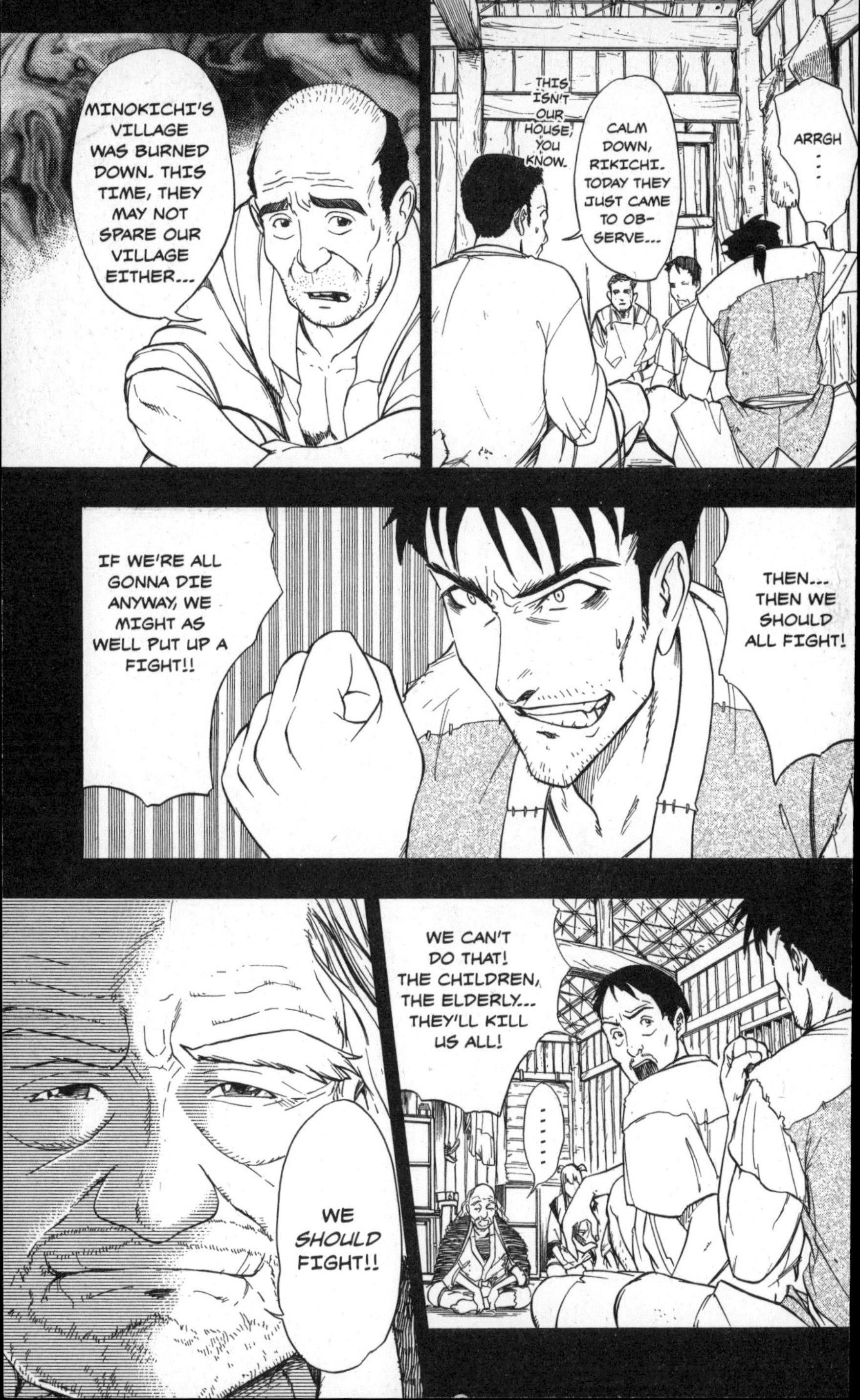
ARRGH...
CALM DOWN, RIKICHI. TODAY THEY JUST CAME TO OBSERVE...
THIS ISN'T OUR HOUSE, YOU KNOW.
MINOKICHI'S VILLAGE WAS BURNED DOWN. THIS TIME, THEY MAY NOT SPARE OUR VILLAGE EITHER...
THEN... THEN WE SHOULD ALL FIGHT!
IF WE'RE ALL GONNA DIE ANYWAY, WE MIGHT AS WELL PUT UP A FIGHT!!
WE CAN'T DO THAT! THE CHILDREN, THE ELDERLY... THEY'LL KILL US ALL!
......
WE SHOULD FIGHT!!

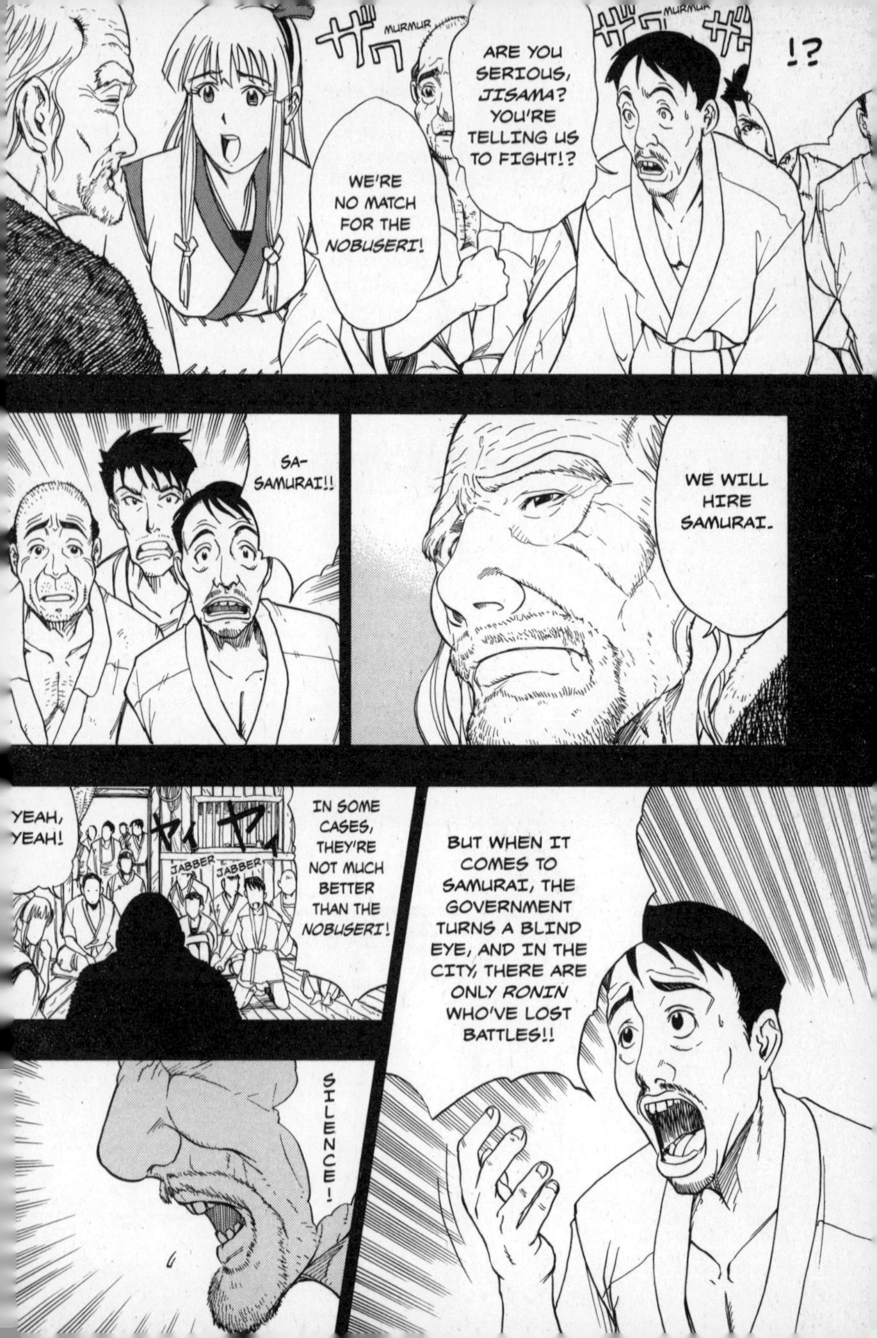
!?
MURMUR
ARE YOU SERIOUS, JISAMA? YOU'RE TELLING US TO FIGHT!?
WE'RE NO MATCH FOR THE NOBUSERI!
MURMUR
WE WILL HIRE SAMURAI.
SA- SAMURAI!!
BUT WHEN IT COMES TO SAMURAI, THE GOVERNMENT TURNS A BLIND EYE, AND IN THE CITY, THERE ARE ONLY RONIN WHO'VE LOST BATTLES!!
IN SOME CASES, THEY'RE NOT MUCH BETTER THAN THE NOBUSERI!
JABBER JABBER
YEAH, YEAH!
SILENCE!

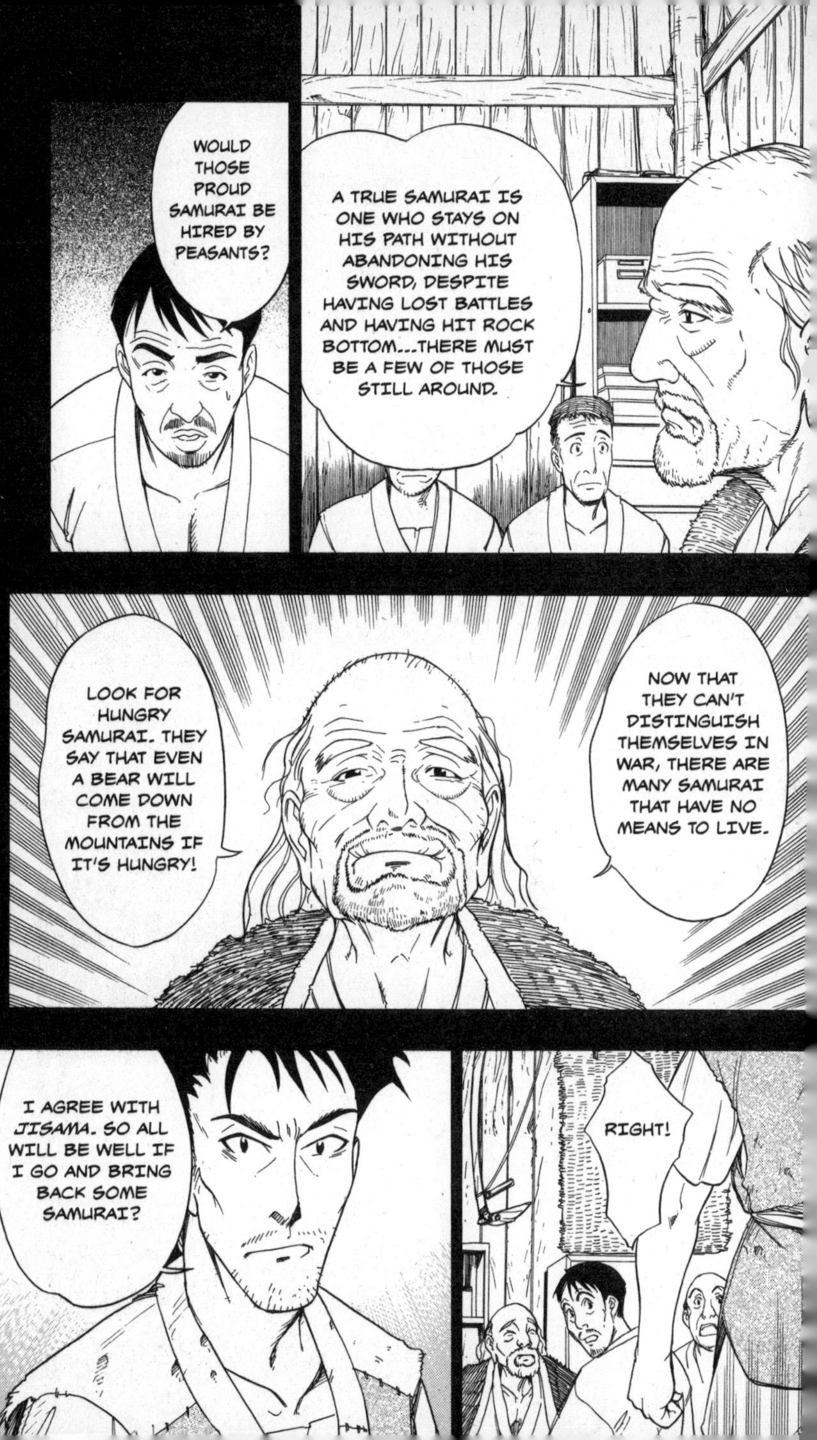
A TRUE SAMURAI IS ONE WHO STAYS ON HIS PATH WITHOUT ABANDONING HIS SWORD, DESPITE HAVING LOST BATTLES AND HAVING HIT ROCK BOTTOM...THERE MUST BE A FEW OF THOSE STILL AROUND.
WOULD THOSE PROUD SAMURAI BE HIRED BY PEASANTS?
NOW THAT THEY CAN'T DISTINGUISH THEMSELVES IN WAR, THERE ARE MANY SAMURAI THAT HAVE NO MEANS TO LIVE.
LOOK FOR HUNGRY SAMURAI. THEY SAY THAT EVEN A BEAR WILL COME DOWN FROM THE MOUNTAINS IF IT'S HUNGRY!
RIGHT!
I AGREE WITH *JISAMA*. SO ALL WILL BE WELL IF I GO AND BRING BACK SOME SAMURAI?

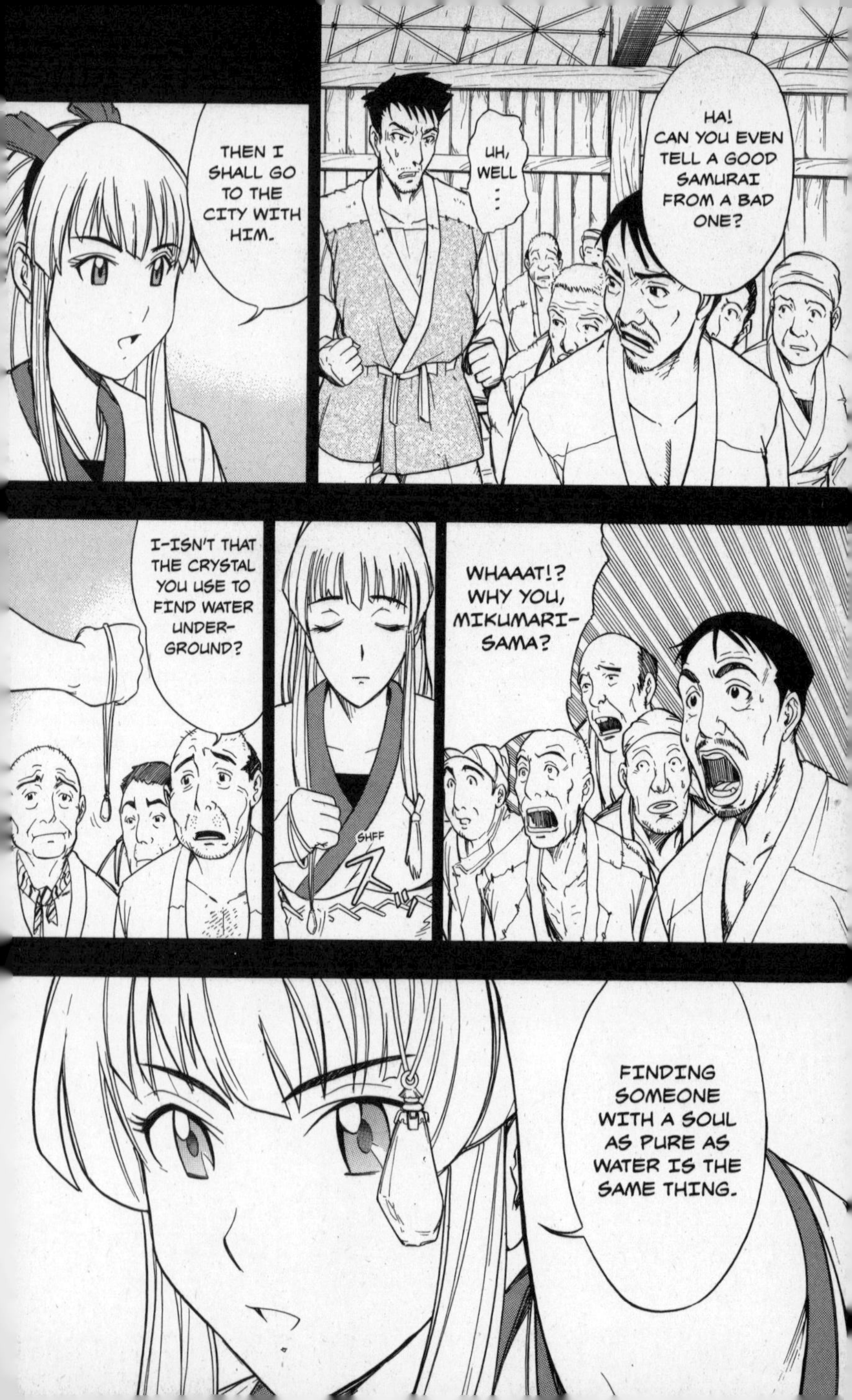
HA! CAN YOU EVEN TELL A GOOD SAMURAI FROM A BAD ONE?
UH, WELL ...
THEN I SHALL GO TO THE CITY WITH HIM.
WHAAAT!? WHY YOU, MIKUMARI-SAMA?
SHFF
I-ISN'T THAT THE CRYSTAL YOU USE TO FIND WATER UNDER-GROUND?
FINDING SOMEONE WITH A SOUL AS PURE AS WATER IS THE SAME THING.

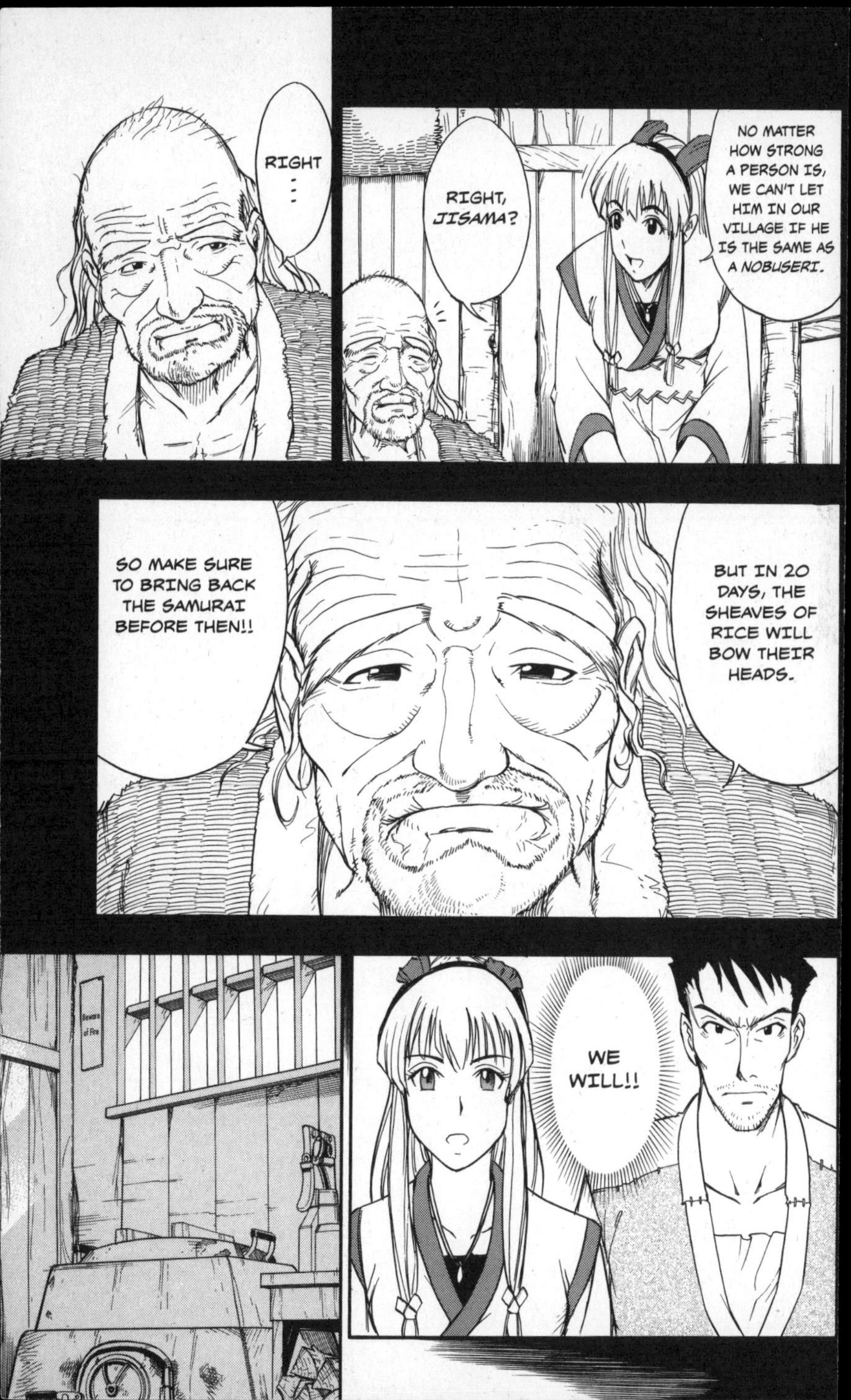
NO MATTER HOW STRONG A PERSON IS, WE CAN'T LET HIM IN OUR VILLAGE IF HE IS THE SAME AS A *NOBUSERI*.
RIGHT, JISAMA?
RIGHT ...
BUT IN 20 DAYS, THE SHEAVES OF RICE WILL BOW THEIR HEADS.
SO MAKE SURE TO BRING BACK THE SAMURAI BEFORE THEN!!
WE WILL!!
Beware of Fire

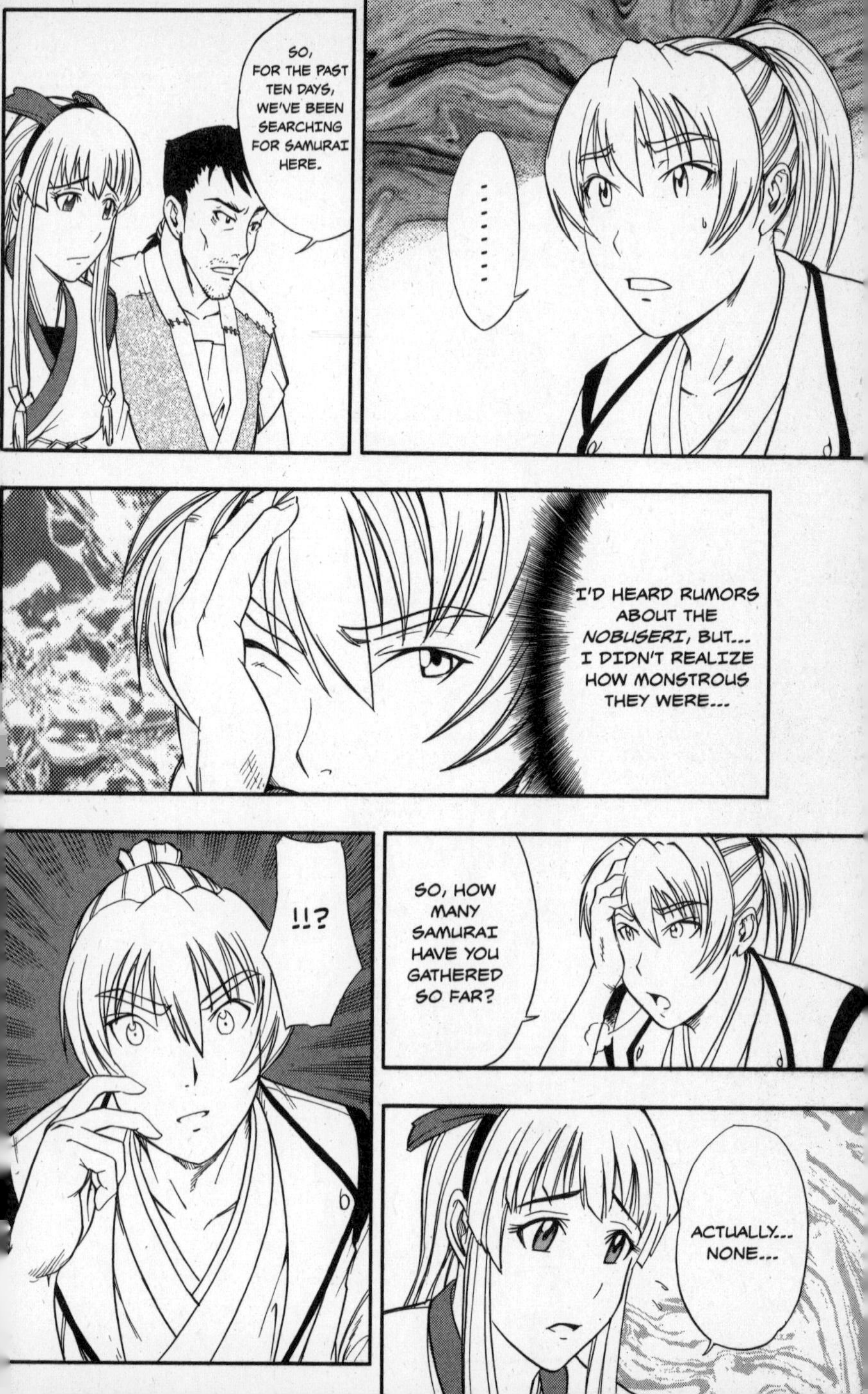
......
SO, FOR THE PAST TEN DAYS, WE'VE BEEN SEARCHING FOR SAMURAI HERE.
I'D HEARD RUMORS ABOUT THE *NOBUSERI*, BUT... I DIDN'T REALIZE HOW MONSTROUS THEY WERE...
SO, HOW MANY SAMURAI HAVE YOU GATHERED SO FAR?
ACTUALLY... NONE...
!!?

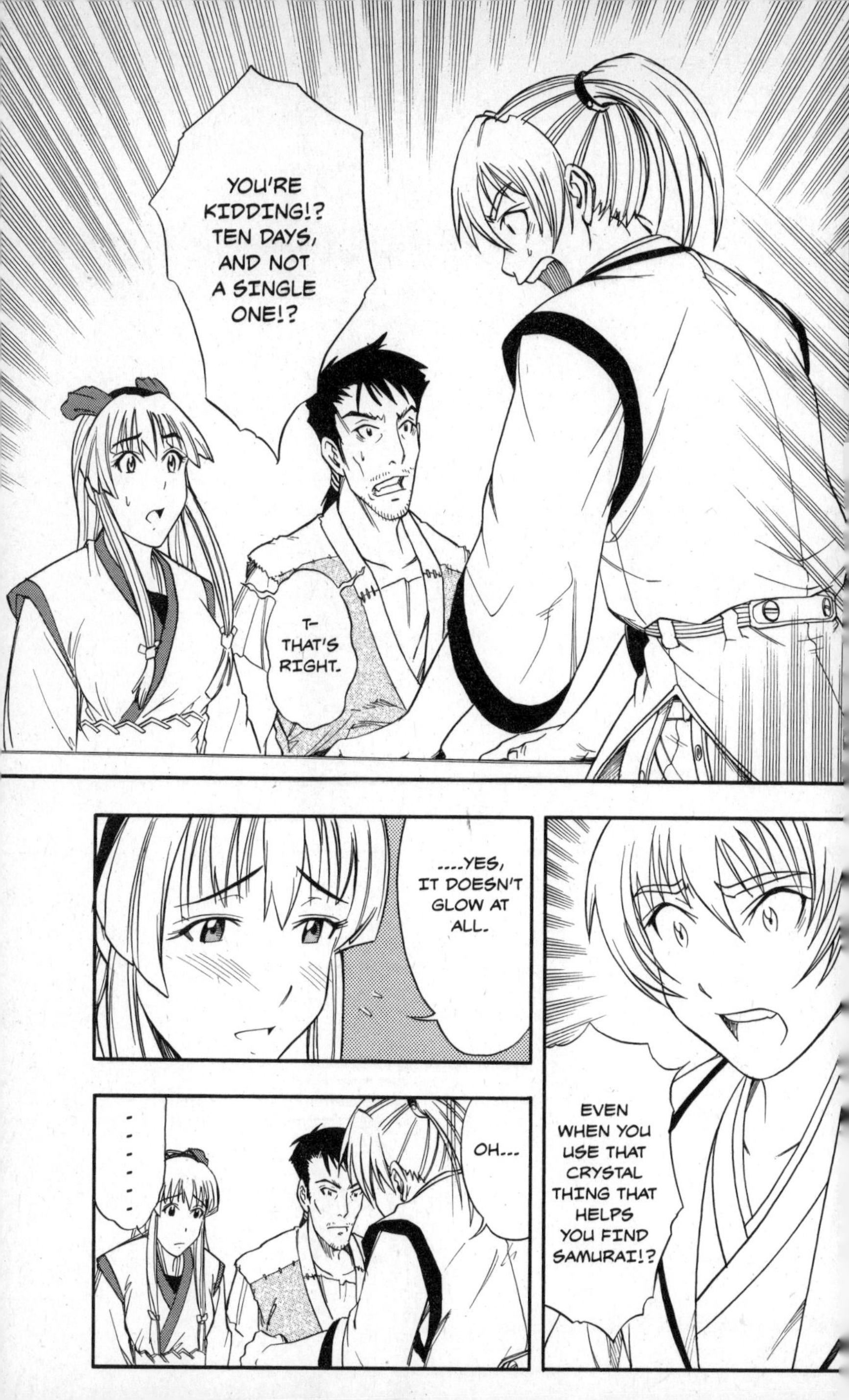
YOU'RE KIDDING!? TEN DAYS, AND NOT A SINGLE ONE!?
T-THAT'S RIGHT.
EVEN WHEN YOU USE THAT CRYSTAL THING THAT HELPS YOU FIND SAMURAI!?
....YES, IT DOESN'T GLOW AT ALL.
OH...
......

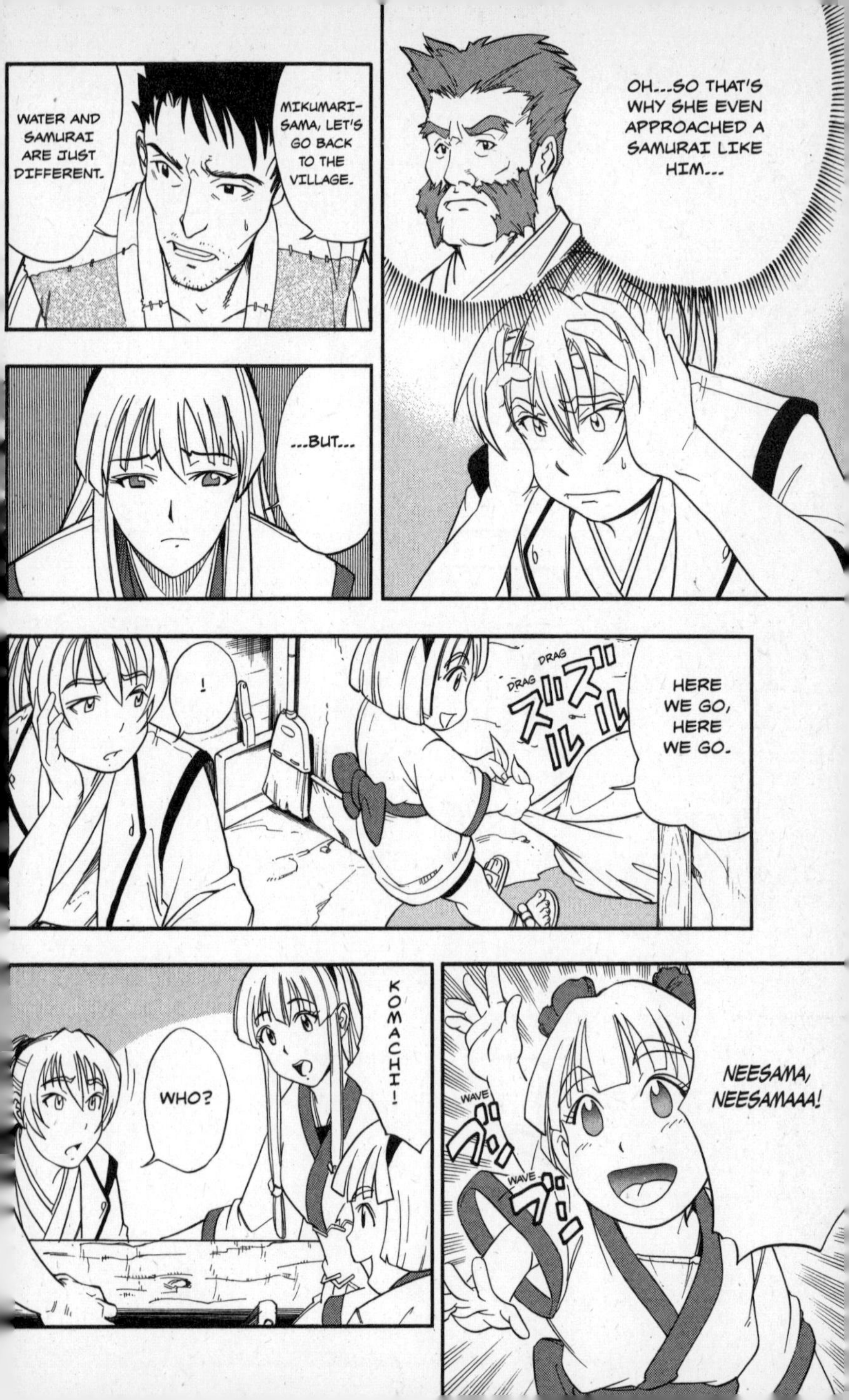
OH...SO THAT'S WHY SHE EVEN APPROACHED A SAMURAI LIKE HIM...
MIKUMARI-SAMA, LET'S GO BACK TO THE VILLAGE.
WATER AND SAMURAI ARE JUST DIFFERENT.
...BUT...
HERE WE GO, HERE WE GO.
DRAG
DRAG
ズルズル
!
NEESAMA, NEESAMAAA!
WAVE
WAVE
KOMACHI!
WHO?

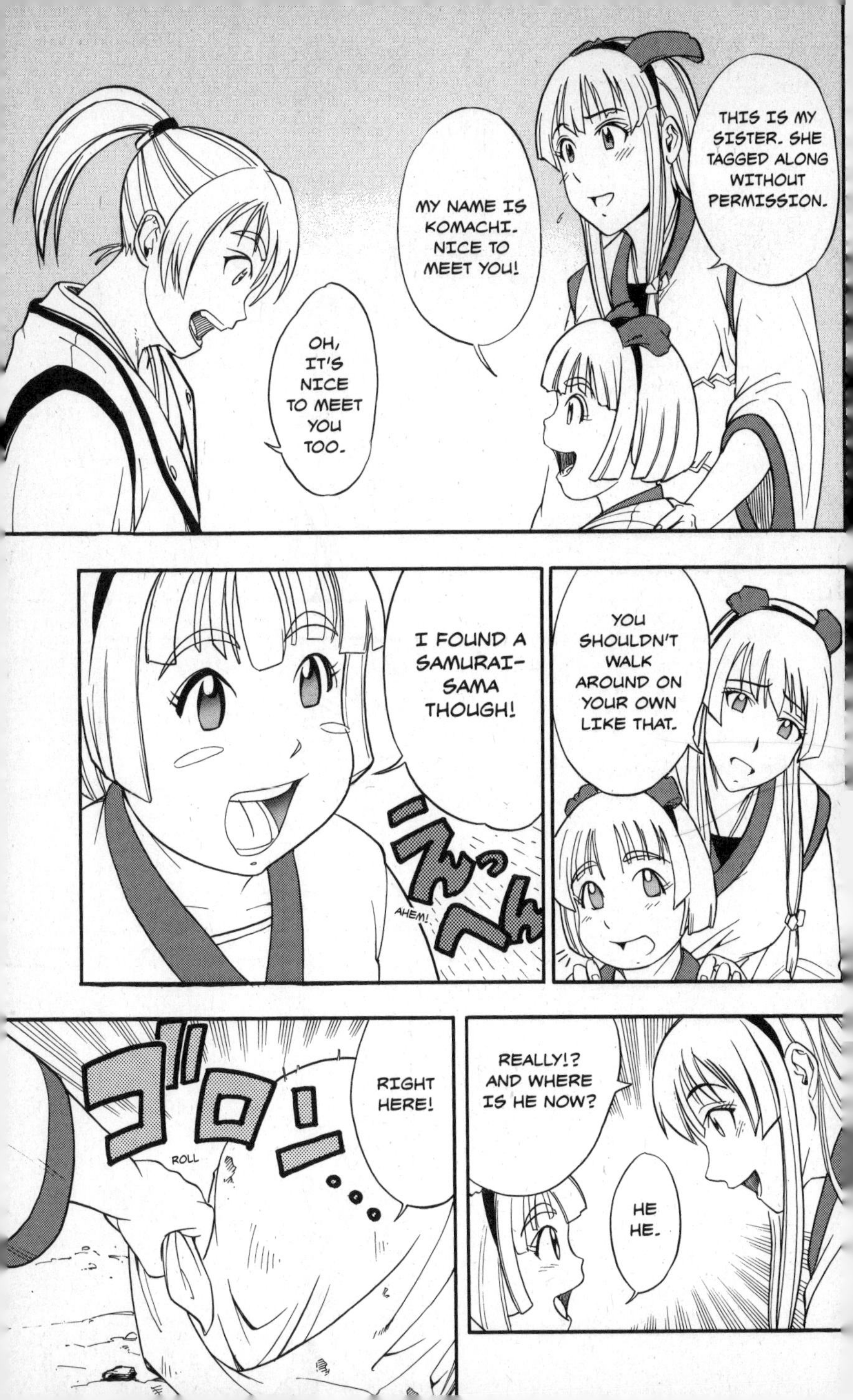
THIS IS MY SISTER. SHE TAGGED ALONG WITHOUT PERMISSION.
MY NAME IS KOMACHI. NICE TO MEET YOU!
OH, IT'S NICE TO MEET YOU TOO.
YOU SHOULDN'T WALK AROUND ON YOUR OWN LIKE THAT.
I FOUND A SAMURAI-SAMA THOUGH!
AHEM!
REALLY!? AND WHERE IS HE NOW?
HE HE.
RIGHT HERE!
ROLL
...

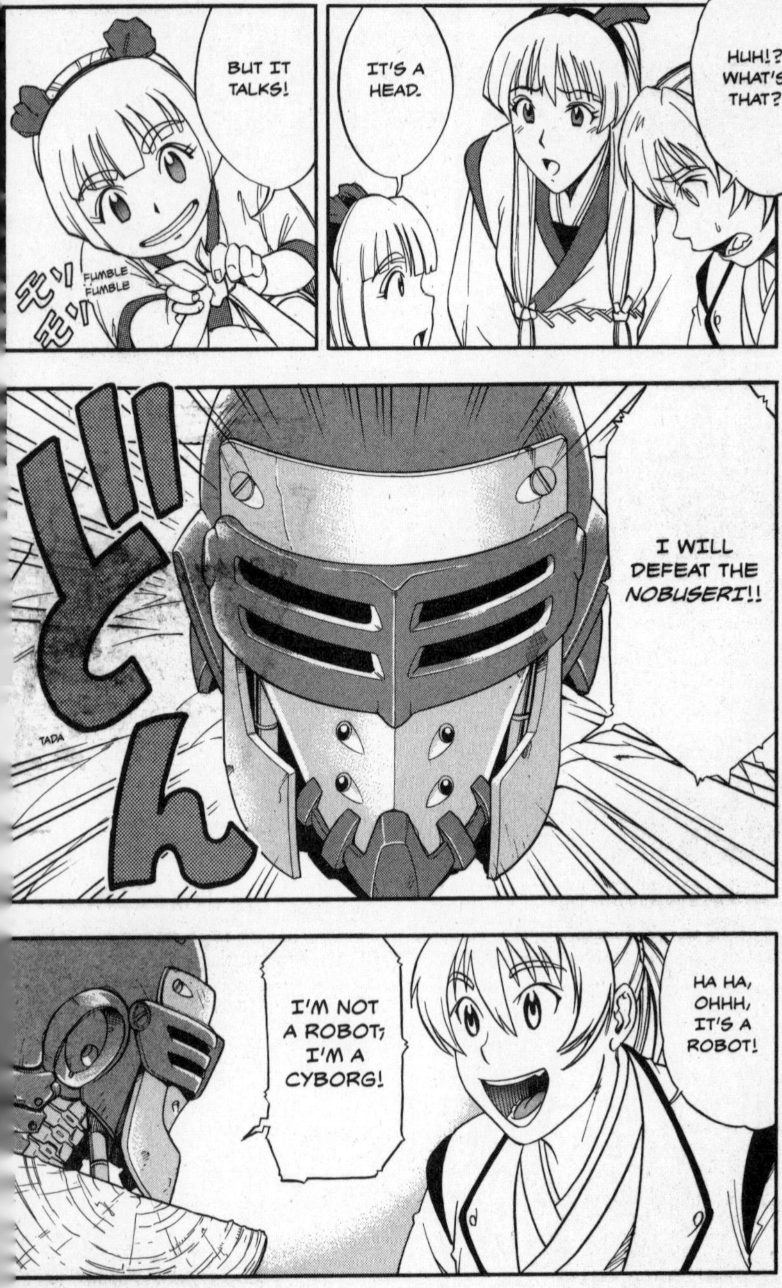
HUH!? WHAT'S THAT?
IT'S A HEAD.
BUT IT TALKS!
FUMBLE FUMBLE
I WILL DEFEAT THE *NOBUSERI*!!
TADA
HA HA, OHHH, IT'S A ROBOT!
I'M NOT A ROBOT; I'M A CYBORG!

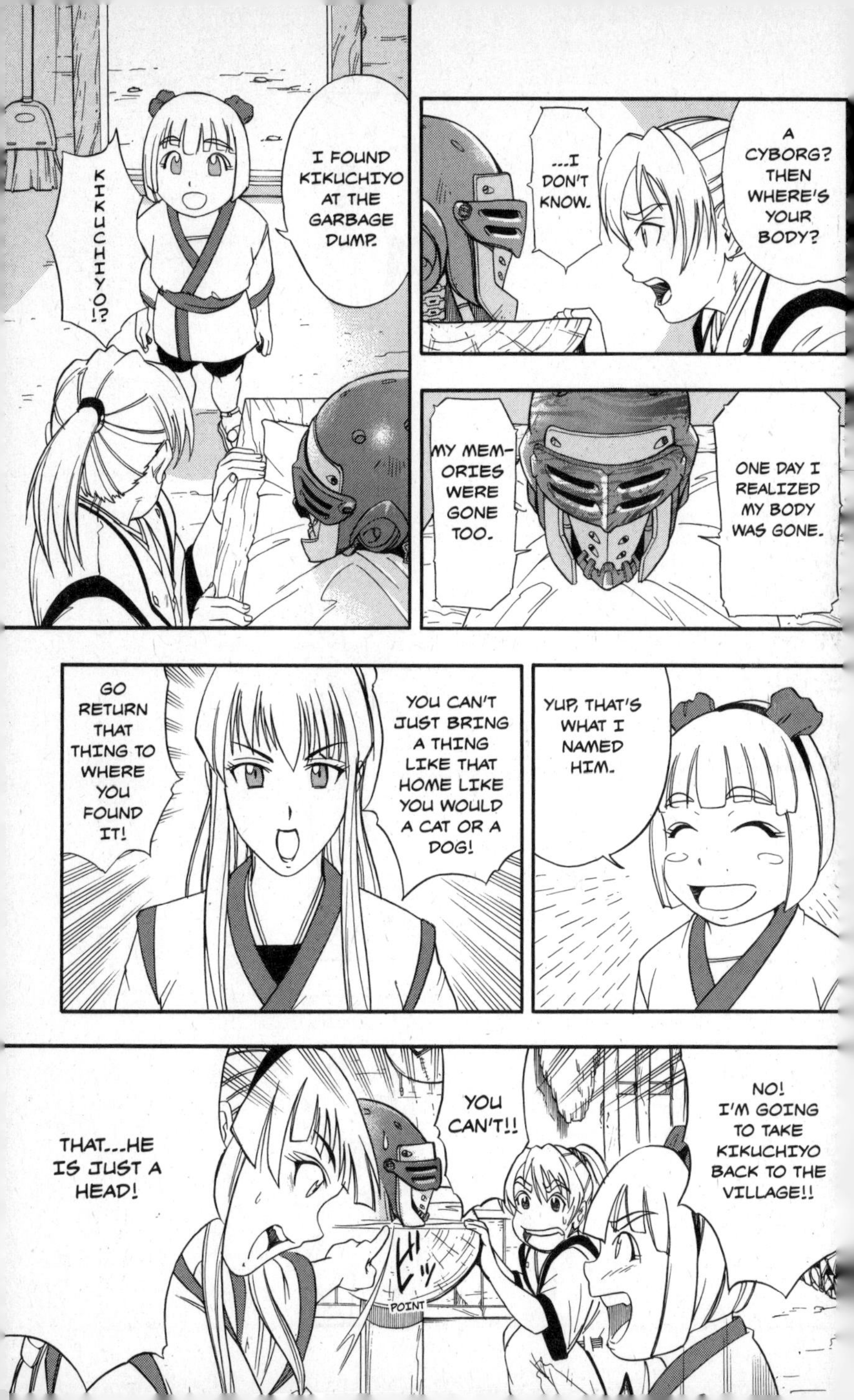

A CYBORG? THEN WHERE'S YOUR BODY?
...I DON'T KNOW.
ONE DAY I REALIZED MY BODY WAS GONE.
MY MEMORIES WERE GONE TOO.
I FOUND KIKUCHIYO AT THE GARBAGE DUMP.
KIKUCHIYO!?
YUP, THAT'S WHAT I NAMED HIM.
YOU CAN'T JUST BRING A THING LIKE THAT HOME LIKE YOU WOULD A CAT OR A DOG!
GO RETURN THAT THING TO WHERE YOU FOUND IT!
NO! I'M GOING TO TAKE KIKUCHIYO BACK TO THE VILLAGE!!
YOU CAN'T!!
THAT...HE IS JUST A HEAD!
ビッ
POINT

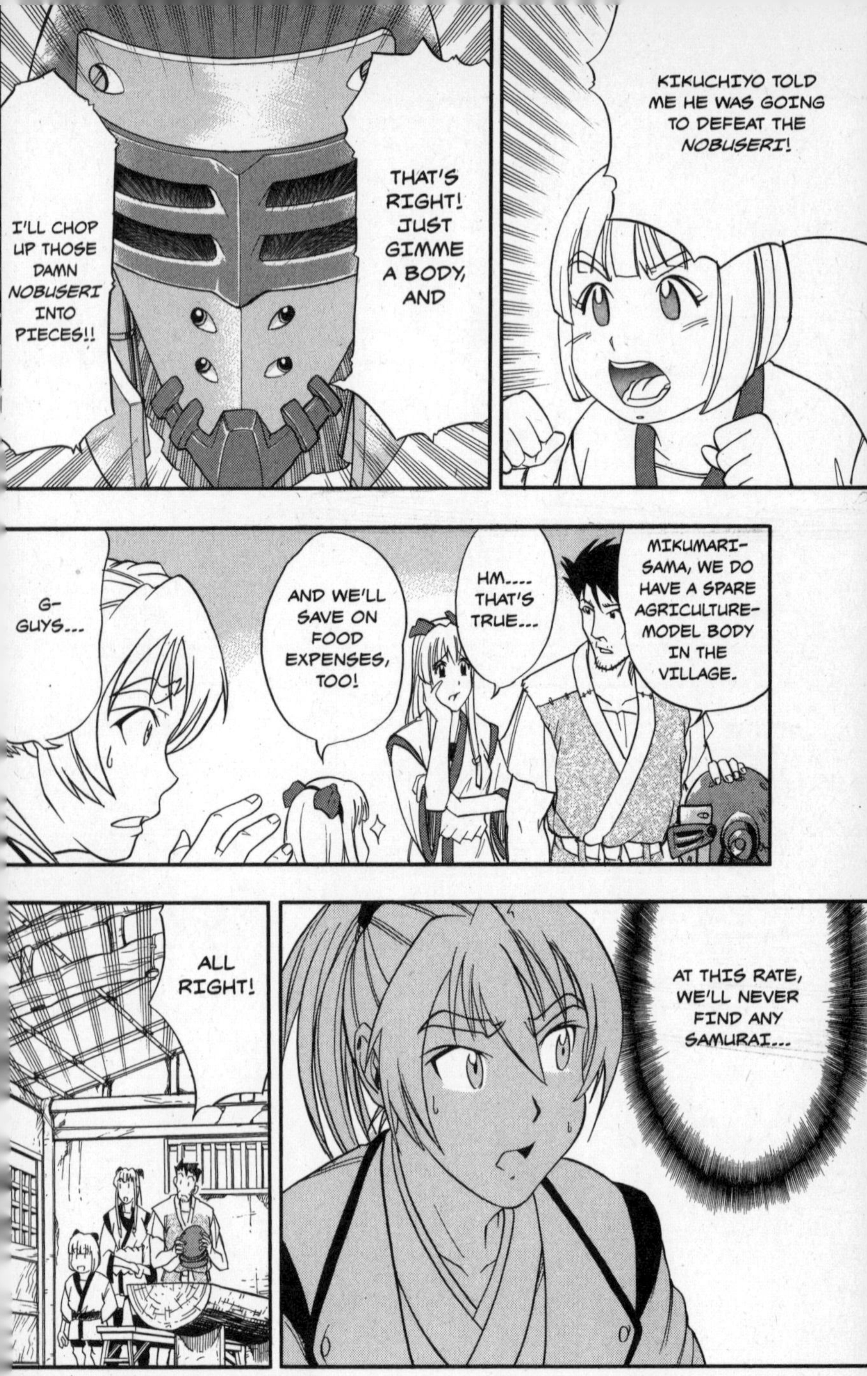
KIKUCHIYO TOLD ME HE WAS GOING TO DEFEAT THE *NOBUSERI*!
THAT'S RIGHT! JUST GIMME A BODY, AND
I'LL CHOP UP THOSE DAMN *NOBUSERI* INTO PIECES!!
MIKUMARI-SAMA, WE DO HAVE A SPARE AGRICULTURE-MODEL BODY IN THE VILLAGE.
HM.... THAT'S TRUE...
AND WE'LL SAVE ON FOOD EXPENSES, TOO!
G-GUYS...
AT THIS RATE, WE'LL NEVER FIND ANY SAMURAI...
ALL RIGHT!

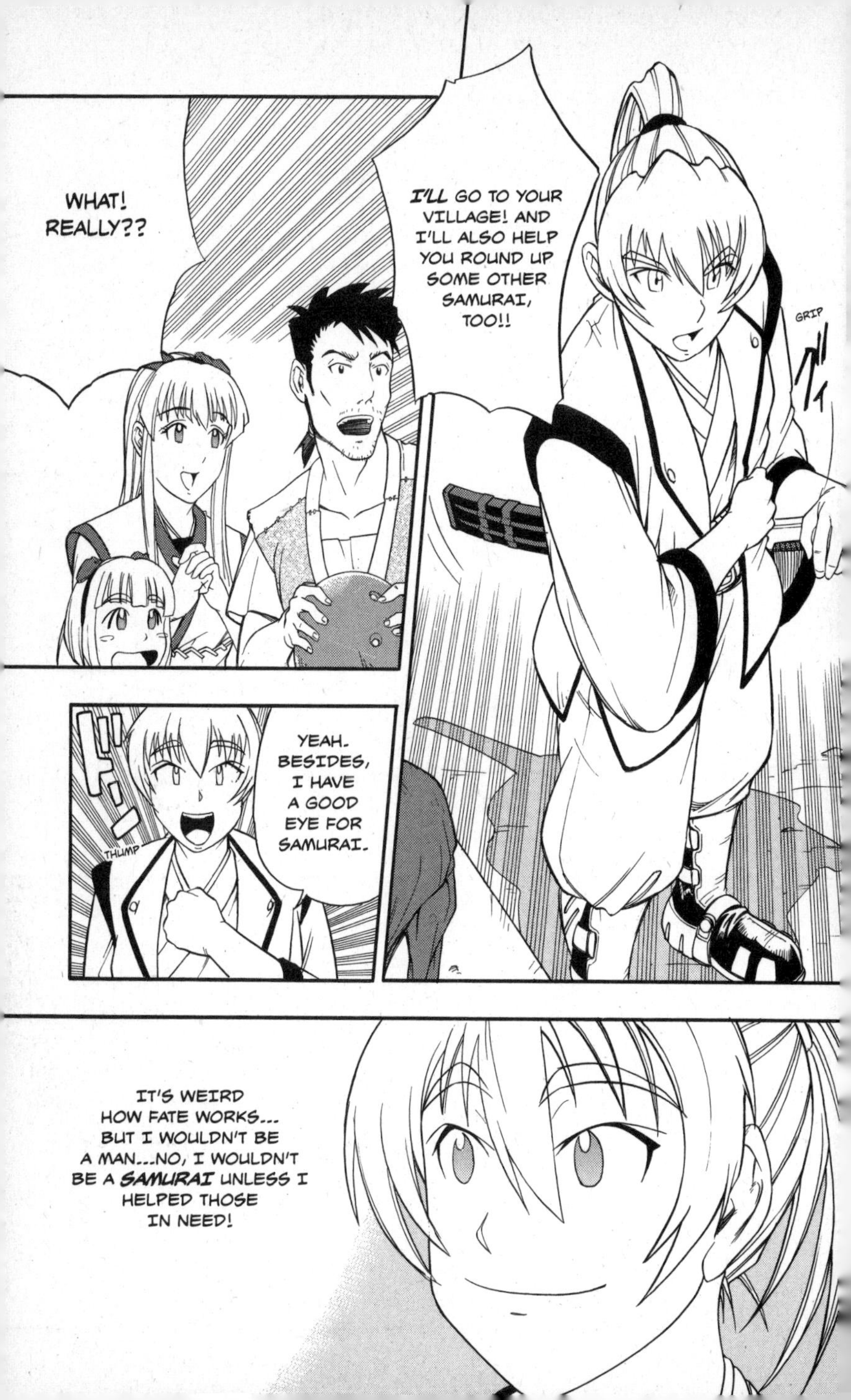
I'LL GO TO YOUR VILLAGE! AND I'LL ALSO HELP YOU ROUND UP SOME OTHER SAMURAI, TOO!!
GRIP
WHAT! REALLY??
YEAH. BESIDES, I HAVE A GOOD EYE FOR SAMURAI.
THUMP
IT'S WEIRD HOW FATE WORKS... BUT I WOULDN'T BE A MAN...NO, I WOULDN'T BE A SAMURAI UNLESS I HELPED THOSE IN NEED!

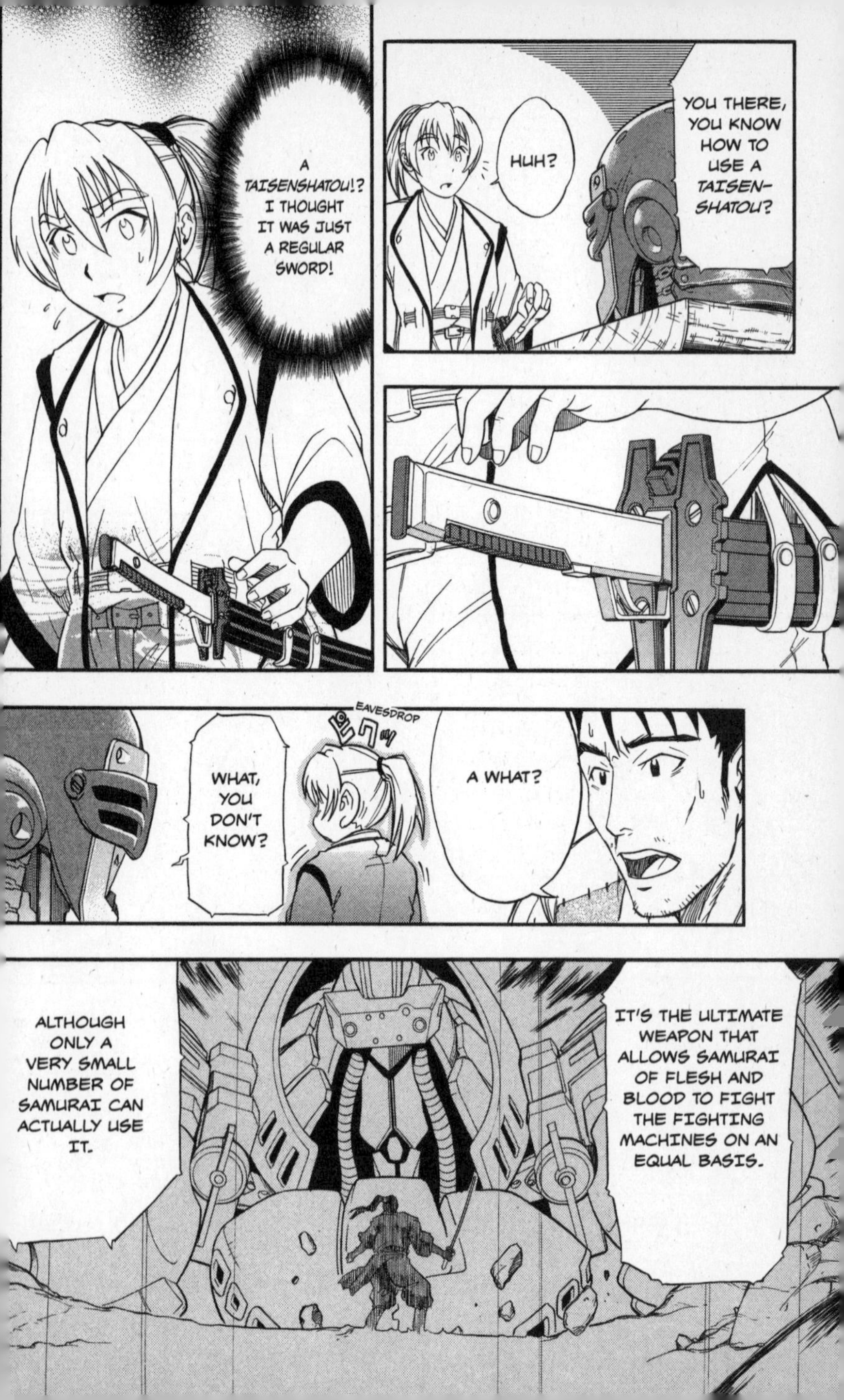
YOU THERE, YOU KNOW HOW TO USE A TAISEN-SHATOU?
HUH?
A TAISENSHATOU!? I THOUGHT IT WAS JUST A REGULAR SWORD!
A WHAT?
EAVESDROP
WHAT, YOU DON'T KNOW?
IT'S THE ULTIMATE WEAPON THAT ALLOWS SAMURAI OF FLESH AND BLOOD TO FIGHT THE FIGHTING MACHINES ON AN EQUAL BASIS.
ALTHOUGH ONLY A VERY SMALL NUMBER OF SAMURAI CAN ACTUALLY USE IT.

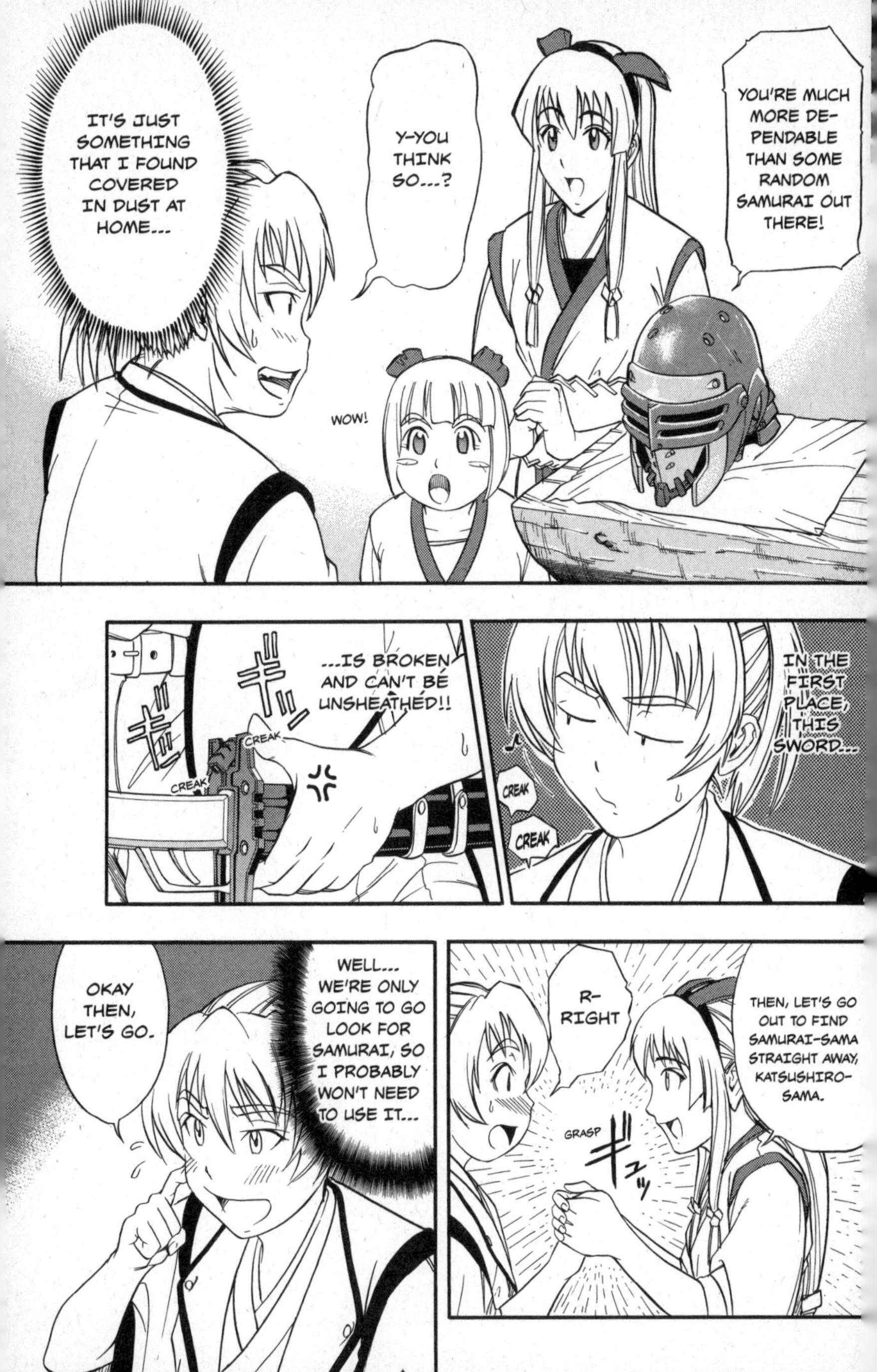
YOU'RE MUCH MORE DE-PENDABLE THAN SOME RANDOM SAMURAI OUT THERE!
Y-YOU THINK SO...?
IT'S JUST SOMETHING THAT I FOUND COVERED IN DUST AT HOME...
WOW!
IN THE FIRST PLACE, THIS SWORD...
CREAK
CREAK
...IS BROKEN AND CAN'T BE UNSHEATHED!!
CREAK
CREAK
THEN, LET'S GO OUT TO FIND SAMURAI-SAMA STRAIGHT AWAY, KATSUSHIRO-SAMA.
R-RIGHT
GRASP
WELL... WE'RE ONLY GOING TO GO LOOK FOR SAMURAI, SO I PROBABLY WON'T NEED TO USE IT...
OKAY THEN, LET'S GO.

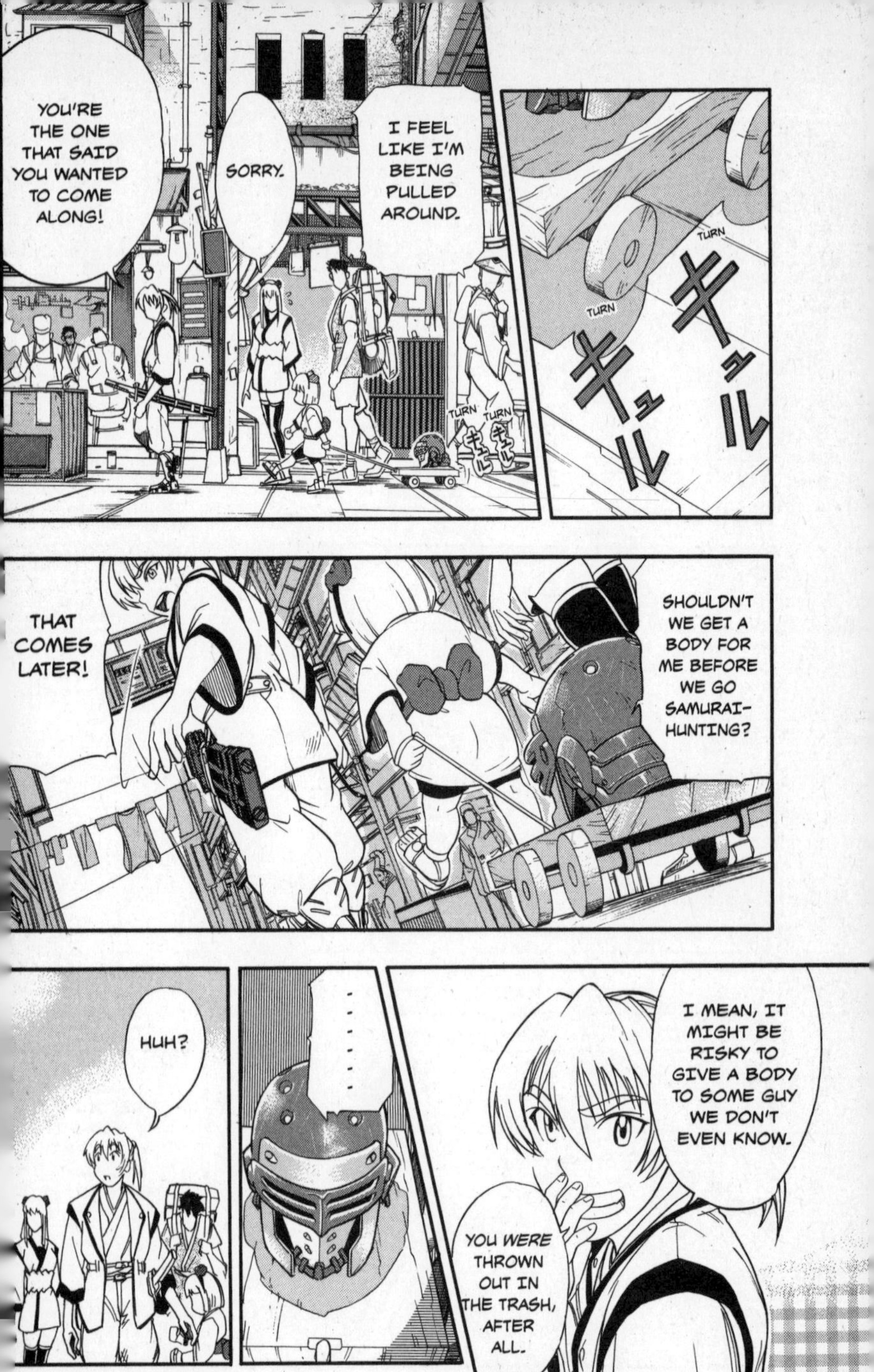
TURN
キュル
TURN
キュル
I FEEL LIKE I'M BEING PULLED AROUND.
SORRY.
YOU'RE THE ONE THAT SAID YOU WANTED TO COME ALONG!
TURN
キュル
TURN
キュル
SHOULDN'T WE GET A BODY FOR ME BEFORE WE GO SAMURAI-HUNTING?
THAT COMES LATER!
I MEAN, IT MIGHT BE RISKY TO GIVE A BODY TO SOME GUY WE DON'T EVEN KNOW.
YOU WERE THROWN OUT IN THE TRASH, AFTER ALL.
......
HUH?

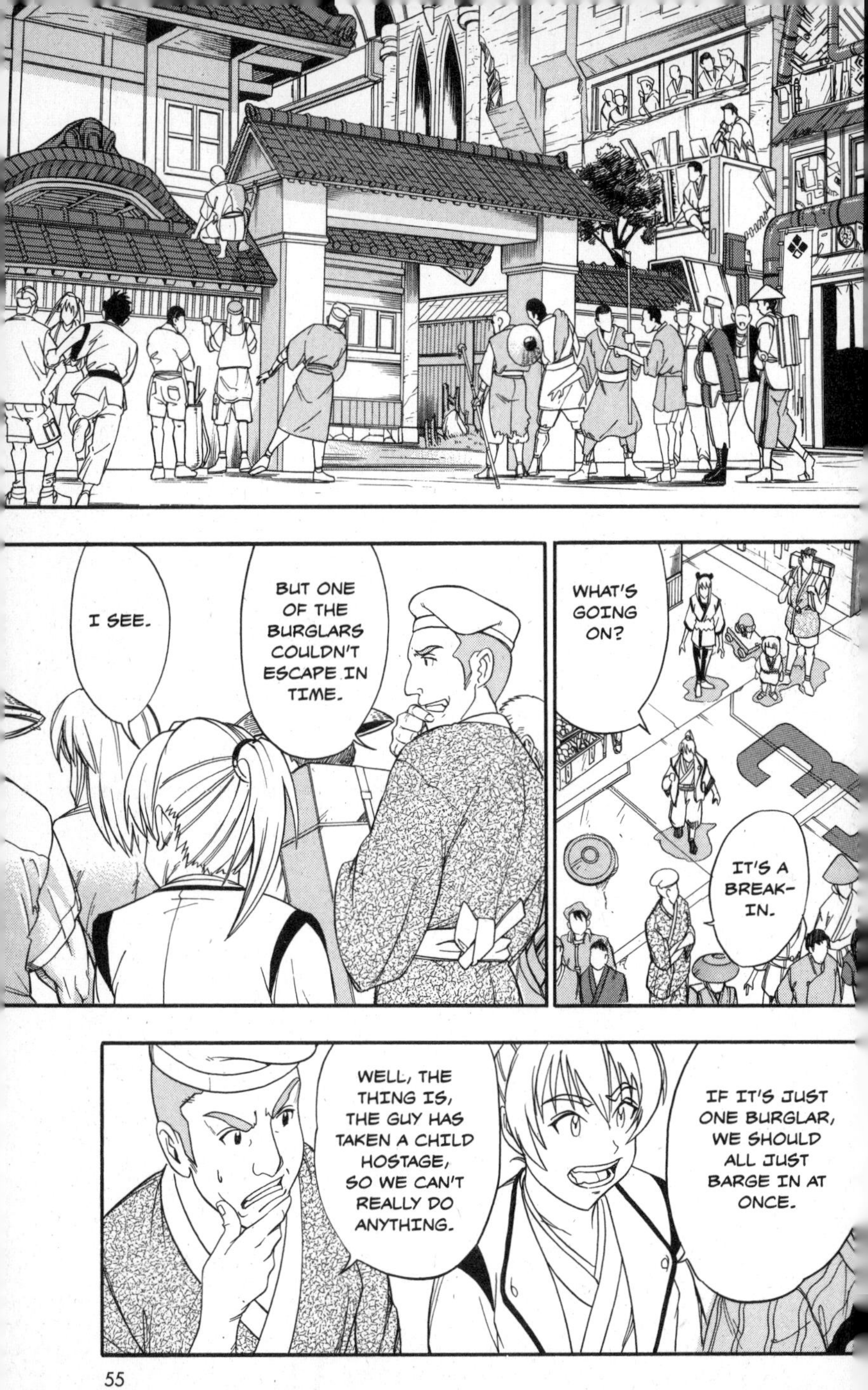
WHAT'S GOING ON?
IT'S A BREAK-IN.
BUT ONE OF THE BURGLARS COULDN'T ESCAPE IN TIME.
I SEE.
IF IT'S JUST ONE BURGLAR, WE SHOULD ALL JUST BARGE IN AT ONCE.
WELL, THE THING IS, THE GUY HAS TAKEN A CHILD HOSTAGE, SO WE CAN'T REALLY DO ANYTHING.

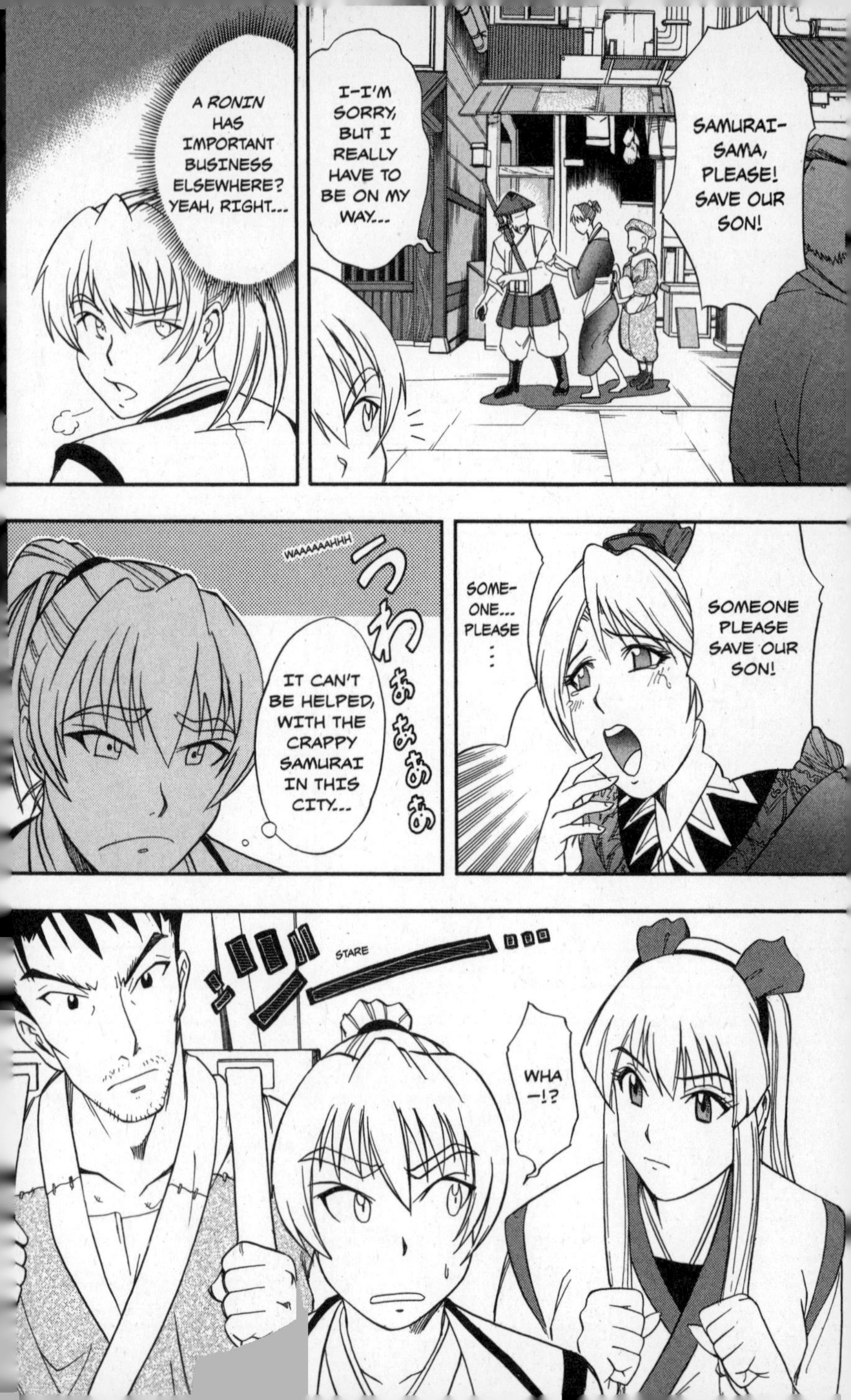
SAMURAI-SAMA, PLEASE! SAVE OUR SON!
I-I'M SORRY, BUT I REALLY HAVE TO BE ON MY WAY...
A RONIN HAS IMPORTANT BUSINESS ELSEWHERE? YEAH, RIGHT...
SOMEONE PLEASE SAVE OUR SON!
SOME-ONE... PLEASE...
WAAAAAAHHH
IT CAN'T BE HELPED, WITH THE CRAPPY SAMURAI IN THIS CITY...
STARE
WHA—!?

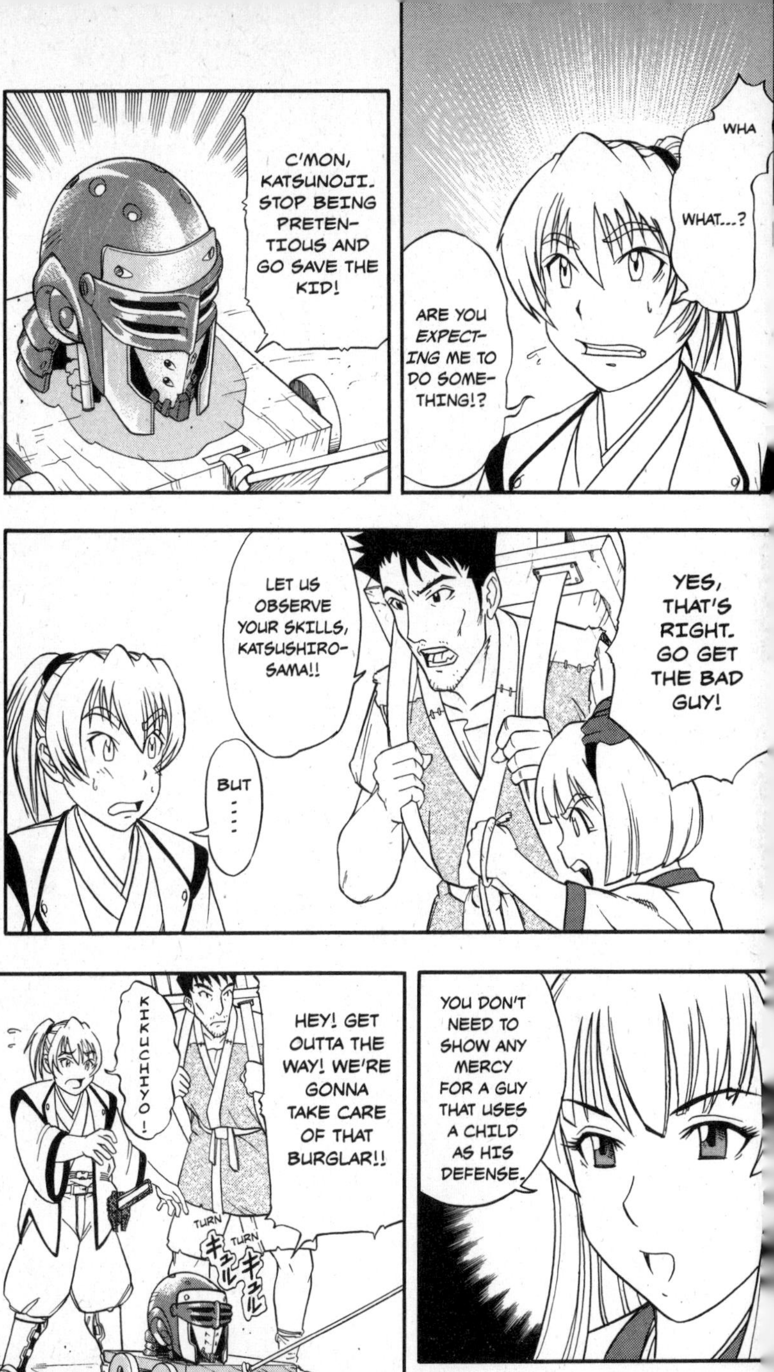
WHA
WHAT...?
ARE YOU EXPECTING ME TO DO SOMETHING!?
C'MON, KATSUNOJI. STOP BEING PRETENTIOUS AND GO SAVE THE KID!
YES, THAT'S RIGHT. GO GET THE BAD GUY!
LET US OBSERVE YOUR SKILLS, KATSUSHIRO-SAMA!!
BUT.....
YOU DON'T NEED TO SHOW ANY MERCY FOR A GUY THAT USES A CHILD AS HIS DEFENSE.
HEY! GET OUTTA THE WAY! WE'RE GONNA TAKE CARE OF THAT BURGLAR!!
KIKUCHIYO!
TURN
キュル
TURN
キュル

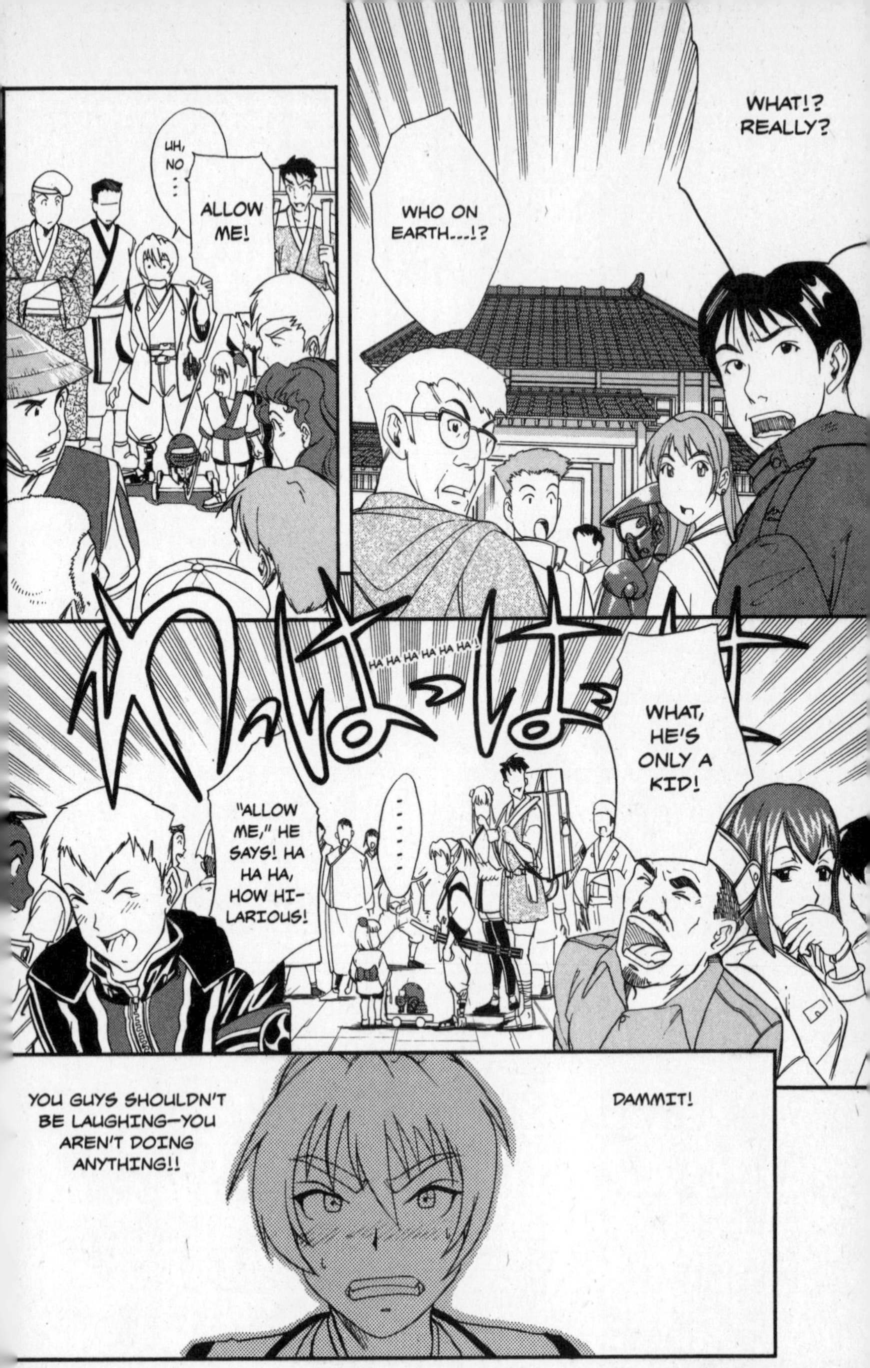
WHAT!? REALLY?
WHO ON EARTH...!?
UH, NO...
ALLOW ME!
HA HA HA HA HA HA!
WHAT, HE'S ONLY A KID!
......
"ALLOW ME," HE SAYS! HA HA HA, HOW HILARIOUS!
DAMMIT!
YOU GUYS SHOULDN'T BE LAUGHING—YOU AREN'T DOING ANYTHING!!

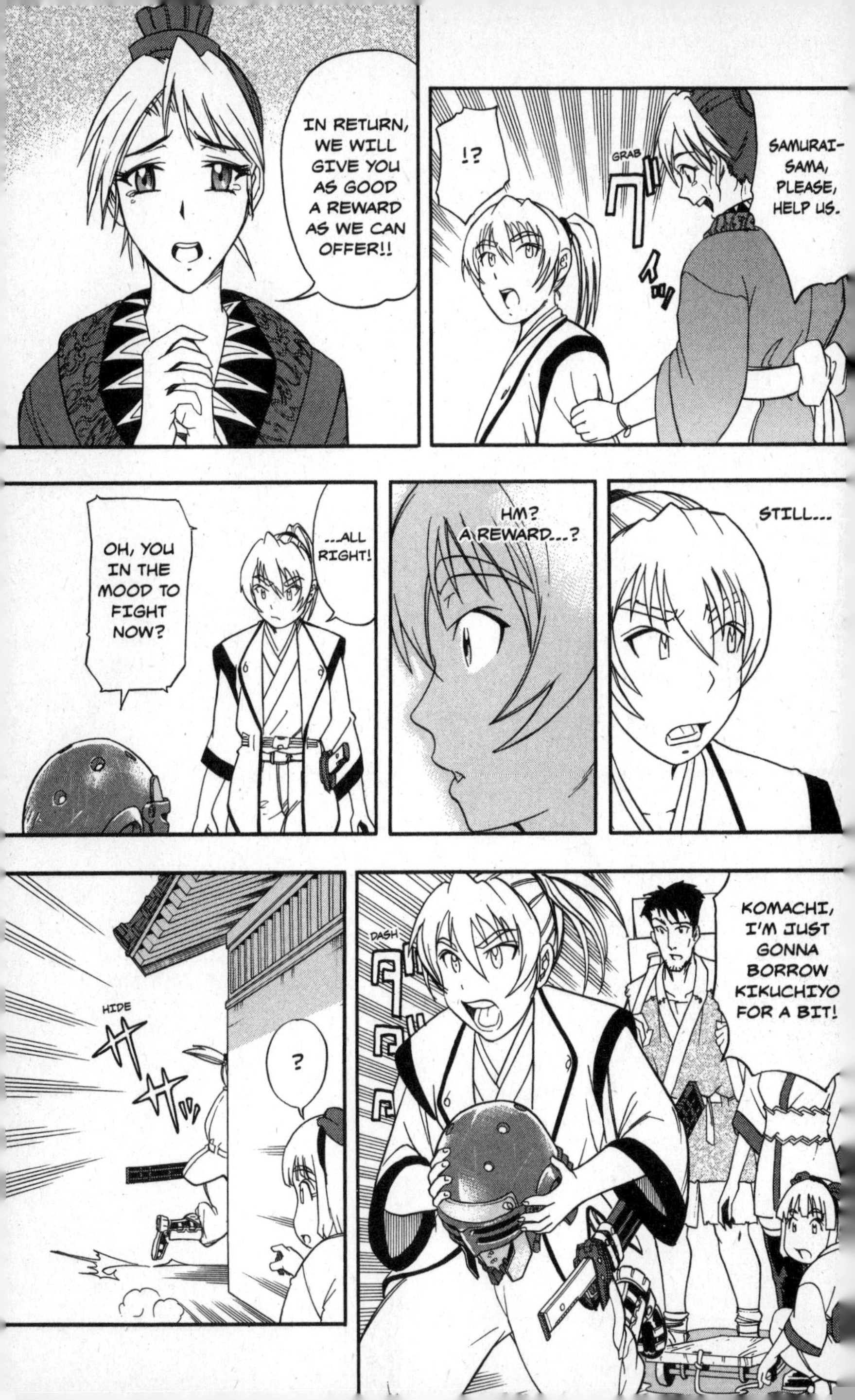
SAMURAI-SAMA, PLEASE, HELP US.
GRAB
!?
IN RETURN, WE WILL GIVE YOU AS GOOD A REWARD AS WE CAN OFFER!!
STILL...
HM? A REWARD...?
...ALL RIGHT!
OH, YOU IN THE MOOD TO FIGHT NOW?
KOMACHI, I'M JUST GONNA BORROW KIKUCHIYO FOR A BIT!
DASH
HIDE
?

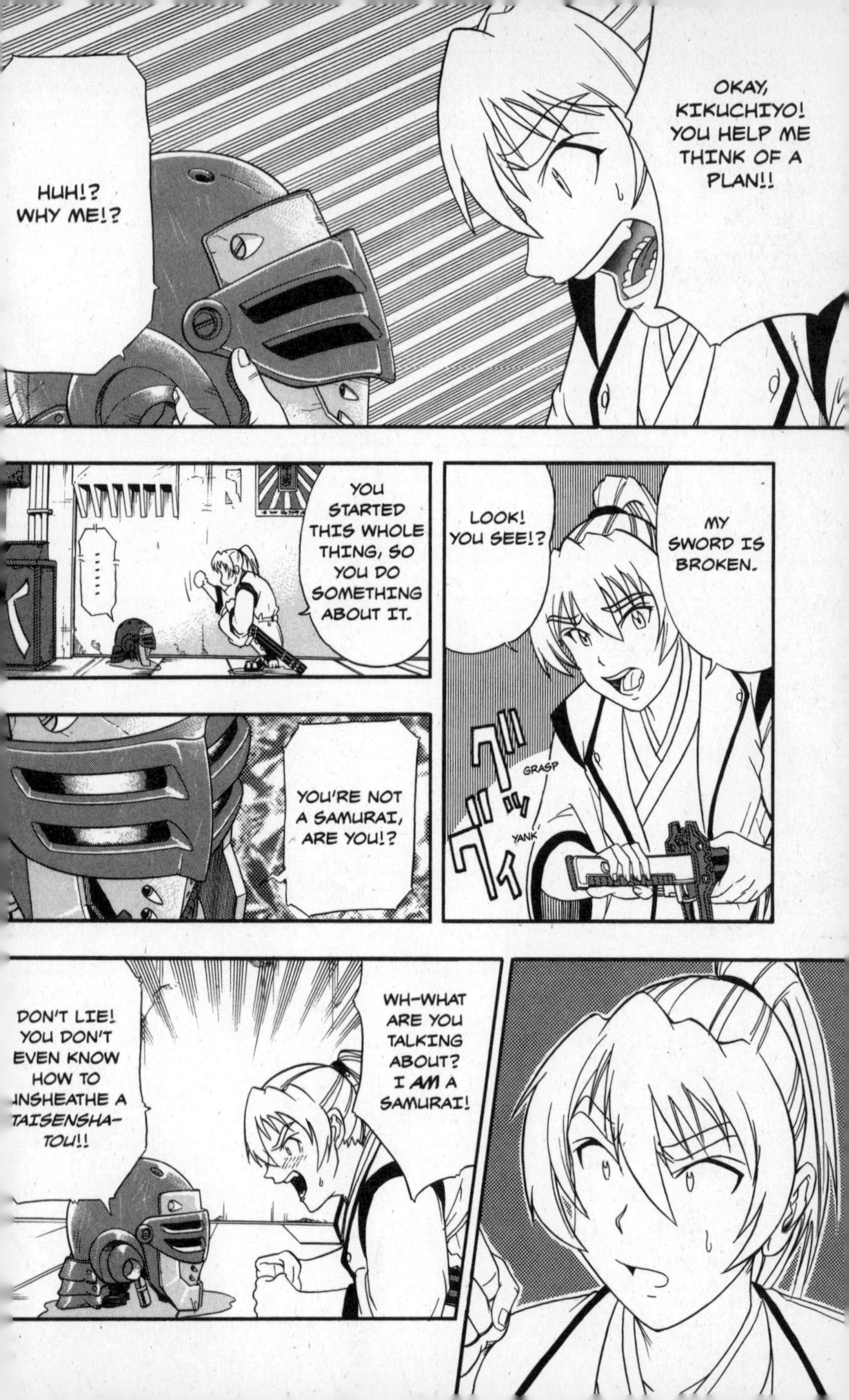
OKAY, KIKUCHIYO! YOU HELP ME THINK OF A PLAN!!
HUH!? WHY ME!?
LOOK! YOU SEE!?
MY SWORD IS BROKEN.
GRASP
YANK
YOU STARTED THIS WHOLE THING, SO YOU DO SOMETHING ABOUT IT.
YOU'RE NOT A SAMURAI, ARE YOU!?
WH-WHAT ARE YOU TALKING ABOUT? I *AM* A SAMURAI!
DON'T LIE! YOU DON'T EVEN KNOW HOW TO UNSHEATHE A TAISENSHA-TOU!!

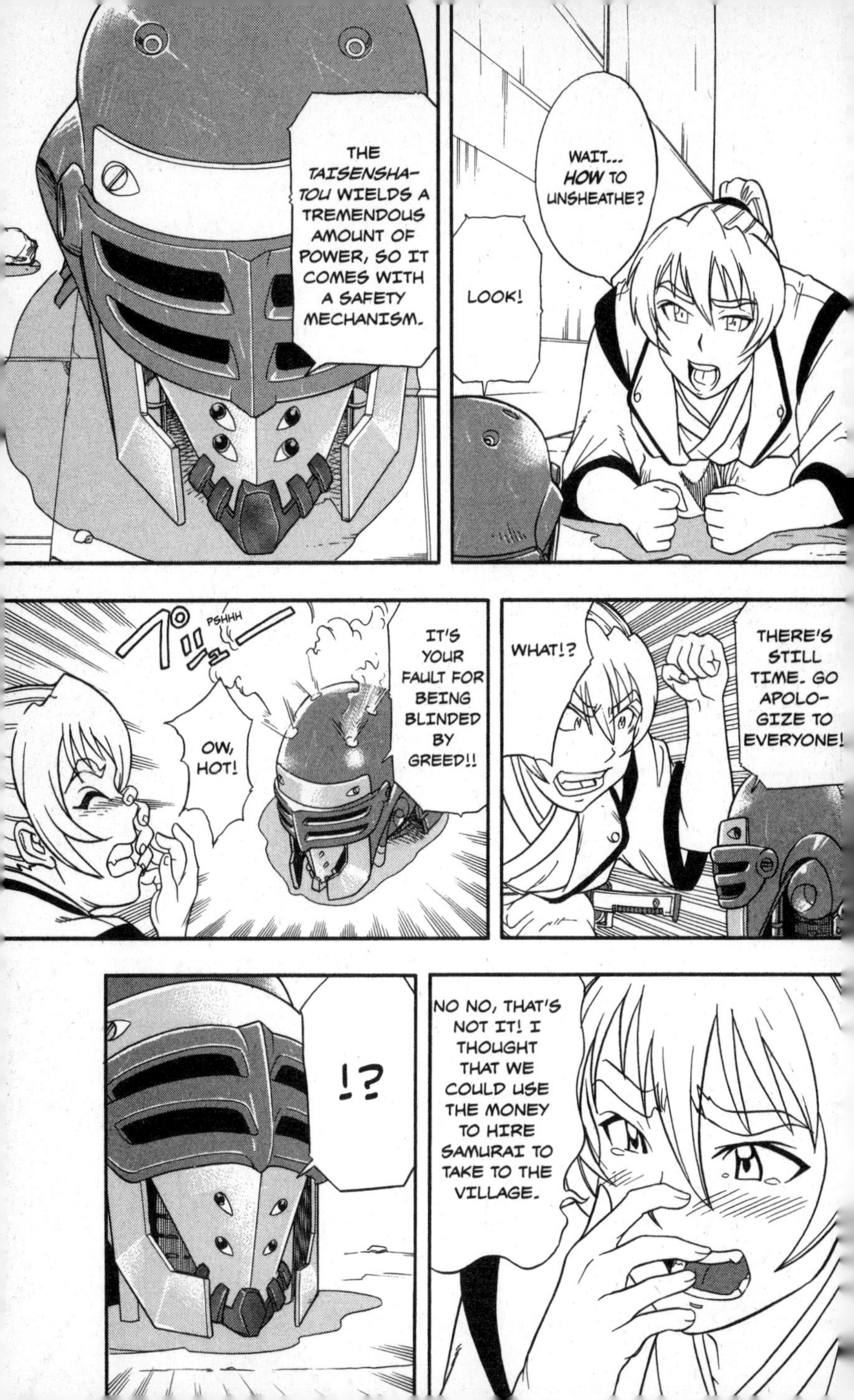
WAIT... HOW TO UNSHEATHE?
LOOK!
THE TAISENSHA-TOU WIELDS A TREMENDOUS AMOUNT OF POWER, SO IT COMES WITH A SAFETY MECHANISM.
THERE'S STILL TIME. GO APOLOGIZE TO EVERYONE!
WHAT!?
IT'S YOUR FAULT FOR BEING BLINDED BY GREED!!
PSHHH
OW, HOT!
NO NO, THAT'S NOT IT! I THOUGHT THAT WE COULD USE THE MONEY TO HIRE SAMURAI TO TAKE TO THE VILLAGE.
!?

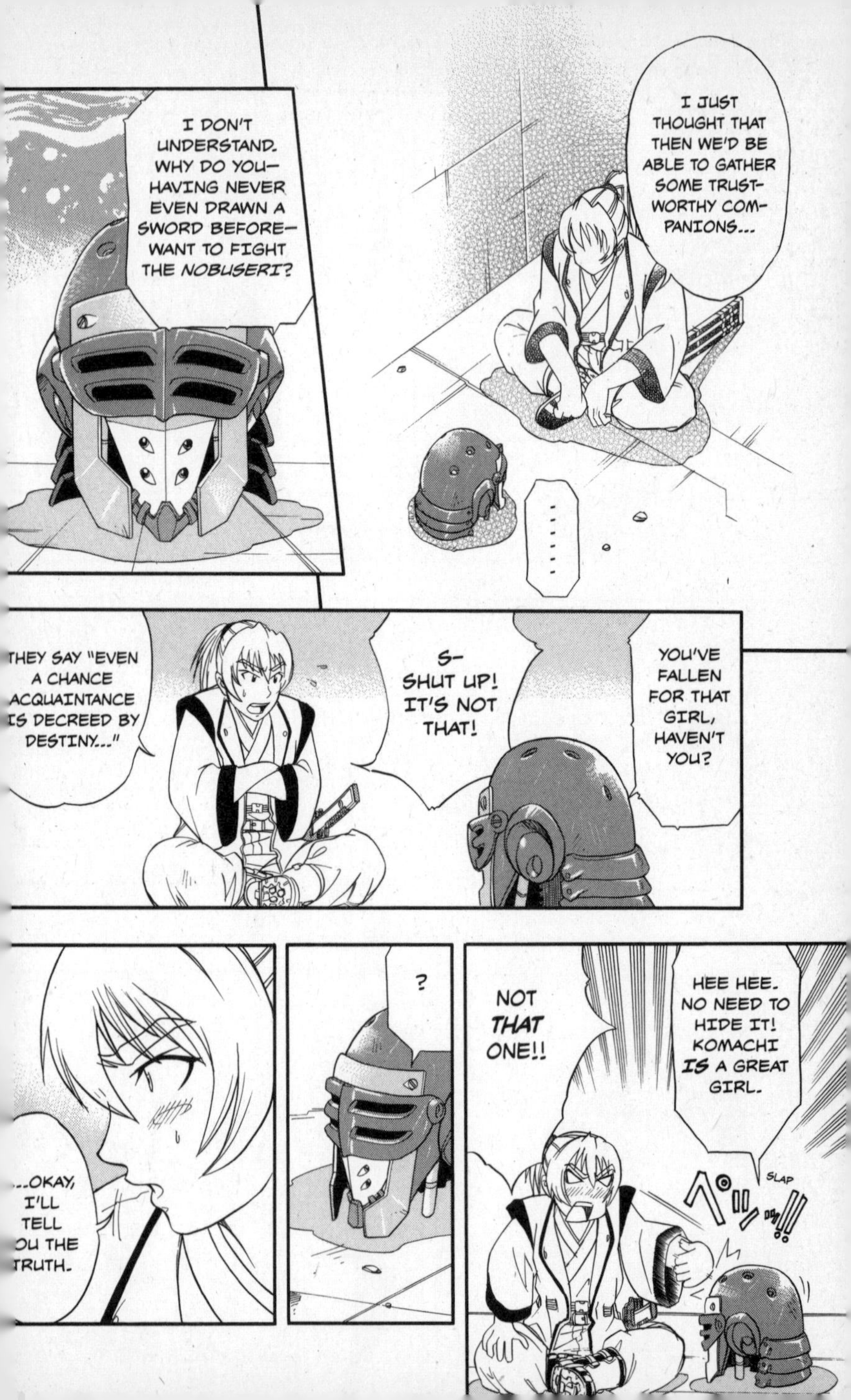
I JUST THOUGHT THAT THEN WE'D BE ABLE TO GATHER SOME TRUST-WORTHY COMPANIONS...
......
I DON'T UNDERSTAND. WHY DO YOU—HAVING NEVER EVEN DRAWN A SWORD BEFORE—WANT TO FIGHT THE *NOBUSERI*?
YOU'VE FALLEN FOR THAT GIRL, HAVEN'T YOU?
S-SHUT UP! IT'S NOT THAT!
THEY SAY "EVEN A CHANCE ACQUAINTANCE IS DECREED BY DESTINY..."
HEE HEE. NO NEED TO HIDE IT! KOMACHI *IS* A GREAT GIRL.
SLAP
NOT *THAT* ONE!!
?
...OKAY, I'LL TELL OU THE TRUTH.

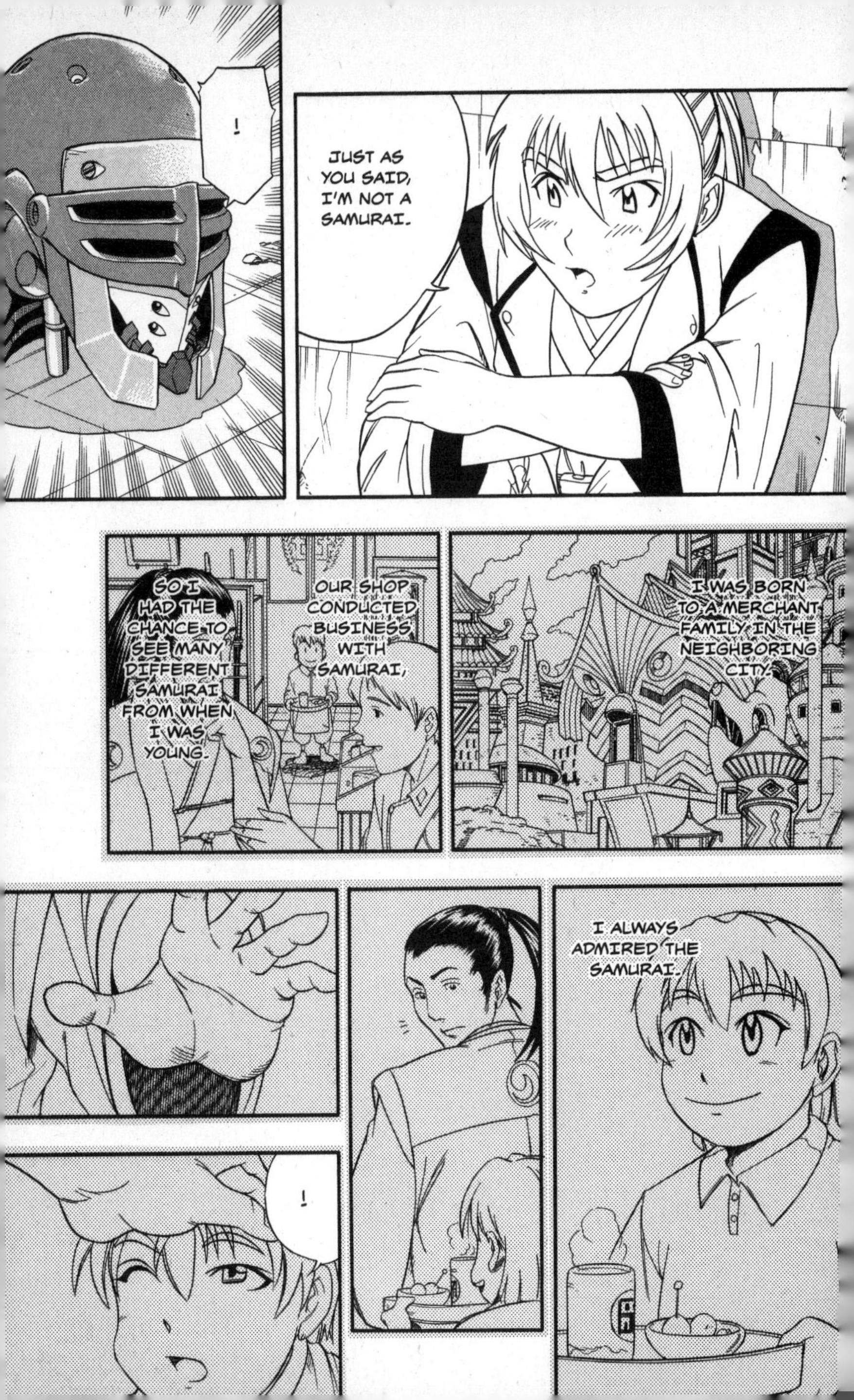
JUST AS YOU SAID, I'M NOT A SAMURAI.
!
I WAS BORN TO A MERCHANT FAMILY IN THE NEIGHBORING CITY.
OUR SHOP CONDUCTED BUSINESS WITH SAMURAI,
SO I HAD THE CHANCE TO SEE MANY DIFFERENT SAMURAI FROM WHEN I WAS YOUNG.
I ALWAYS ADMIRED THE SAMURAI.
!

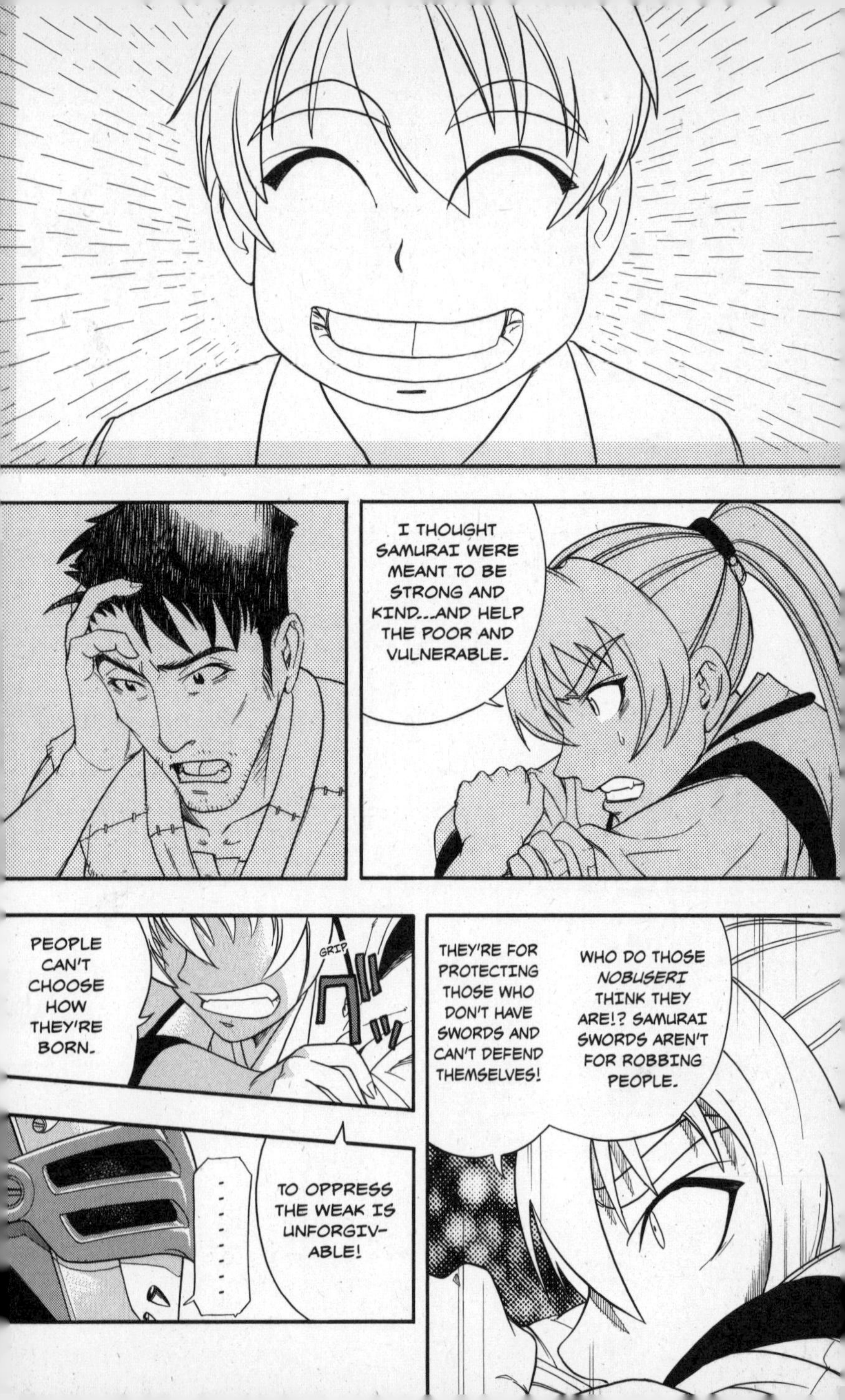
I THOUGHT SAMURAI WERE MEANT TO BE STRONG AND KIND...AND HELP THE POOR AND VULNERABLE.
WHO DO THOSE *NOBUSERI* THINK THEY ARE!? SAMURAI SWORDS AREN'T FOR ROBBING PEOPLE.
THEY'RE FOR PROTECTING THOSE WHO DON'T HAVE SWORDS AND CAN'T DEFEND THEMSELVES!
GRIP
PEOPLE CAN'T CHOOSE HOW THEY'RE BORN.
TO OPPRESS THE WEAK IS UNFORGIV-ABLE!
....

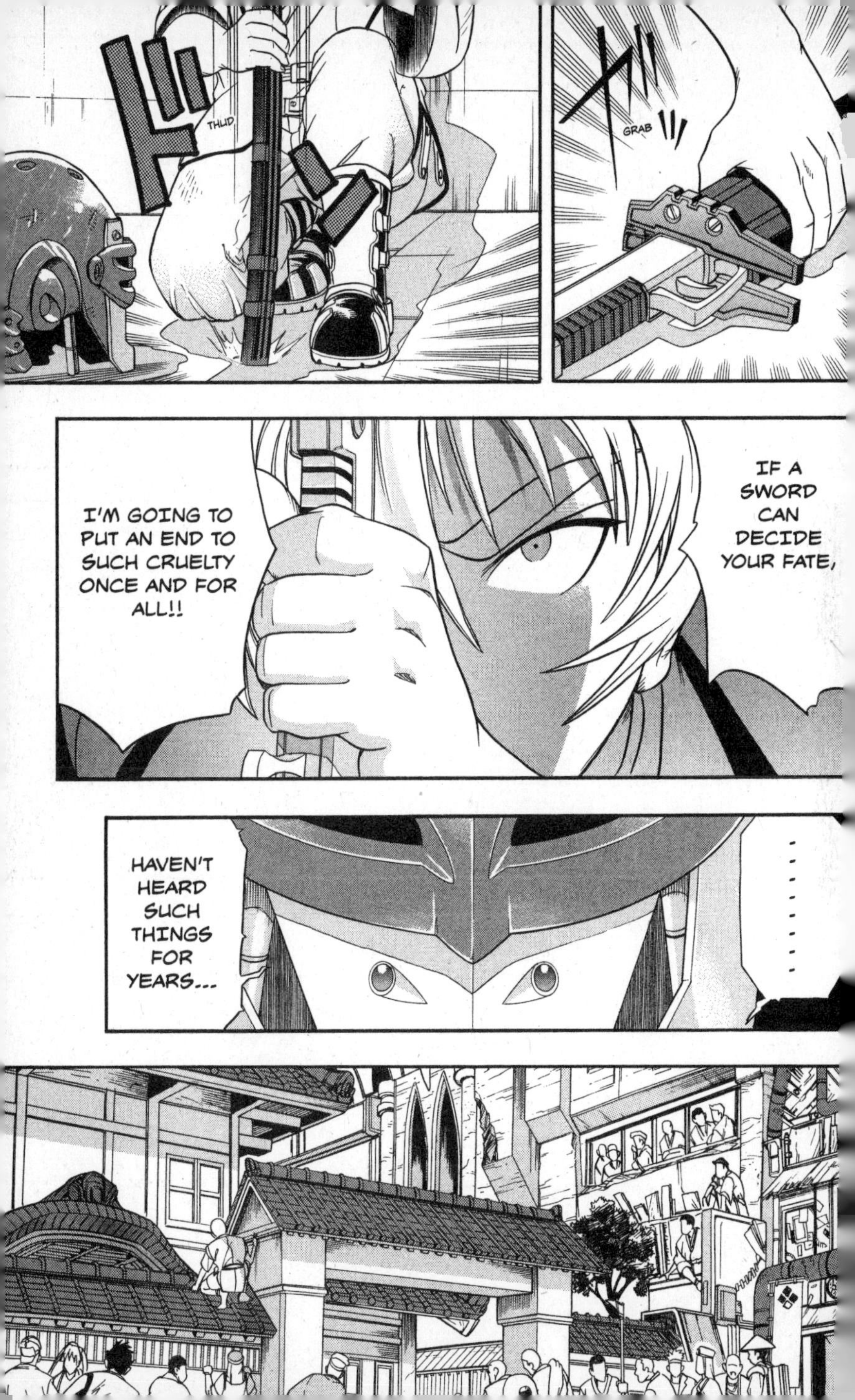
GRAB
THUD
IF A SWORD CAN DECIDE YOUR FATE,
I'M GOING TO PUT AN END TO SUCH CRUELTY ONCE AND FOR ALL!!
......
HAVEN'T HEARD SUCH THINGS FOR YEARS...

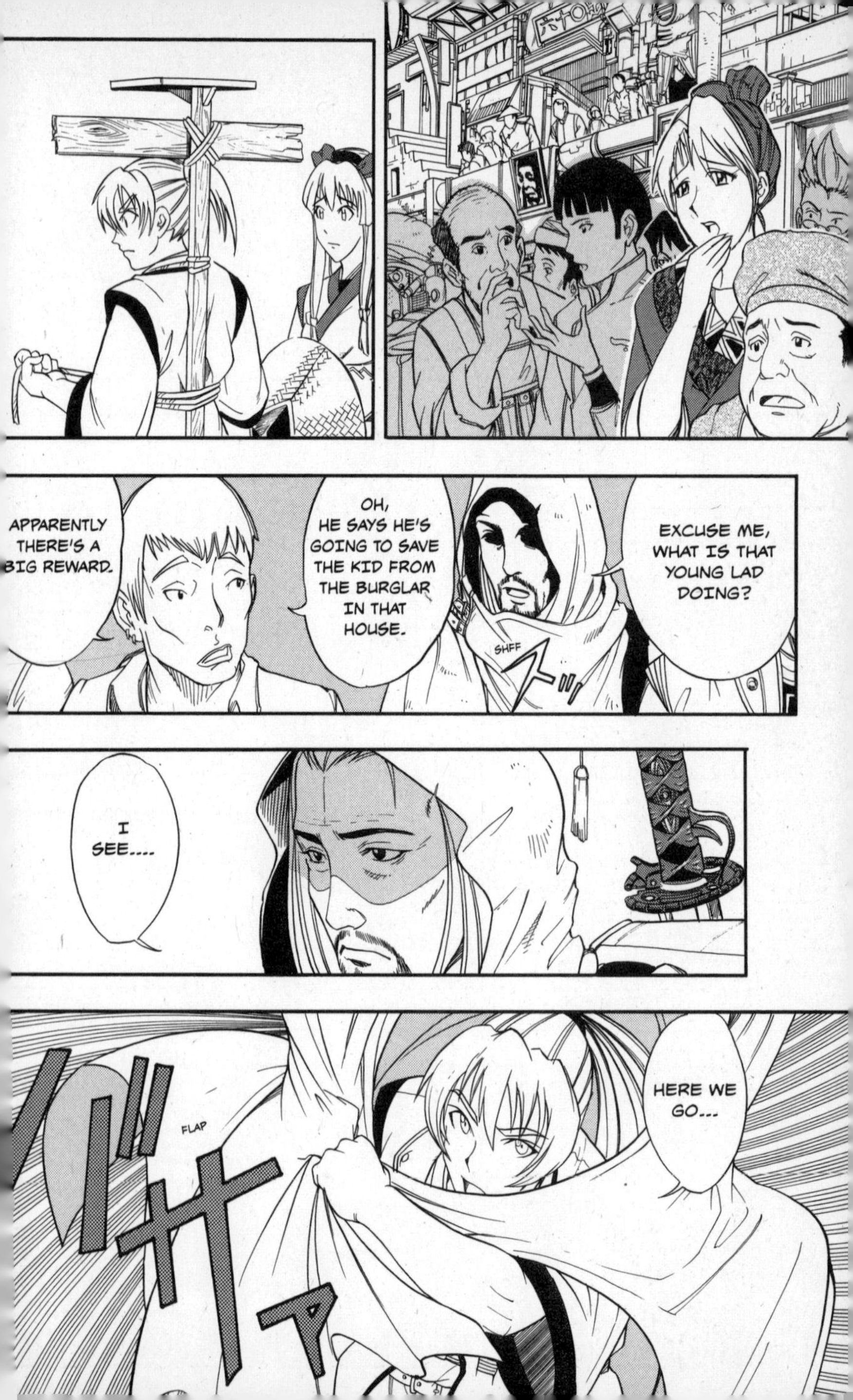
EXCUSE ME, WHAT IS THAT YOUNG LAD DOING?
SHFF
OH, HE SAYS HE'S GOING TO SAVE THE KID FROM THE BURGLAR IN THAT HOUSE.
APPARENTLY THERE'S A BIG REWARD.
I SEE....
HERE WE GO...
FLAP

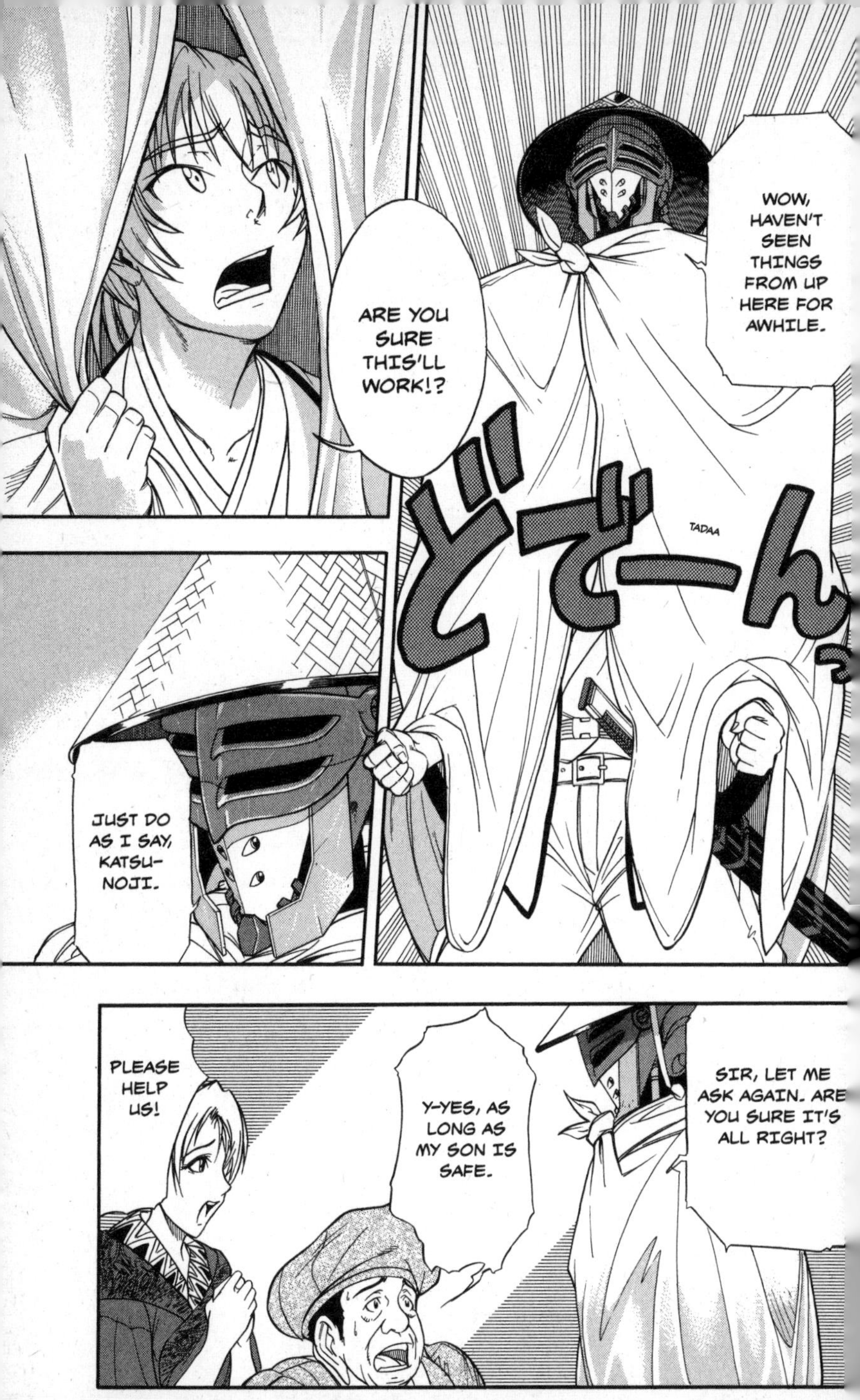
WOW, HAVEN'T SEEN THINGS FROM UP HERE FOR AWHILE.
どでーんっ
TADAA
ARE YOU SURE THIS'LL WORK!?
JUST DO AS I SAY, KATSU-NOJI.
SIR, LET ME ASK AGAIN. ARE YOU SURE IT'S ALL RIGHT?
Y-YES, AS LONG AS MY SON IS SAFE.
PLEASE HELP US!

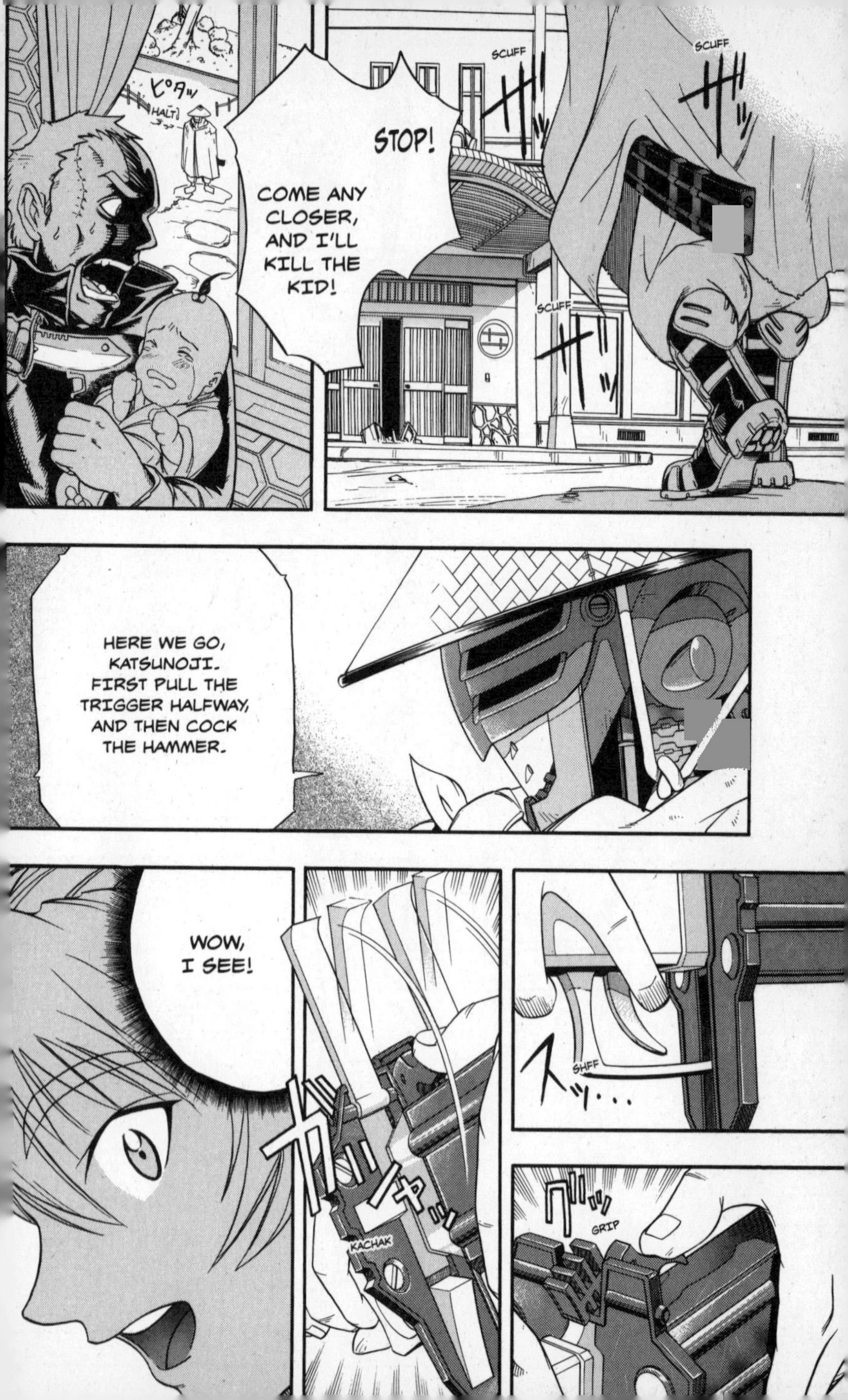

SCUFF
SCUFF
SCUFF
HALT!
STOP!
COME ANY CLOSER, AND I'LL KILL THE KID!
HERE WE GO, KATSUNOJI. FIRST PULL THE TRIGGER HALFWAY, AND THEN COCK THE HAMMER.
SHFF
GRIP
KACHAK
WOW, I SEE!

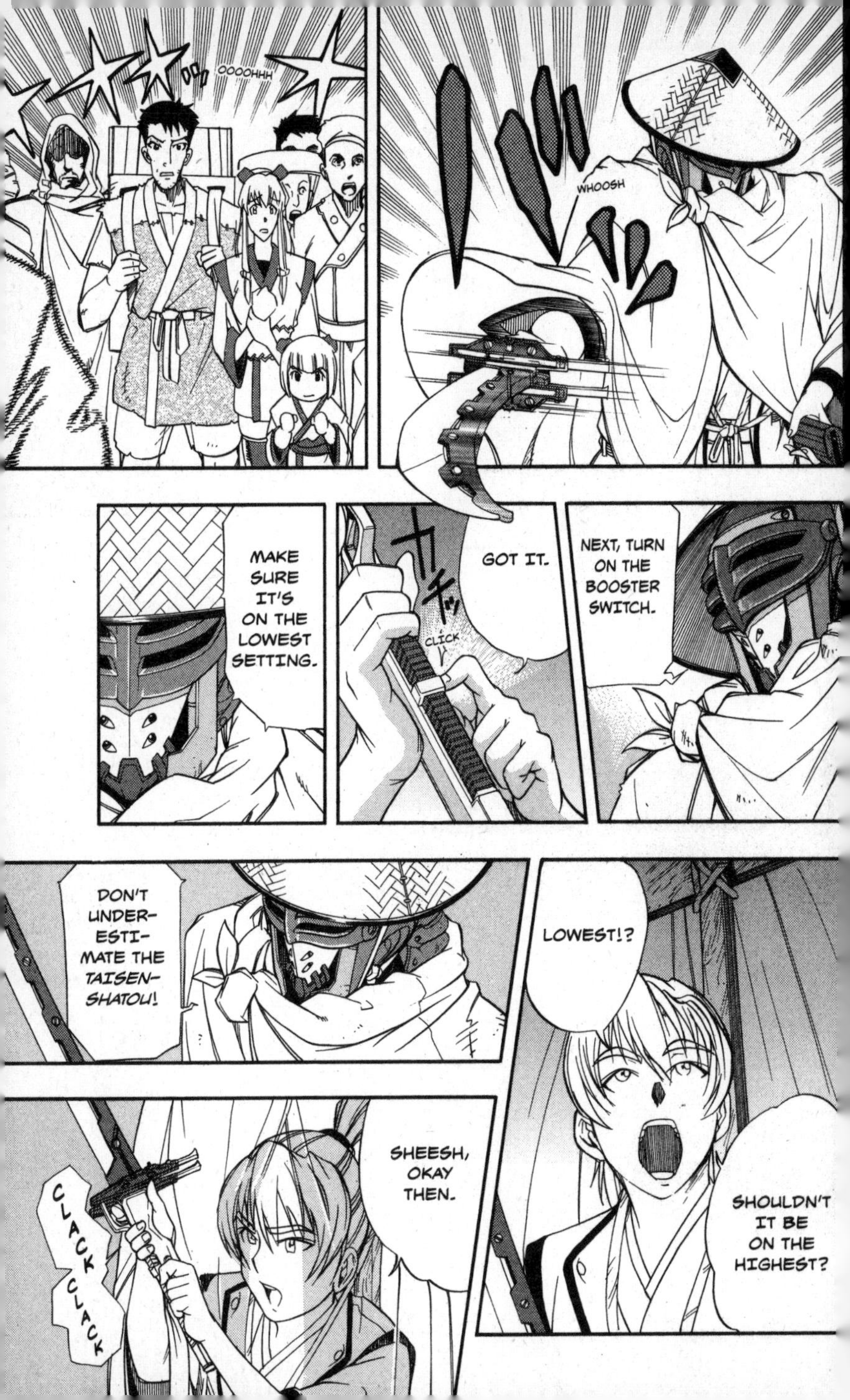
WHOOSH
OOOOHHH
NEXT, TURN ON THE BOOSTER SWITCH.
GOT IT.
CLICK
MAKE SURE IT'S ON THE LOWEST SETTING.
LOWEST!?
SHOULDN'T IT BE ON THE HIGHEST?
DON'T UNDER-ESTI-MATE THE TAISEN-SHATOU!
SHEESH, OKAY THEN.
CLACK CLACK

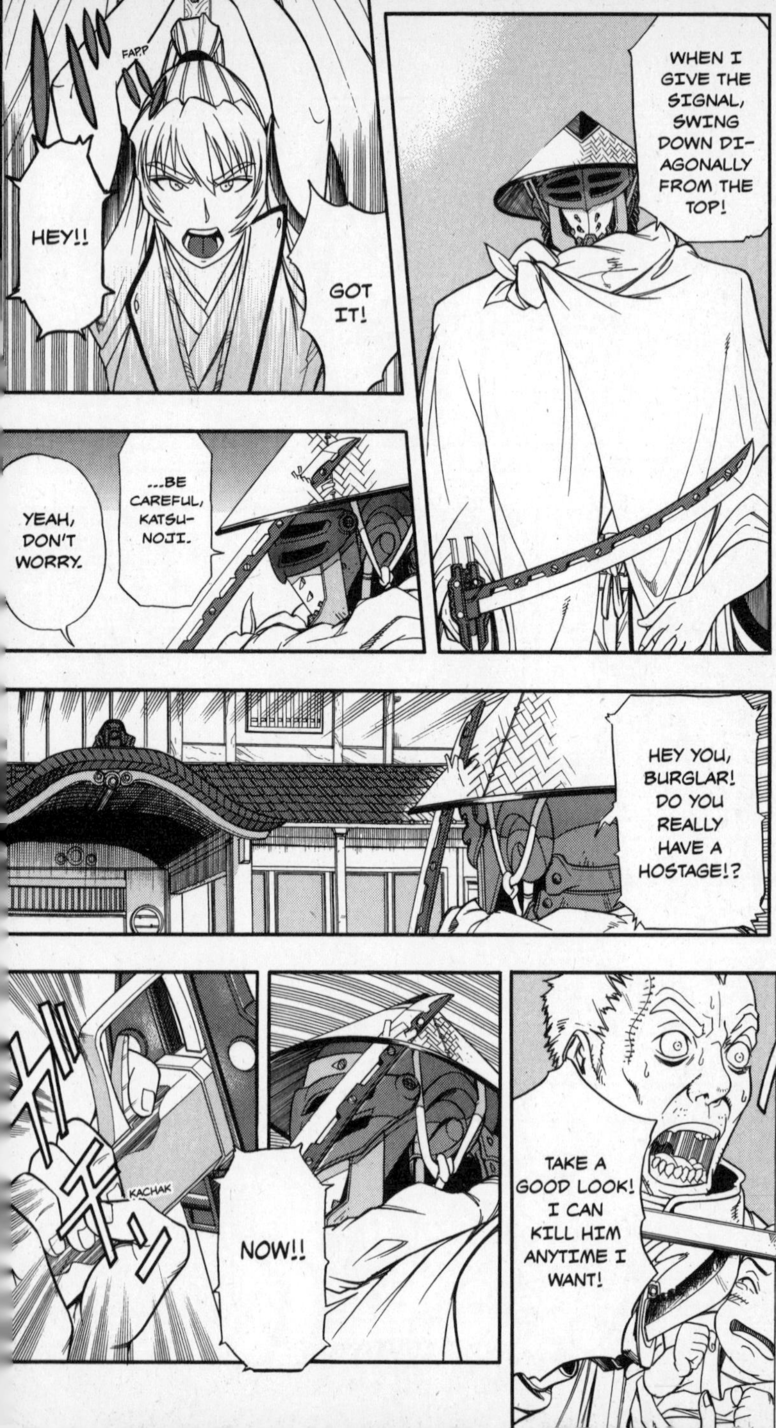
WHEN I GIVE THE SIGNAL, SWING DOWN DI-AGONALLY FROM THE TOP!
FAPP
GOT IT!
HEY!!
...BE CAREFUL, KATSU-NOJI.
YEAH, DON'T WORRY.
HEY YOU, BURGLAR! DO YOU REALLY HAVE A HOSTAGE!?
TAKE A GOOD LOOK! I CAN KILL HIM ANYTIME I WANT!
FAPP
NOW!!
KACHAK

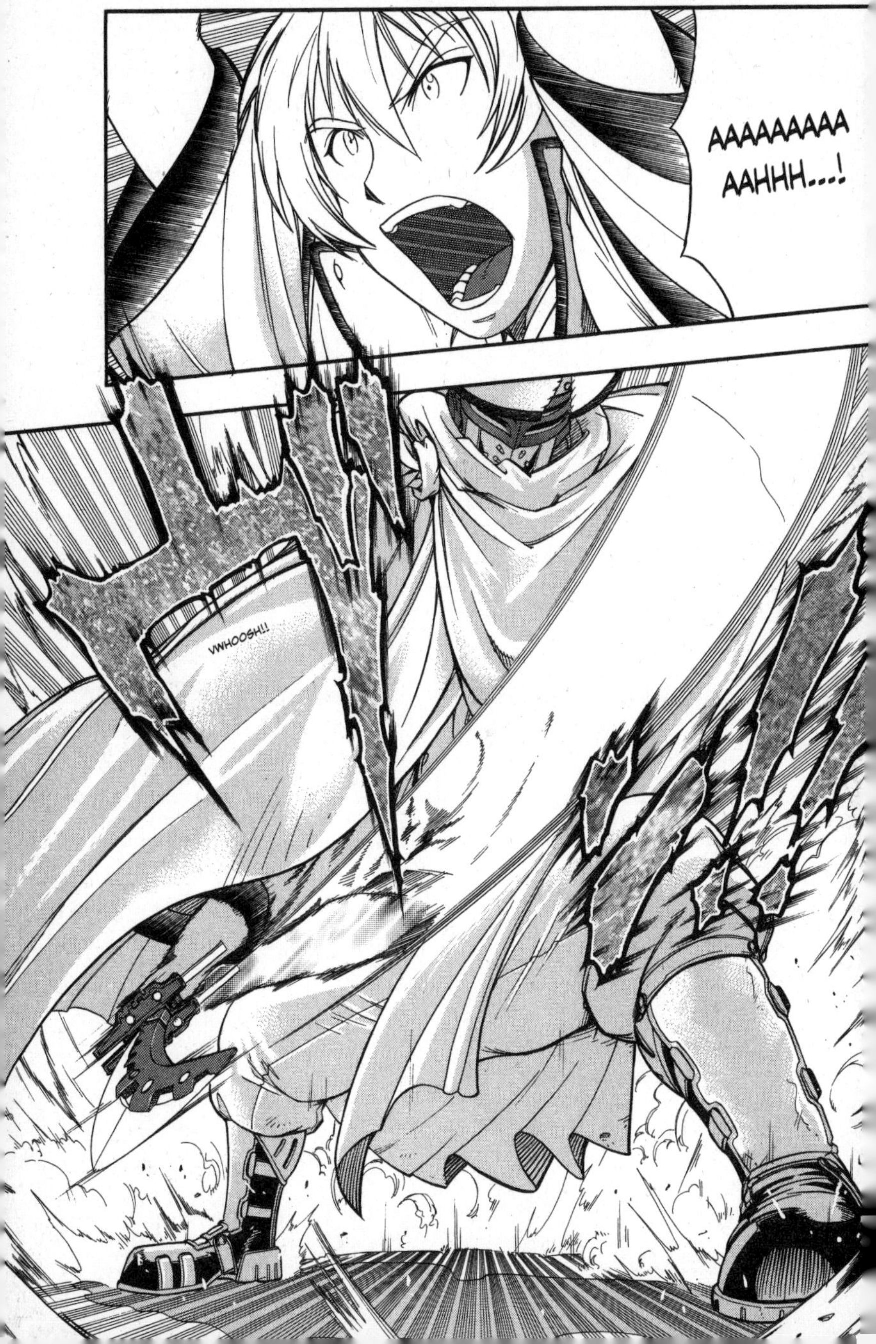
AAAAAAAAA
AAHHH...!
VWHOOSH!!

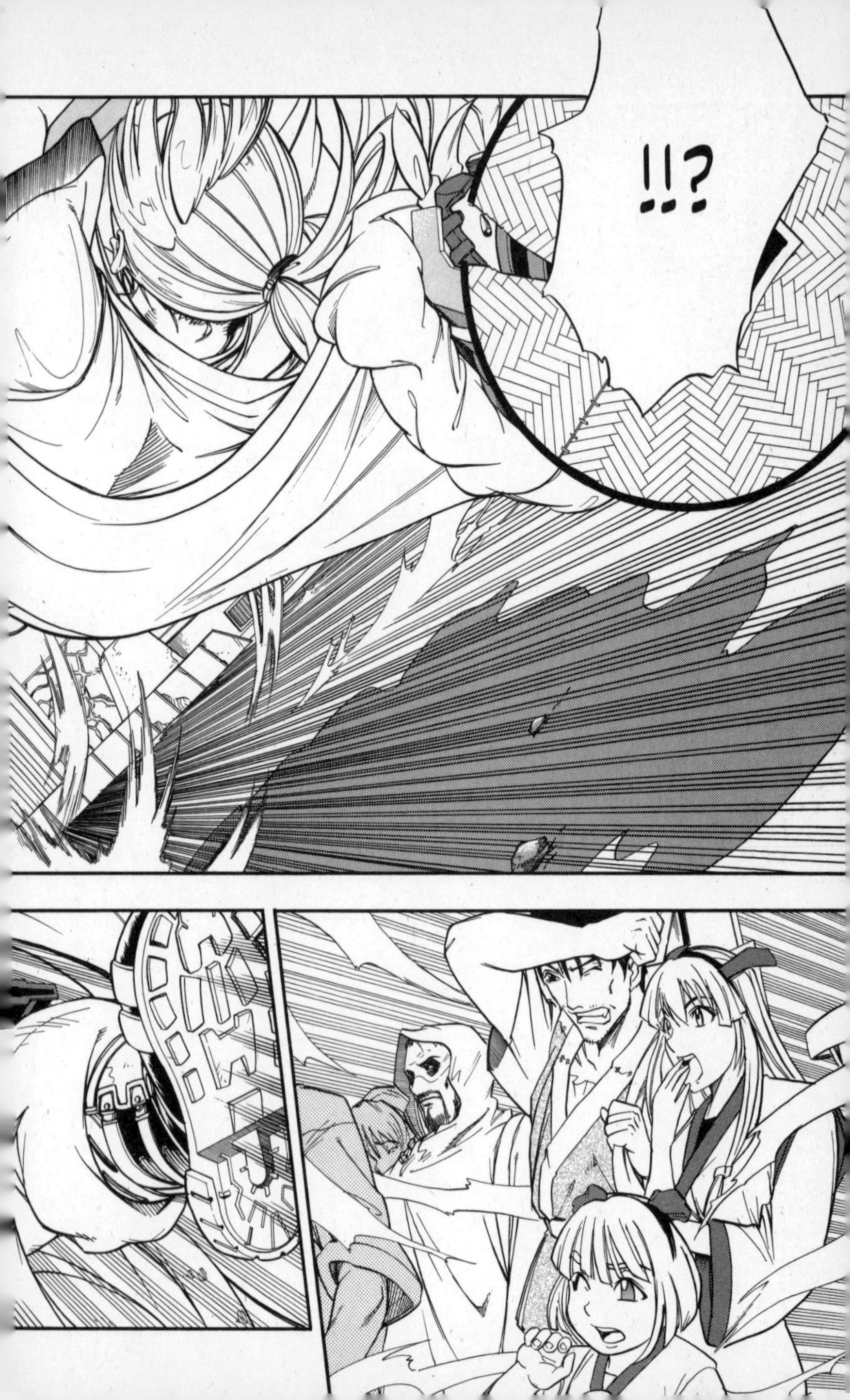
!!?

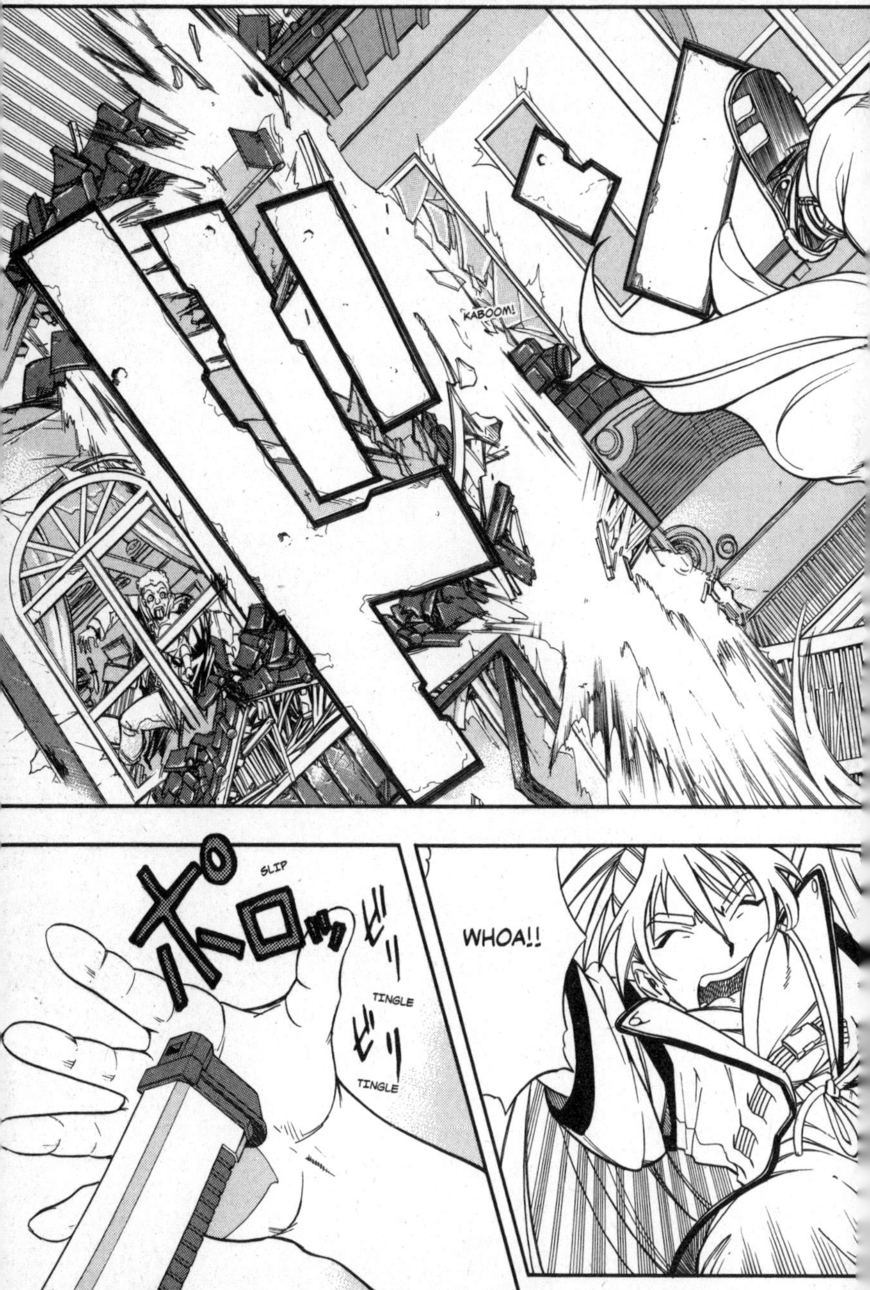

KABOOM!
WHOA!!
ポロッ
SLIP
ビリ
TINGLE
ビリ
TINGLE

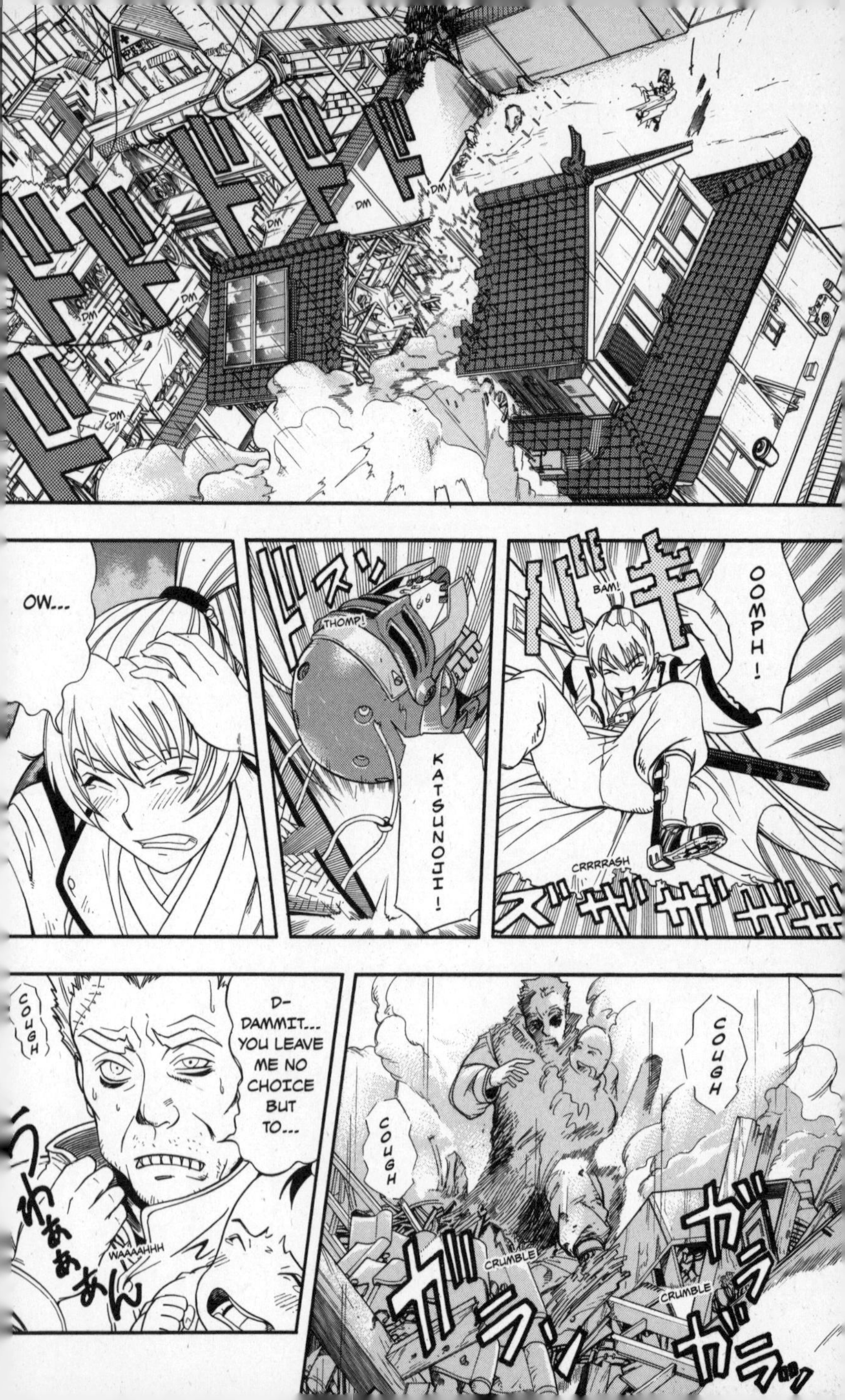

DM
DM
DM
DM
DM
DM
ドドドドドド
バキ
BAM!
OOMPH!
CRRRRASH
ズザザザザ
ドスッ
THOMP!
KATSUNOJI!
OW...
COUGH
COUGH
CRUMBLE
CRUMBLE
ガラッ
ガラガラッ
COUGH
D-DAMMIT... YOU LEAVE ME NO CHOICE BUT TO...
WAAAAHHH
うわああああん

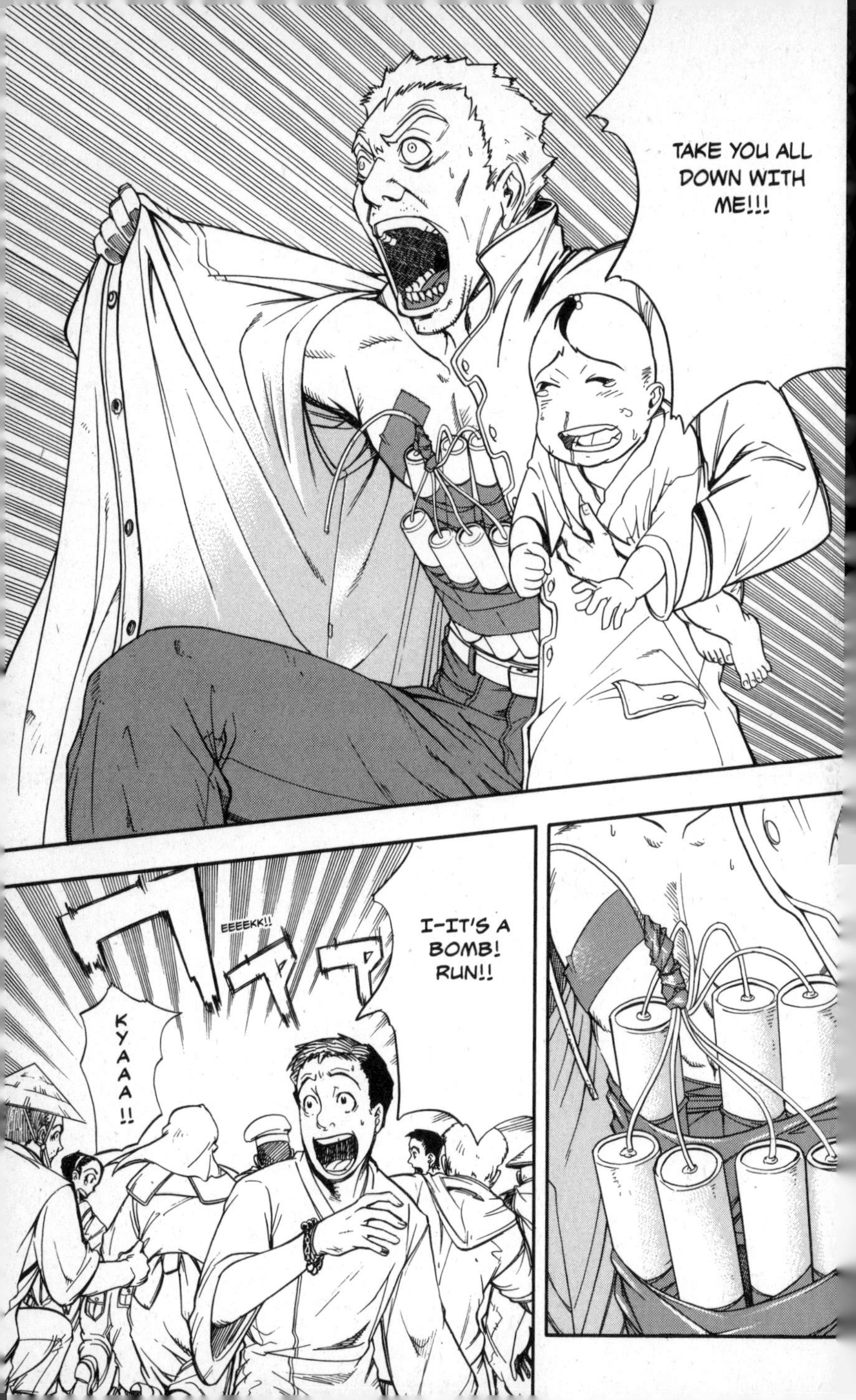
TAKE YOU ALL DOWN WITH ME!!!
I-IT'S A BOMB! RUN!!
EEEEKK!!
KYAAAA!!

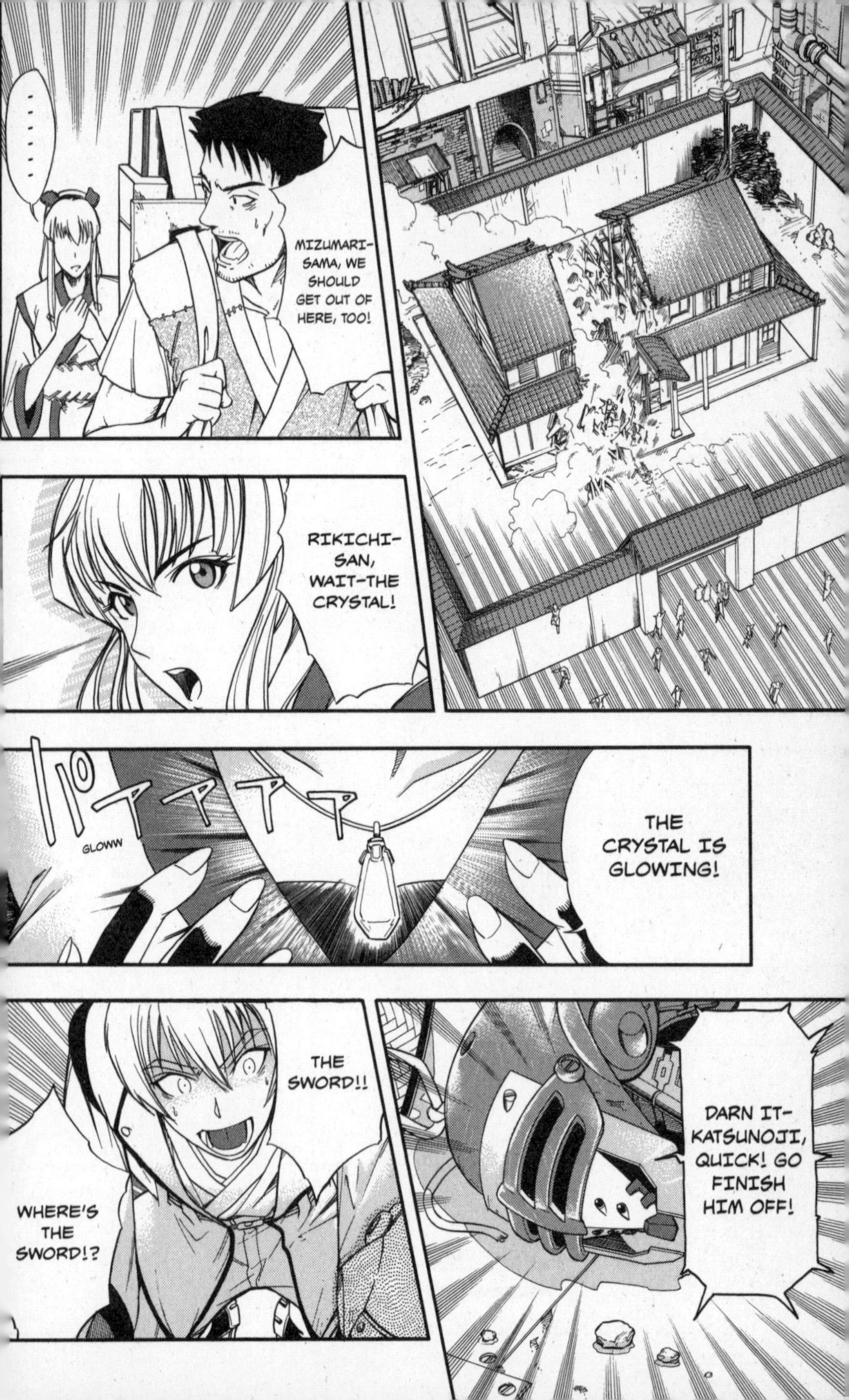
MIZUMARI-SAMA, WE SHOULD GET OUT OF HERE, TOO!
......
RIKICHI-SAN, WAIT—THE CRYSTAL!
THE CRYSTAL IS GLOWING!
GLOWW
DARN IT-KATSUNOJI, QUICK! GO FINISH HIM OFF!
THE SWORD!!
WHERE'S THE SWORD!?

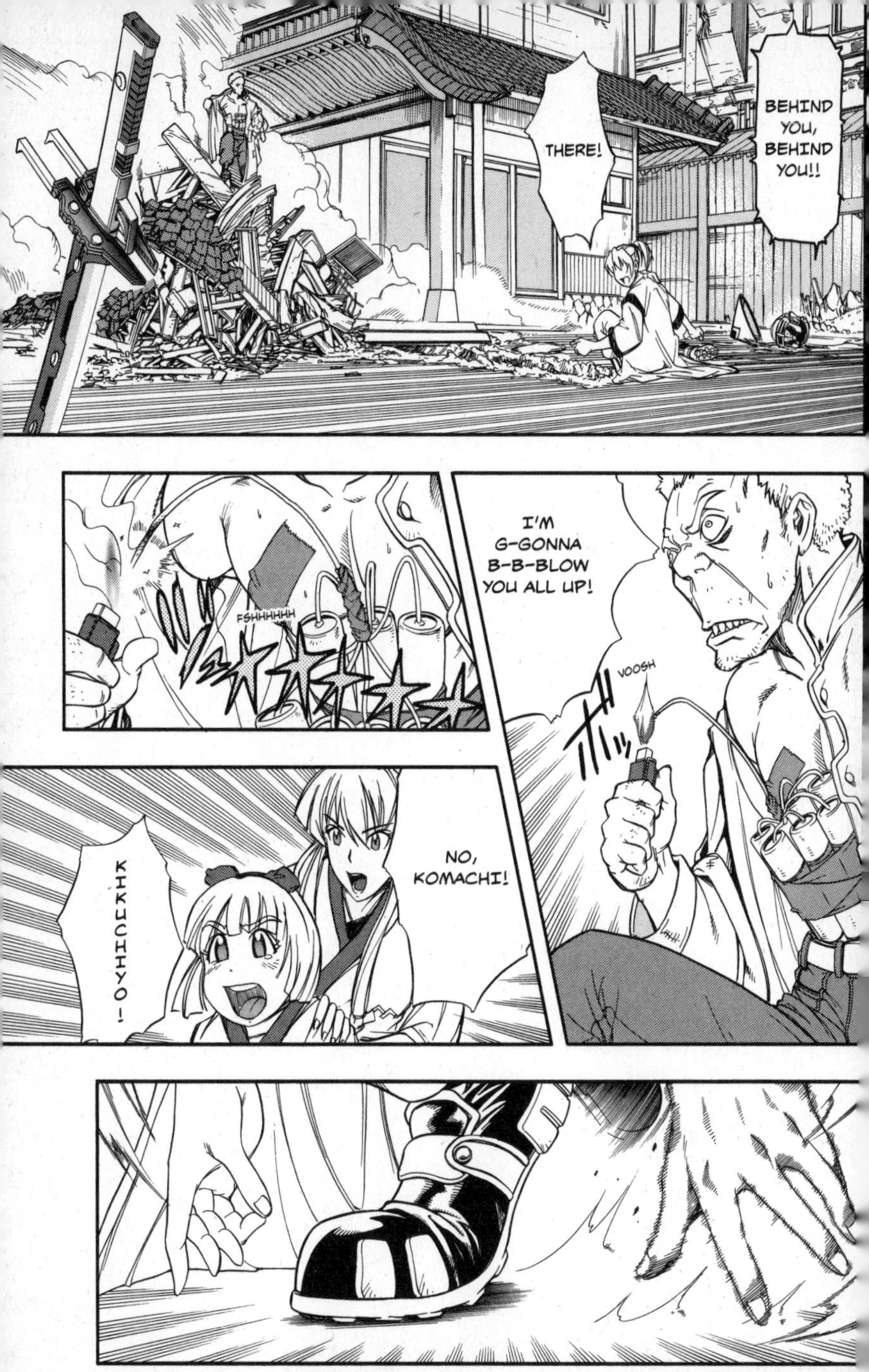
BEHIND YOU, BEHIND YOU!!
THERE!
I'M G-GONNA B-B-BLOW YOU ALL UP!
VOOSH
FSHHHHHH
NO, KOMACHI!
KIKUCHIYO!

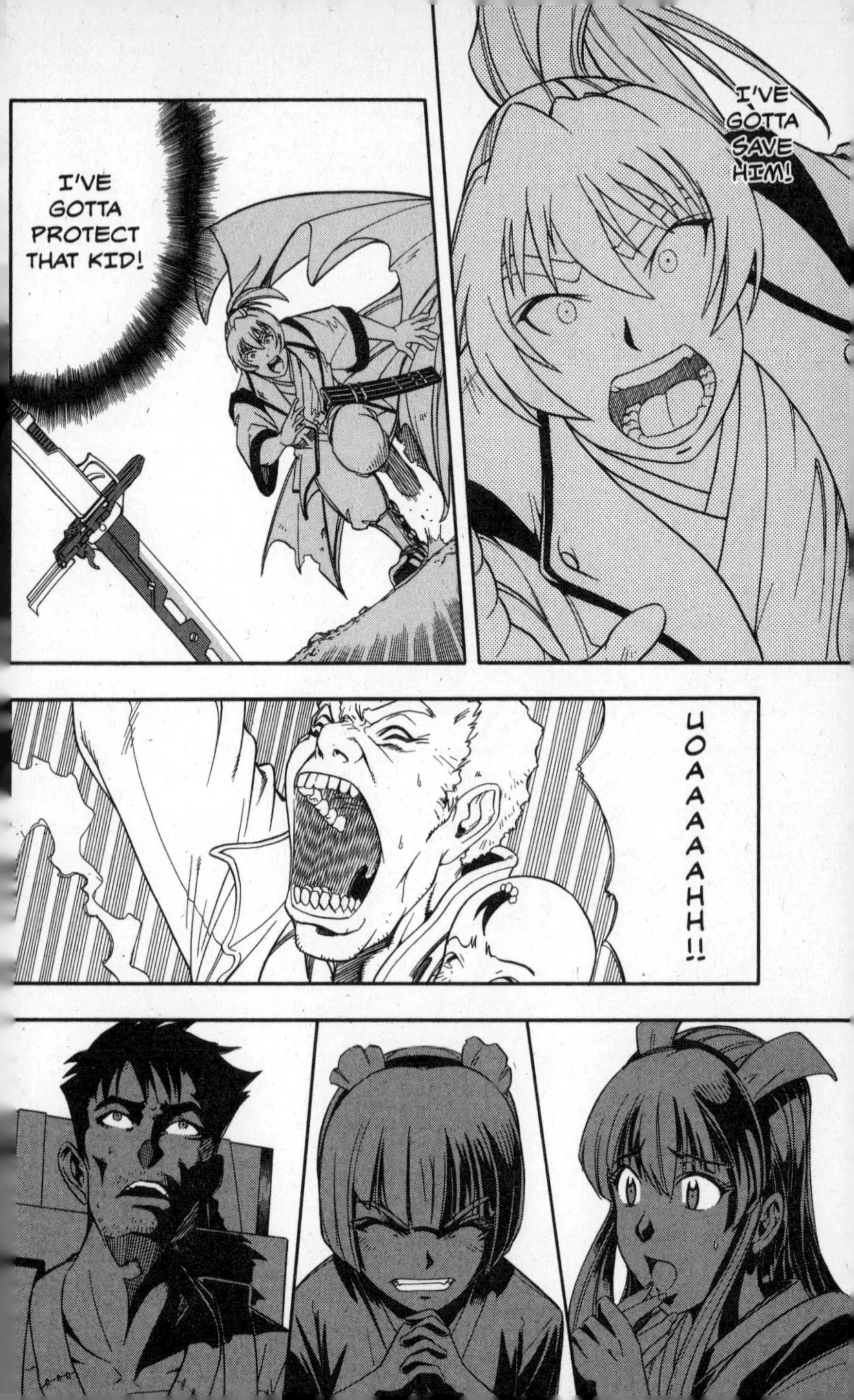
I'VE GOTTA SAVE HIM!
I'VE GOTTA PROTECT THAT KID!
UOAAAAAAHH!!

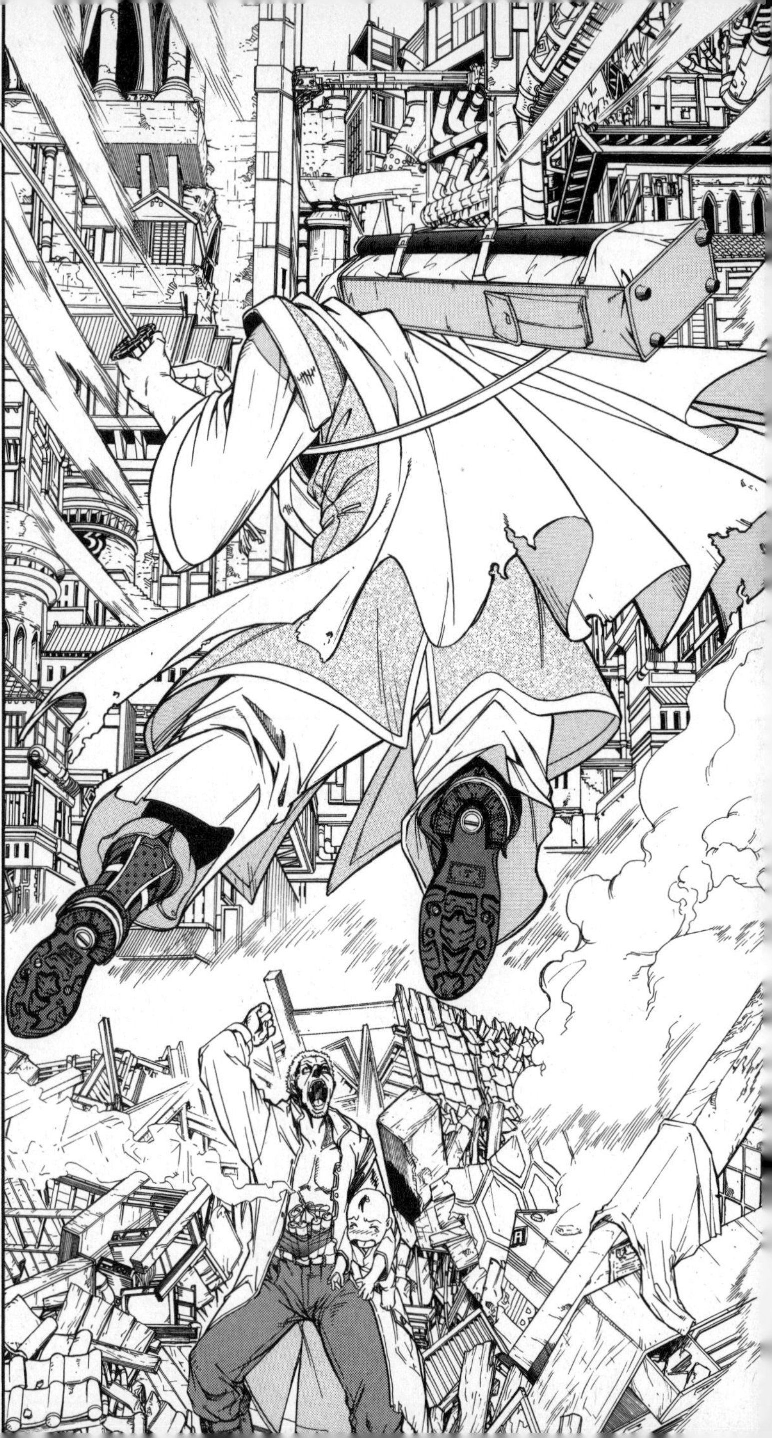

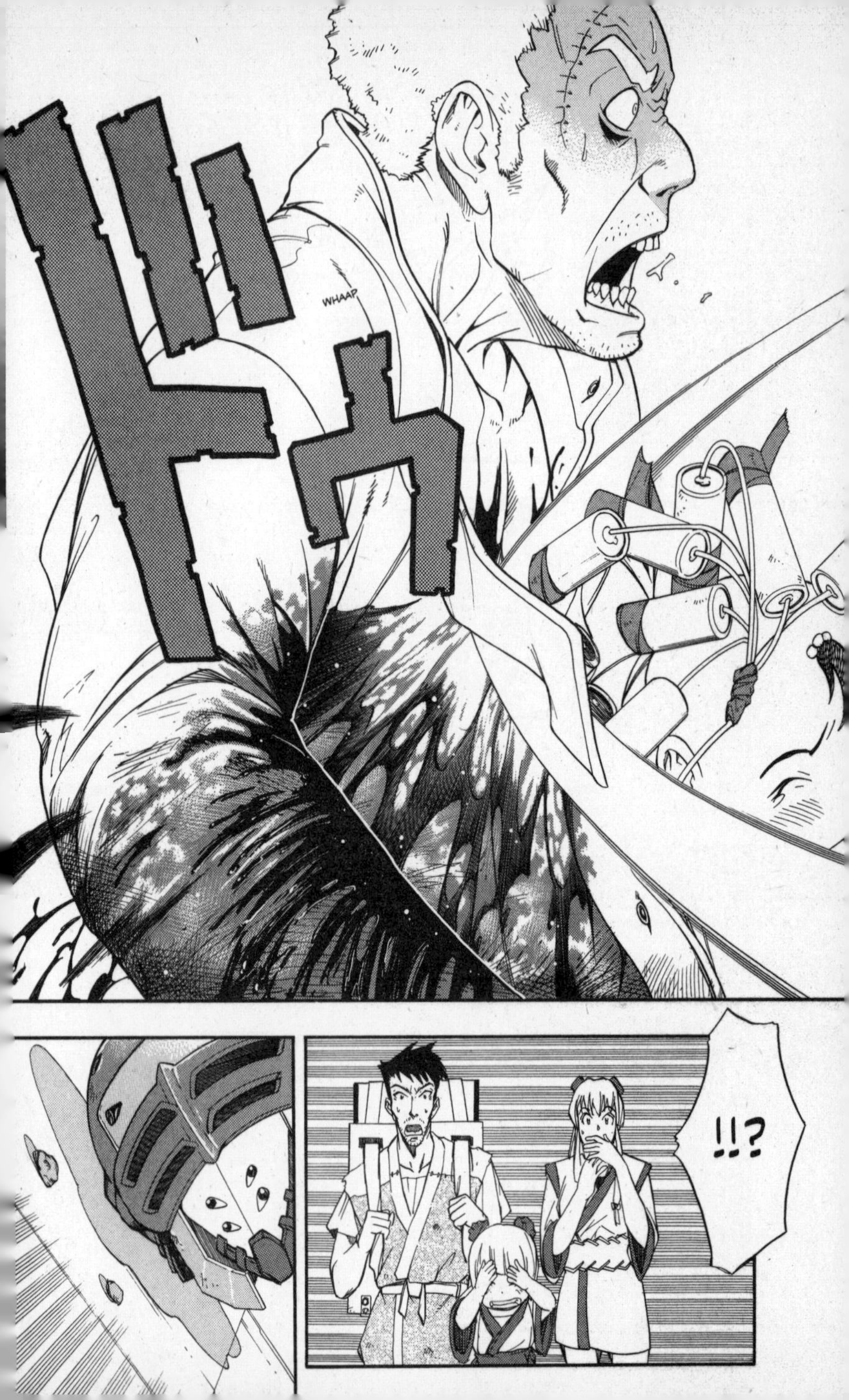
ドカ
WHAAP
!!?

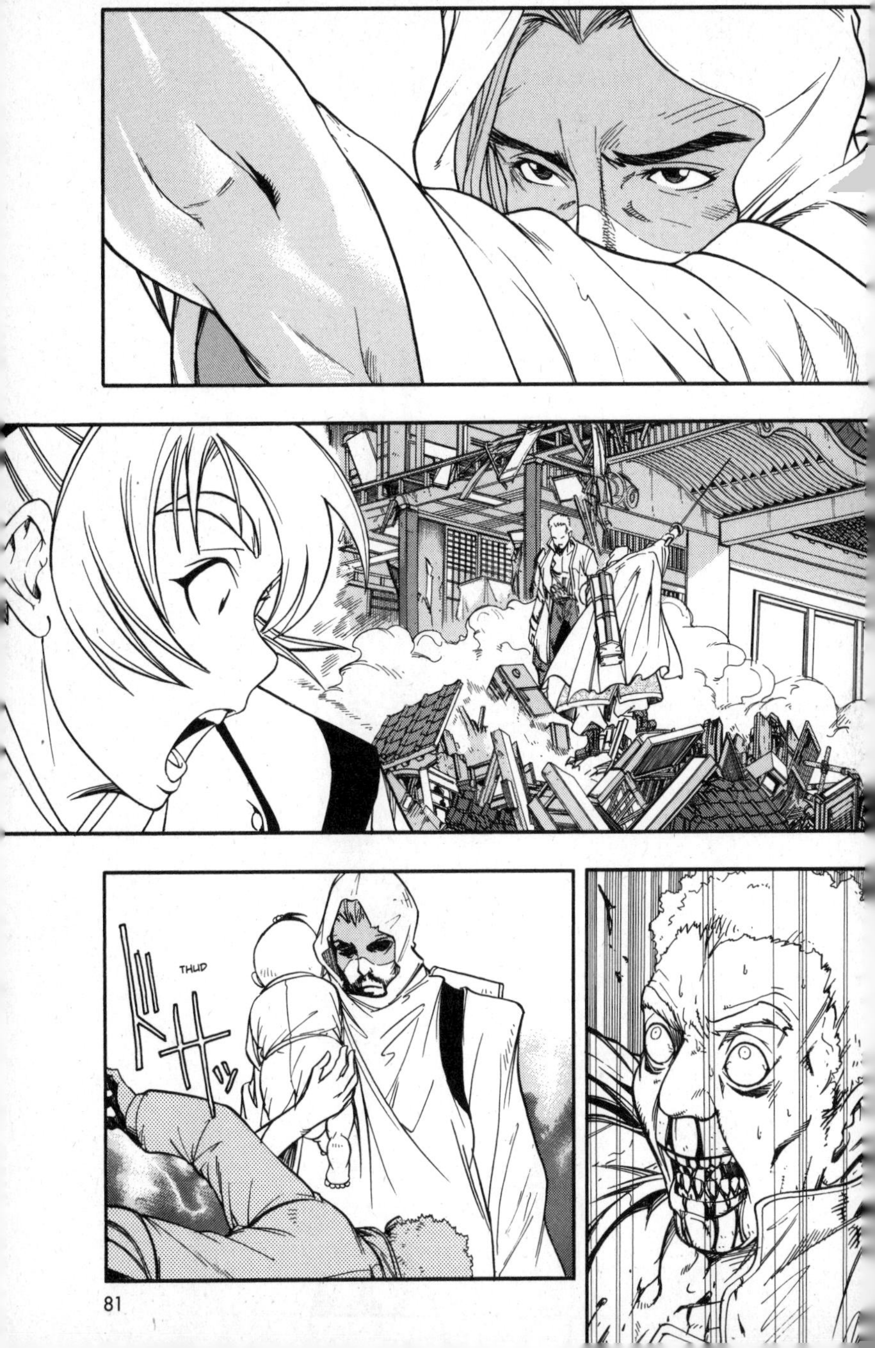
THUD
ドサッ

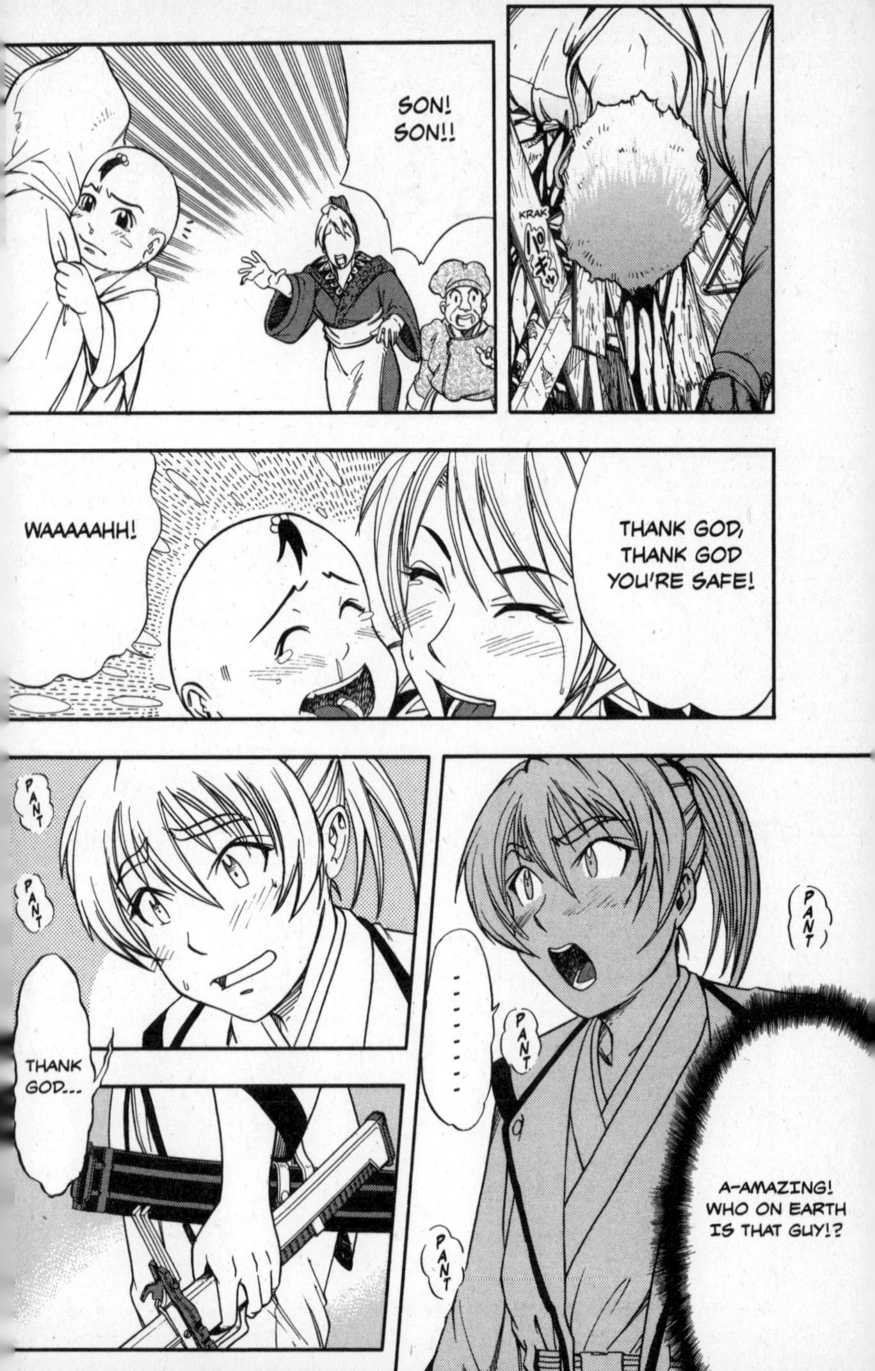
KRAK
パキッ
SON! SON!!
THANK GOD, THANK GOD YOU'RE SAFE!
WAAAAAHH!
PANT
A-AMAZING! WHO ON EARTH IS THAT GUY!?
PANT
PANT
......
PANT
PANT
THANK GOD...

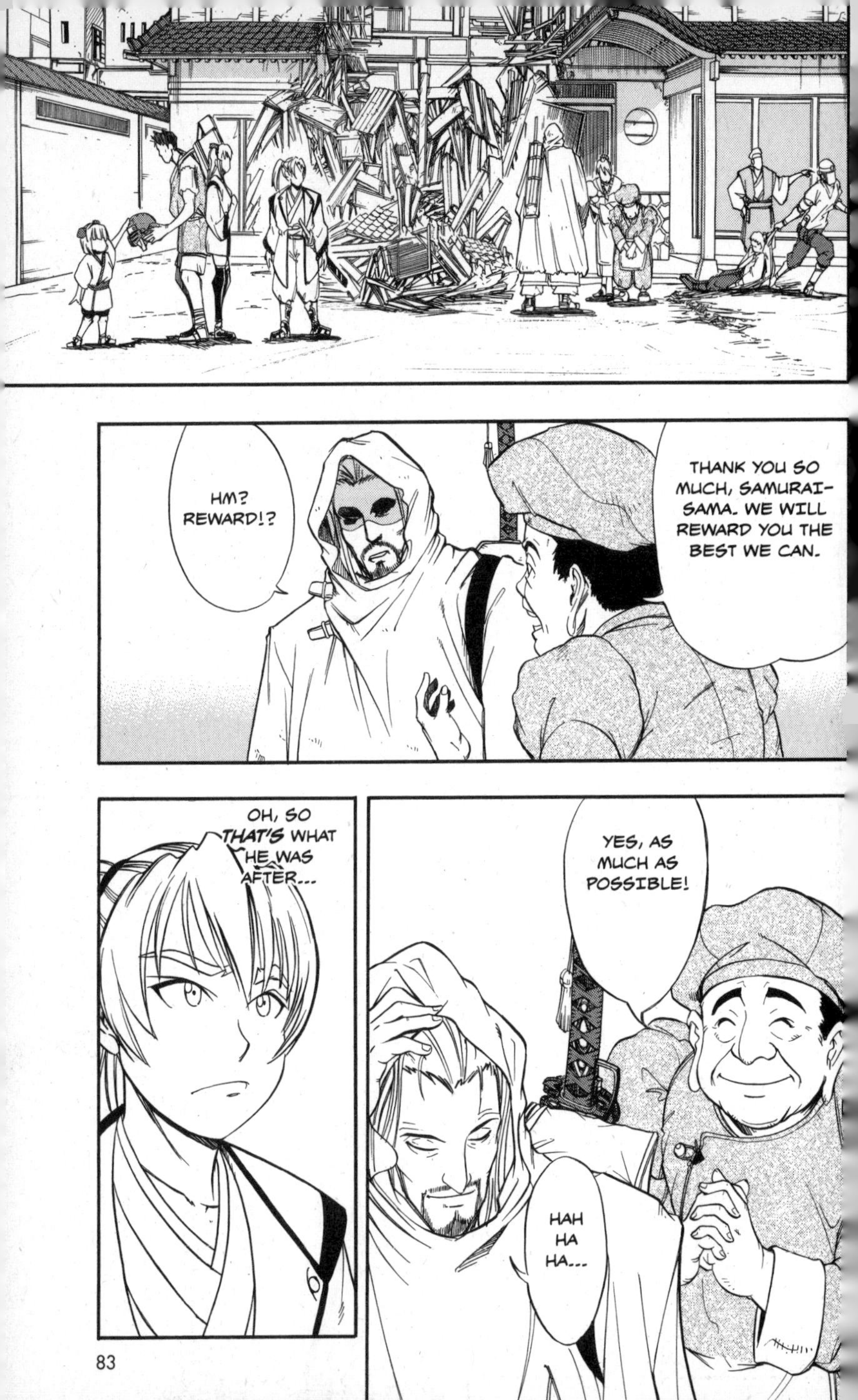
THANK YOU SO MUCH, SAMURAI-SAMA. WE WILL REWARD YOU THE BEST WE CAN.
HM? REWARD!?
YES, AS MUCH AS POSSIBLE!
HAH HA HA...
OH, SO *THAT'S* WHAT HE WAS AFTER...

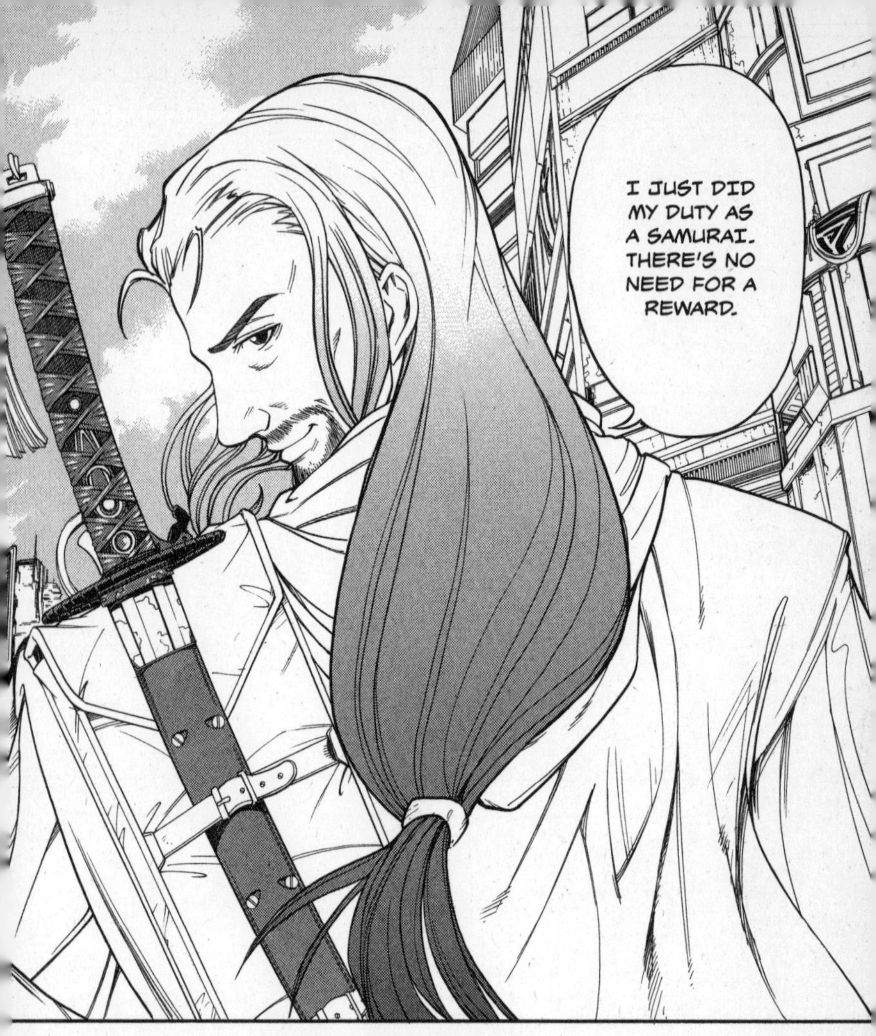
I JUST DID MY DUTY AS A SAMURAI. THERE'S NO NEED FOR A REWARD.

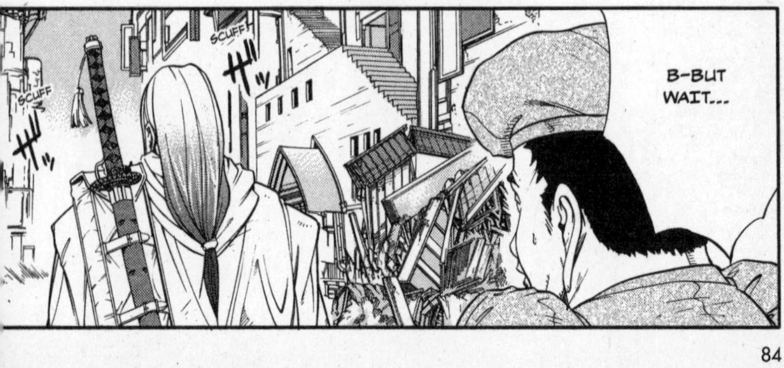
B-BUT WAIT...
SCUFF
SCUFF

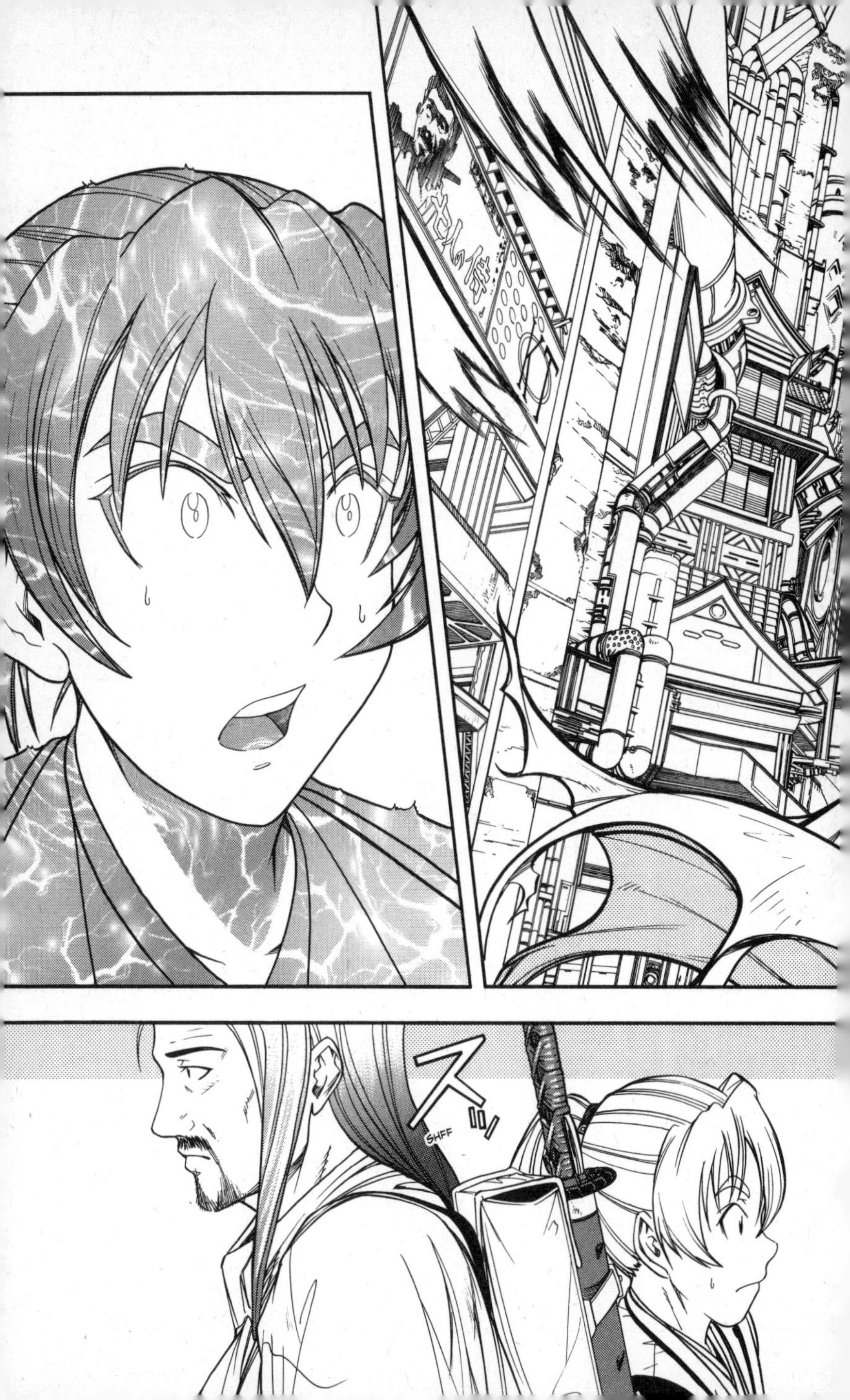
ス
SHFF

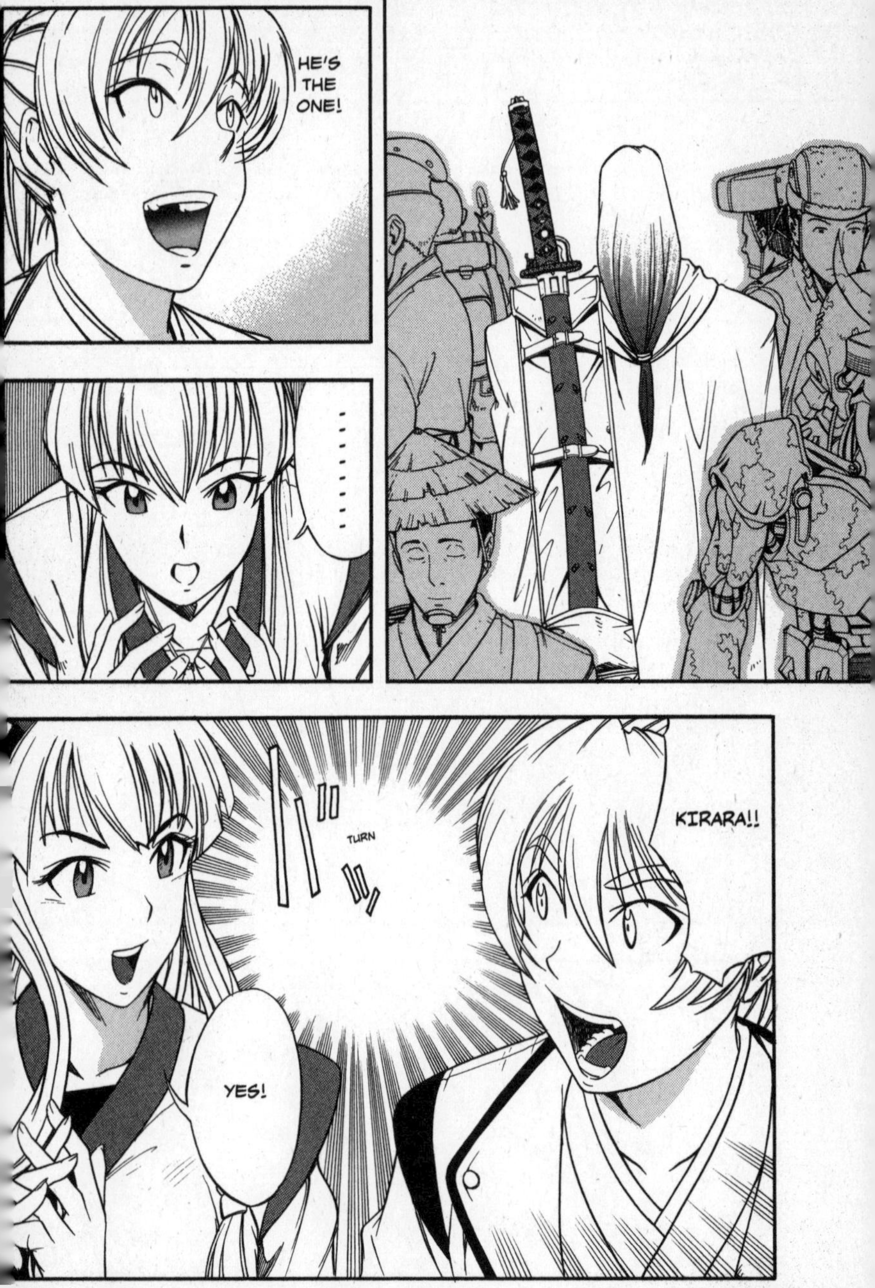
HE'S THE ONE!
......
KIRARA!!
TURN
YES!

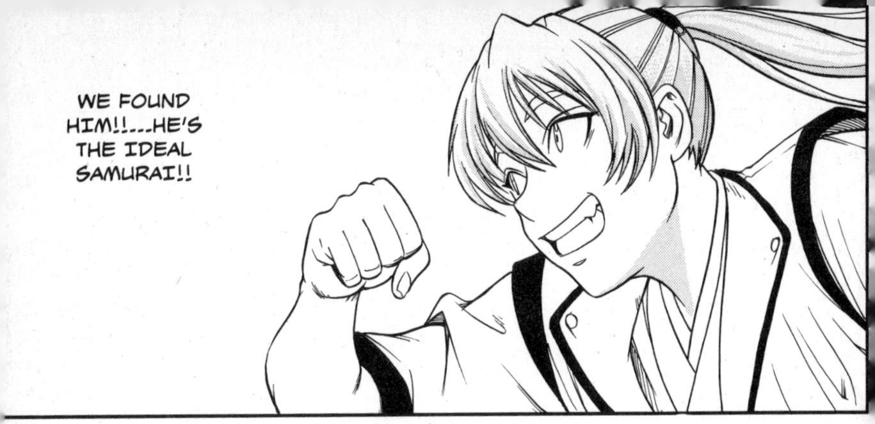
WE FOUND HIM!!...HE'S THE IDEAL SAMURAI!!

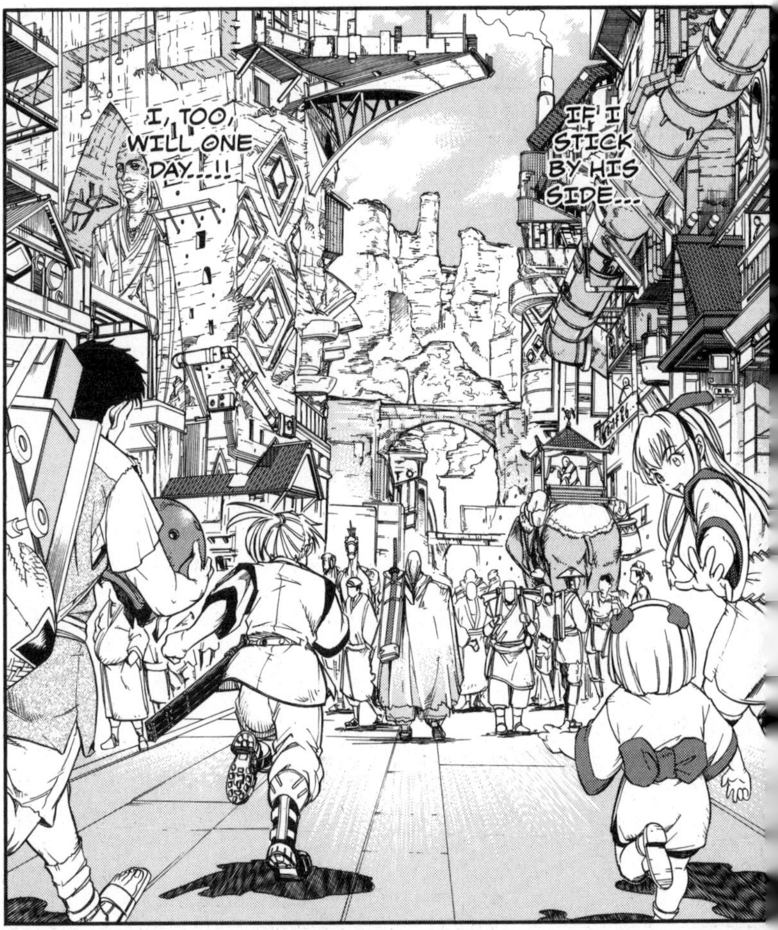
IF I STICK BY HIS SIDE...
I, TOO, WILL ONE DAY...!!

Chapter 1/End

Katsushiro

Kambei

Kikuchiyo

Kyuzo

Shichiroji

Heihachi

Gorobei

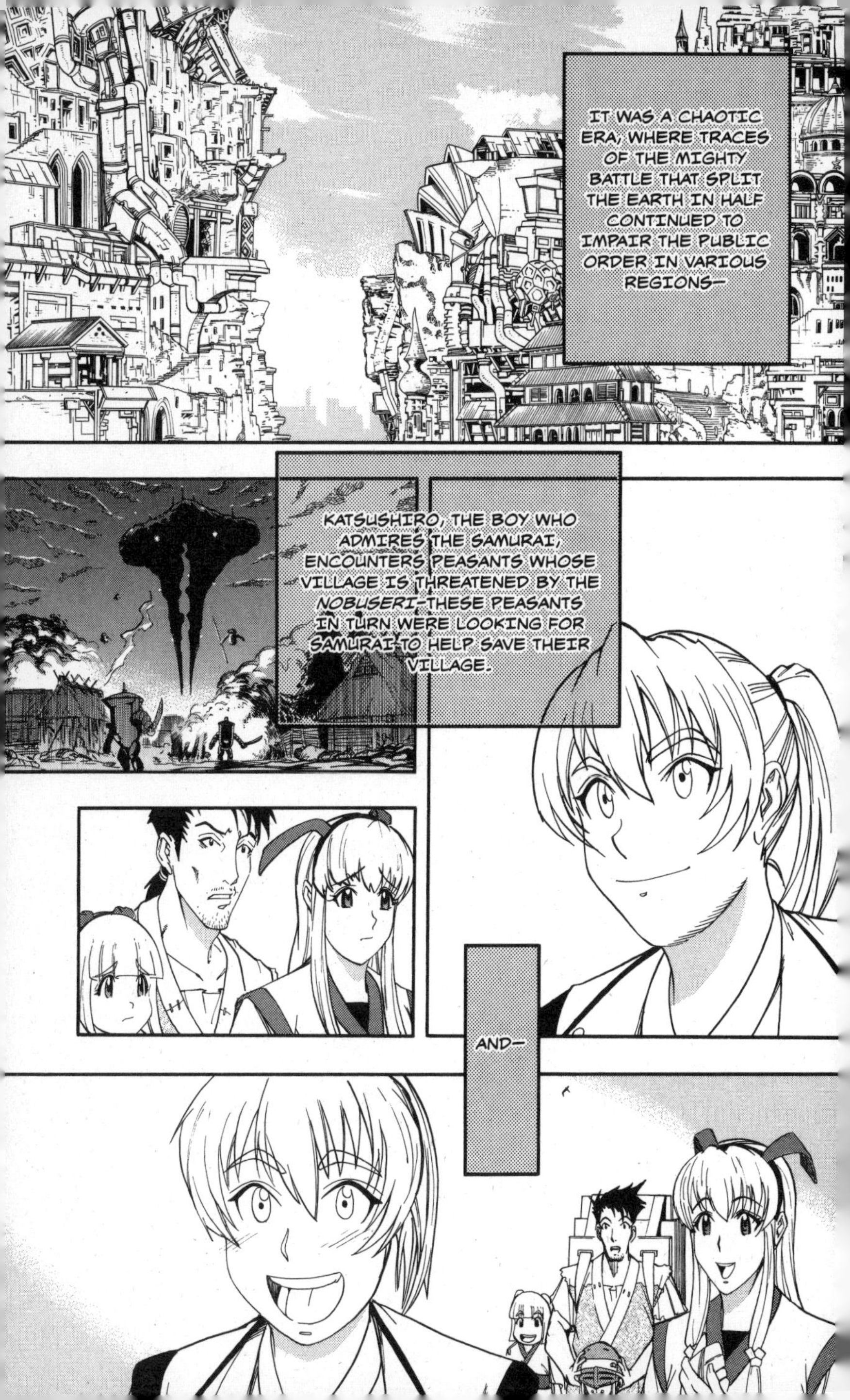
IT WAS A CHAOTIC ERA, WHERE TRACES OF THE MIGHTY BATTLE THAT SPLIT THE EARTH IN HALF CONTINUED TO IMPAIR THE PUBLIC ORDER IN VARIOUS REGIONS—
KATSUSHIRO, THE BOY WHO ADMIRES THE SAMURAI, ENCOUNTERS PEASANTS WHOSE VILLAGE IS THREATENED BY THE *NOBUSERI*—THESE PEASANTS IN TURN WERE LOOKING FOR SAMURAI TO HELP SAVE THEIR VILLAGE.
AND—

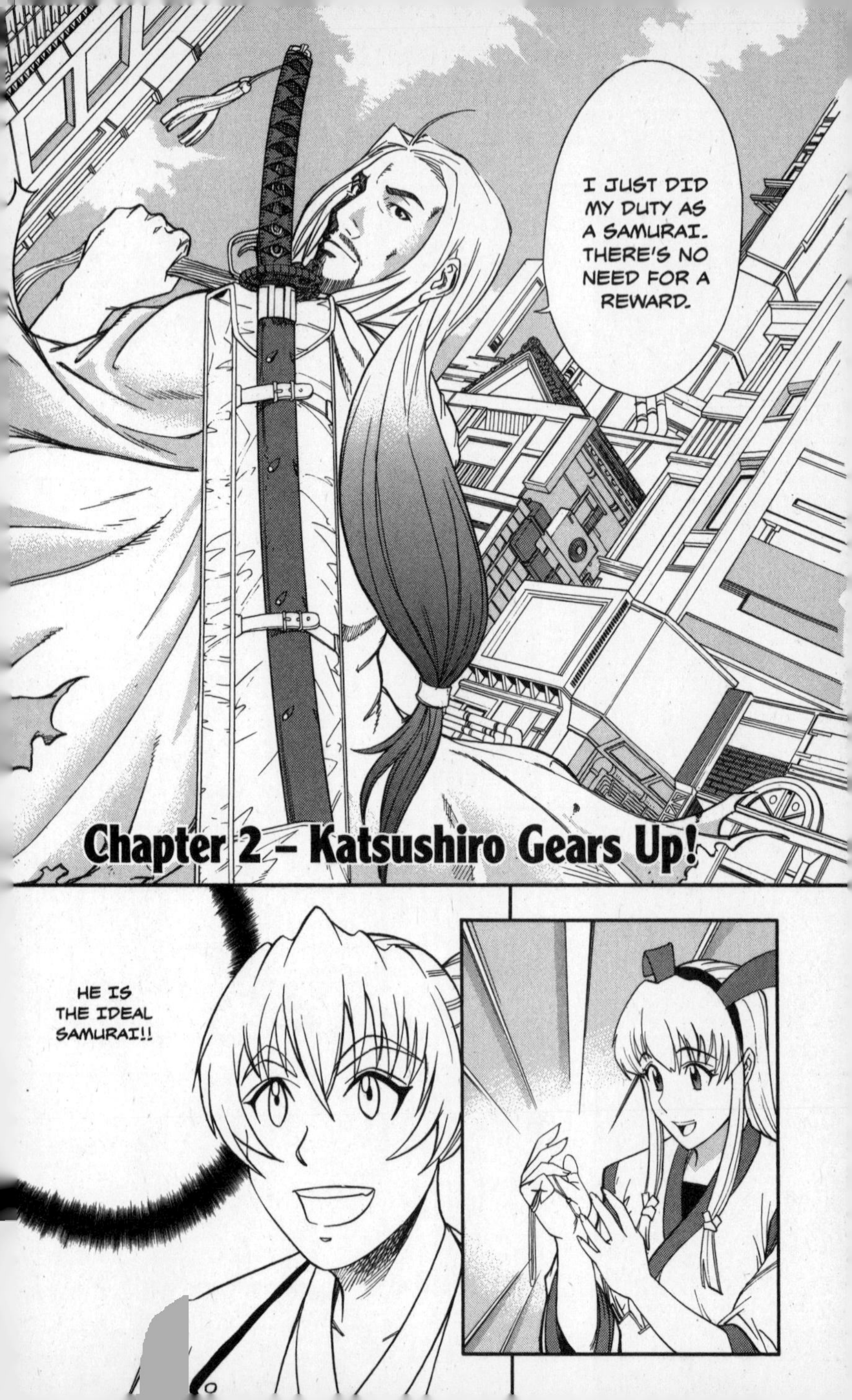
I JUST DID MY DUTY AS A SAMURAI. THERE'S NO NEED FOR A REWARD.
Chapter 2 – Katsushiro Gears Up!
HE IS THE IDEAL SAMURAI!!

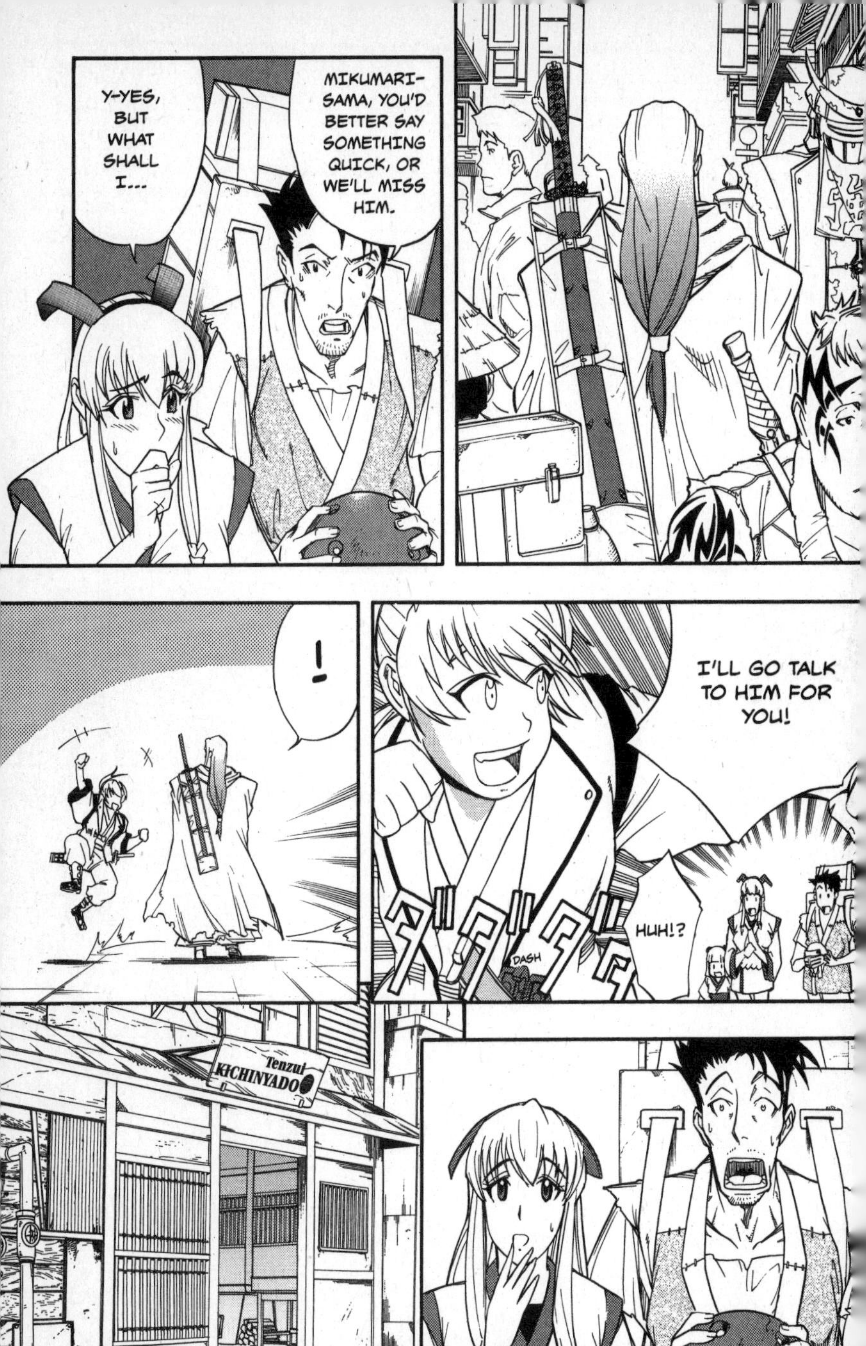
MIKUMARI-SAMA, YOU'D BETTER SAY SOMETHING QUICK, OR WE'LL MISS HIM.
Y-YES, BUT WHAT SHALL I...
I'LL GO TALK TO HIM FOR YOU!
DASH
HUH!?
!
Tenzui KICHINYADO

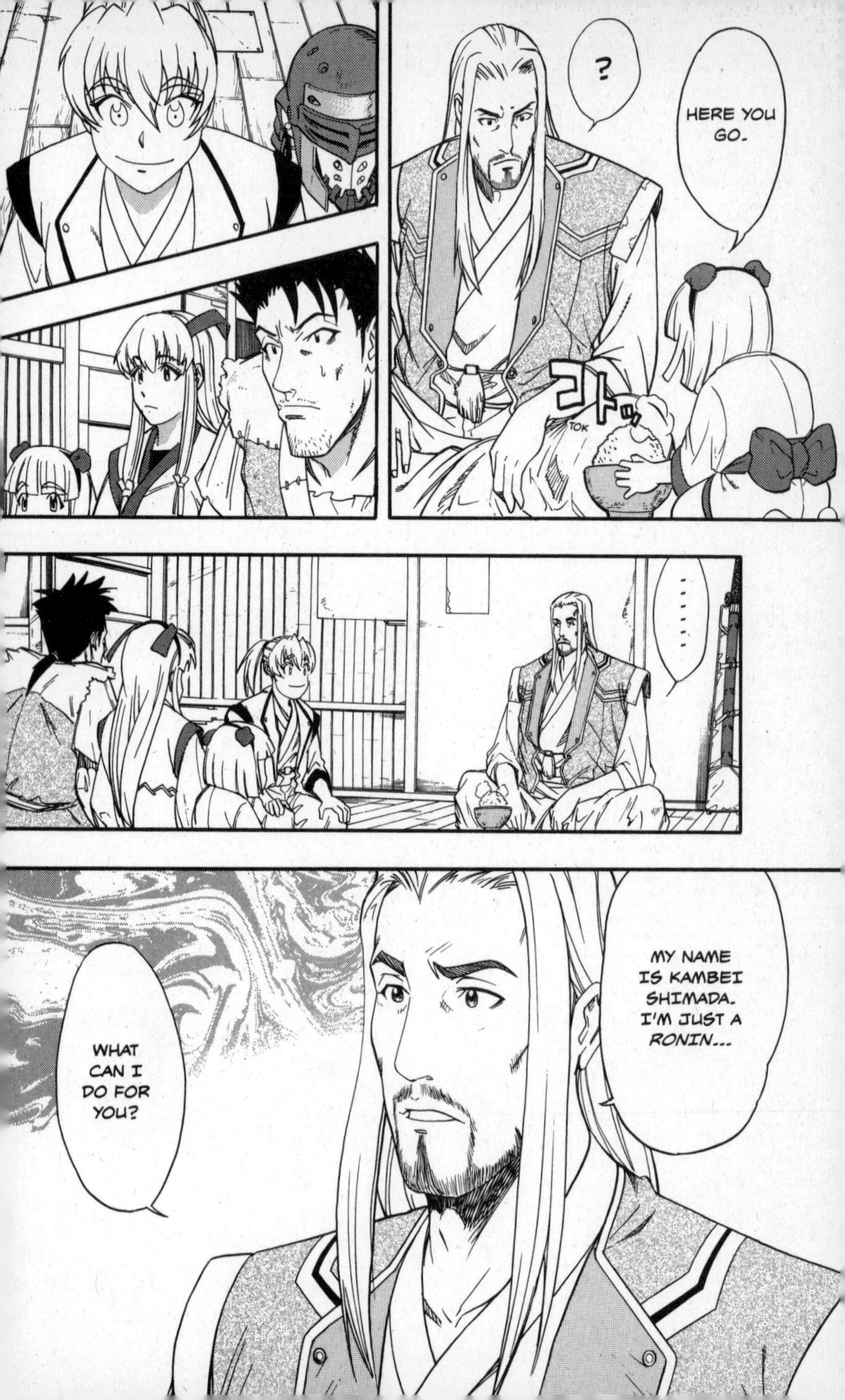
HERE YOU GO.
?
コトッ
TOK
......
MY NAME IS KAMBEI SHIMADA. I'M JUST A RONIN...
WHAT CAN I DO FOR YOU?

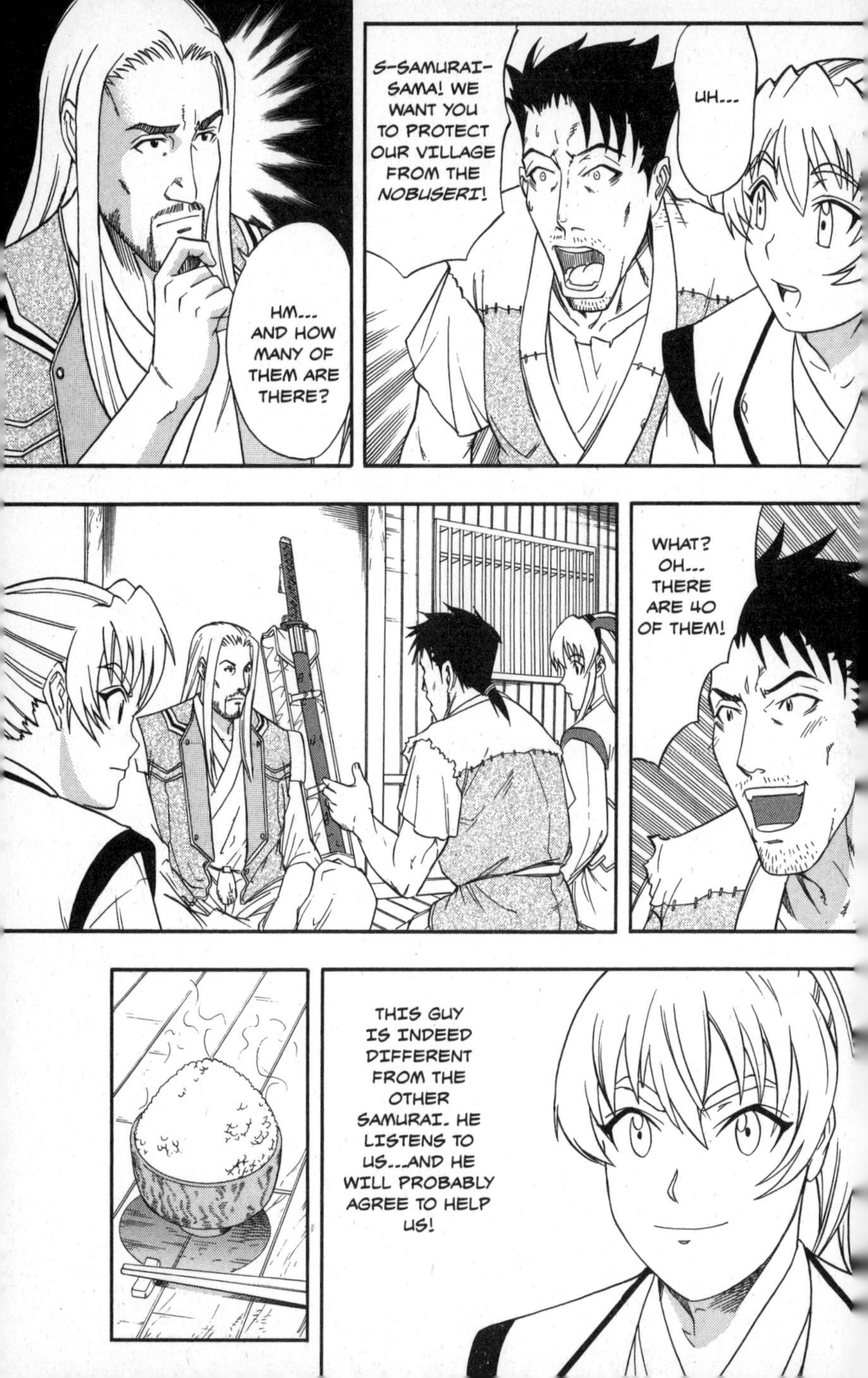
UH...
S-SAMURAI-SAMA! WE WANT YOU TO PROTECT OUR VILLAGE FROM THE *NOBUSERI*!
HM... AND HOW MANY OF THEM ARE THERE?
WHAT? OH... THERE ARE 40 OF THEM!
THIS GUY IS INDEED DIFFERENT FROM THE OTHER SAMURAI. HE LISTENS TO US...AND HE WILL PROBABLY AGREE TO HELP US!

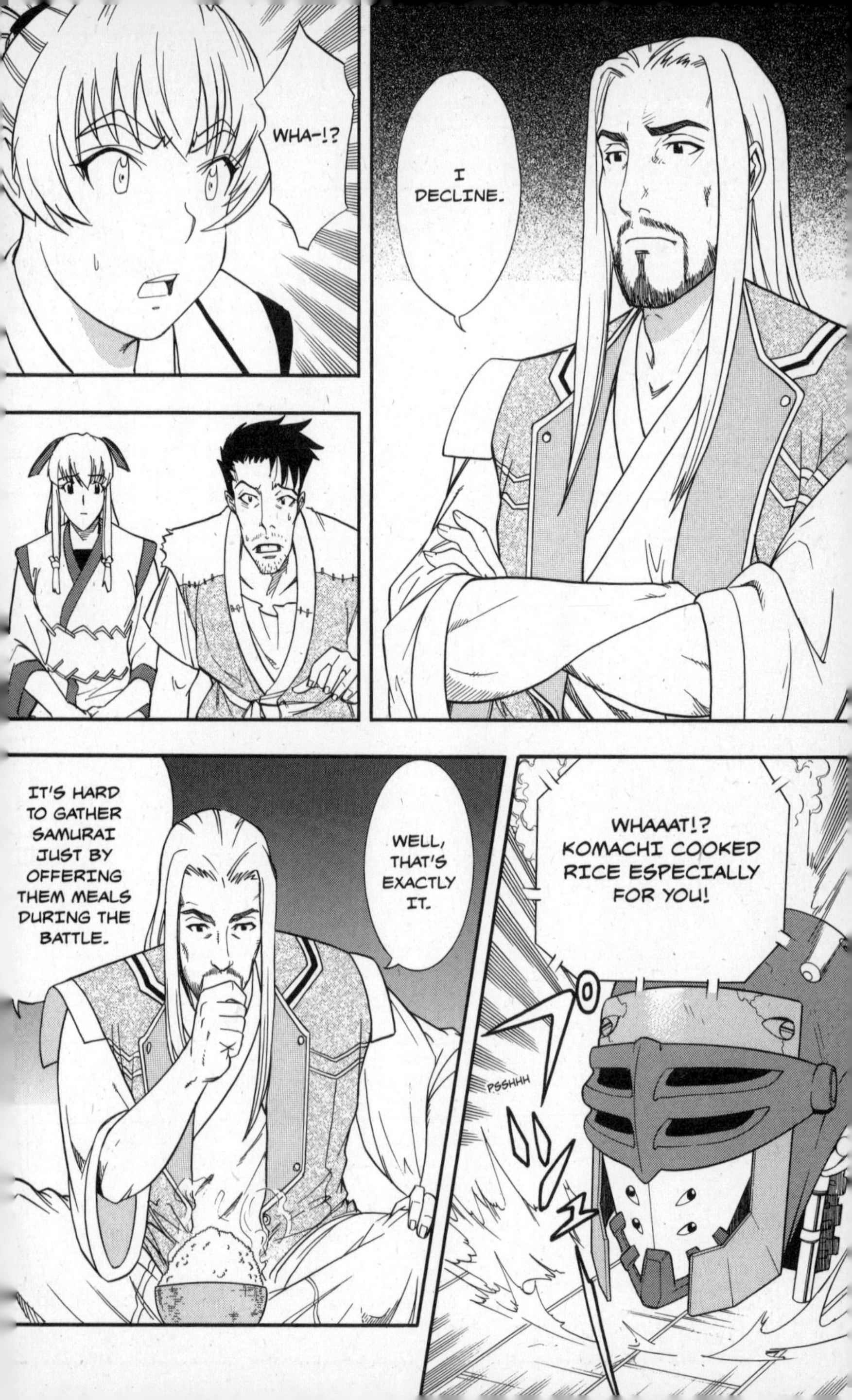
I DECLINE.
WHA-!?
WHAAAT!? KOMACHI COOKED RICE ESPECIALLY FOR YOU!
PSSHHH
WELL, THAT'S EXACTLY IT.
IT'S HARD TO GATHER SAMURAI JUST BY OFFERING THEM MEALS DURING THE BATTLE.

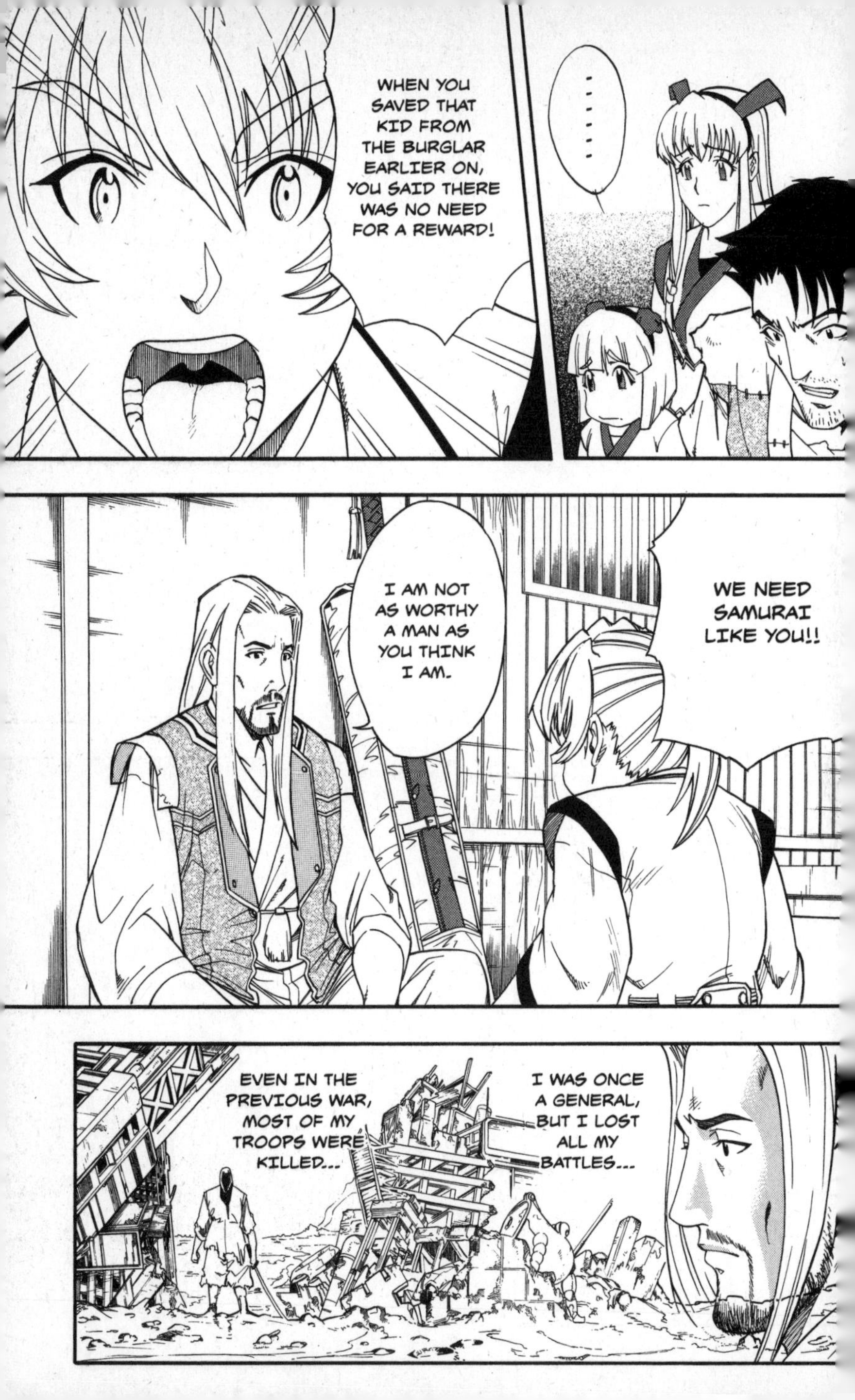
......
WHEN YOU SAVED THAT KID FROM THE BURGLAR EARLIER ON, YOU SAID THERE WAS NO NEED FOR A REWARD!
WE NEED SAMURAI LIKE YOU!!
I AM NOT AS WORTHY A MAN AS YOU THINK I AM.
I WAS ONCE A GENERAL, BUT I LOST ALL MY BATTLES...
EVEN IN THE PREVIOUS WAR, MOST OF MY TROOPS WERE KILLED...

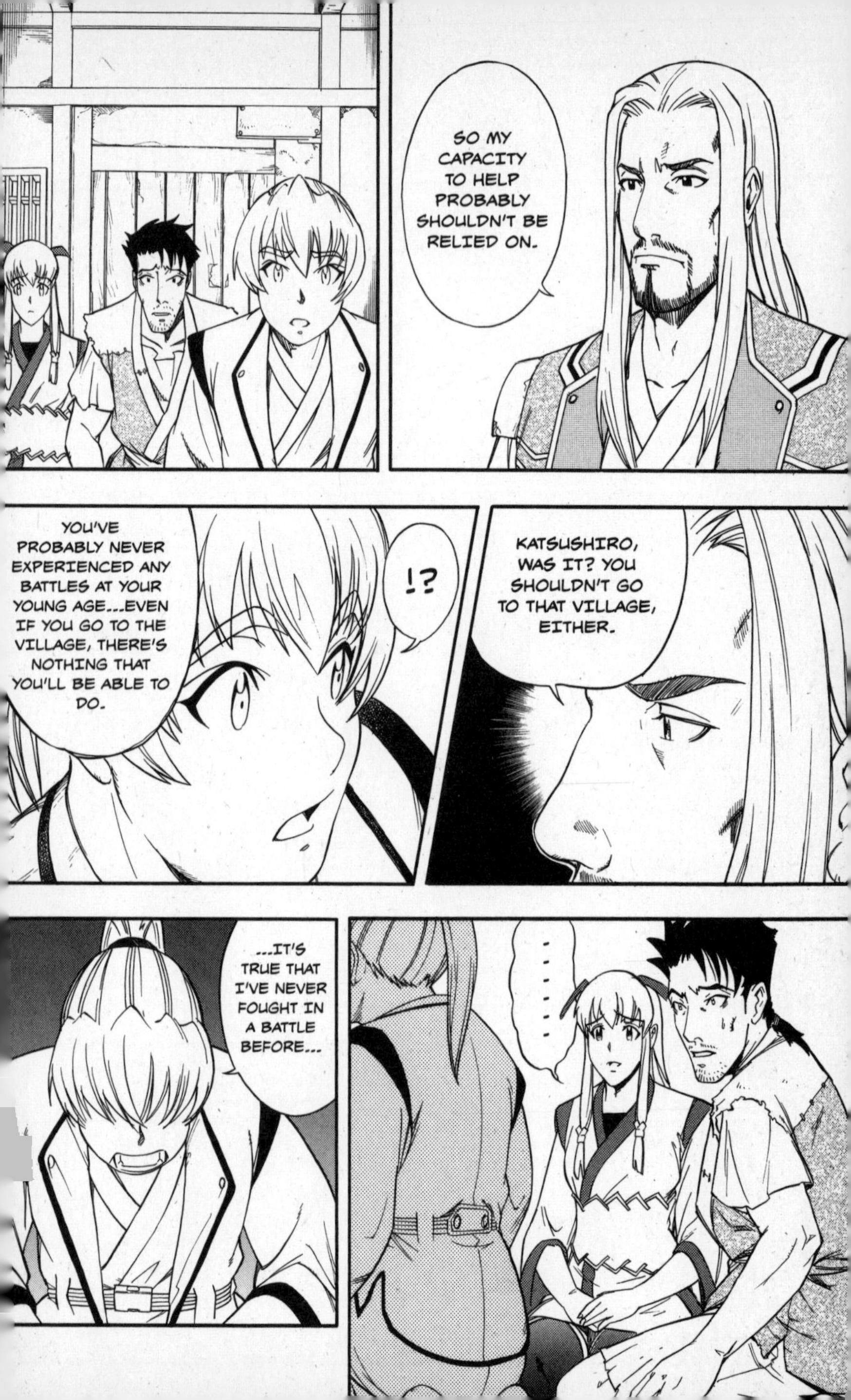
SO MY CAPACITY TO HELP PROBABLY SHOULDN'T BE RELIED ON.
KATSUSHIRO, WAS IT? YOU SHOULDN'T GO TO THAT VILLAGE, EITHER.
!?
YOU'VE PROBABLY NEVER EXPERIENCED ANY BATTLES AT YOUR YOUNG AGE...EVEN IF YOU GO TO THE VILLAGE, THERE'S NOTHING THAT YOU'LL BE ABLE TO DO.
......
...IT'S TRUE THAT I'VE NEVER FOUGHT IN A BATTLE BEFORE...

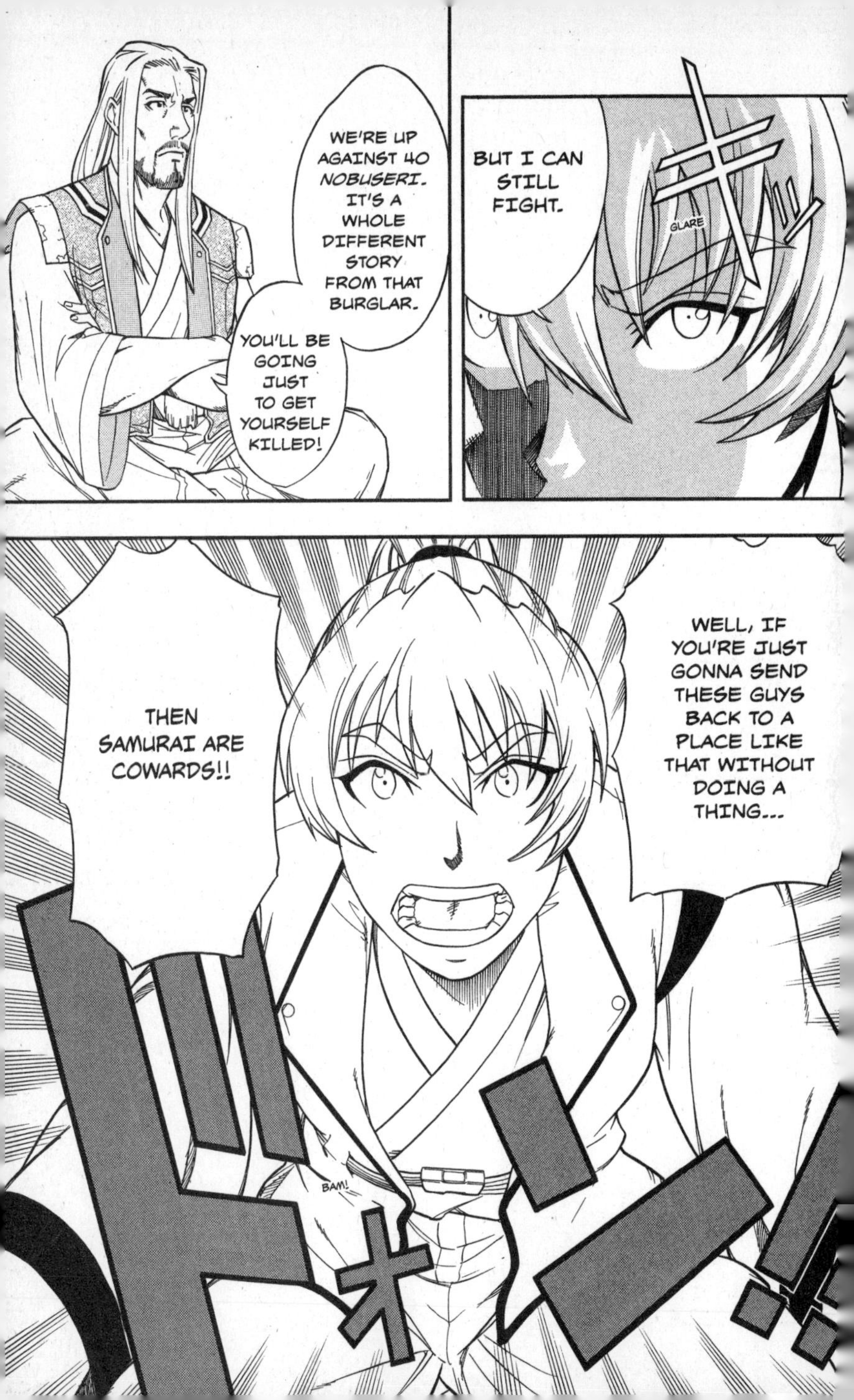
BUT I CAN STILL FIGHT.
GLARE
WE'RE UP AGAINST 40 *NOBUSERI*. IT'S A WHOLE DIFFERENT STORY FROM THAT BURGLAR.
YOU'LL BE GOING JUST TO GET YOURSELF KILLED!
WELL, IF YOU'RE JUST GONNA SEND THESE GUYS BACK TO A PLACE LIKE THAT WITHOUT DOING A THING...
THEN SAMURAI ARE COWARDS!!
BAM!

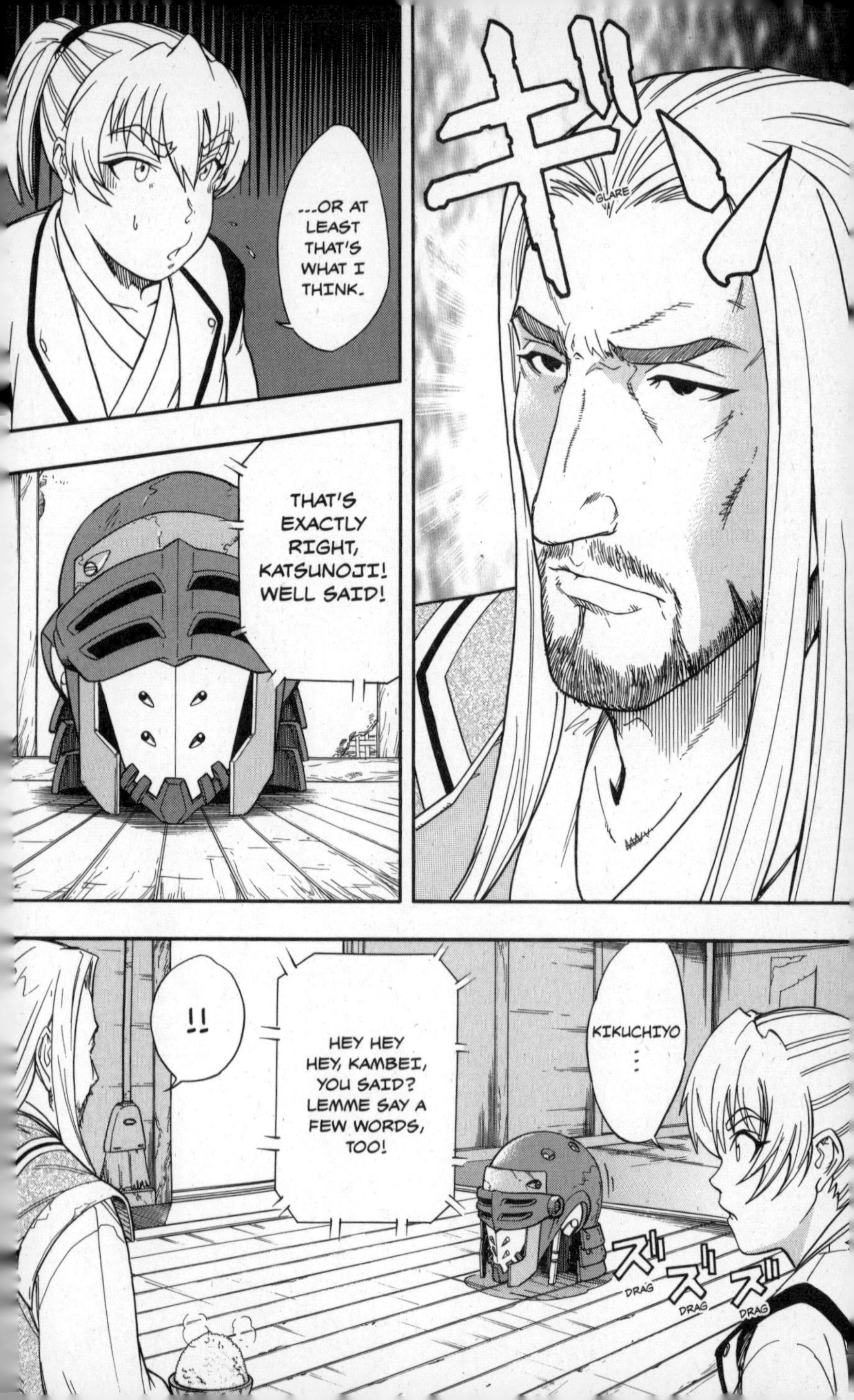
GLARE
...OR AT LEAST THAT'S WHAT I THINK.
THAT'S EXACTLY RIGHT, KATSUNOJI! WELL SAID!
KIKUCHIYO ...
HEY HEY HEY, KAMBEI, YOU SAID? LEMME SAY A FEW WORDS, TOO!
!!
DRAG
DRAG
DRAG

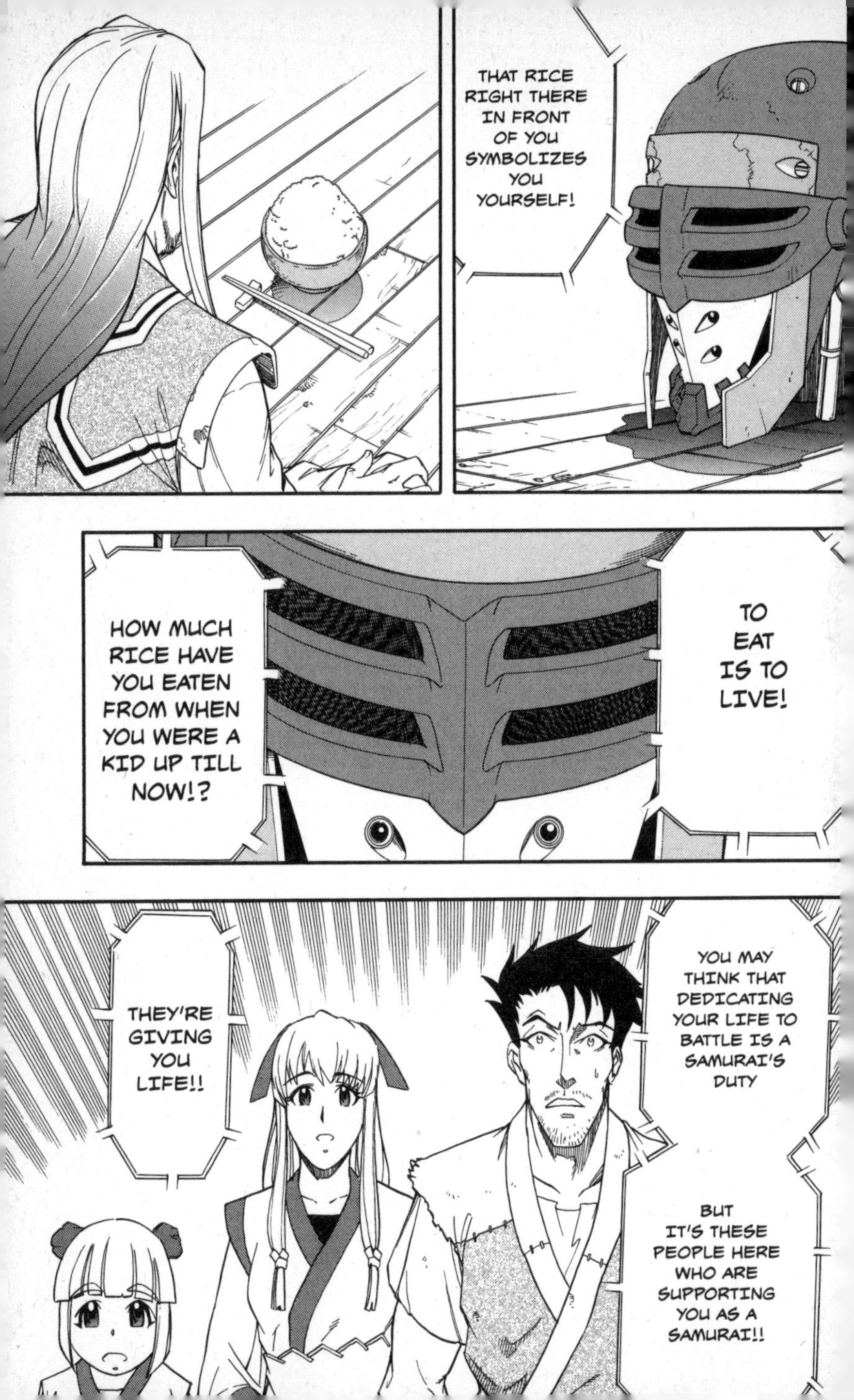
THAT RICE RIGHT THERE IN FRONT OF YOU SYMBOLIZES YOU YOURSELF!
TO EAT IS TO LIVE!
HOW MUCH RICE HAVE YOU EATEN FROM WHEN YOU WERE A KID UP TILL NOW!?
YOU MAY THINK THAT DEDICATING YOUR LIFE TO BATTLE IS A SAMURAI'S DUTY
BUT IT'S THESE PEOPLE HERE WHO ARE SUPPORTING YOU AS A SAMURAI!!
THEY'RE GIVING YOU LIFE!!

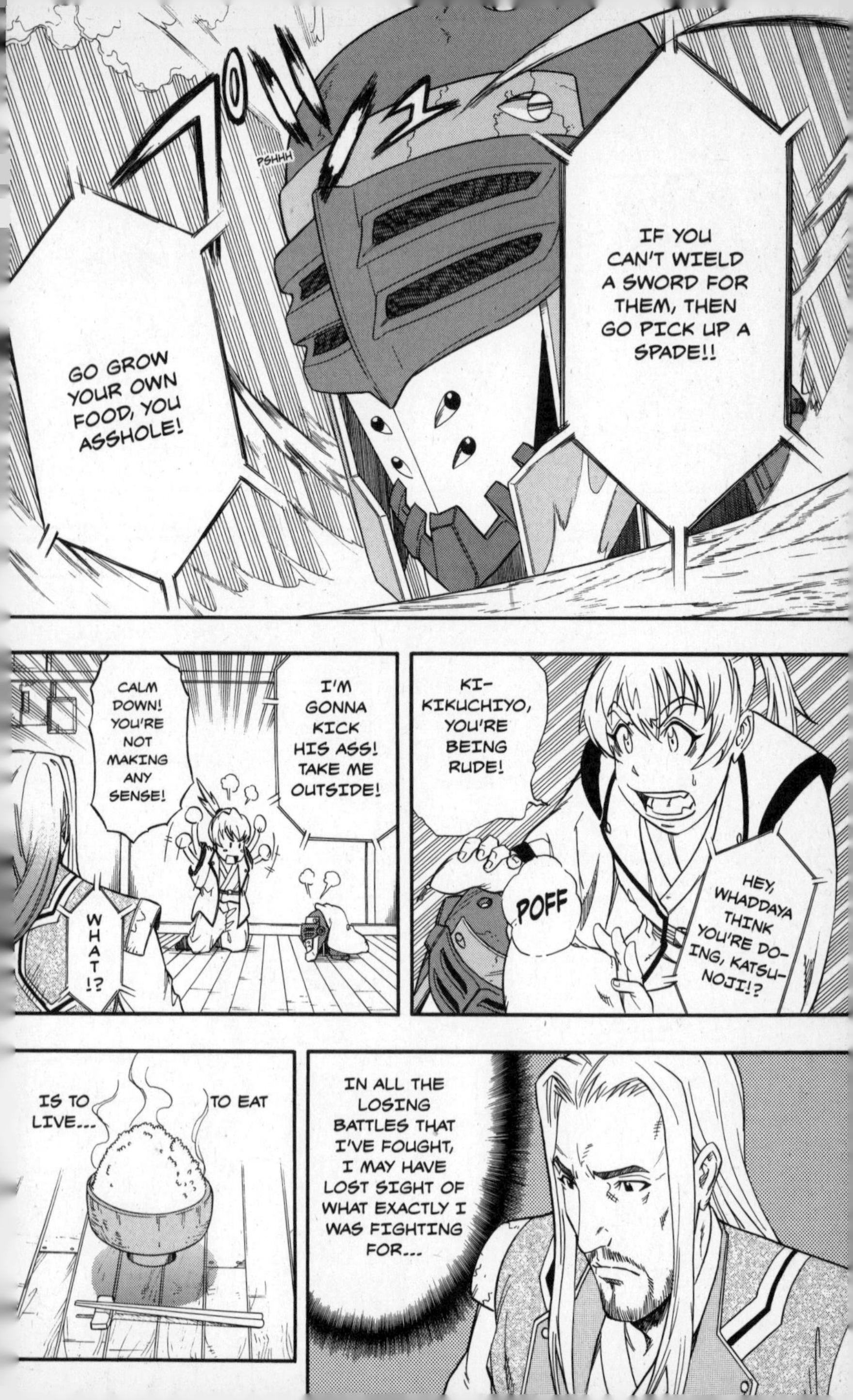
IF YOU CAN'T WIELD A SWORD FOR THEM, THEN GO PICK UP A SPADE!!
PSHHH
GO GROW YOUR OWN FOOD, YOU ASSHOLE!
KI-KIKUCHIYO, YOU'RE BEING RUDE!
POFF
HEY, WHADDAYA THINK YOU'RE DO-ING, KATSU-NOJI!?
I'M GONNA KICK HIS ASS! TAKE ME OUTSIDE!
CALM DOWN! YOU'RE NOT MAKING ANY SENSE!
WHAT!?
IN ALL THE LOSING BATTLES THAT I'VE FOUGHT, I MAY HAVE LOST SIGHT OF WHAT EXACTLY I WAS FIGHTING FOR...
TO EAT
IS TO LIVE...

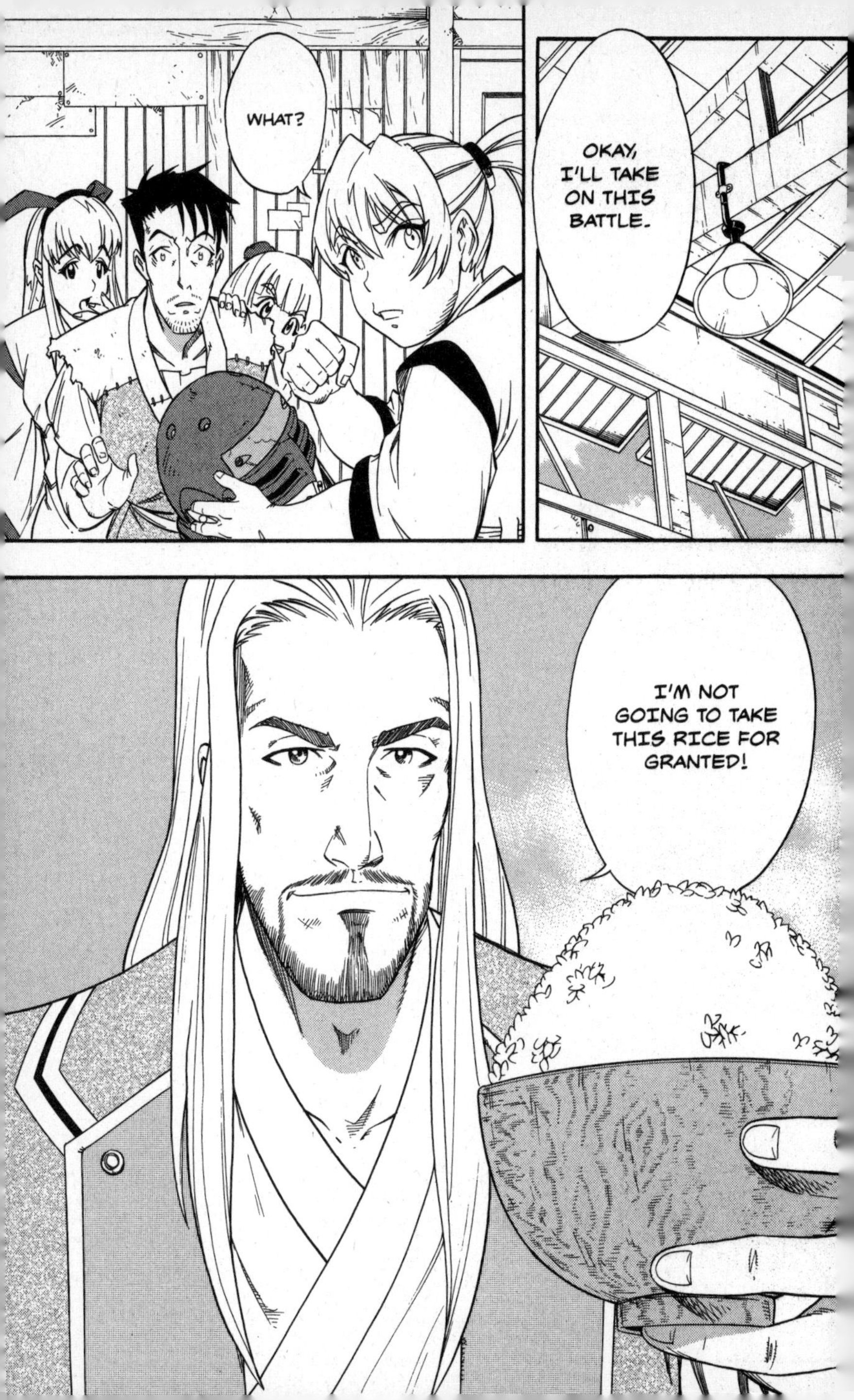
OKAY, I'LL TAKE ON THIS BATTLE.
WHAT?
I'M NOT GOING TO TAKE THIS RICE FOR GRANTED!

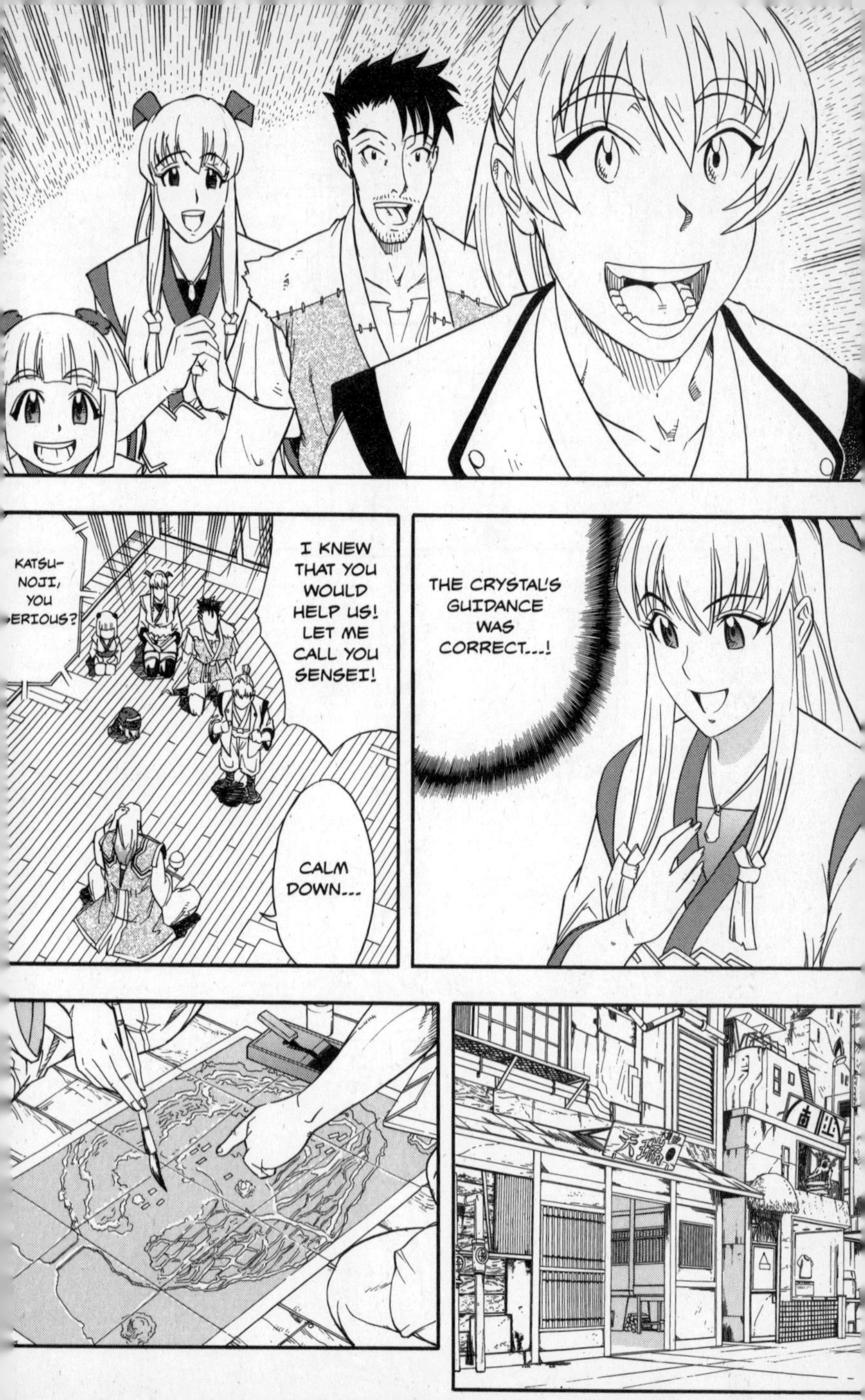
THE CRYSTAL'S GUIDANCE WAS CORRECT...!
I KNEW THAT YOU WOULD HELP US! LET ME CALL YOU SENSEI!
KATSU-NOJI, YOU ERIOUS?
CALM DOWN...

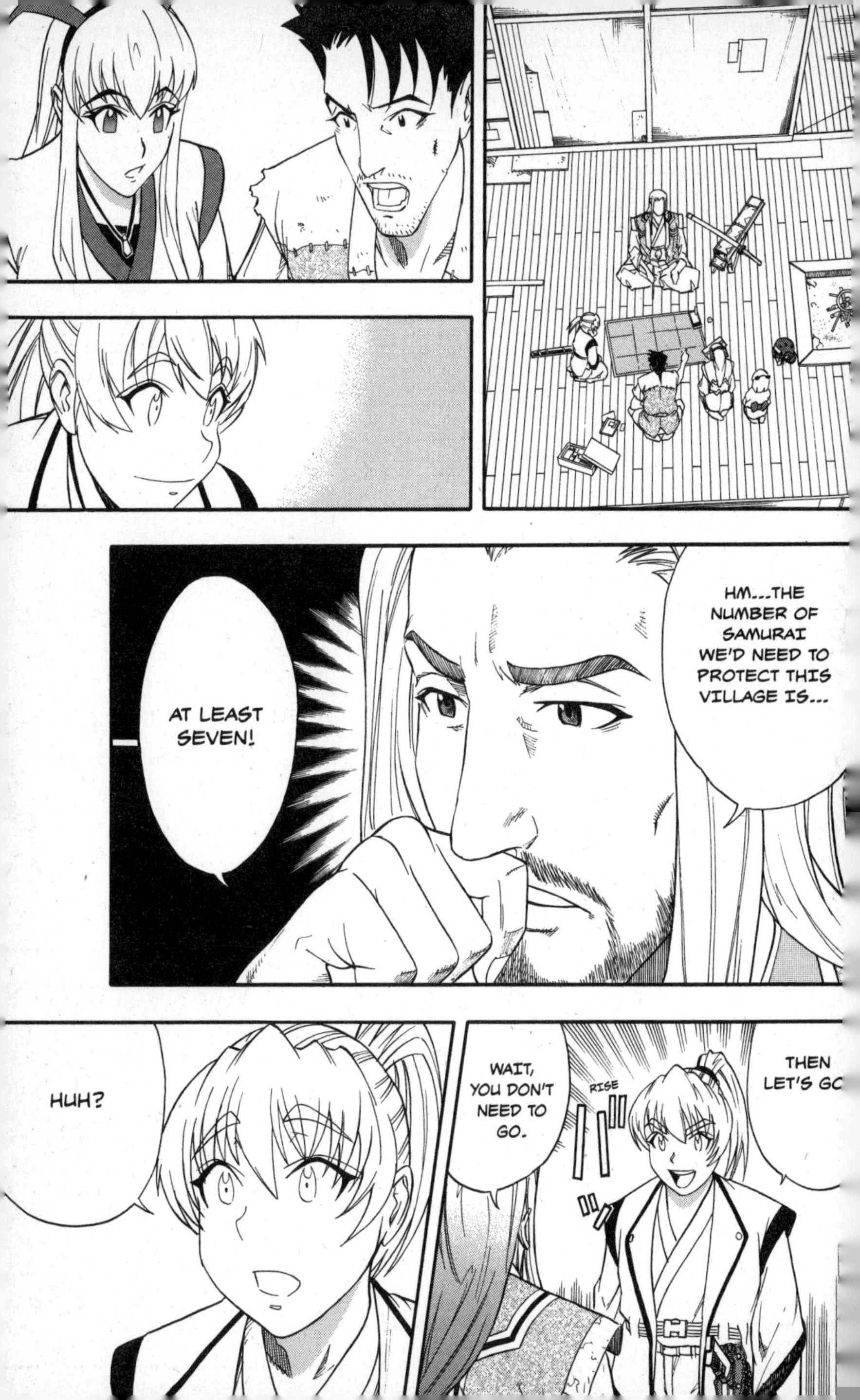
HM...THE NUMBER OF SAMURAI WE'D NEED TO PROTECT THIS VILLAGE IS...
AT LEAST SEVEN!
THEN LET'S GO
RISE
WAIT, YOU DON'T NEED TO GO.
HUH?

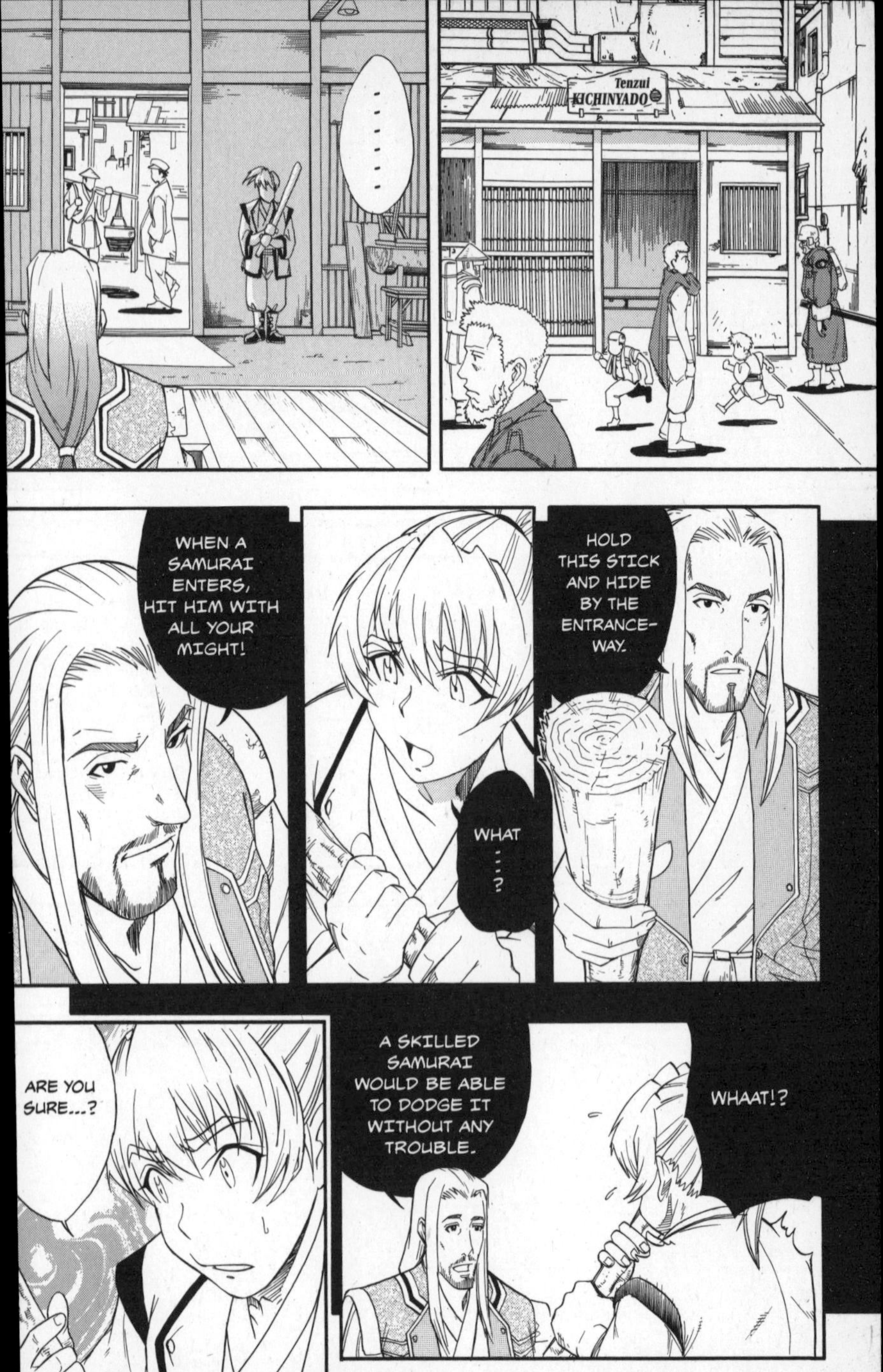
Tenzui
KICHINYADO
......
HOLD THIS STICK AND HIDE BY THE ENTRANCE-WAY.
WHAT...?
WHEN A SAMURAI ENTERS, HIT HIM WITH ALL YOUR MIGHT!
WHAAT!?
A SKILLED SAMURAI WOULD BE ABLE TO DODGE IT WITHOUT ANY TROUBLE.
ARE YOU SURE...?

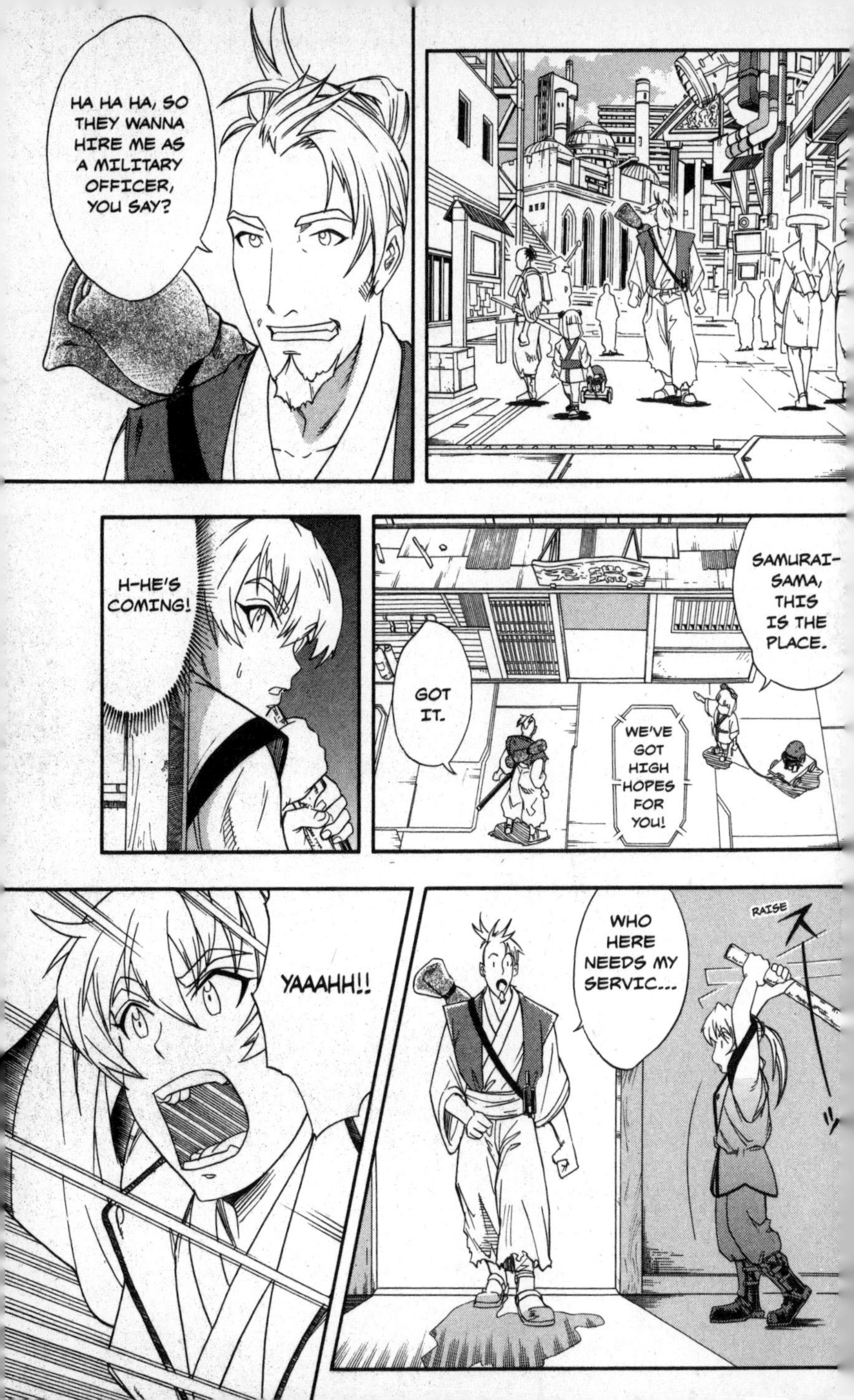
HA HA HA, SO THEY WANNA HIRE ME AS A MILITARY OFFICER, YOU SAY?
SAMURAI-SAMA, THIS IS THE PLACE.
WE'VE GOT HIGH HOPES FOR YOU!
GOT IT.
H-HE'S COMING!
WHO HERE NEEDS MY SERVIC...
RAISE
YAAAHH!!

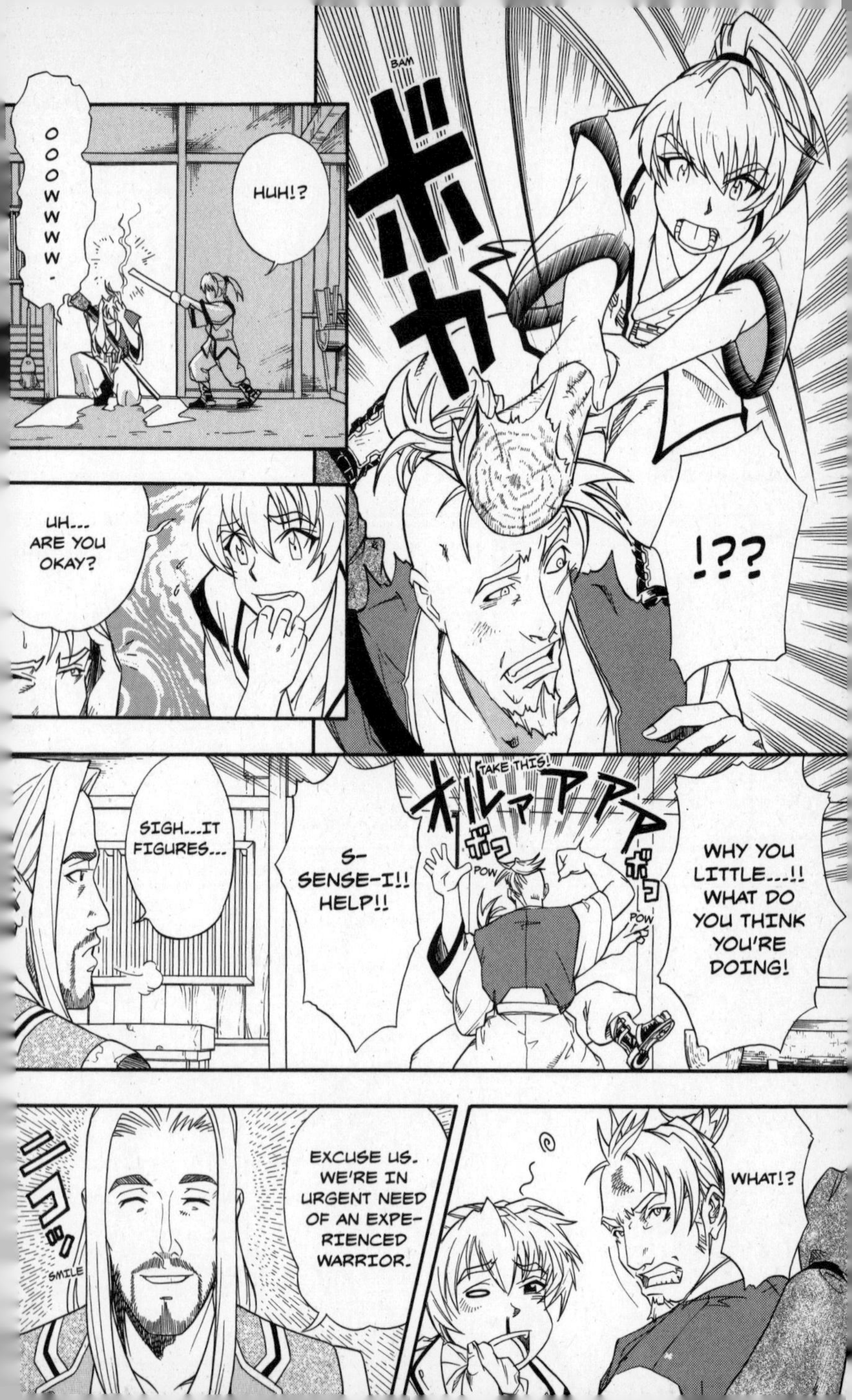
BAM
ボカ
!??
HUH!?
OOOWWWWWW.
UH... ARE YOU OKAY?
WHY YOU LITTLE...!! WHAT DO YOU THINK YOU'RE DOING!
TAKE THIS!
POW
POW
S-SENSE-I!! HELP!!
SIGH...IT FIGURES...
WHAT!?
EXCUSE US. WE'RE IN URGENT NEED OF AN EXPE-RIENCED WARRIOR.
SMILE

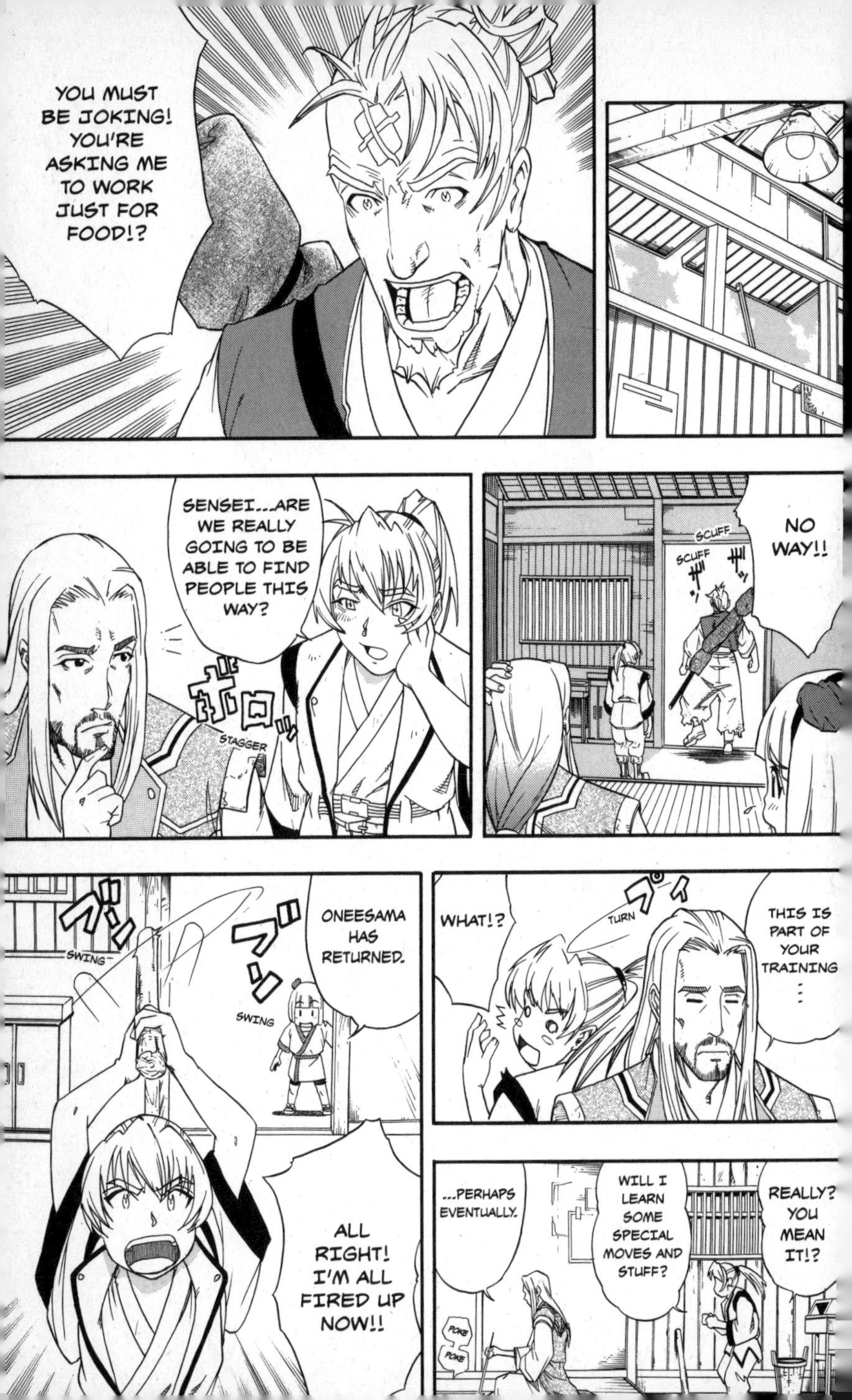

YOU MUST BE JOKING! YOU'RE ASKING ME TO WORK JUST FOR FOOD!?
NO WAY!!
SCUFF
SCUFF
SENSEI...ARE WE REALLY GOING TO BE ABLE TO FIND PEOPLE THIS WAY?
STAGGER
THIS IS PART OF YOUR TRAINING...
TURN
WHAT!?
REALLY? YOU MEAN IT!?
WILL I LEARN SOME SPECIAL MOVES AND STUFF?
...PERHAPS EVENTUALLY.
POKE
POKE
ONEESAMA HAS RETURNED.
SWING
SWING
ALL RIGHT! I'M ALL FIRED UP NOW!!

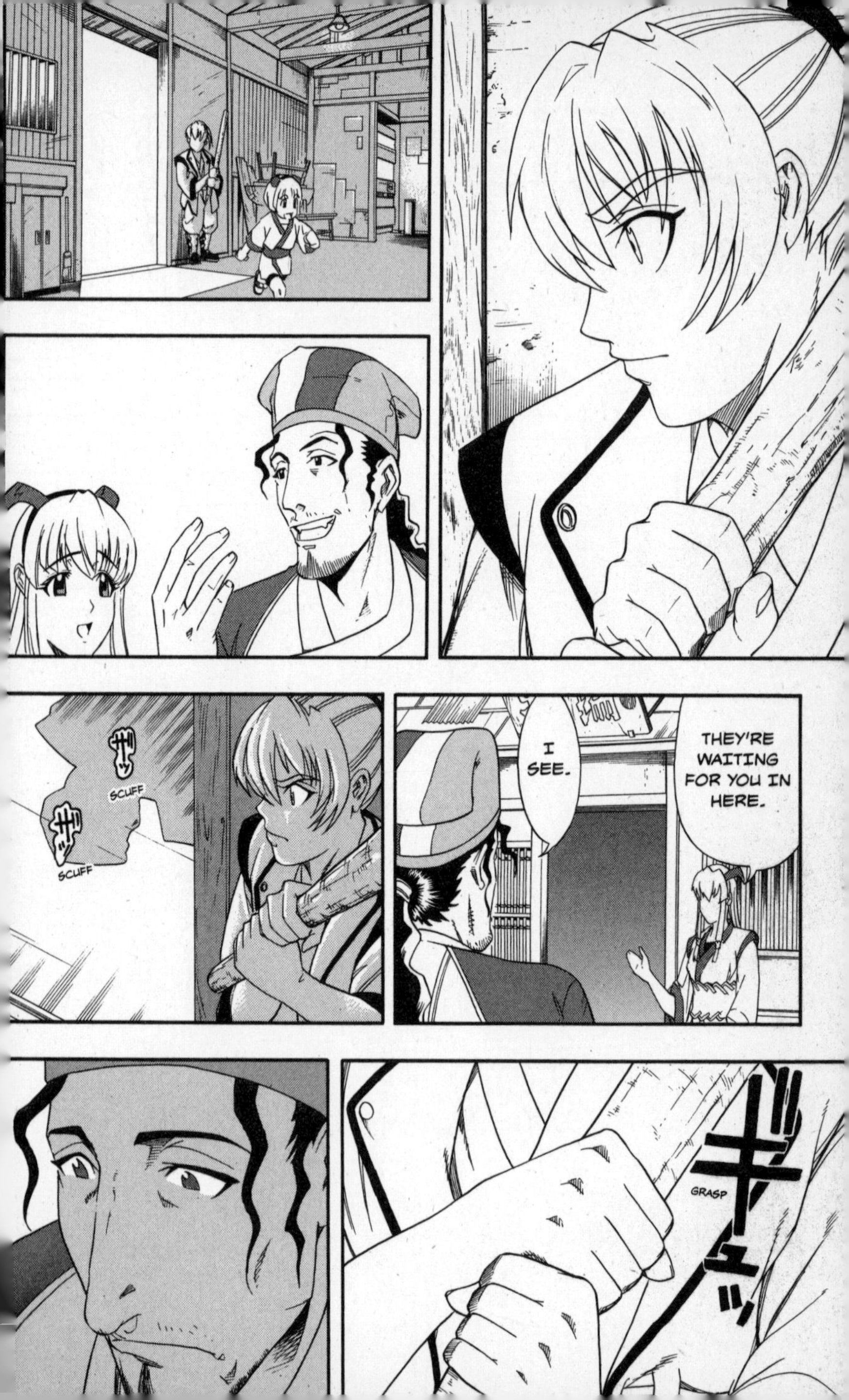
THEY'RE WAITING FOR YOU IN HERE.
I SEE.
ザッ
SCUFF
ザッ
SCUFF
ギュッ
GRASP

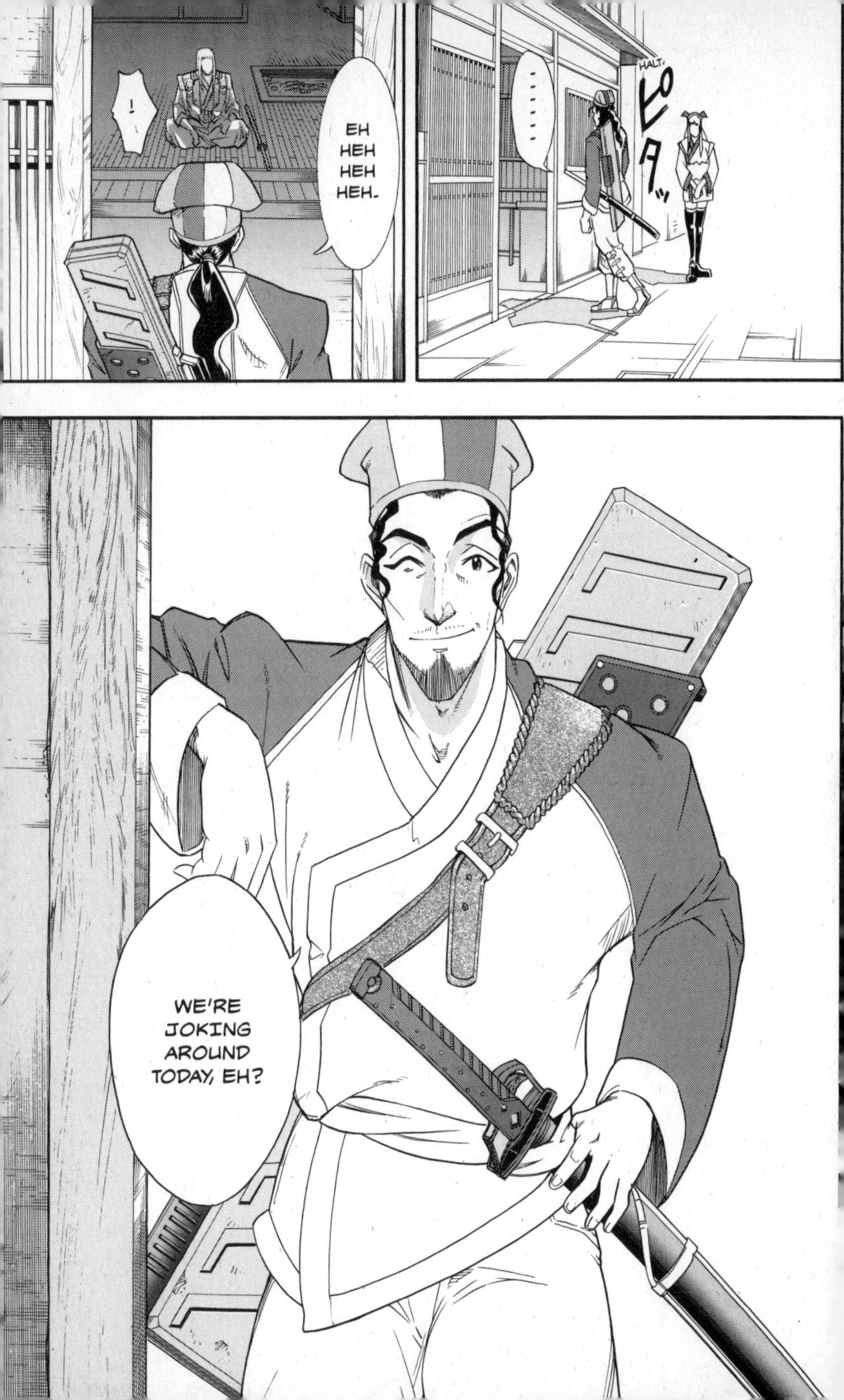
HALT.
ピタッ
......
!
EH HEH HEH HEH.
WE'RE JOKING AROUND TODAY, EH?

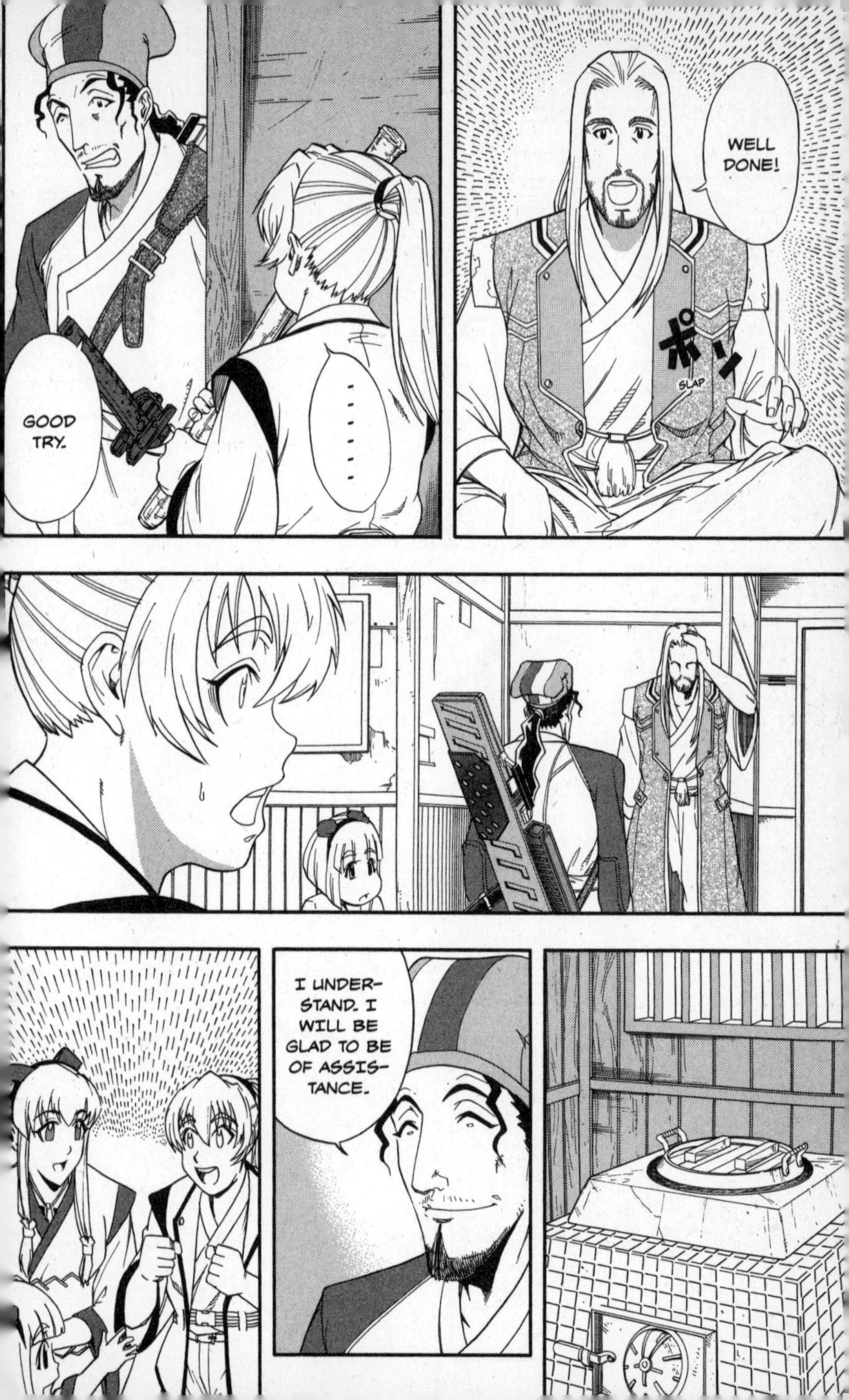
WELL DONE!
ポン
SLAP
......
GOOD TRY.
I UNDER-STAND. I WILL BE GLAD TO BE OF ASSIS-TANCE.

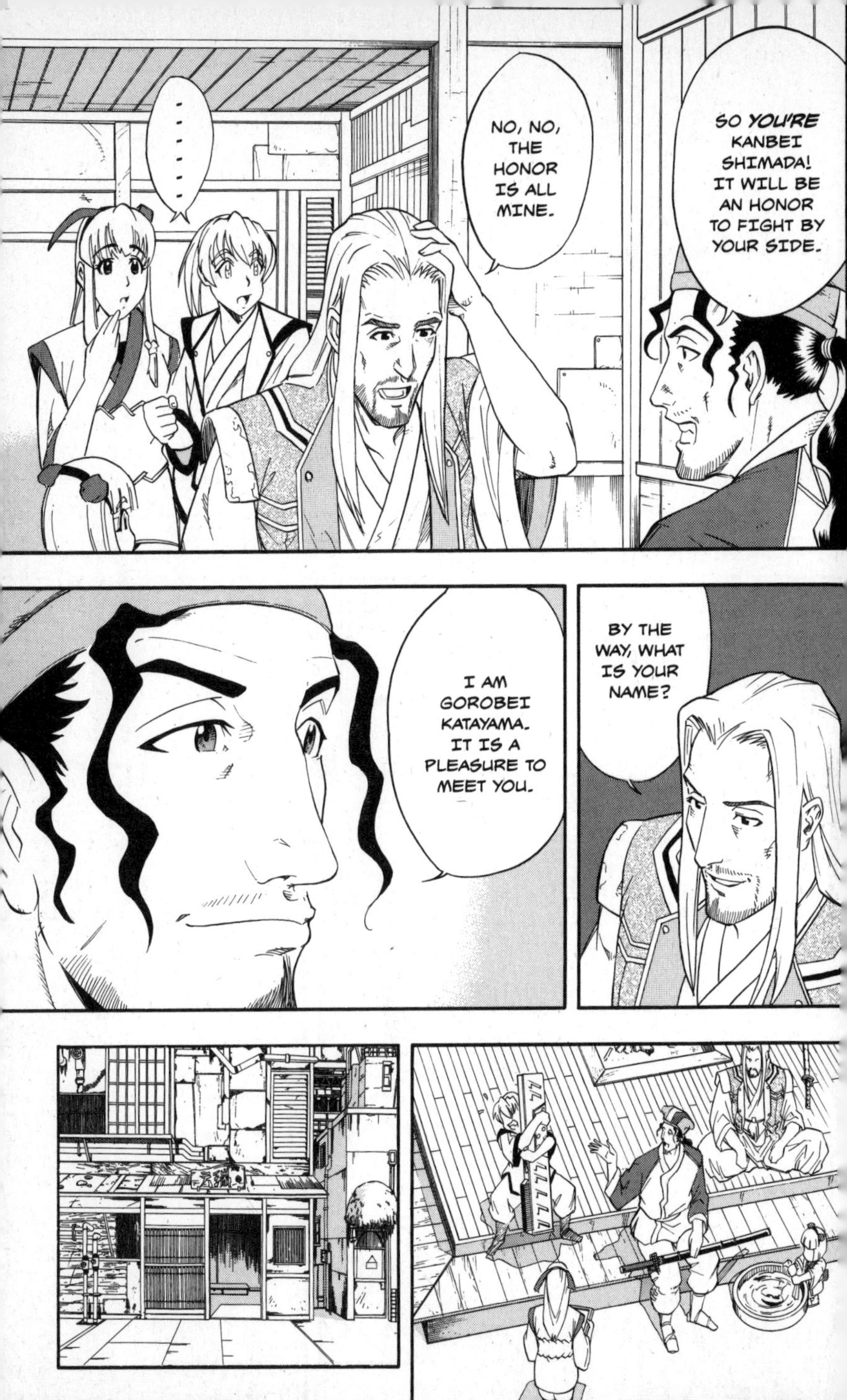
SO *YOU'RE* KANBEI SHIMADA! IT WILL BE AN HONOR TO FIGHT BY YOUR SIDE.
NO, NO, THE HONOR IS ALL MINE.
......
BY THE WAY, WHAT IS YOUR NAME?
I AM GOROBEI KATAYAMA. IT IS A PLEASURE TO MEET YOU.

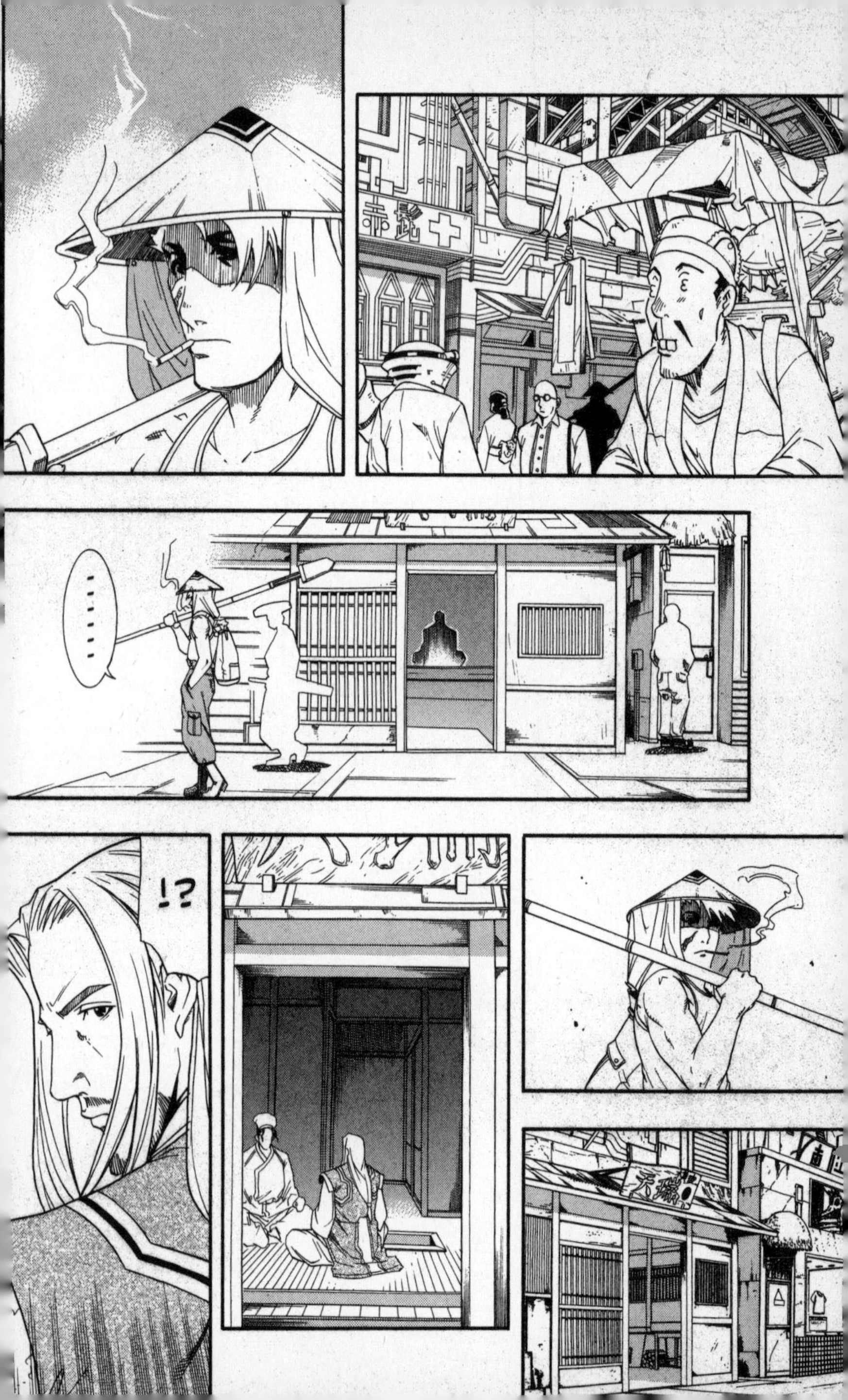
......
!?

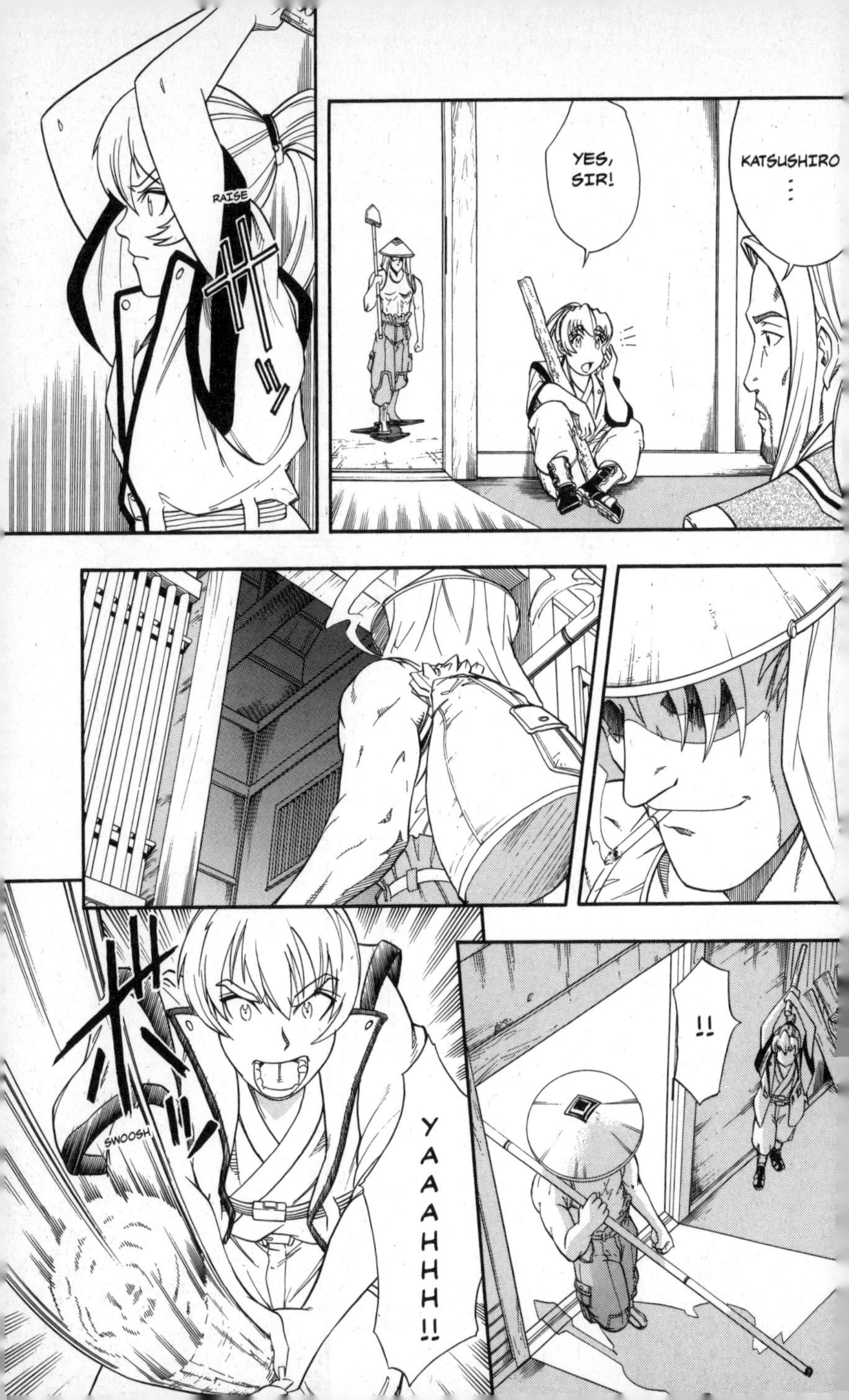
KATSUSHIRO ...
YES, SIR!
RAISE
!!
YAAAHHH!!
SWOOSH

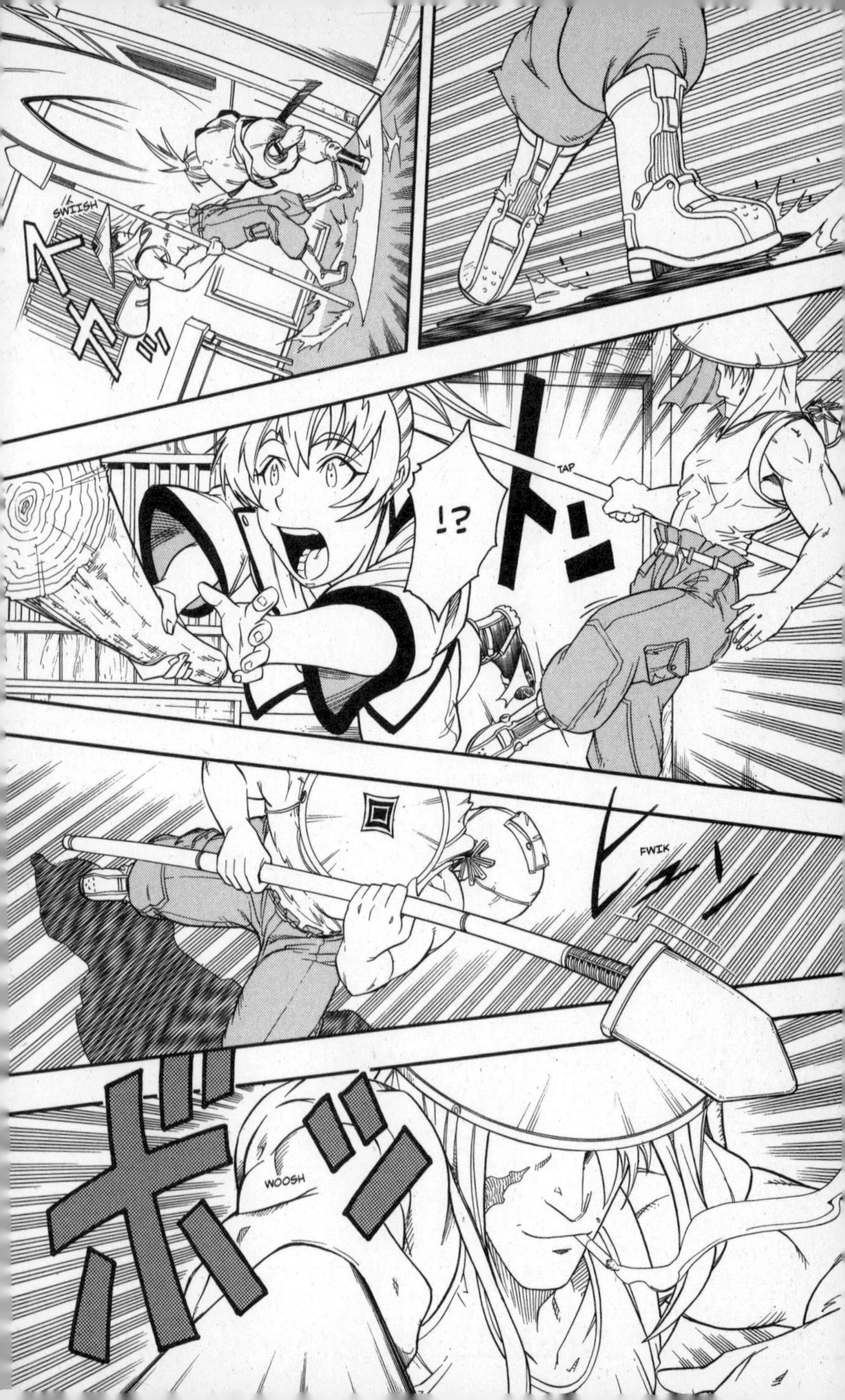
SWIISH
!?
TAP
FWIK
WOOSH

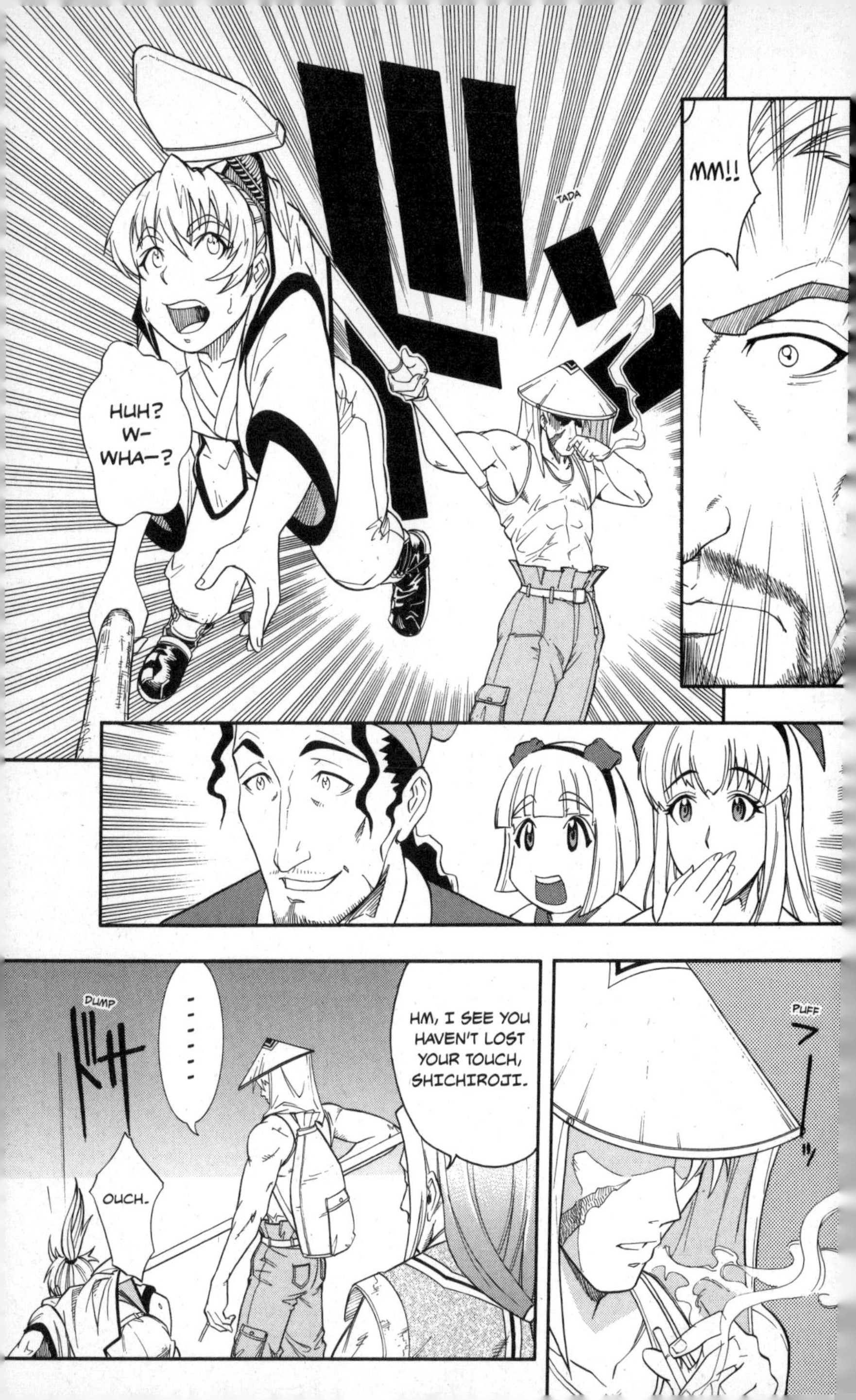
MM!!
TADA
HUH? W- WHA—?
PUFF
HM, I SEE YOU HAVEN'T LOST YOUR TOUCH, SHICHIROJI.
......
DUMP
OUCH.

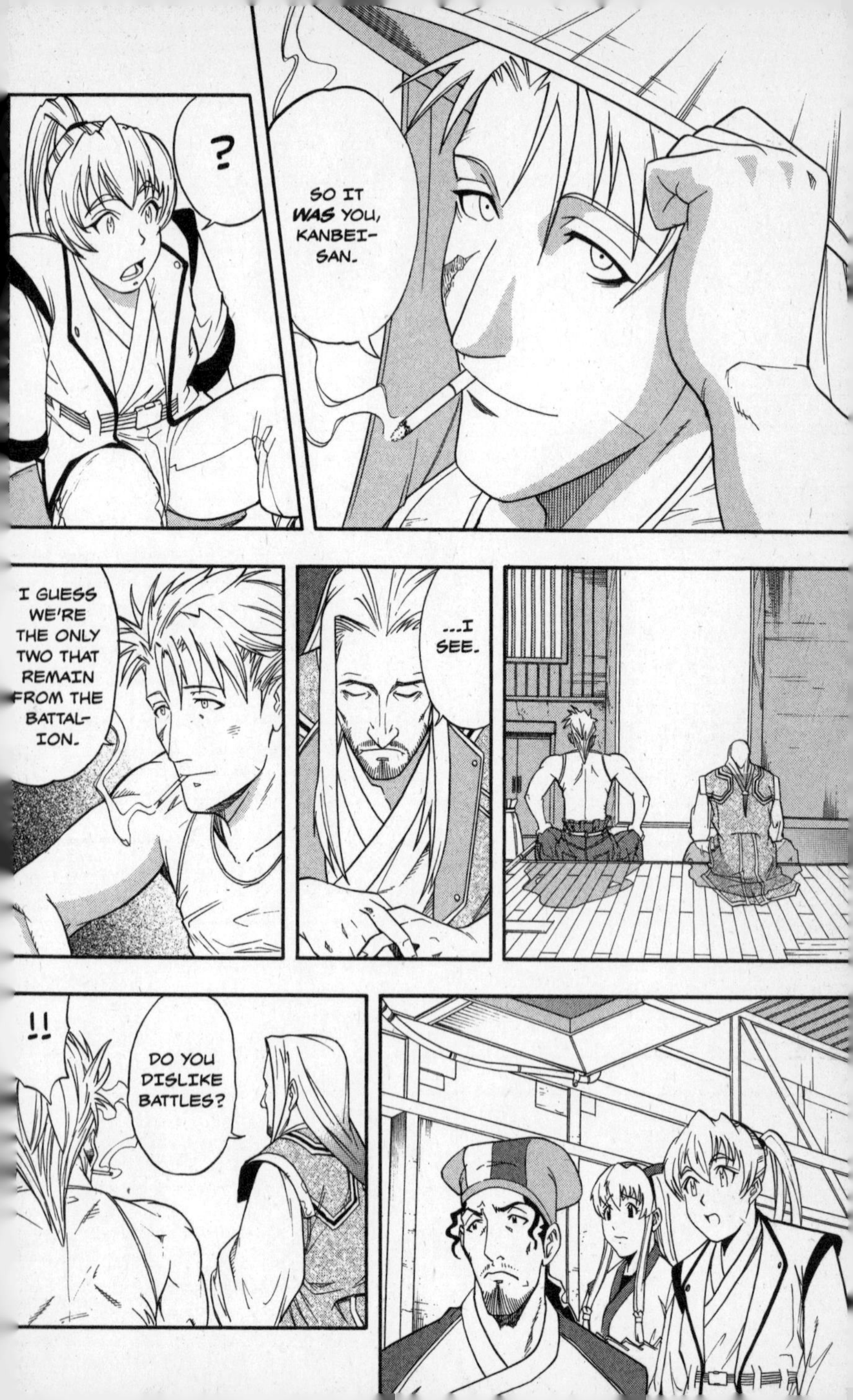
SO IT WAS YOU, KANBEI-SAN.
?
...I SEE.
I GUESS WE'RE THE ONLY TWO THAT REMAIN FROM THE BATTALION.
DO YOU DISLIKE BATTLES?
!!

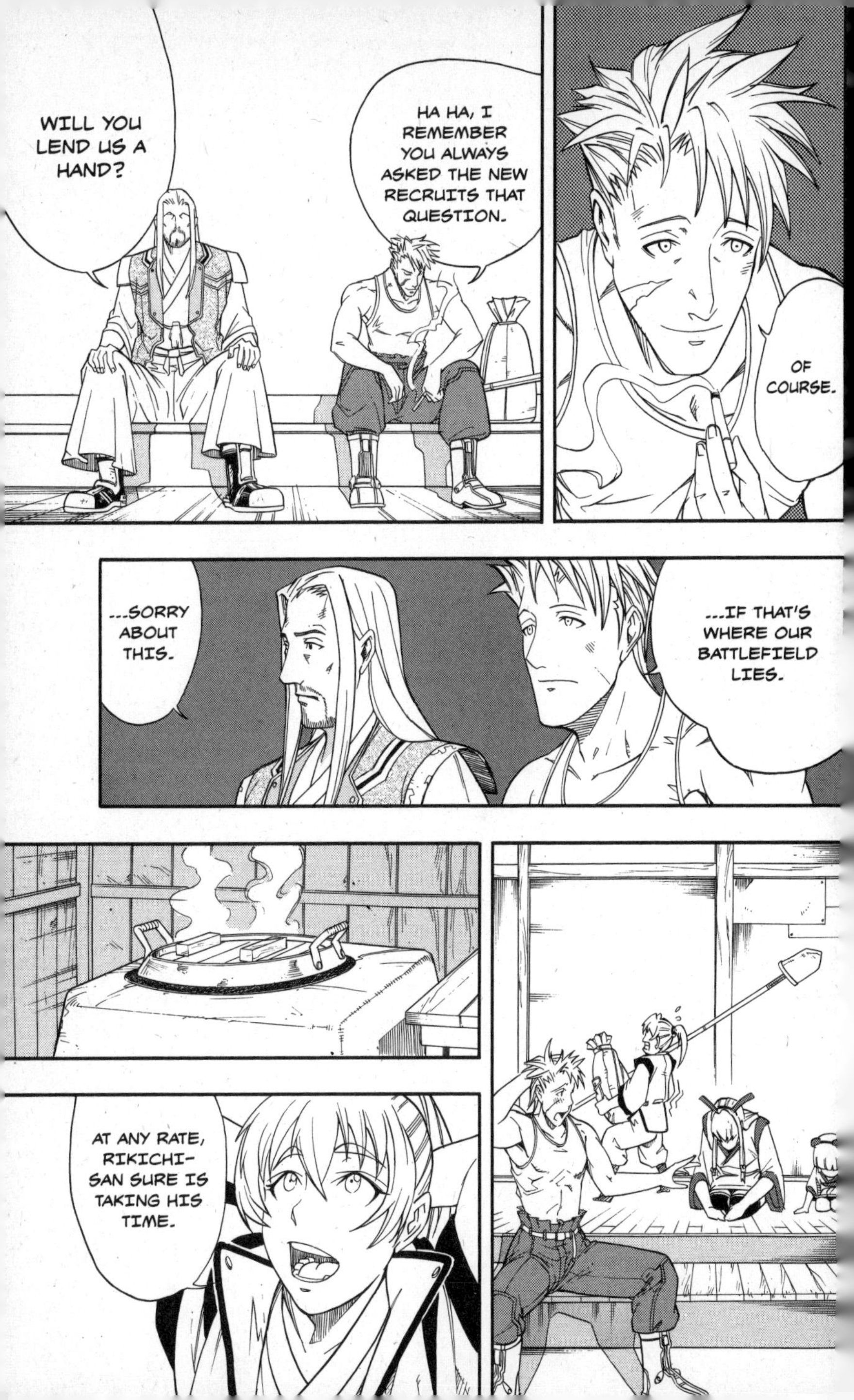
OF COURSE.
HA HA, I REMEMBER YOU ALWAYS ASKED THE NEW RECRUITS THAT QUESTION.
WILL YOU LEND US A HAND?
...IF THAT'S WHERE OUR BATTLEFIELD LIES.
...SORRY ABOUT THIS.
AT ANY RATE, RIKICHI-SAN SURE IS TAKING HIS TIME.

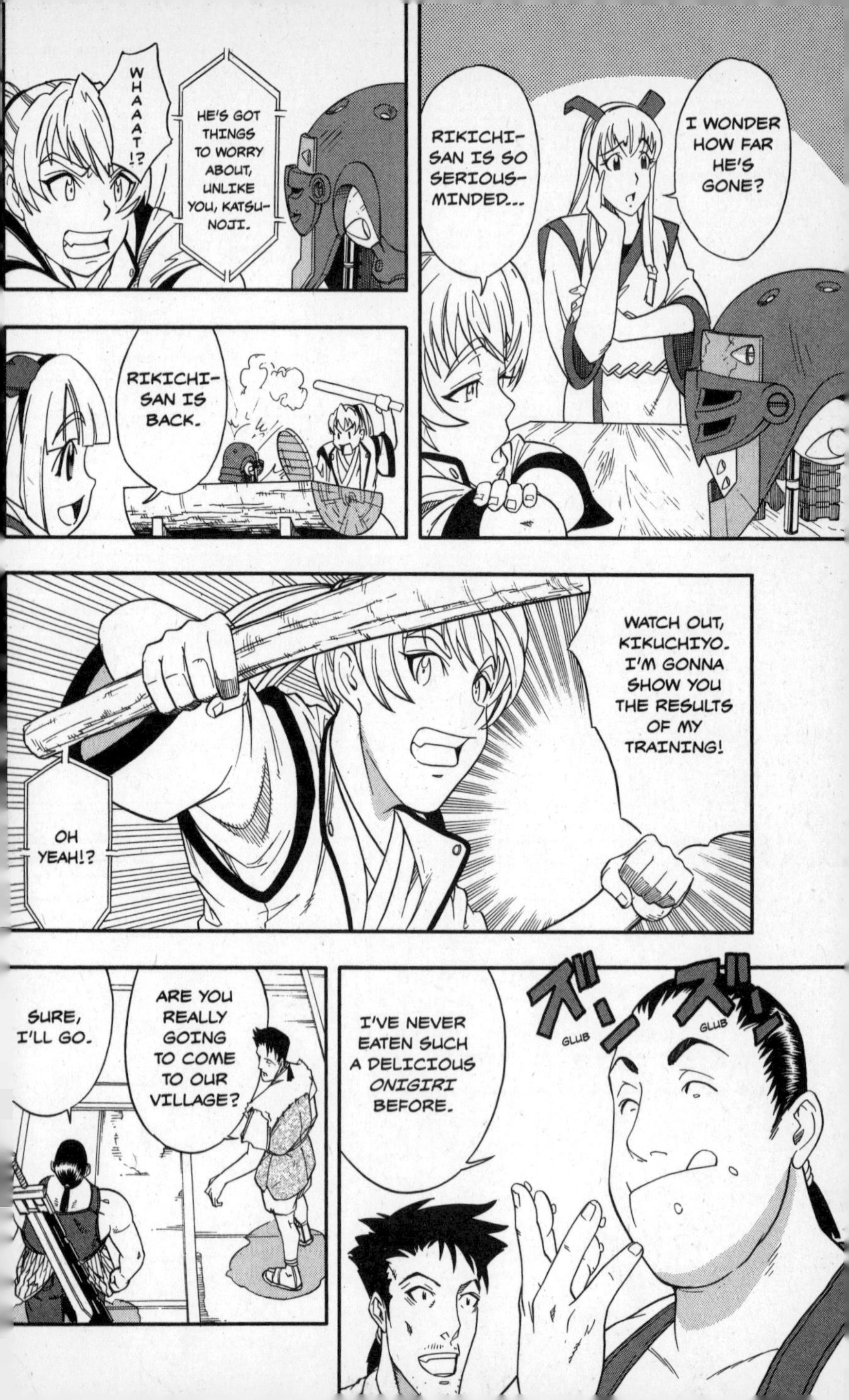
I WONDER HOW FAR HE'S GONE?
RIKICHI-SAN IS SO SERIOUS-MINDED...
HE'S GOT THINGS TO WORRY ABOUT, UNLIKE YOU, KATSUNOJI.
WHAAAT!?
RIKICHI-SAN IS BACK.
WATCH OUT, KIKUCHIYO. I'M GONNA SHOW YOU THE RESULTS OF MY TRAINING!
OH YEAH!?
ズー ズー
GLUB
GLUB
I'VE NEVER EATEN SUCH A DELICIOUS *ONIGIRI* BEFORE.
ARE YOU REALLY GOING TO COME TO OUR VILLAGE?
SURE, I'LL GO.

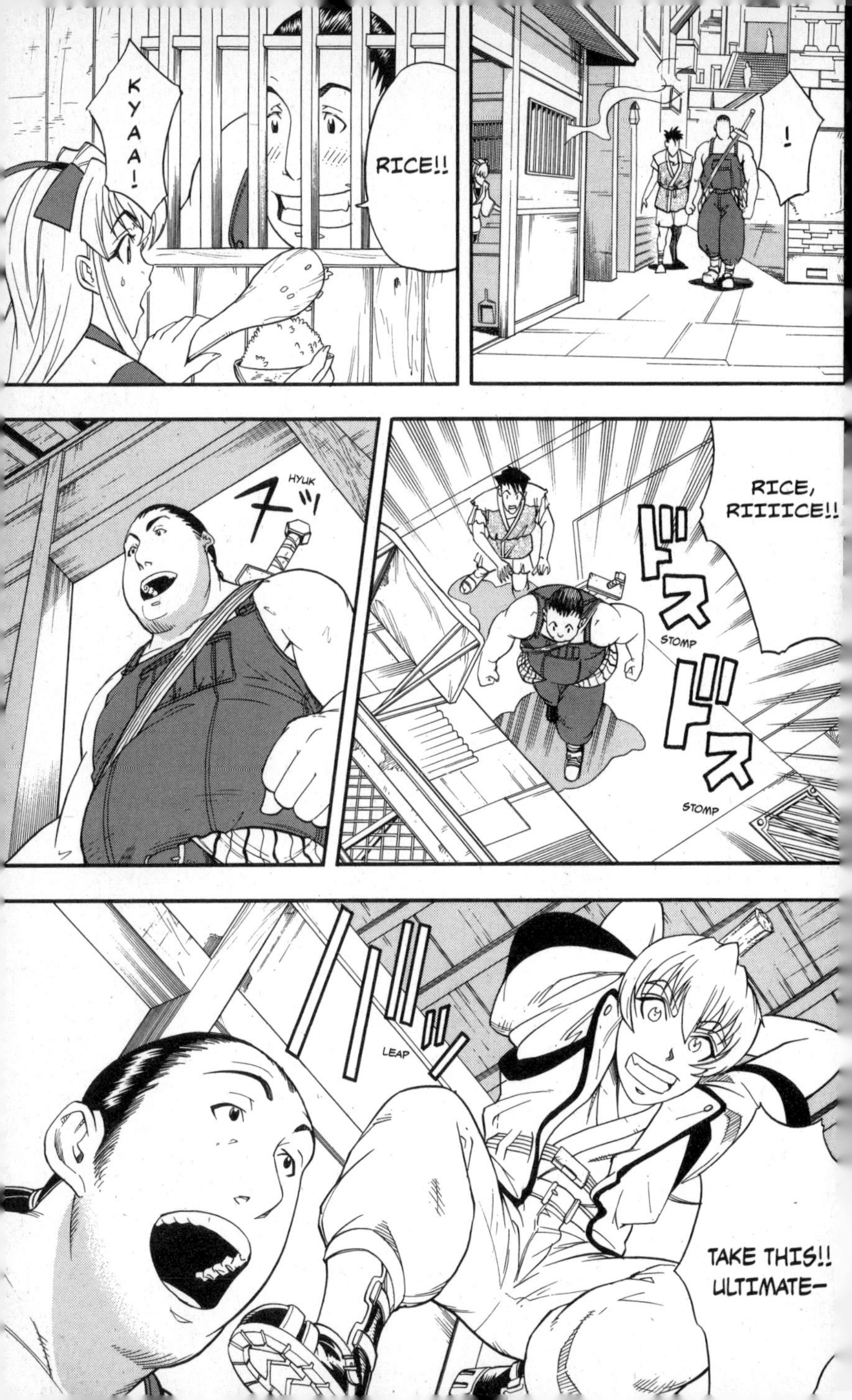
!
RICE!!
KYAA!
RICE, RIIIICE!!
ドス
STOMP
ドス
STOMP
HYUK
TAKE THIS!! ULTIMATE—
LEAP

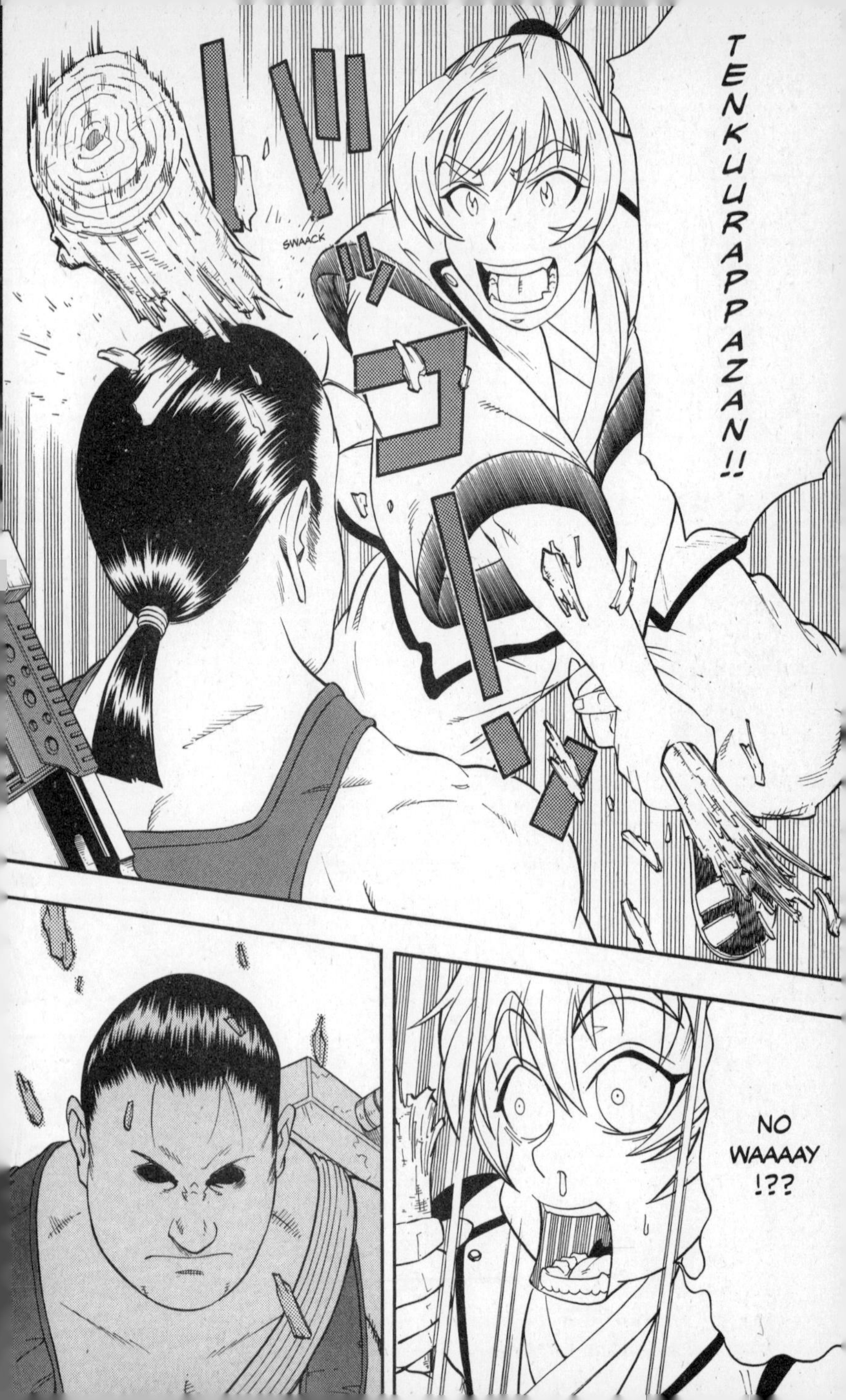
TENKUURAPPAZAN!!
SWAACK
NO WAAAAY !??

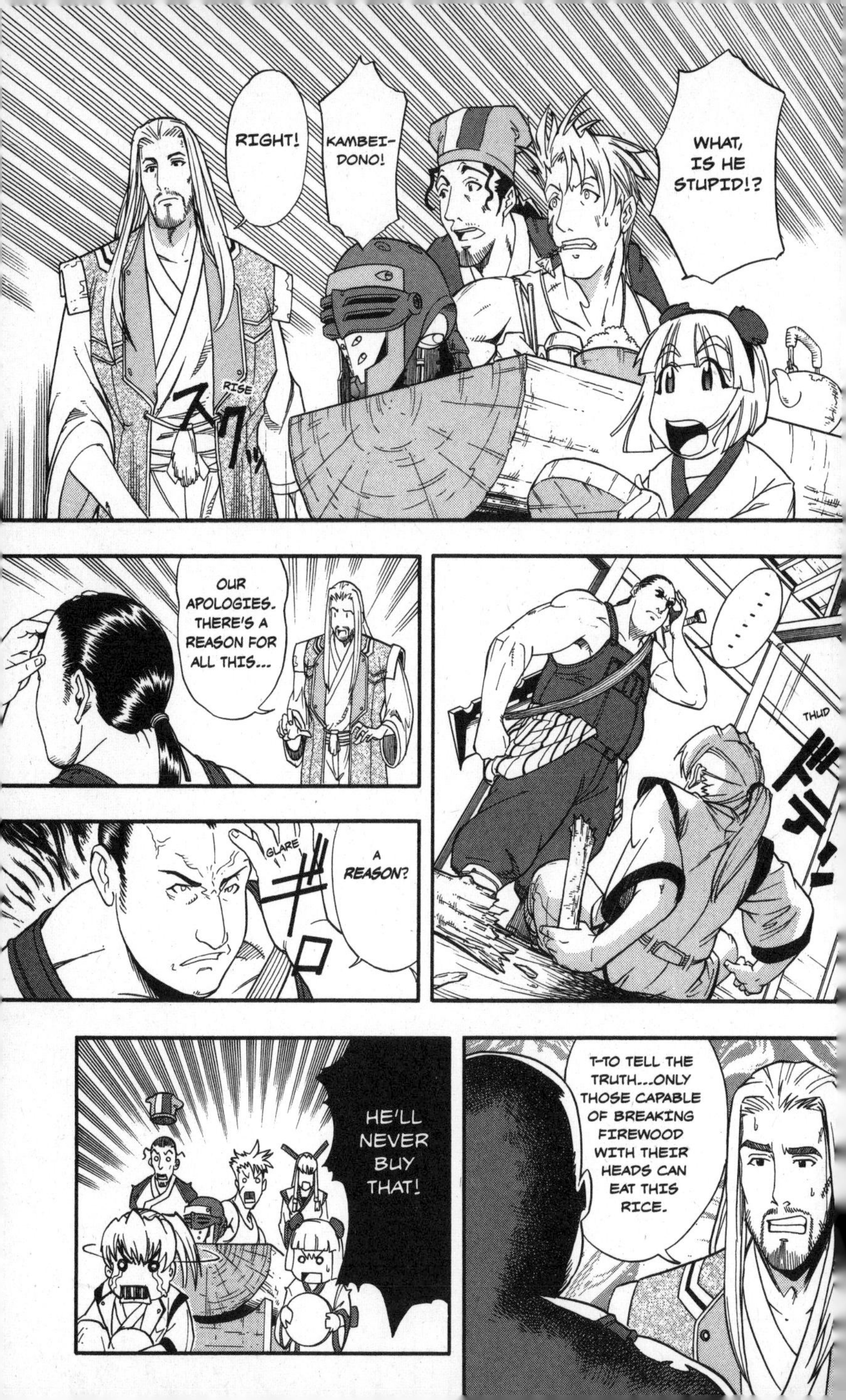
WHAT, IS HE STUPID!?
KAMBEI-DONO!
RIGHT!
RISE
......
THUD
OUR APOLOGIES. THERE'S A REASON FOR ALL THIS...
GLARE
A *REASON*?
T-TO TELL THE TRUTH...ONLY THOSE CAPABLE OF BREAKING FIREWOOD WITH THEIR HEADS CAN EAT THIS RICE.
HE'LL NEVER BUY THAT!

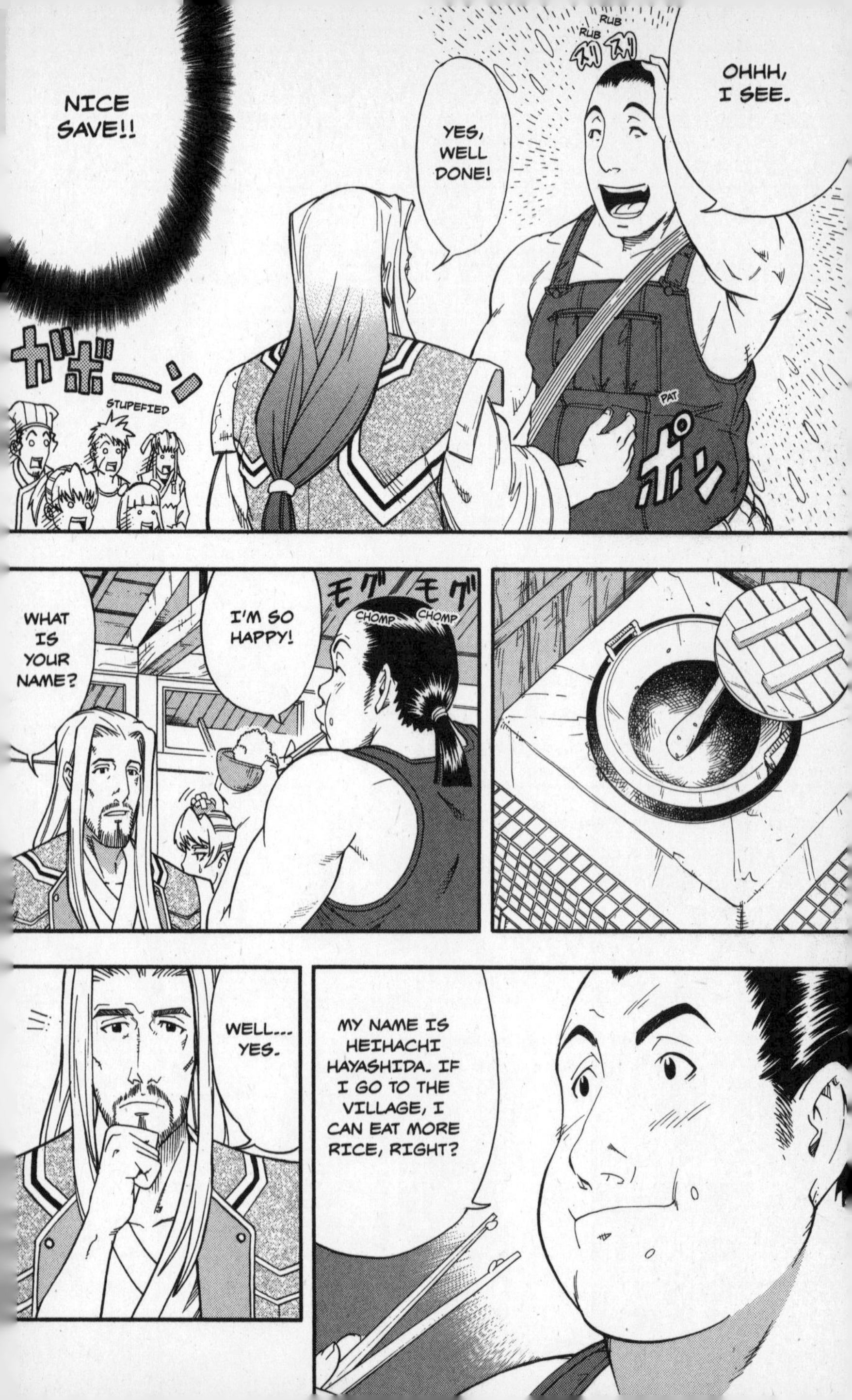

OHHH, I SEE.
RUB RUB
スリスリ
YES, WELL DONE!
PAT
ポン
NICE SAVE!!
ガボーン
STUPEFIED
モグモグ
CHOMP CHOMP
I'M SO HAPPY!
WHAT IS YOUR NAME?
MY NAME IS HEIHACHI HAYASHIDA. IF I GO TO THE VILLAGE, I CAN EAT MORE RICE, RIGHT?
WELL... YES.

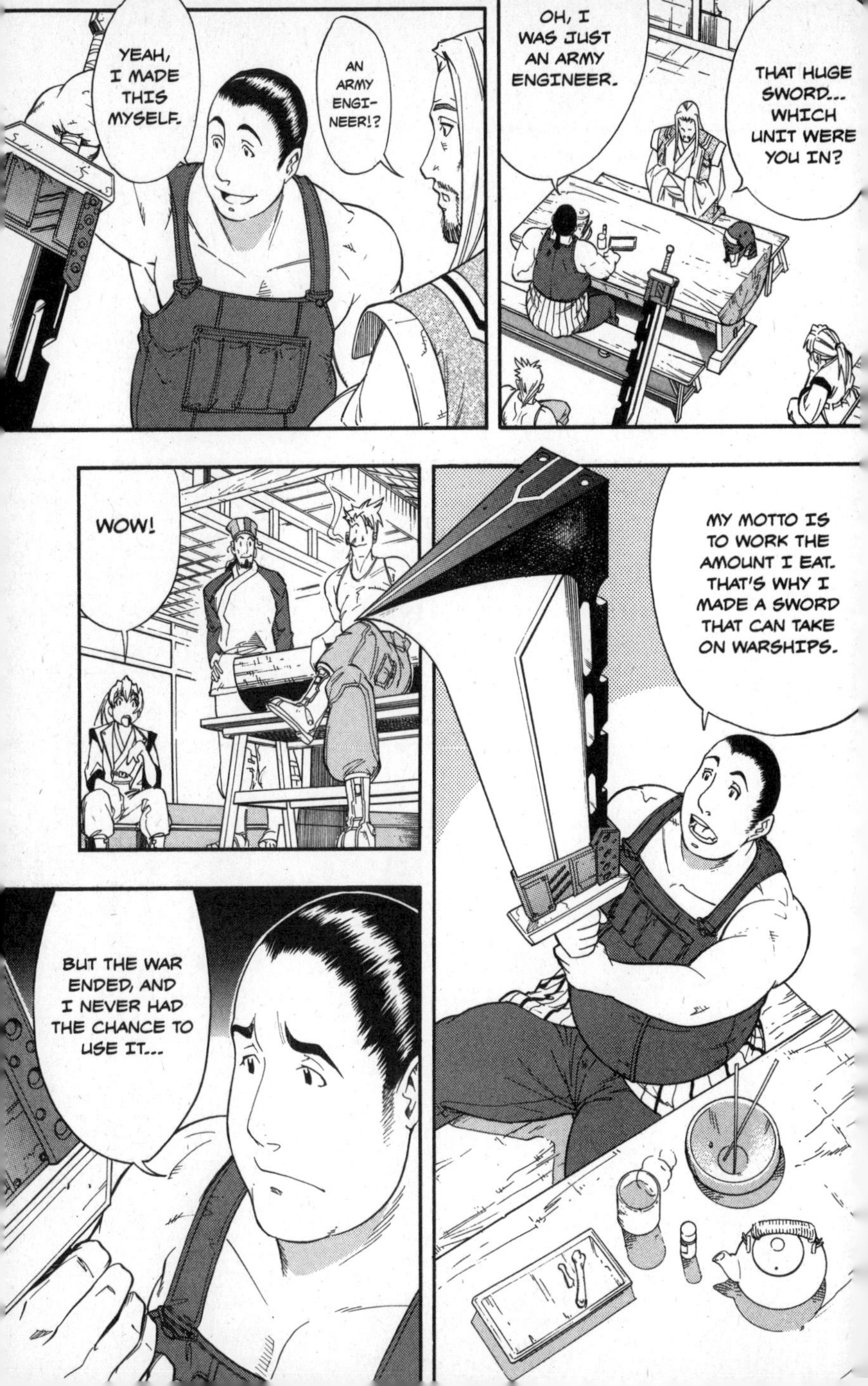
THAT HUGE SWORD... WHICH UNIT WERE YOU IN?
OH, I WAS JUST AN ARMY ENGINEER.
AN ARMY ENGI-NEER!?
YEAH, I MADE THIS MYSELF.
MY MOTTO IS TO WORK THE AMOUNT I EAT. THAT'S WHY I MADE A SWORD THAT CAN TAKE ON WARSHIPS.
WOW!
BUT THE WAR ENDED, AND I NEVER HAD THE CHANCE TO USE IT...

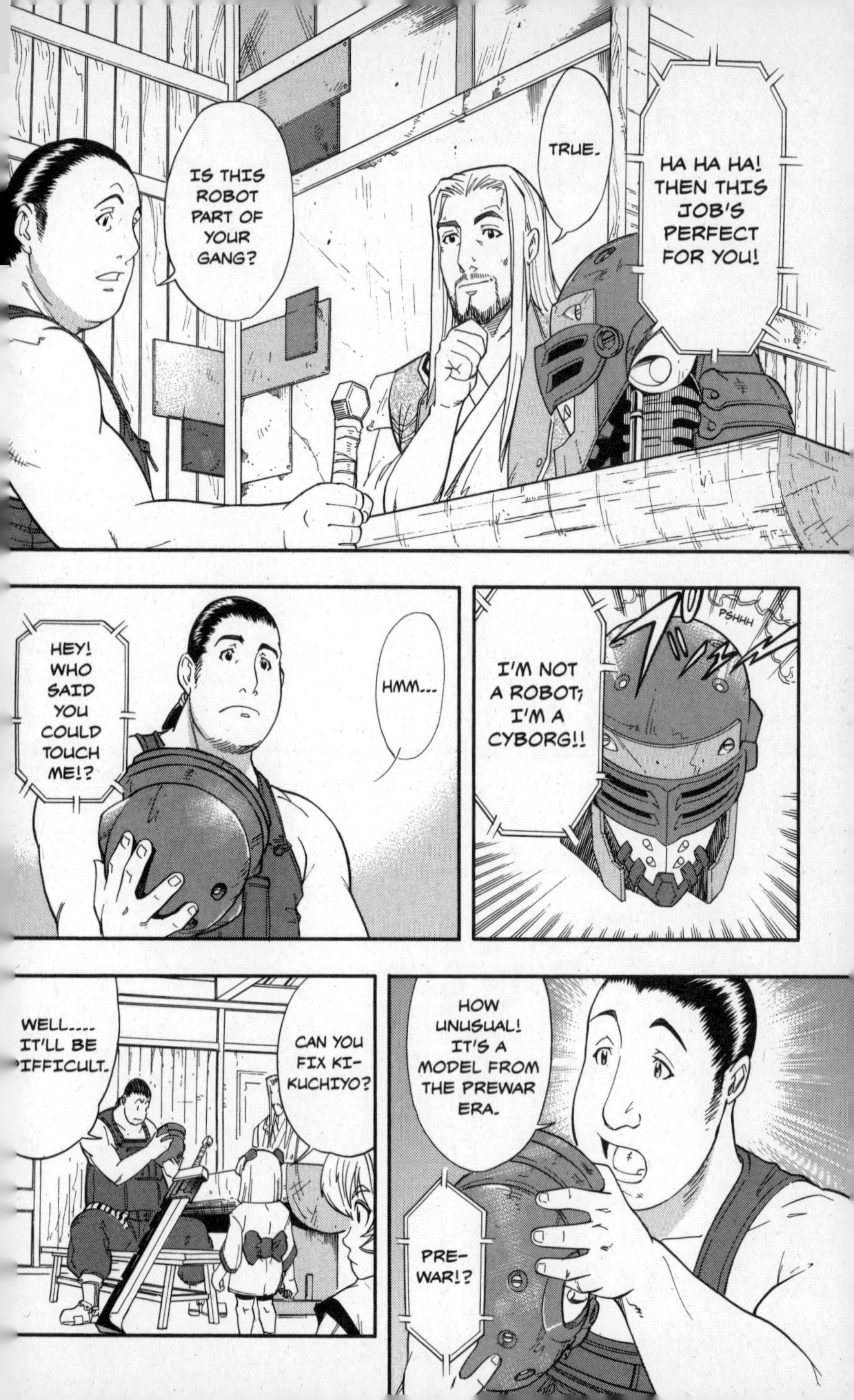
IS THIS ROBOT PART OF YOUR GANG?
TRUE.
HA HA HA! THEN THIS JOB'S PERFECT FOR YOU!
PSHHH
I'M NOT A ROBOT; I'M A CYBORG!!
HEY! WHO SAID YOU COULD TOUCH ME!?
HMM...
HOW UNUSUAL! IT'S A MODEL FROM THE PREWAR ERA.
PRE-WAR!?
CAN YOU FIX KI-KUCHIYO?
WELL.... IT'LL BE DIFFICULT.

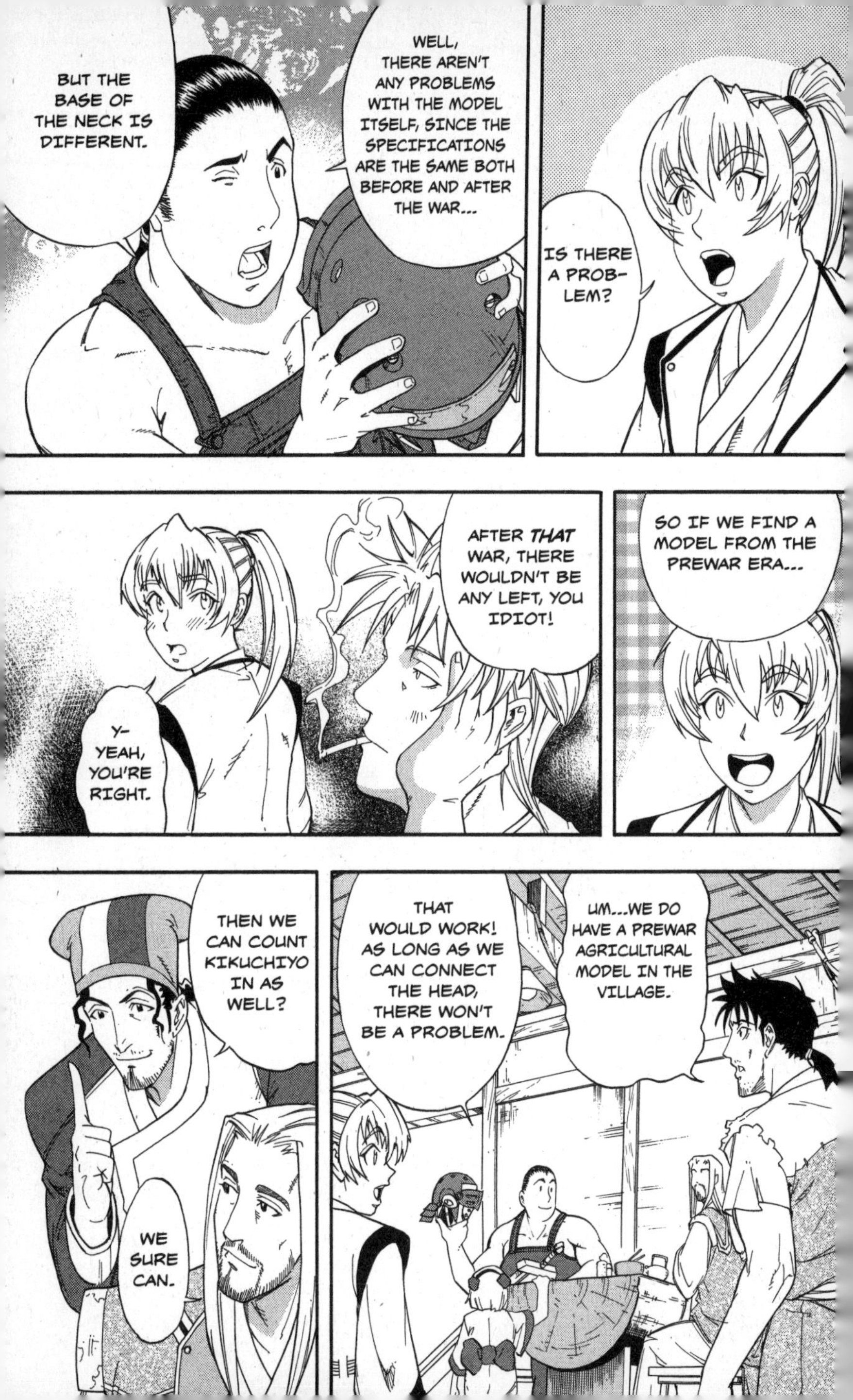
IS THERE A PROBLEM?
WELL, THERE AREN'T ANY PROBLEMS WITH THE MODEL ITSELF, SINCE THE SPECIFICATIONS ARE THE SAME BOTH BEFORE AND AFTER THE WAR...
BUT THE BASE OF THE NECK IS DIFFERENT.
SO IF WE FIND A MODEL FROM THE PREWAR ERA...
AFTER *THAT* WAR, THERE WOULDN'T BE ANY LEFT, YOU IDIOT!
Y-YEAH, YOU'RE RIGHT.
UM...WE DO HAVE A PREWAR AGRICULTURAL MODEL IN THE VILLAGE.
THAT WOULD WORK! AS LONG AS WE CAN CONNECT THE HEAD, THERE WON'T BE A PROBLEM.
THEN WE CAN COUNT KIKUCHIYO IN AS WELL?
WE SURE CAN.

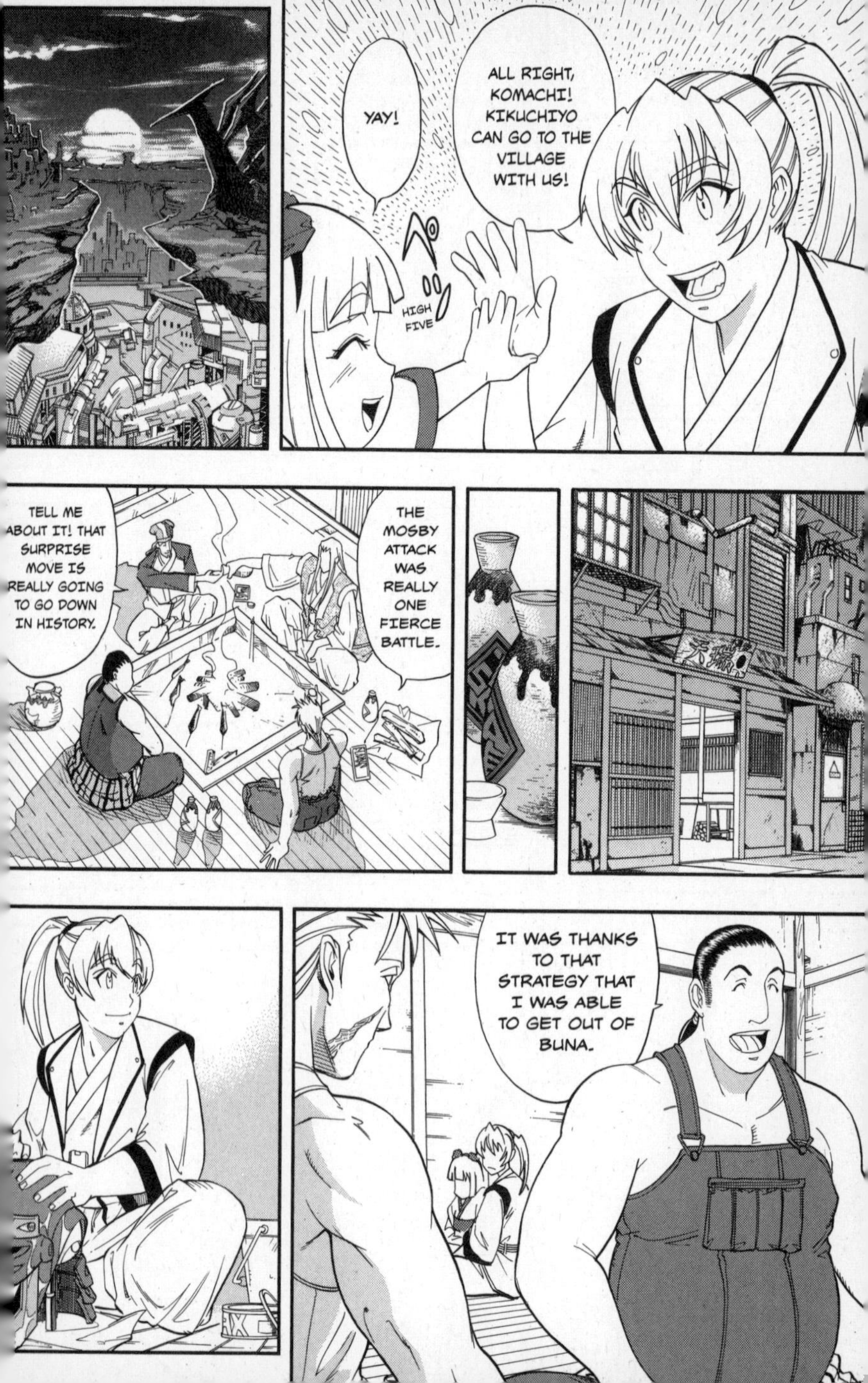
ALL RIGHT, KOMACHI! KIKUCHIYO CAN GO TO THE VILLAGE WITH US!
YAY!
HIGH FIVE
THE MOSBY ATTACK WAS REALLY ONE FIERCE BATTLE.
TELL ME ABOUT IT! THAT SURPRISE MOVE IS REALLY GOING TO GO DOWN IN HISTORY.
IT WAS THANKS TO THAT STRATEGY THAT I WAS ABLE TO GET OUT OF BUNA.

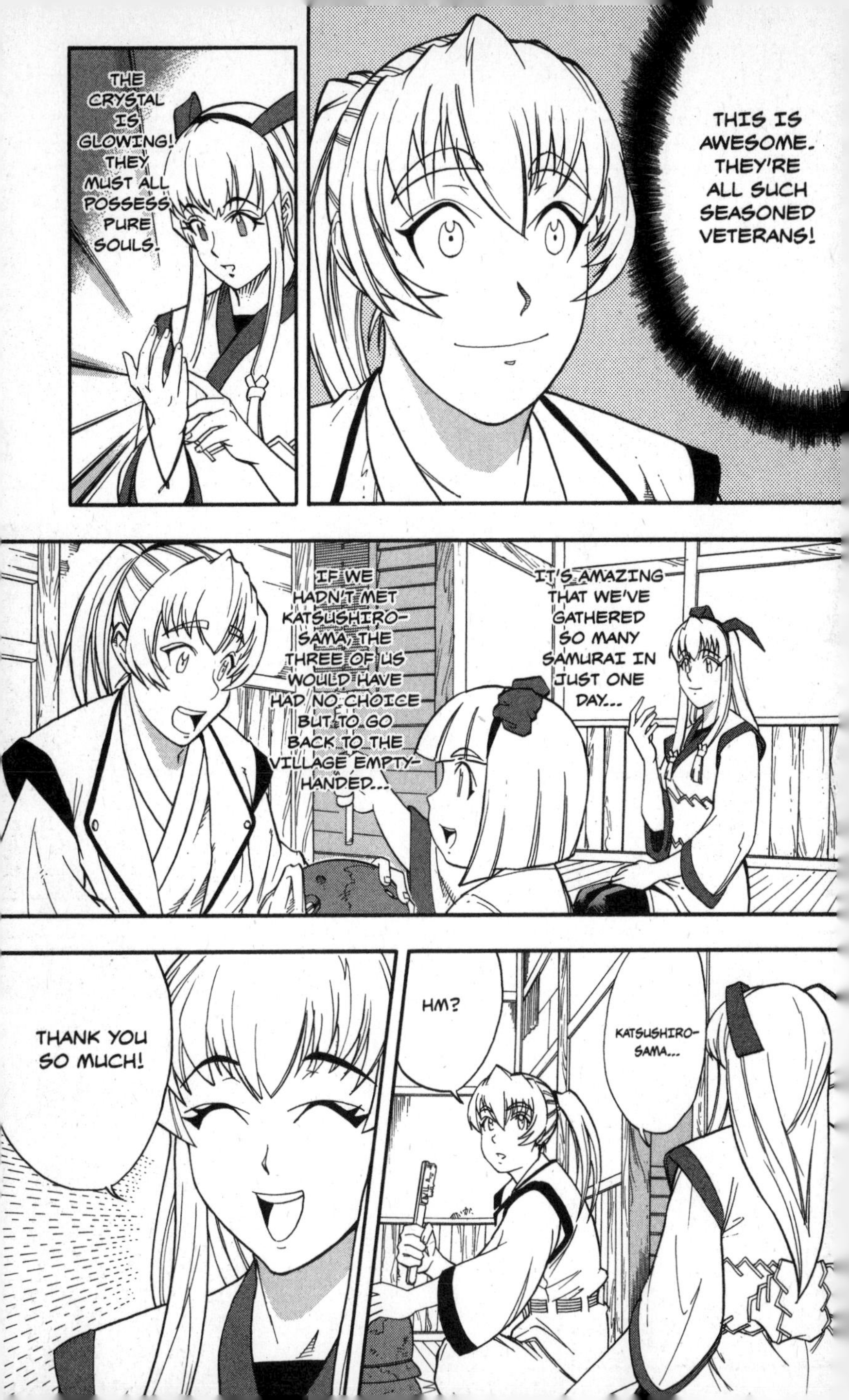
THIS IS AWESOME. THEY'RE ALL SUCH SEASONED VETERANS!
THE CRYSTAL IS GLOWING! THEY MUST ALL POSSESS PURE SOULS.
IT'S AMAZING THAT WE'VE GATHERED SO MANY SAMURAI IN JUST ONE DAY...
IF WE HADN'T MET KATSUSHIRO-SAMA, THE THREE OF US WOULD HAVE HAD NO CHOICE BUT TO GO BACK TO THE VILLAGE EMPTY-HANDED...
KATSUSHIRO-SAMA...
HM?
THANK YOU SO MUCH!

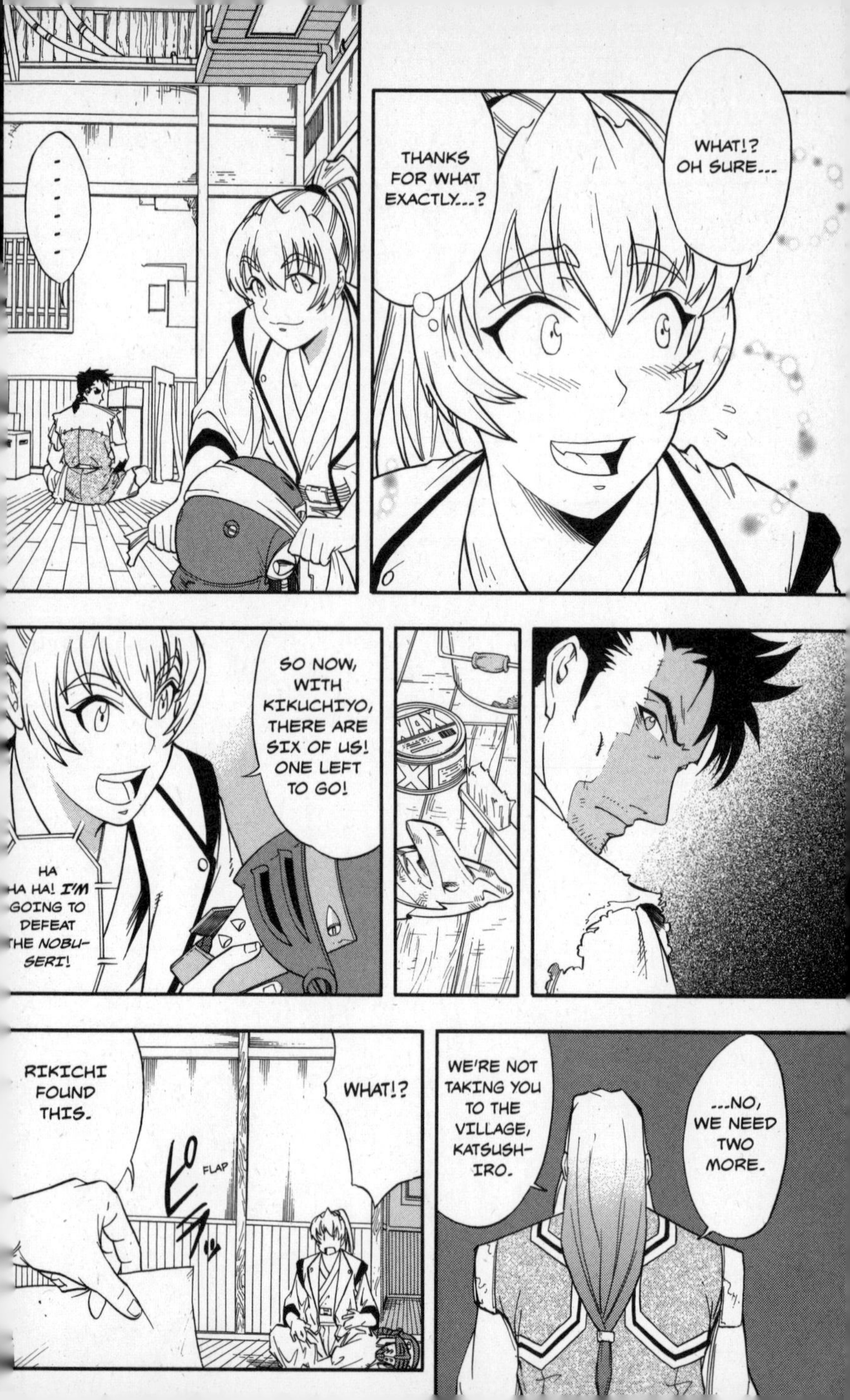
WHAT!? OH SURE...
THANKS FOR WHAT EXACTLY...?
......
SO NOW, WITH KIKUCHIYO, THERE ARE SIX OF US! ONE LEFT TO GO!
HA HA HA! I'M GOING TO DEFEAT THE NOBU-SERI!
...NO, WE NEED TWO MORE.
WE'RE NOT TAKING YOU TO THE VILLAGE, KATSUSH-IRO.
WHAT!?
FLAP
RIKICHI FOUND THIS.

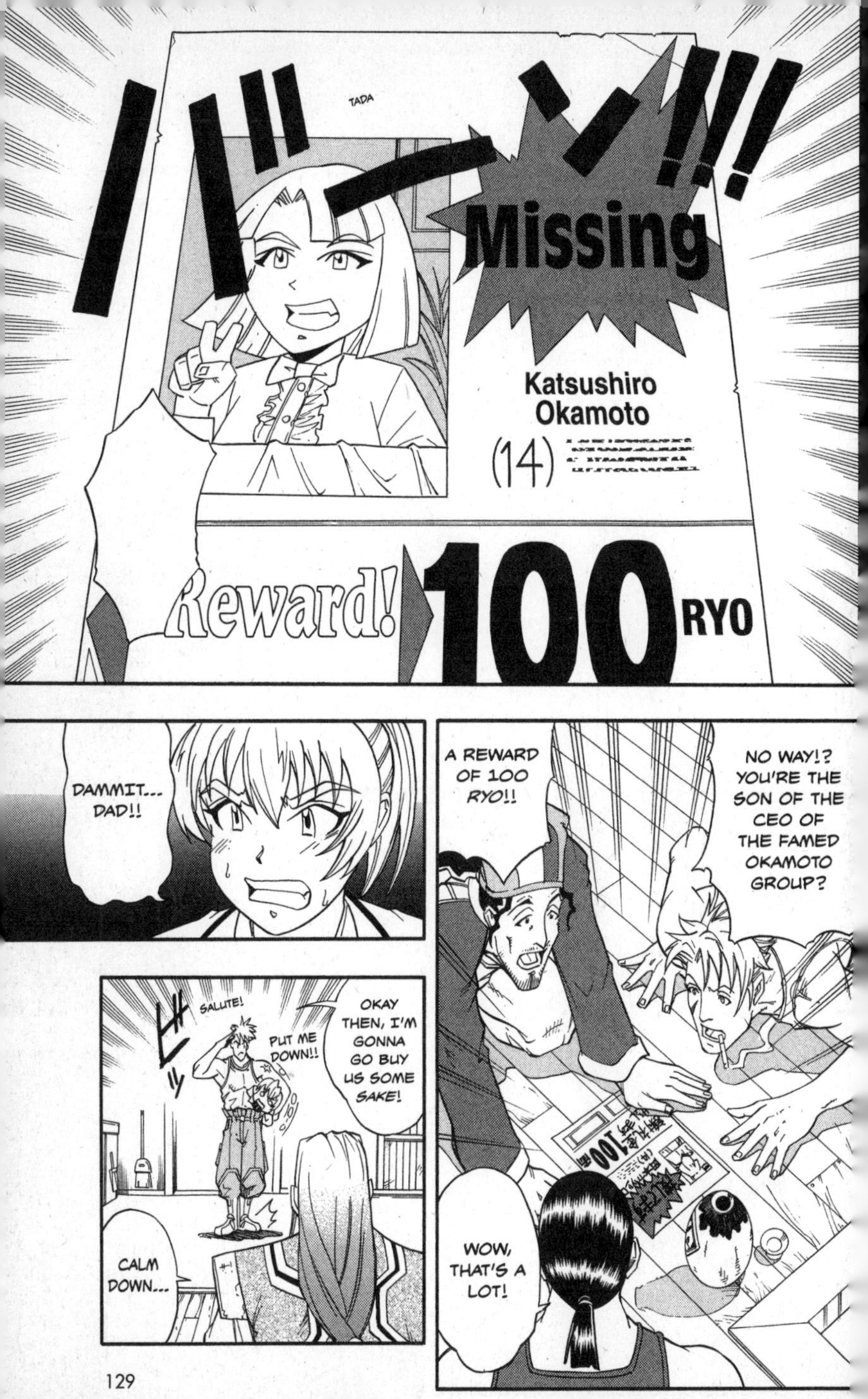
TADA
Missing
Katsushiro Okamoto
(14)
Reward! 100 RYO
NO WAY!? YOU'RE THE SON OF THE CEO OF THE FAMED OKAMOTO GROUP?
A REWARD OF 100 RYO!!
WOW, THAT'S A LOT!
DAMMIT... DAD!!
OKAY THEN, I'M GONNA GO BUY US SOME SAKE!
PUT ME DOWN!!
SALUTE!
CALM DOWN...

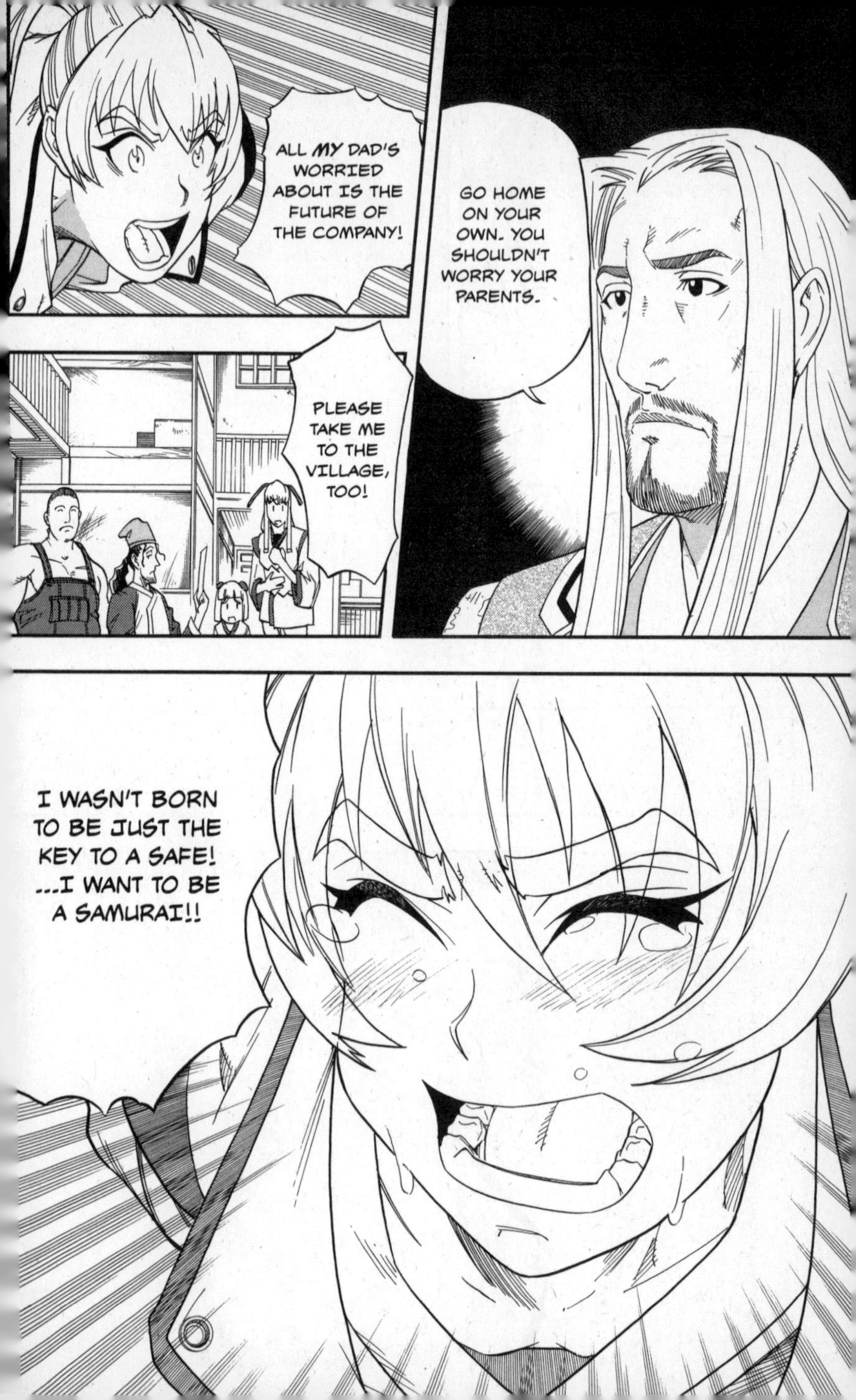
GO HOME ON YOUR OWN. YOU SHOULDN'T WORRY YOUR PARENTS.
ALL *MY* DAD'S WORRIED ABOUT IS THE FUTURE OF THE COMPANY!
PLEASE TAKE ME TO THE VILLAGE, TOO!
I WASN'T BORN TO BE JUST THE KEY TO A SAFE! ...I WANT TO BE A SAMURAI!!

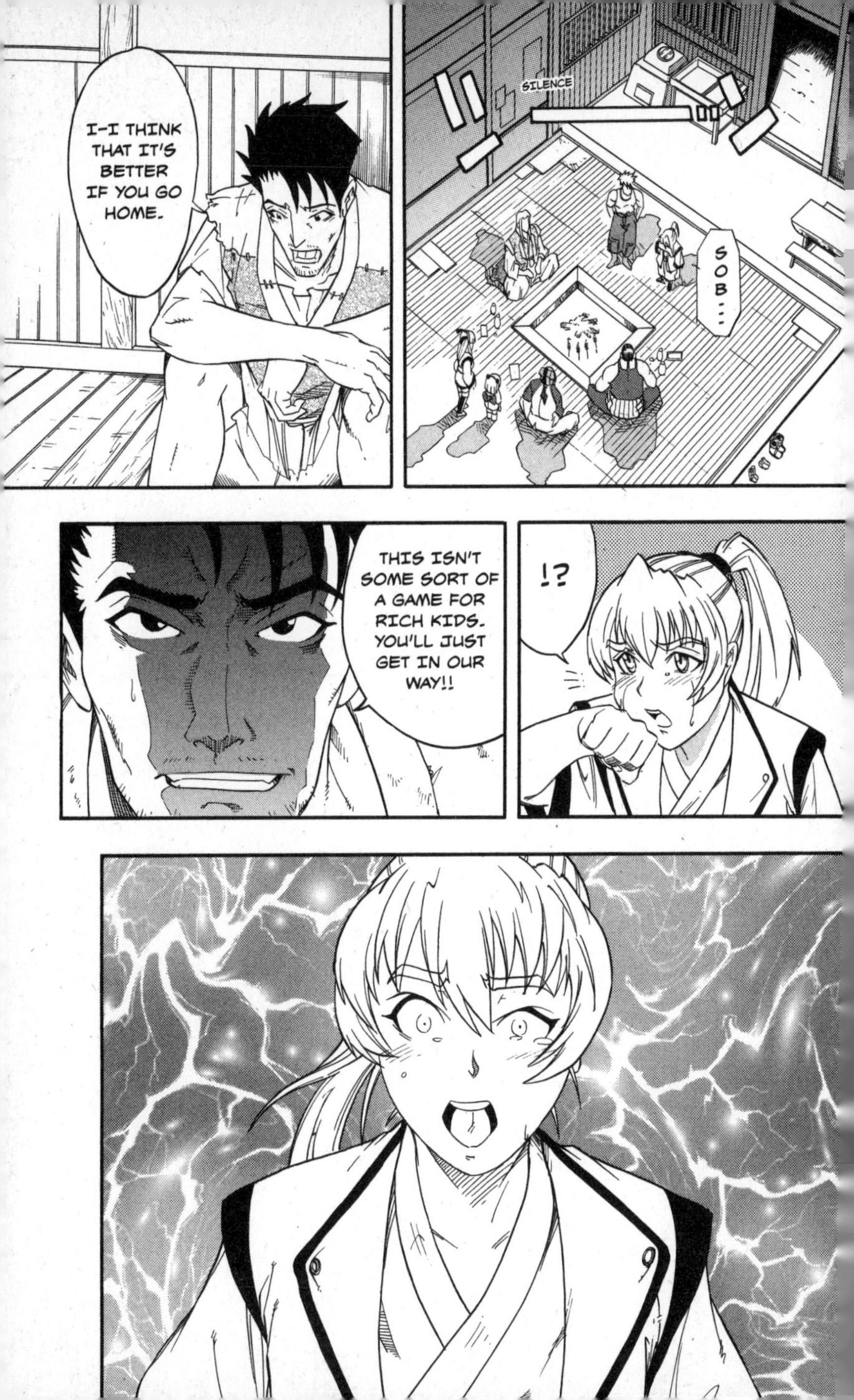
SILENCE
SOB...
I-I THINK THAT IT'S BETTER IF YOU GO HOME.
!?
THIS ISN'T SOME SORT OF A GAME FOR RICH KIDS. YOU'LL JUST GET IN OUR WAY!!

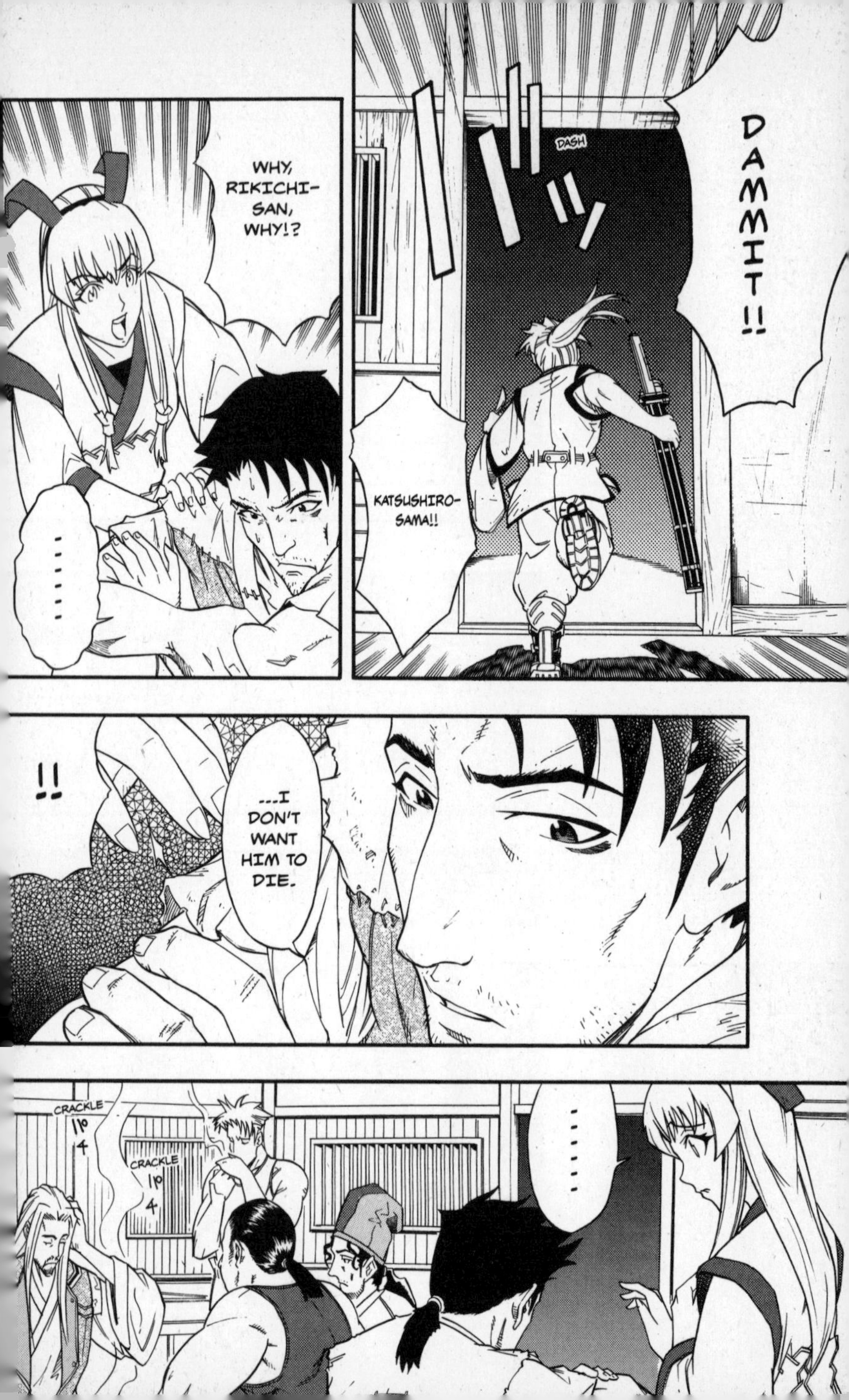
DAMMIT!!
DASH
KATSUSHIRO-SAMA!!
WHY, RIKICHI-SAN, WHY!?
......
...I DON'T WANT HIM TO DIE.
!!
......
CRACKLE
CRACKLE

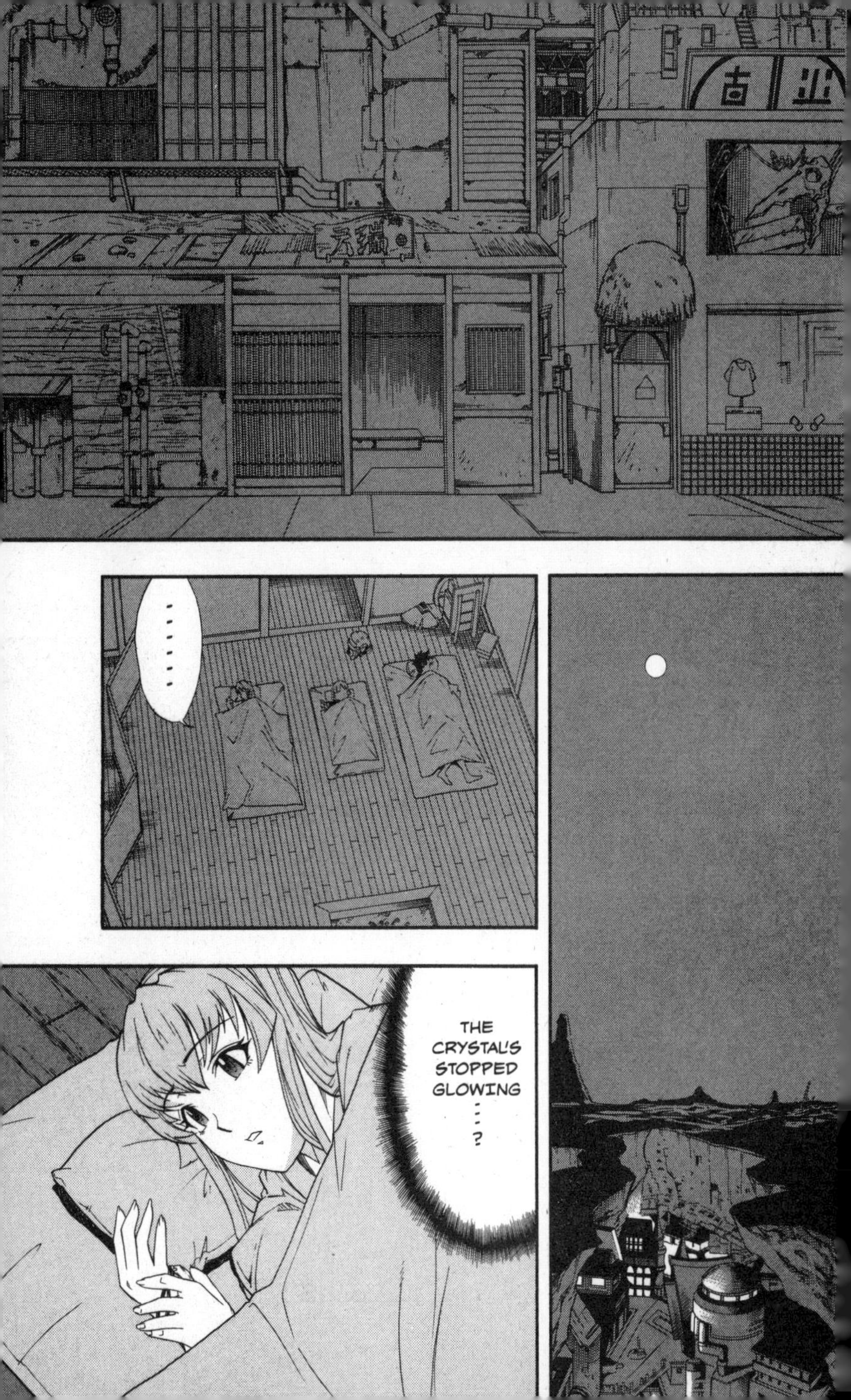
......
THE CRYSTAL'S STOPPED GLOWING ...?

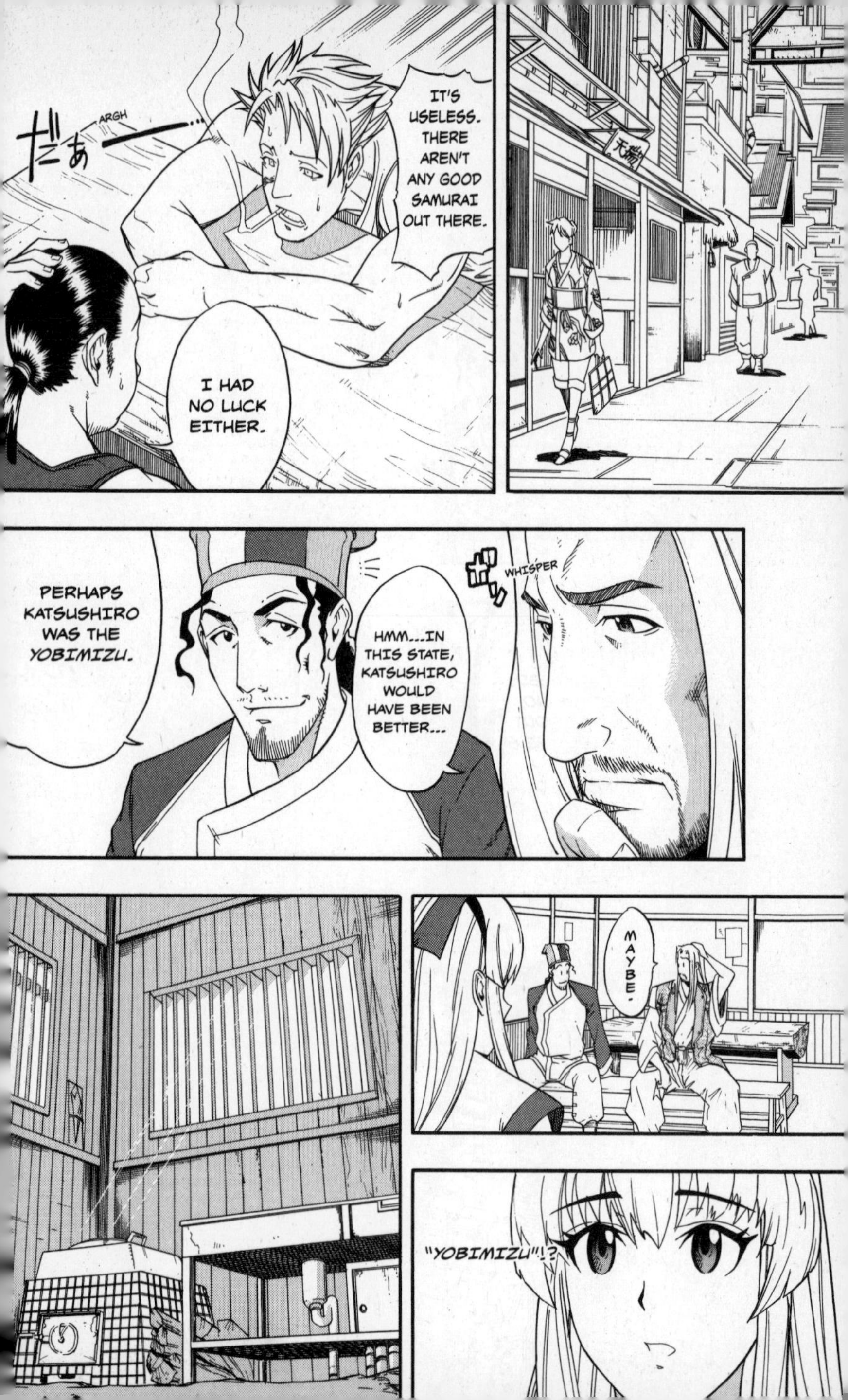IT'S USELESS. THERE AREN'T ANY GOOD SAMURAI OUT THERE.
だあ
ARGH
I HAD NO LUCK EITHER.
WHISPER
HMM...IN THIS STATE, KATSUSHIRO WOULD HAVE BEEN BETTER...
PERHAPS KATSUSHIRO WAS THE *YOBIMIZU*.
MAYBE.
"*YOBIMIZU*"!?

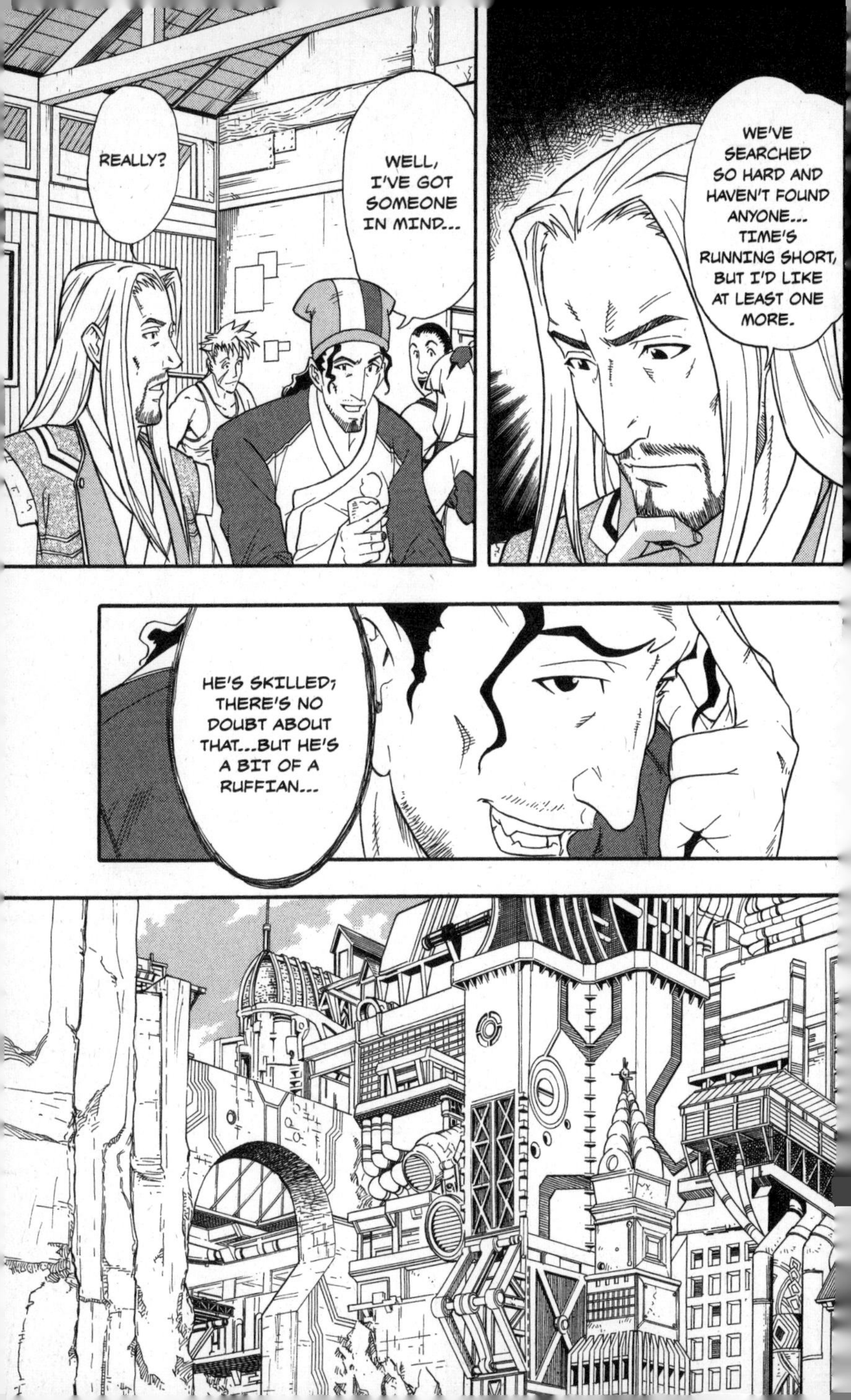
WE'VE SEARCHED SO HARD AND HAVEN'T FOUND ANYONE... TIME'S RUNNING SHORT, BUT I'D LIKE AT LEAST ONE MORE.
WELL, I'VE GOT SOMEONE IN MIND...
REALLY?
HE'S SKILLED; THERE'S NO DOUBT ABOUT THAT...BUT HE'S A BIT OF A RUFFIAN...

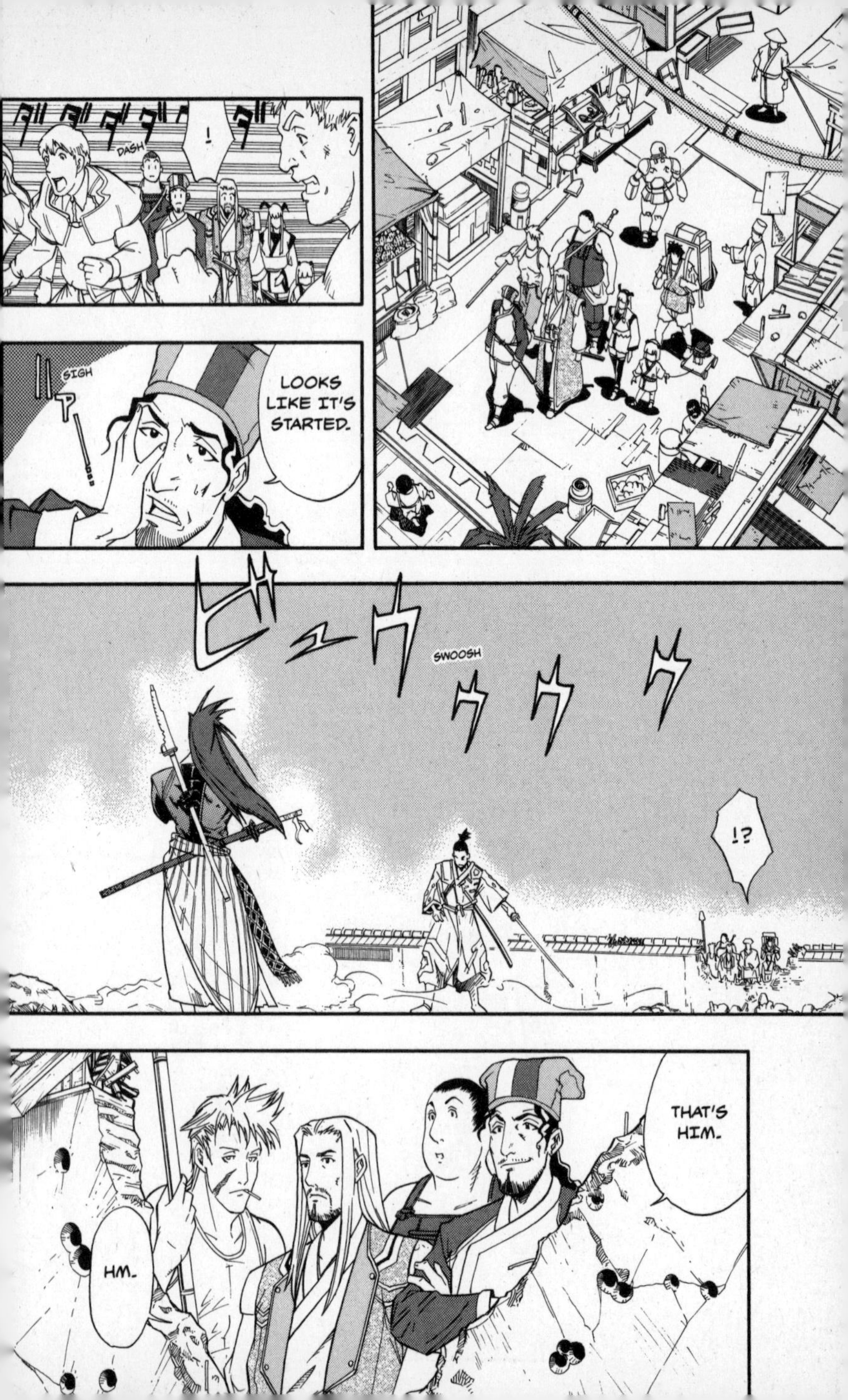
DASH
!
SIGH
LOOKS LIKE IT'S STARTED.
SWOOSH
!?
THAT'S HIM.
HM.

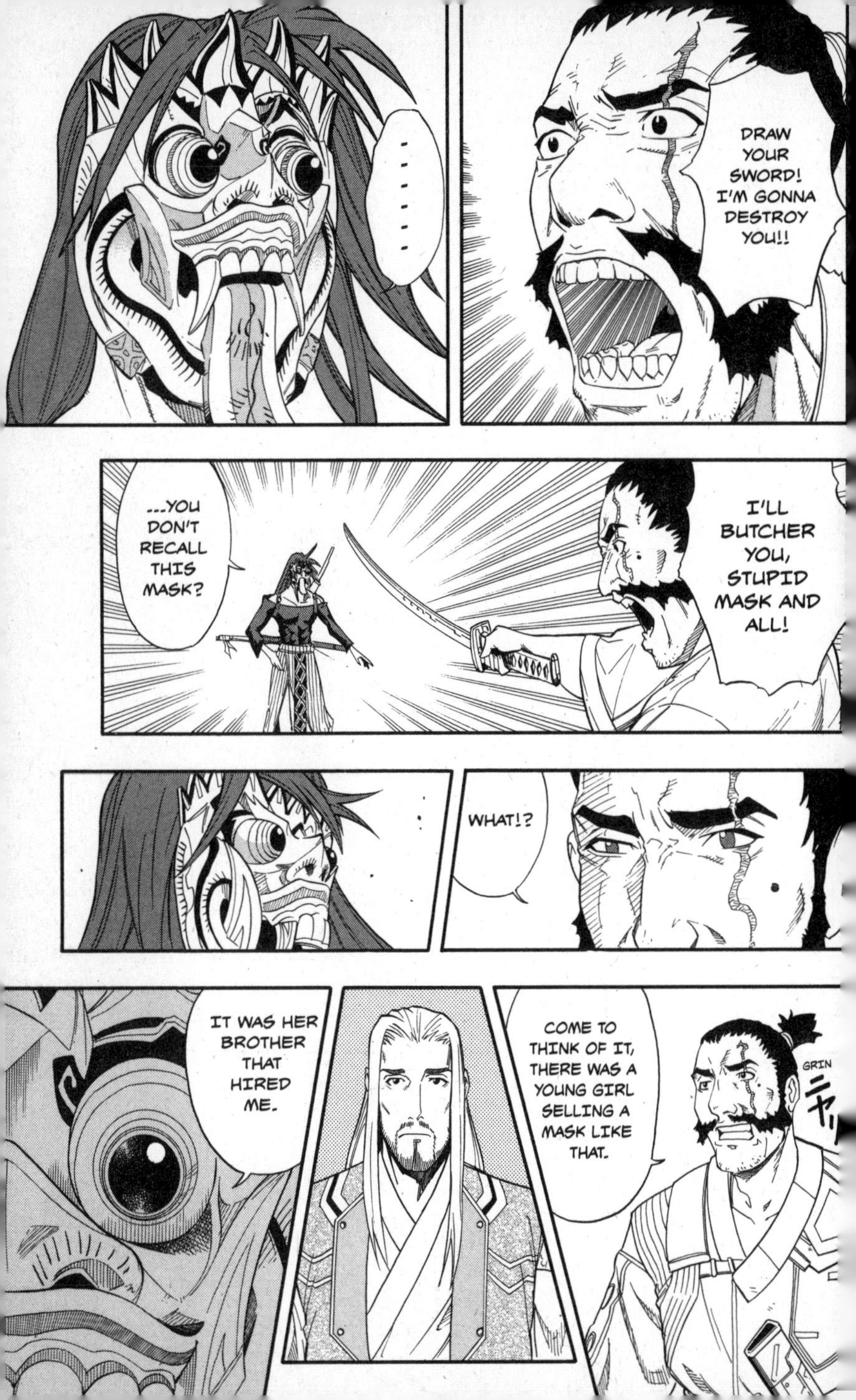
DRAW YOUR SWORD! I'M GONNA DESTROY YOU!!
......
I'LL BUTCHER YOU, STUPID MASK AND ALL!
...YOU DON'T RECALL THIS MASK?
WHAT!?
COME TO THINK OF IT, THERE WAS A YOUNG GIRL SELLING A MASK LIKE THAT.
GRIN
ニヤ
IT WAS HER BROTHER THAT HIRED ME.

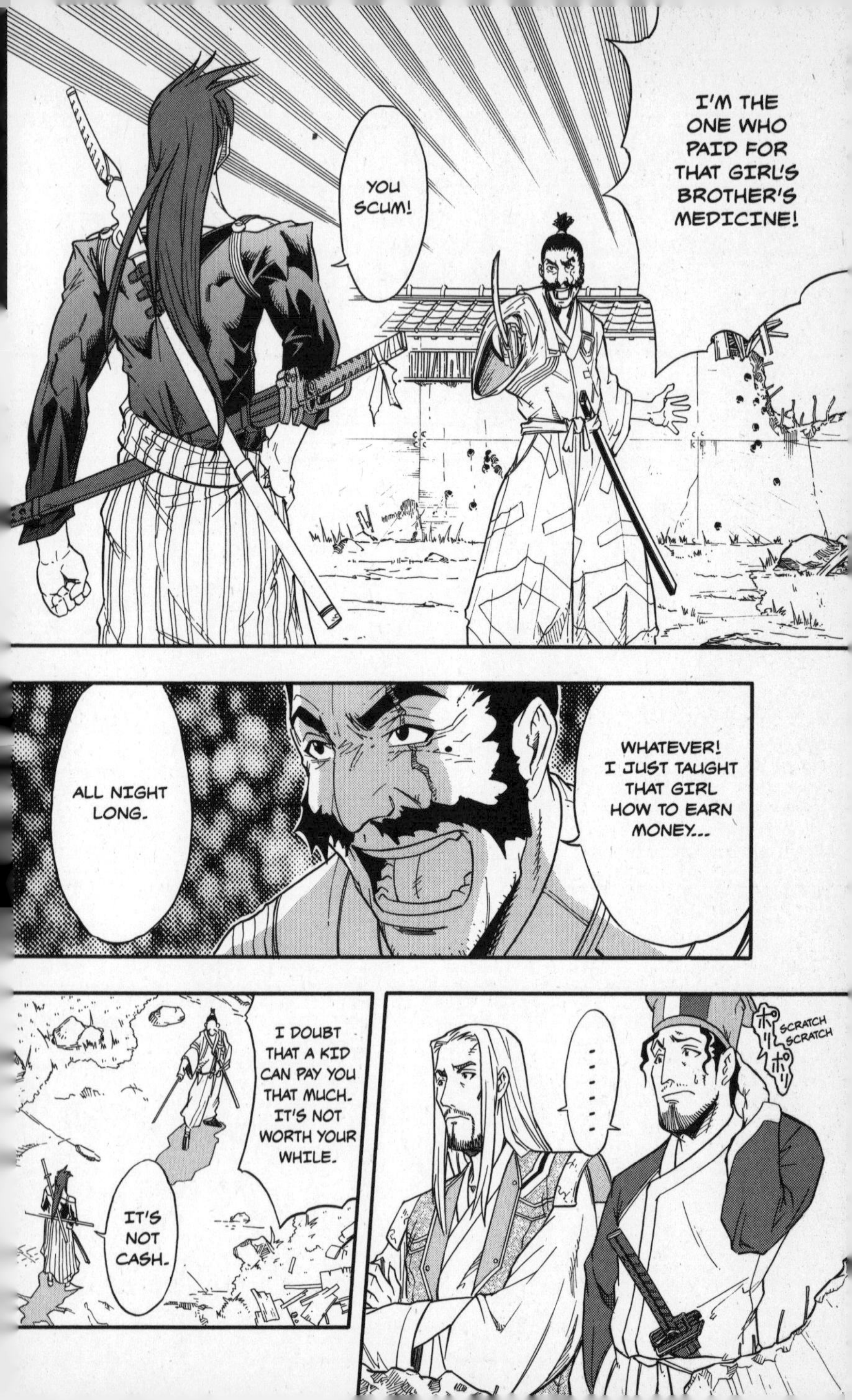

I'M THE ONE WHO PAID FOR THAT GIRL'S BROTHER'S MEDICINE!
YOU SCUM!
WHATEVER! I JUST TAUGHT THAT GIRL HOW TO EARN MONEY...
ALL NIGHT LONG.
ポリポリ
SCRATCH SCRATCH
......
I DOUBT THAT A KID CAN PAY YOU THAT MUCH. IT'S NOT WORTH YOUR WHILE.
IT'S NOT CASH.

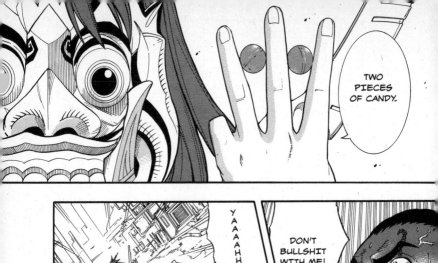

TWO
PIECES
OF CANDY.

YAAAAHHH!!

DON'T
BULLSHIT
WITH ME!

DM
DM
DM
DM

!?

LEAP

TAH!

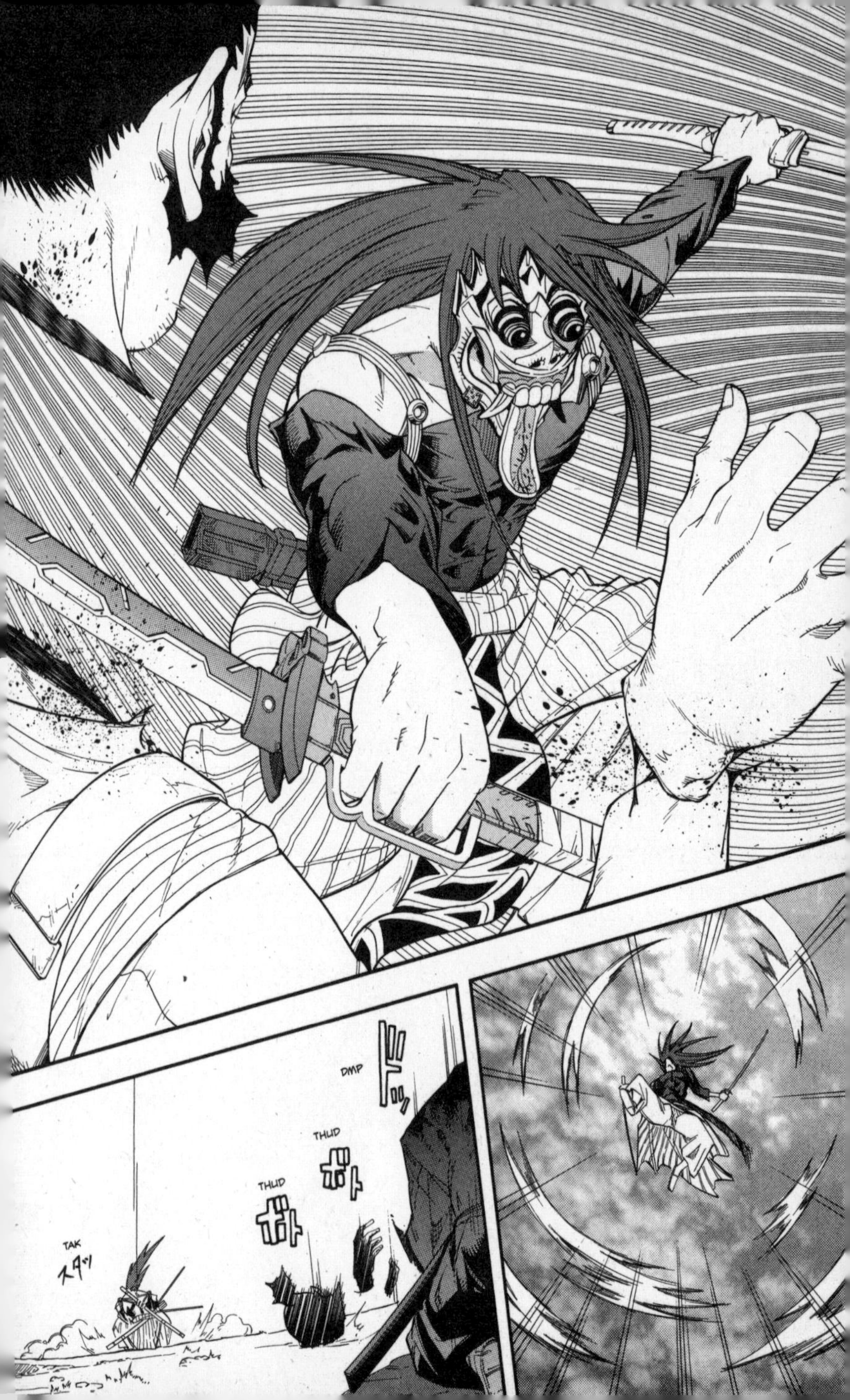
DMP
ドッ
THUD
ボト
THUD
ボト
TAK
スタッ

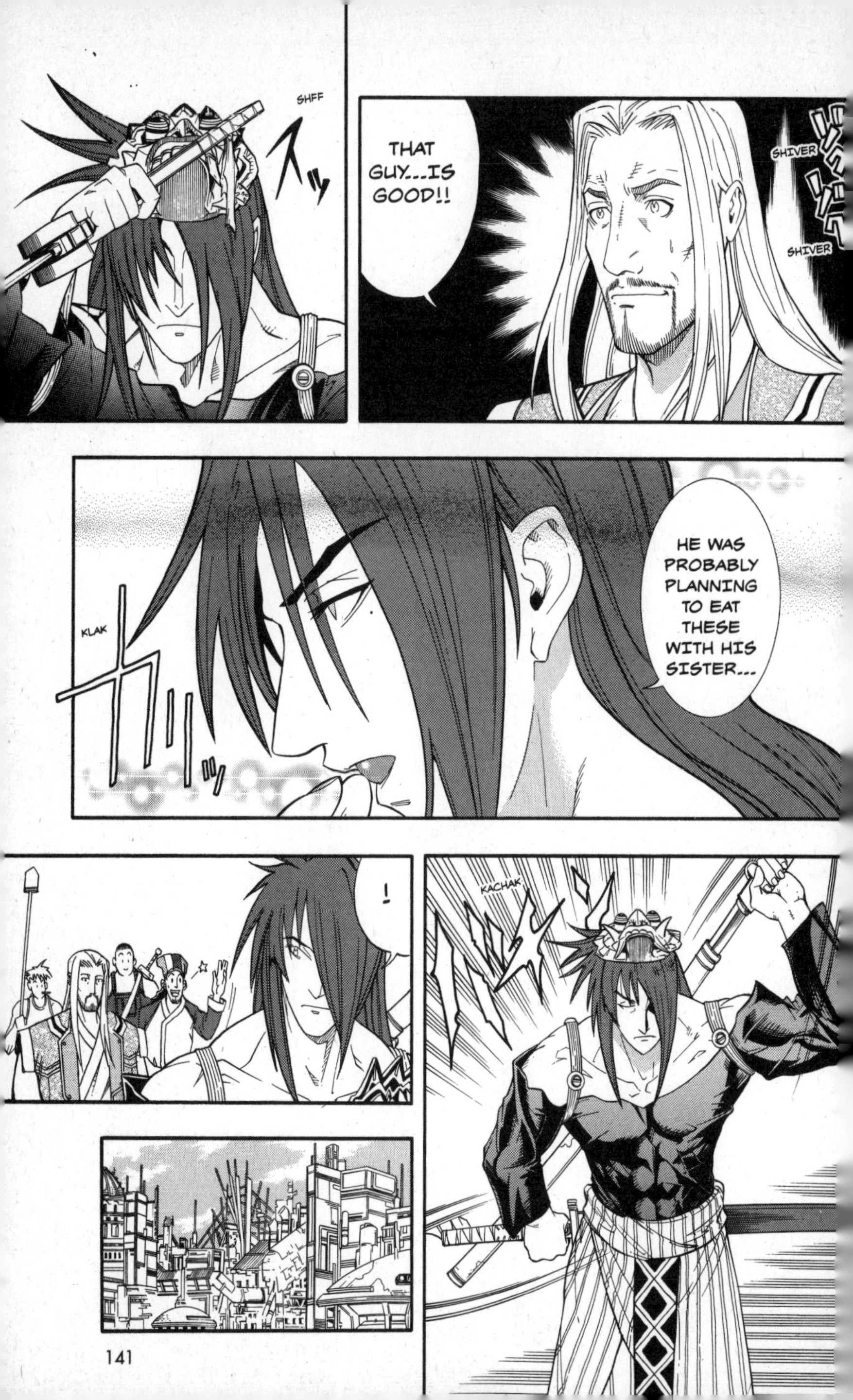
SHIVER
SHIVER
THAT GUY...IS GOOD!!
SHFF
HE WAS PROBABLY PLANNING TO EAT THESE WITH HIS SISTER...
KLAK
KACHAK
!

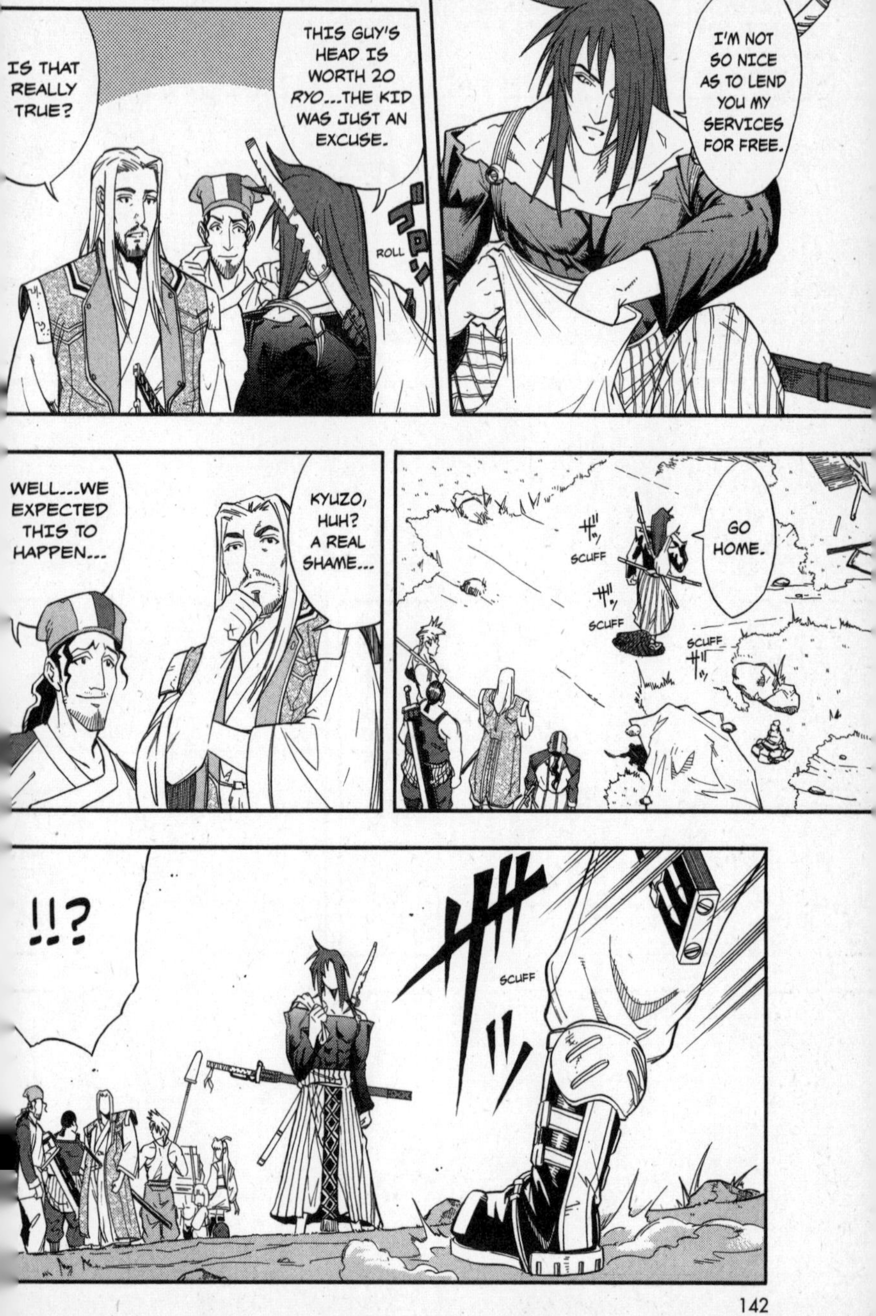
I'M NOT SO NICE AS TO LEND YOU MY SERVICES FOR FREE.
THIS GUY'S HEAD IS WORTH 20 RYO...THE KID WAS JUST AN EXCUSE.
ROLL
IS THAT REALLY TRUE?
GO HOME.
SCUFF
SCUFF
SCUFF
KYUZO, HUH? A REAL SHAME...
WELL...WE EXPECTED THIS TO HAPPEN...
SCUFF
!!?

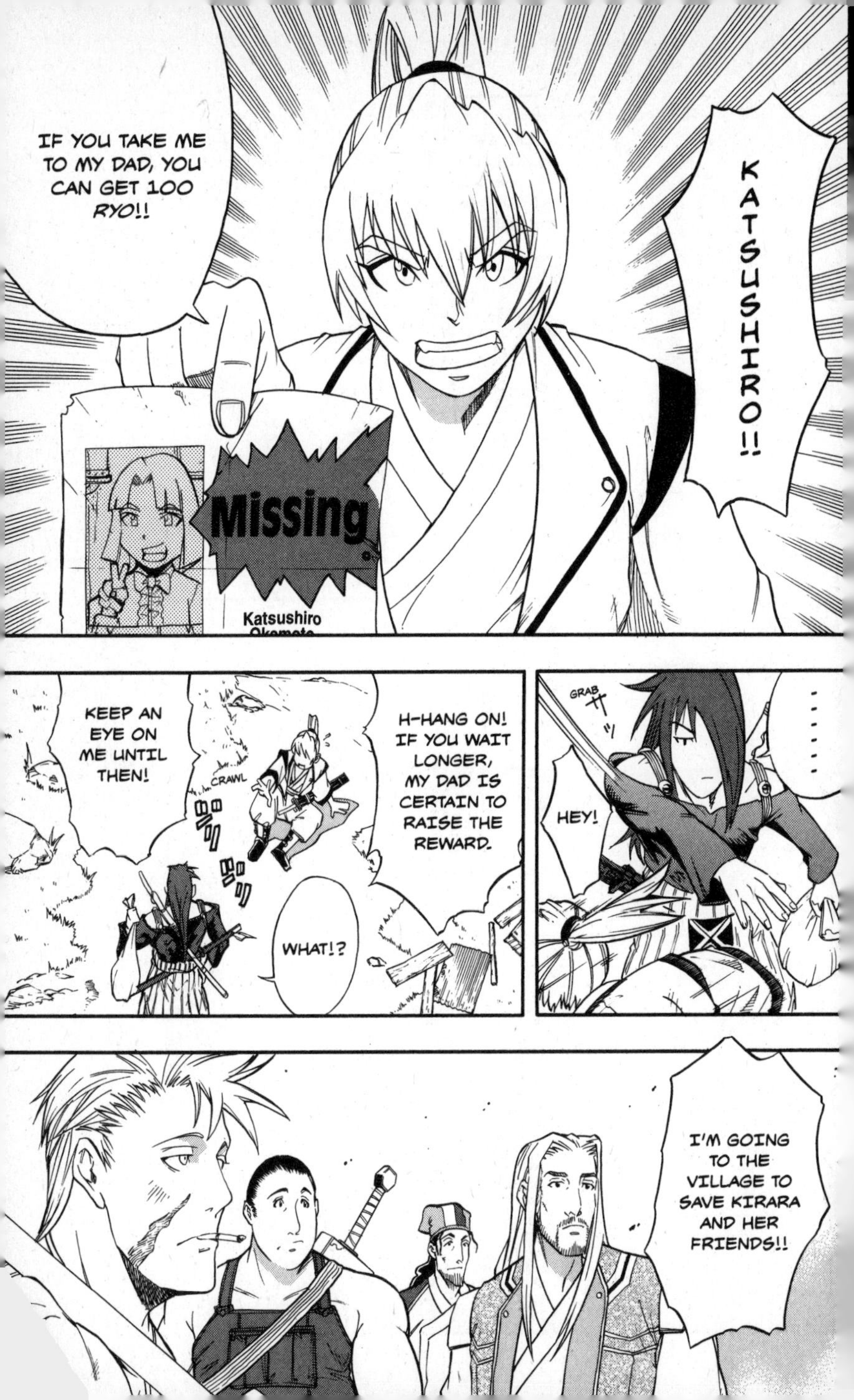
KATSUSHIRO!!
IF YOU TAKE ME TO MY DAD, YOU CAN GET 100 RYO!!
Missing
Katsushiro
......
GRAB
HEY!
H-HANG ON! IF YOU WAIT LONGER, MY DAD IS CERTAIN TO RAISE THE REWARD.
KEEP AN EYE ON ME UNTIL THEN!
CRAWL
WHAT!?
I'M GOING TO THE VILLAGE TO SAVE KIRARA AND HER FRIENDS!!

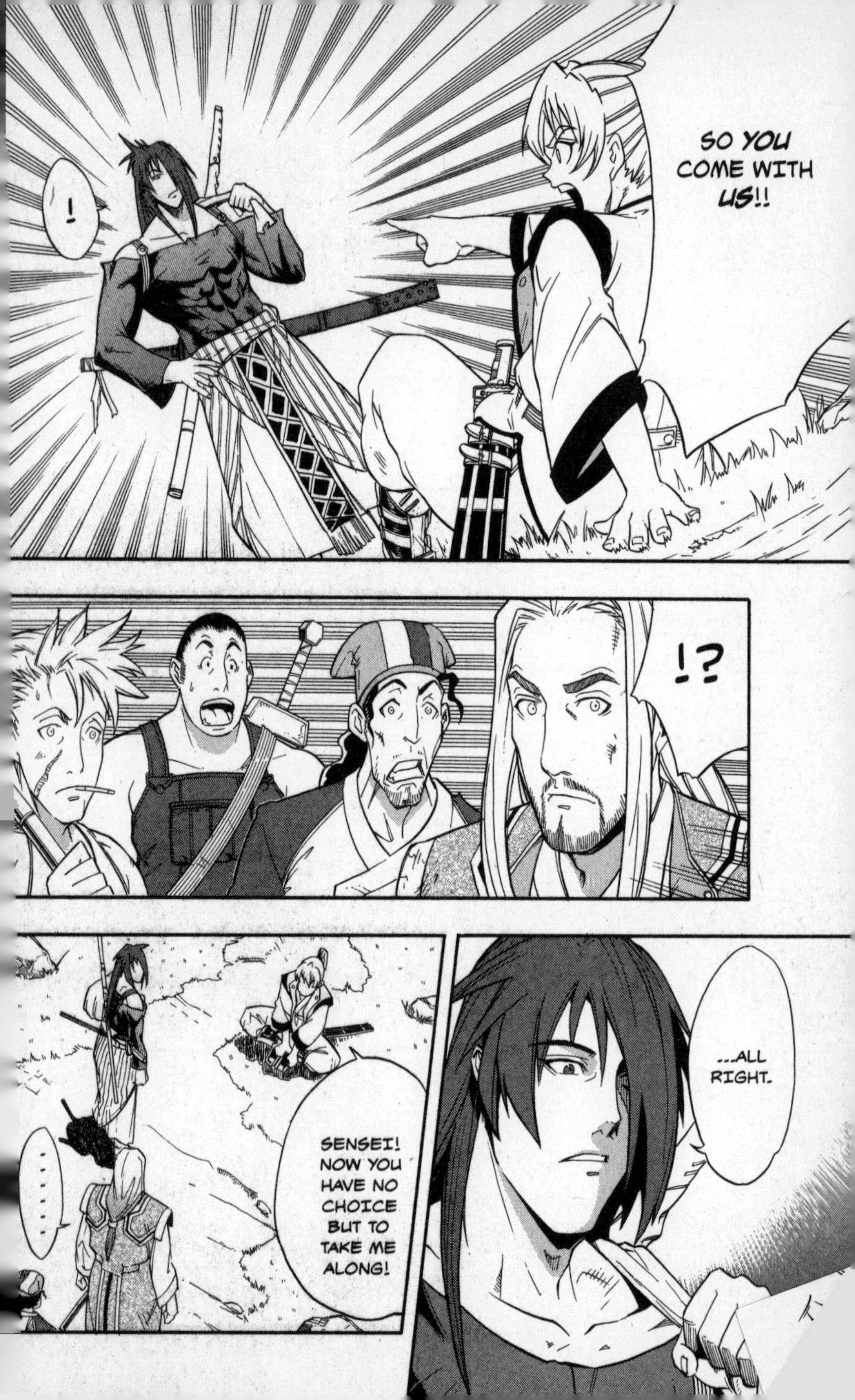
SO YOU COME WITH US!!
!
!?
...ALL RIGHT.
SENSEI! NOW YOU HAVE NO CHOICE BUT TO TAKE ME ALONG!
......

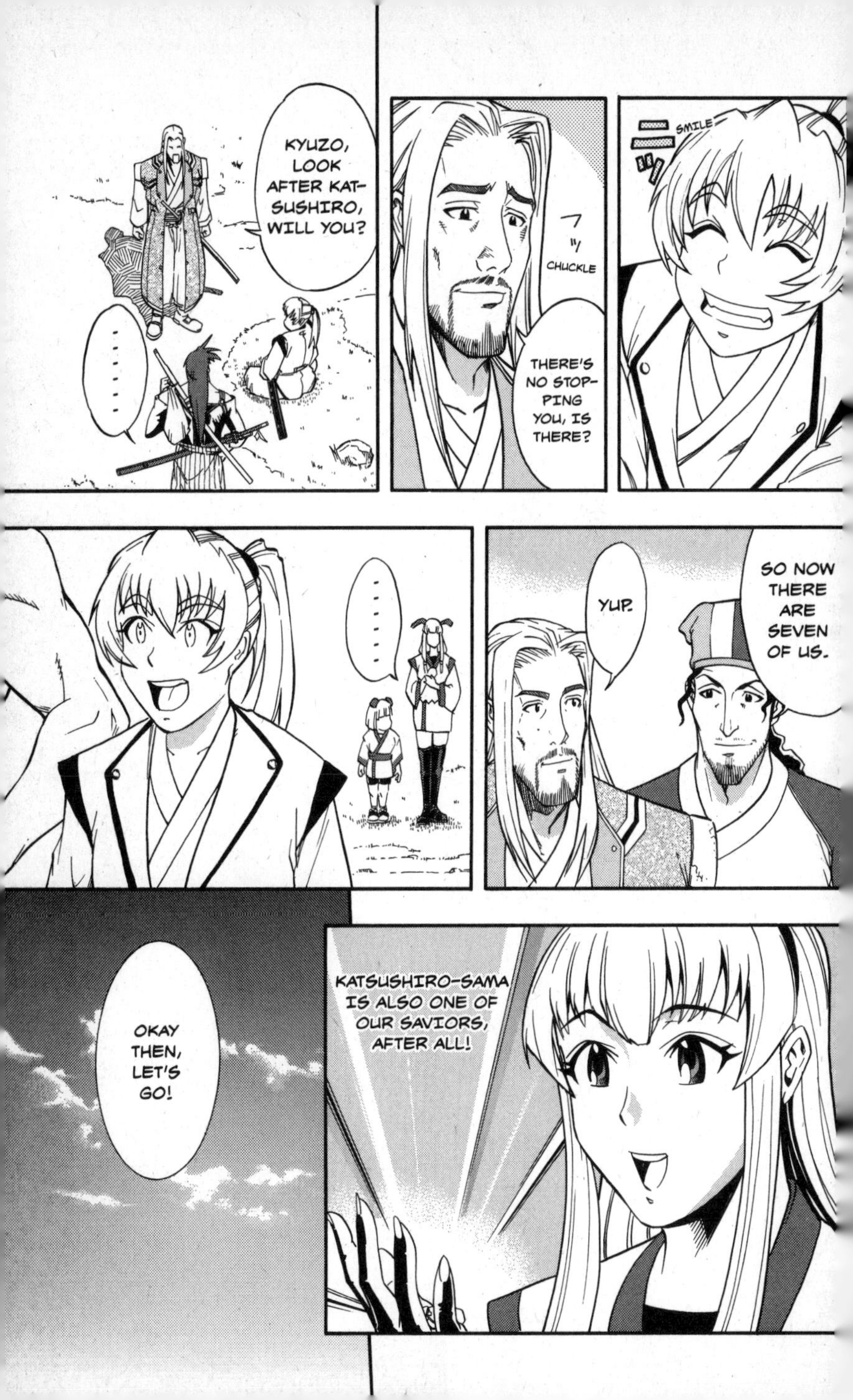
SMILE
CHUCKLE
THERE'S NO STOPPING YOU, IS THERE?
KYUZO, LOOK AFTER KATSUSHIRO, WILL YOU?
......
SO NOW THERE ARE SEVEN OF US.
YUP.
......
KATSUSHIRO-SAMA IS ALSO ONE OF OUR SAVIORS, AFTER ALL!
OKAY THEN, LET'S GO!

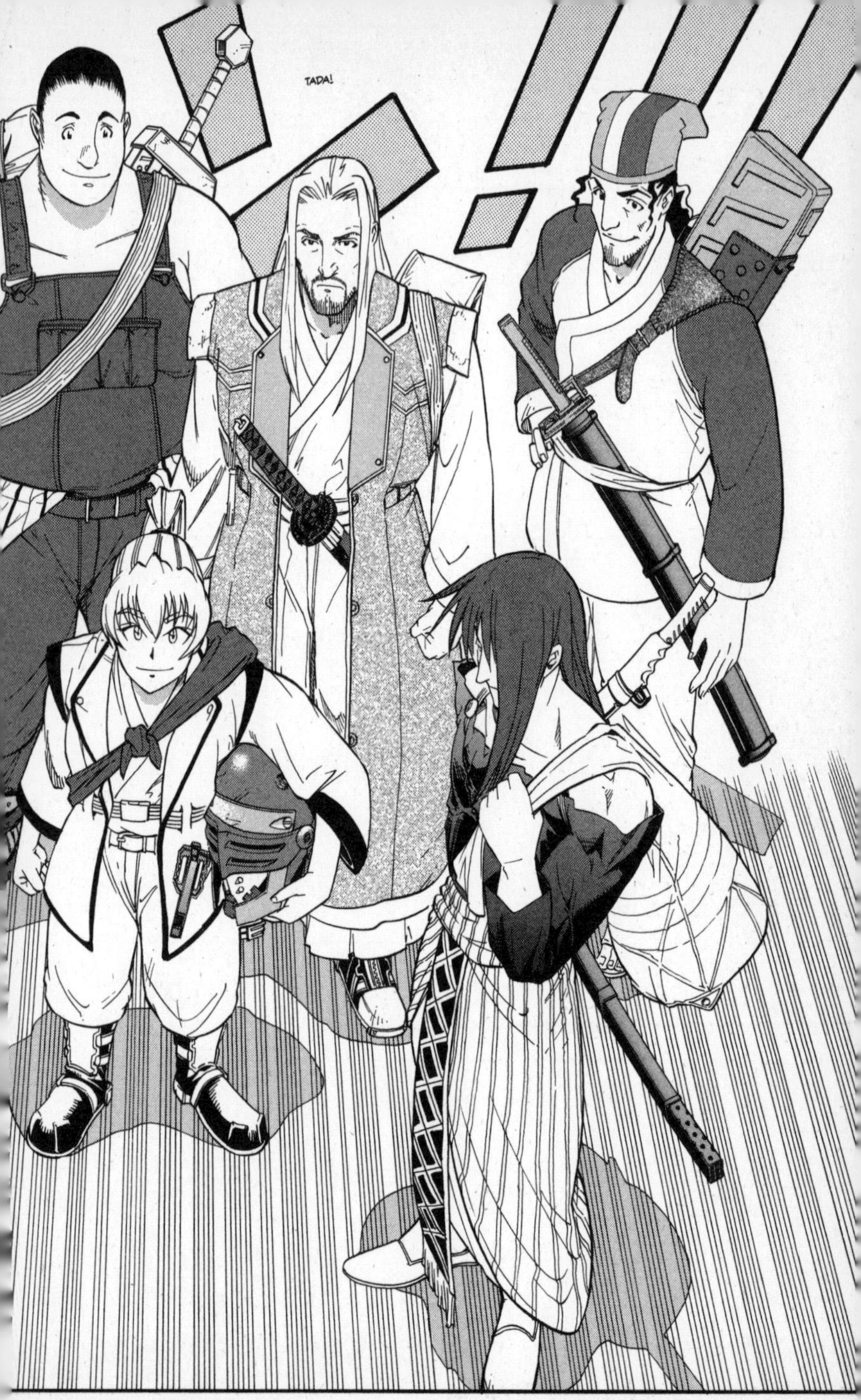
TADA!

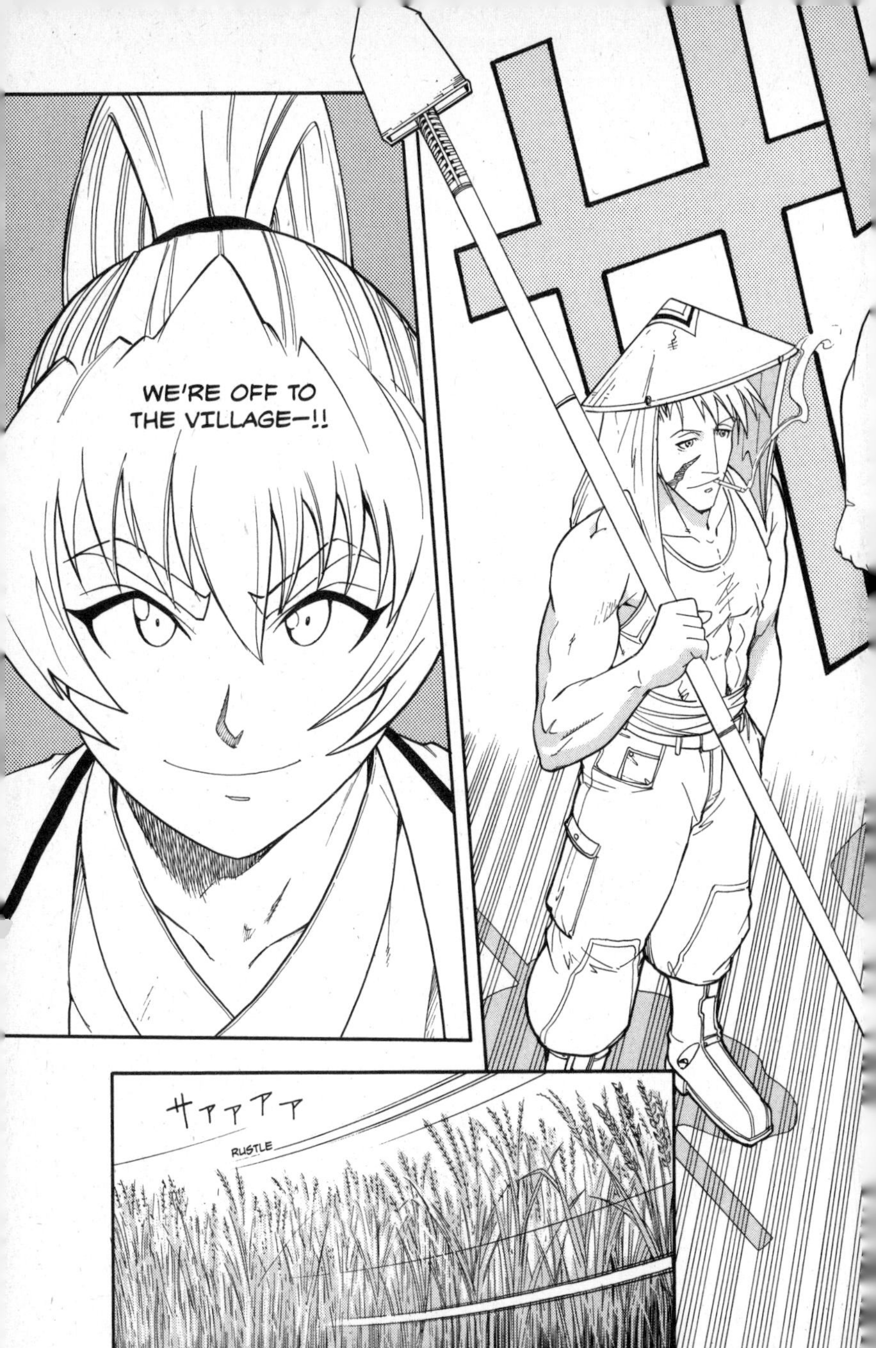
WE'RE OFF TO THE VILLAGE—!!
サァァアァ
RUSTLE

Chapter 2/End

Katsushiro

Kambei

Kikuchiyo

Kyuzo

Shichiroji

Heihachi

Gorobei

Chapter 3 – Katsushiro Freaks Out!

SHICHIROJI   GOROBEI   KAMBEI   KATSUSHIRO   KIKUCHIYO   KYUZO   HEIHACHI

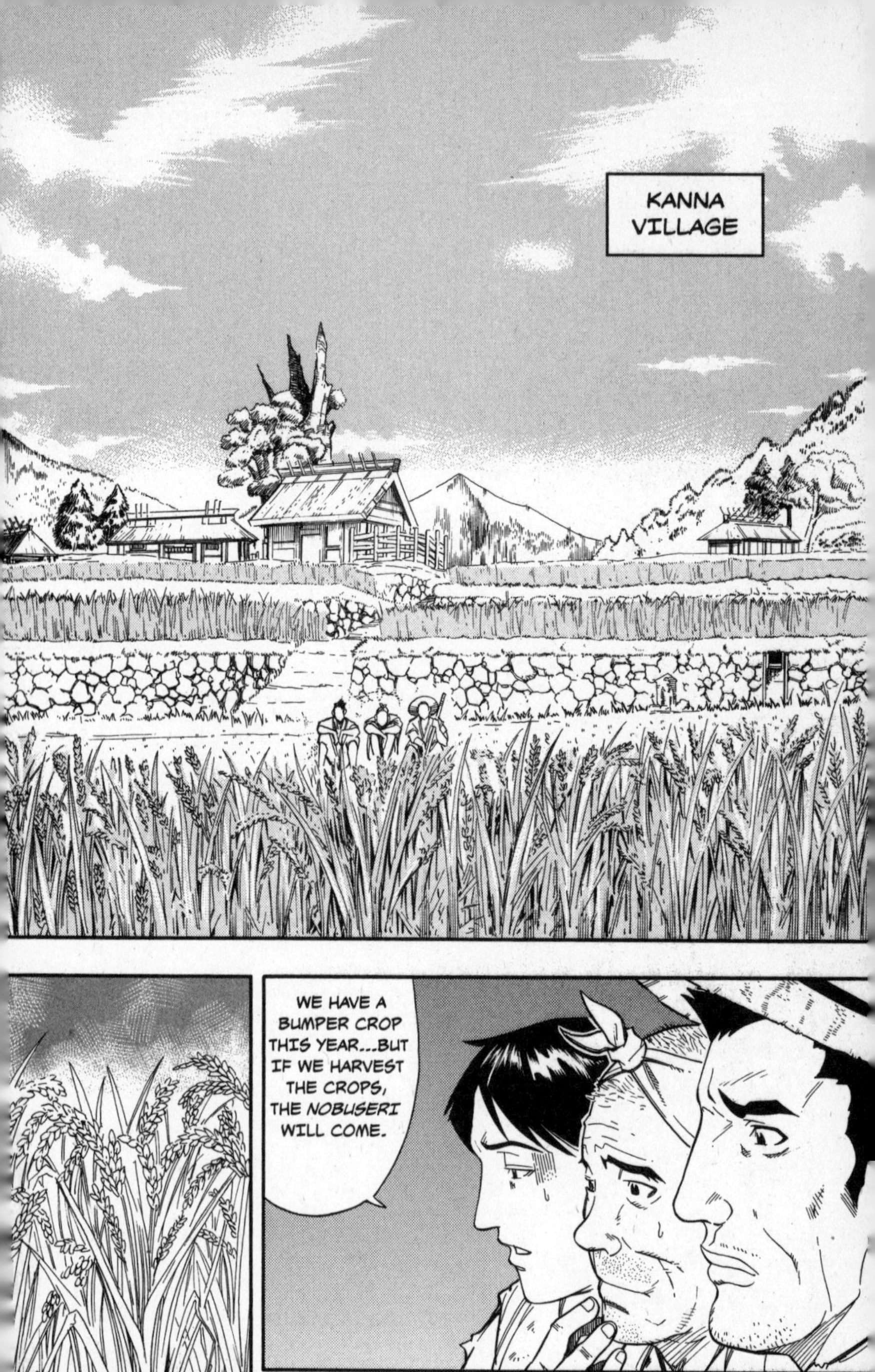
KANNA VILLAGE
WE HAVE A BUMPER CROP THIS YEAR...BUT IF WE HARVEST THE CROPS, THE *NOBUSERI* WILL COME.

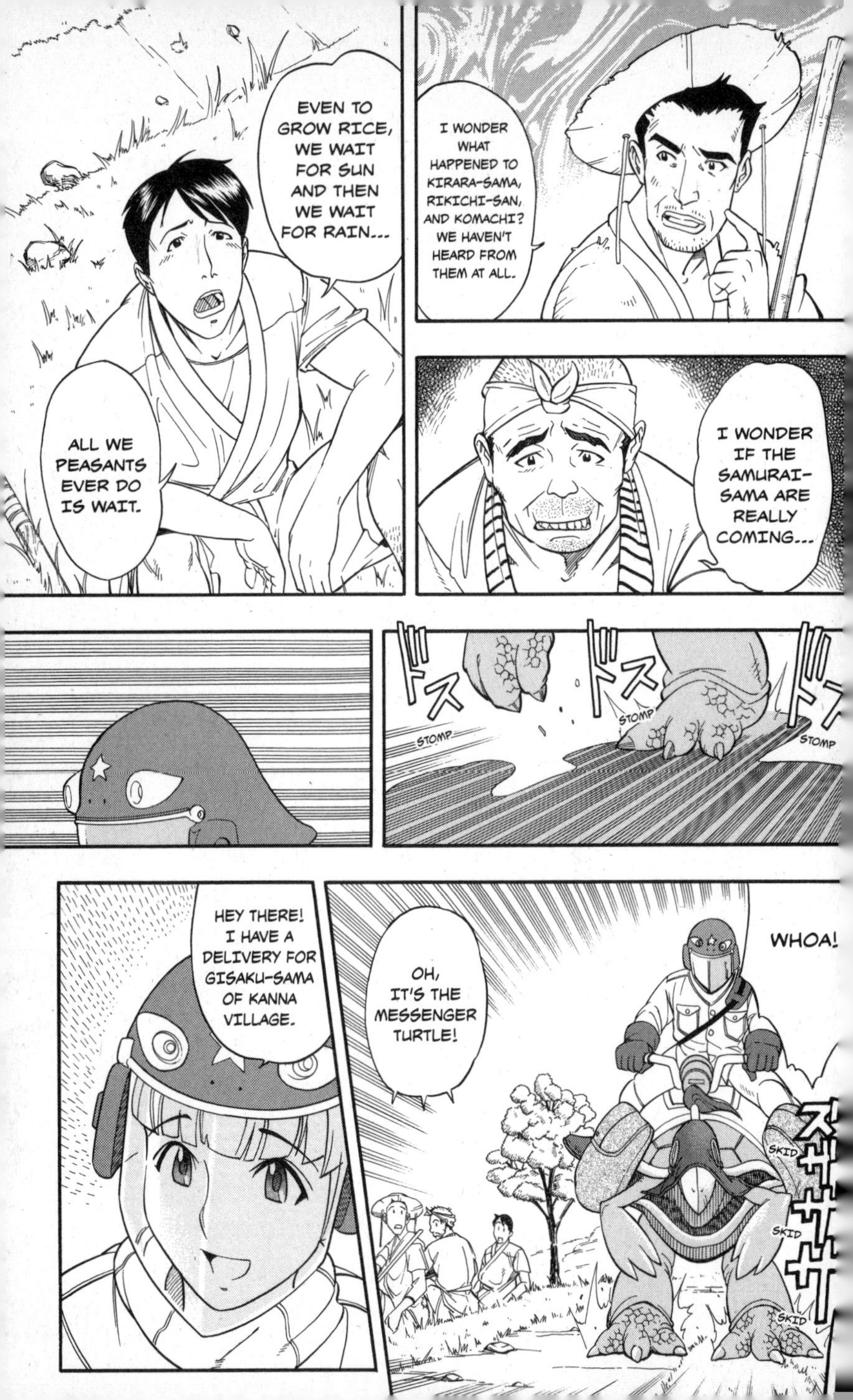
I WONDER WHAT HAPPENED TO KIRARA-SAMA, RIKICHI-SAN, AND KOMACHI? WE HAVEN'T HEARD FROM THEM AT ALL.
I WONDER IF THE SAMURAI-SAMA ARE REALLY COMING...
EVEN TO GROW RICE, WE WAIT FOR SUN AND THEN WE WAIT FOR RAIN...
ALL WE PEASANTS EVER DO IS WAIT.
ドス
STOMP
ドス
STOMP
STOMP
WHOA!
SKID
SKID
SKID
OH, IT'S THE MESSENGER TURTLE!
HEY THERE! I HAVE A DELIVERY FOR GISAKU-SAMA OF KANNA VILLAGE.

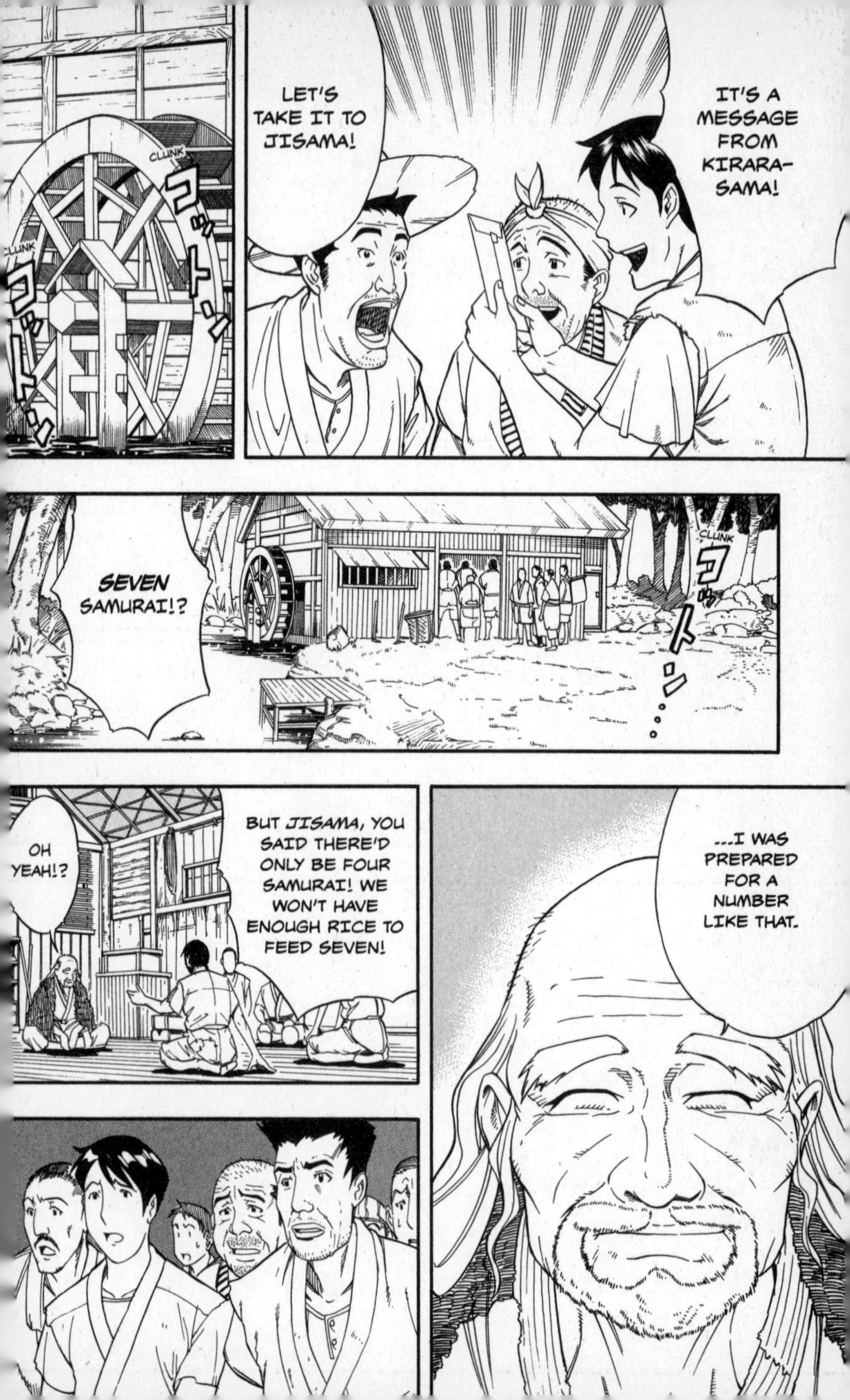
IT'S A MESSAGE FROM KIRARA-SAMA!
LET'S TAKE IT TO JISAMA!
CLUNK
CLUNK
CLUNK
SEVEN SAMURAI!?
...I WAS PREPARED FOR A NUMBER LIKE THAT.
BUT JISAMA, YOU SAID THERE'D ONLY BE FOUR SAMURAI! WE WON'T HAVE ENOUGH RICE TO FEED SEVEN!
OH YEAH!?

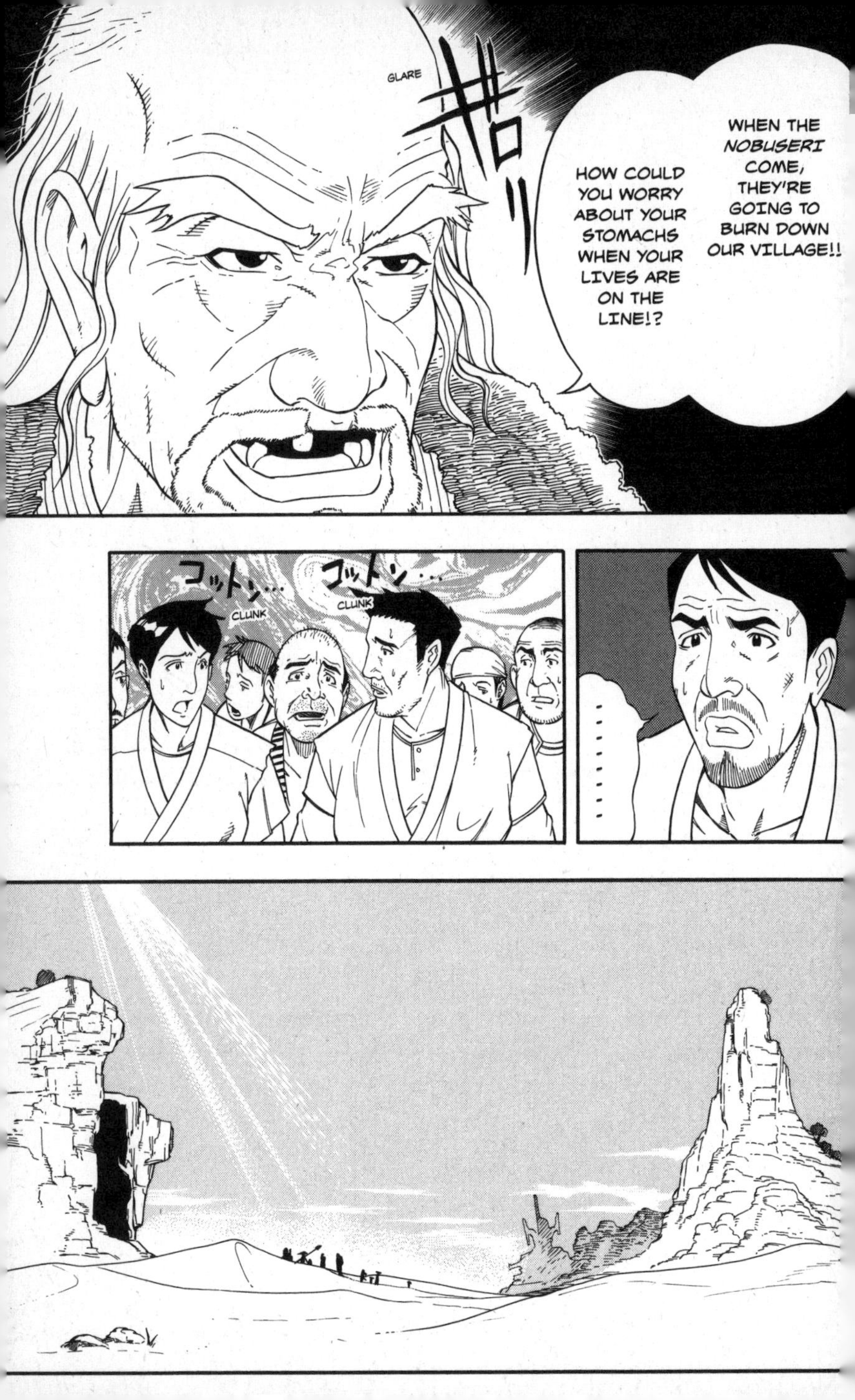
GLARE
WHEN THE *NOBUSERI* COME, THEY'RE GOING TO BURN DOWN OUR VILLAGE!!
HOW COULD YOU WORRY ABOUT YOUR STOMACHS WHEN YOUR LIVES ARE ON THE LINE!?
......
コットン...
CLUNK
コットン...
CLUNK

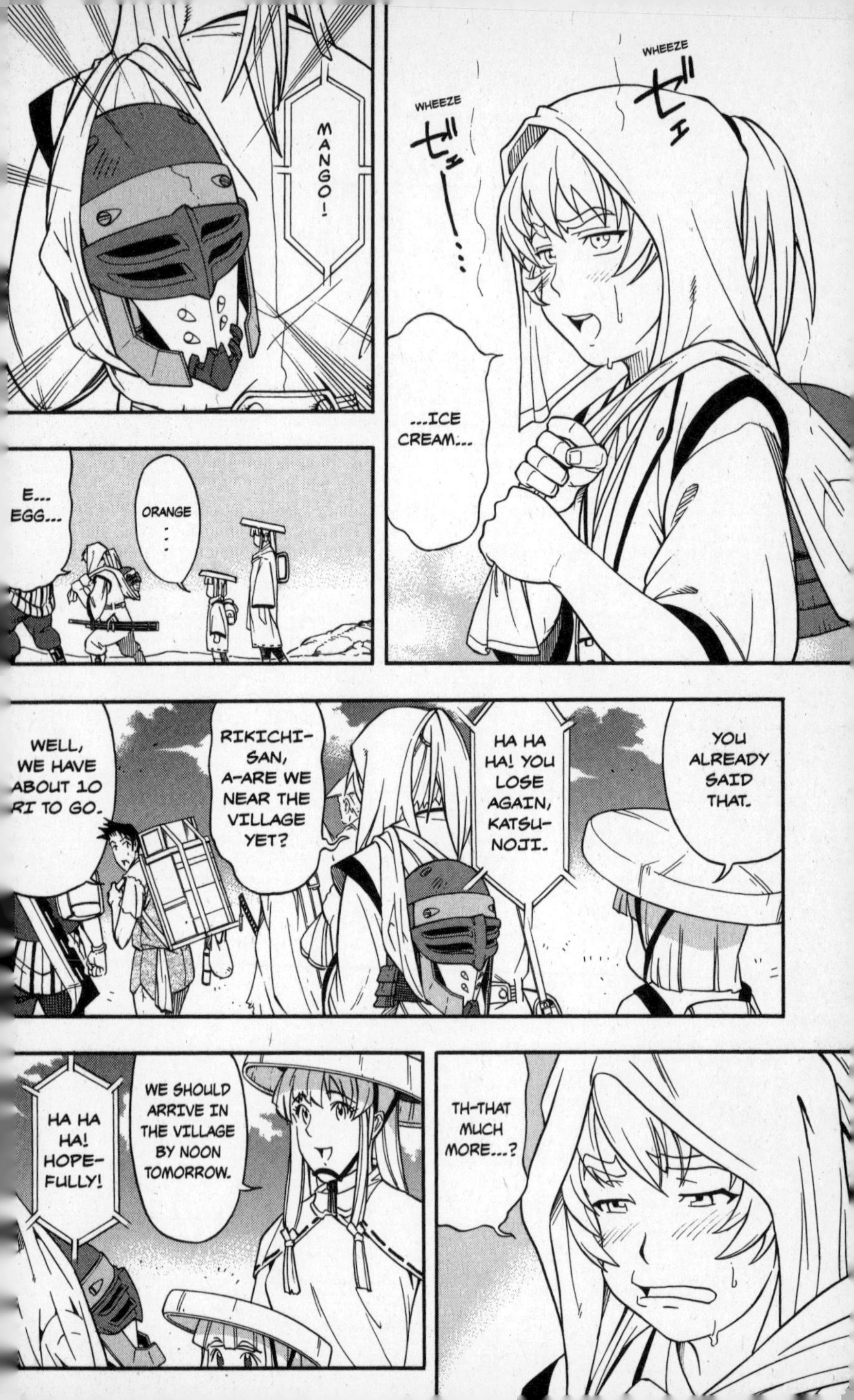
WHEEZE
WHEEZE
...ICE CREAM...
MANGO!
ORANGE...
E... EGG...
YOU ALREADY SAID THAT.
HA HA HA! YOU LOSE AGAIN, KATSUNOJI.
RIKICHI-SAN, A-ARE WE NEAR THE VILLAGE YET?
WELL, WE HAVE ABOUT 10 RI TO GO.
TH-THAT MUCH MORE...?
WE SHOULD ARRIVE IN THE VILLAGE BY NOON TOMORROW.
HA HA HA! HOPEFULLY!

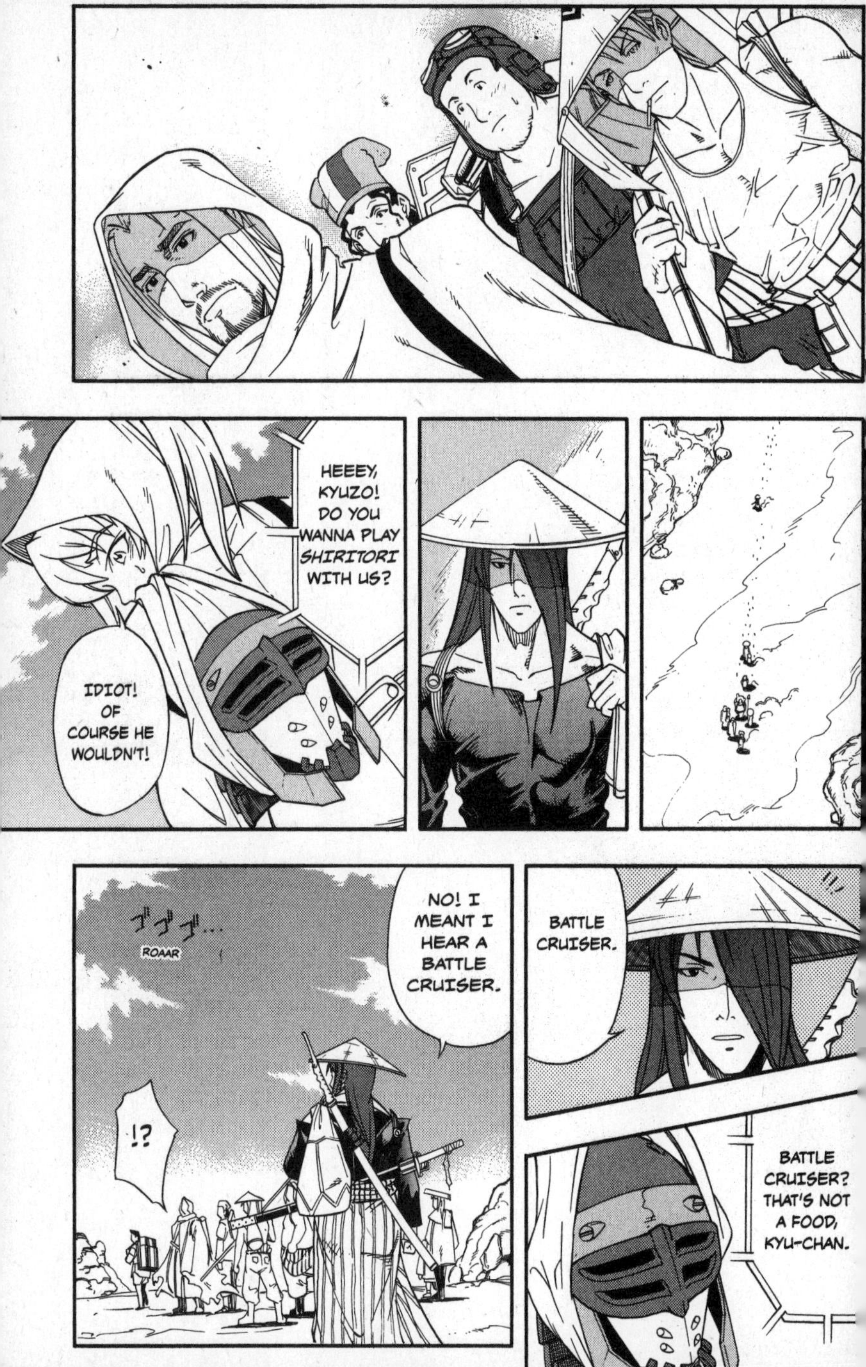
HEEEY, KYUZO! DO YOU WANNA PLAY SHIRITORI WITH US?
IDIOT! OF COURSE HE WOULDN'T!
BATTLE CRUISER.
BATTLE CRUISER? THAT'S NOT A FOOD, KYU-CHAN.
NO! I MEANT I HEAR A BATTLE CRUISER.
ゴゴゴ…
ROAAR
!?

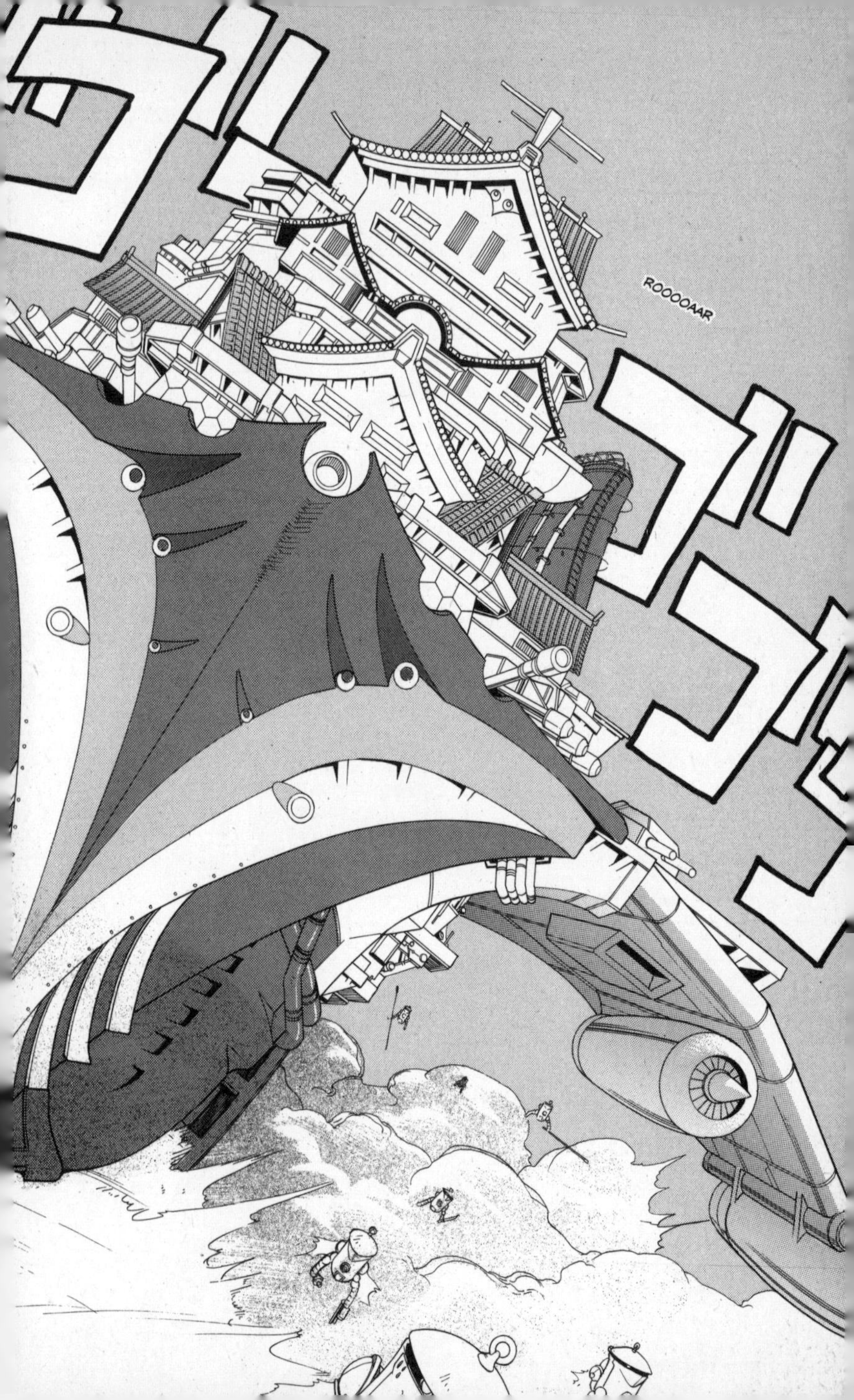
ROOOOAAR

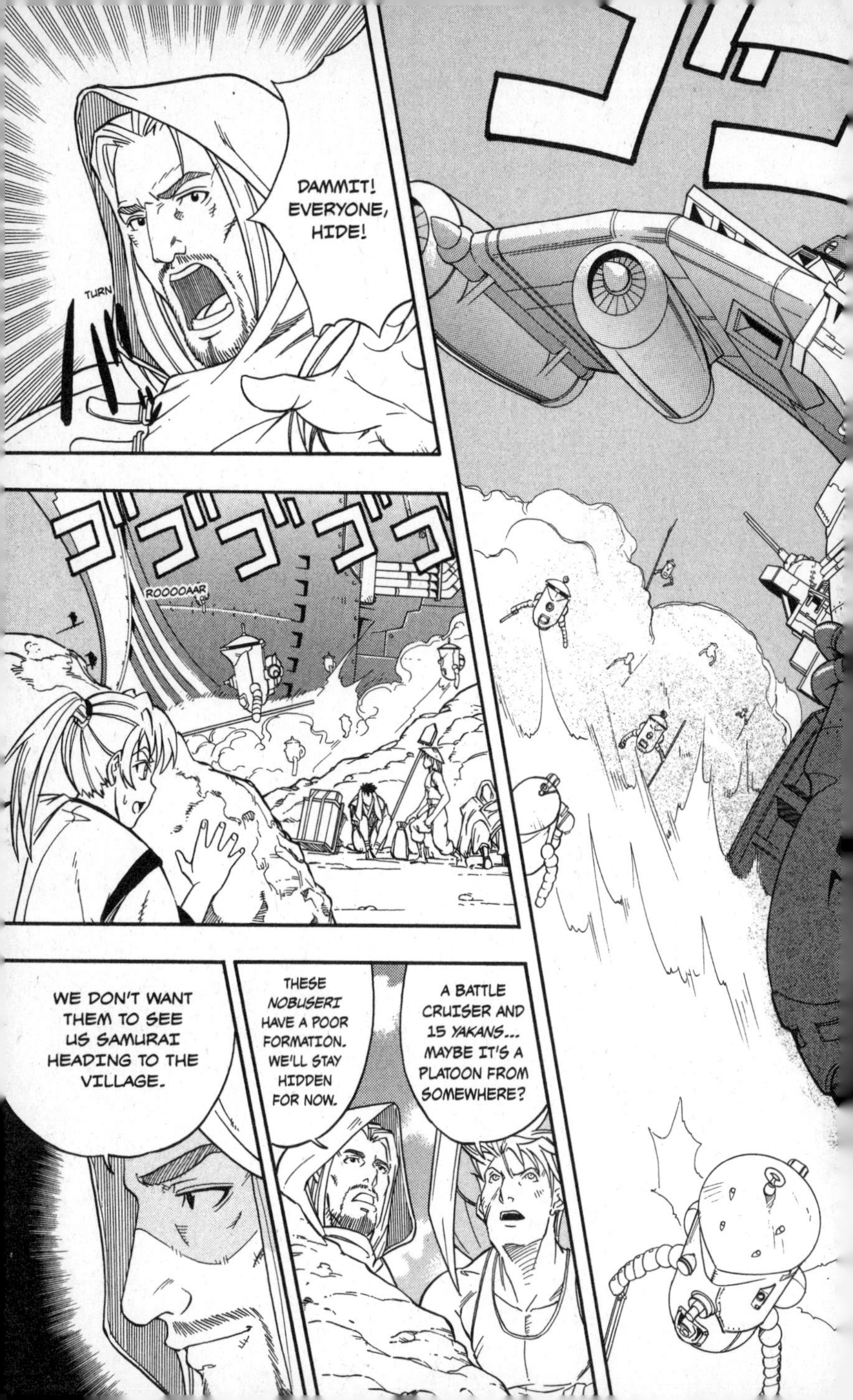
DAMMIT! EVERYONE, HIDE!
TURN
ROOOOAAR
A BATTLE CRUISER AND 15 *YAKANS*... MAYBE IT'S A PLATOON FROM SOMEWHERE?
THESE *NOBUSERI* HAVE A POOR FORMATION. WE'LL STAY HIDDEN FOR NOW.
WE DON'T WANT THEM TO SEE US SAMURAI HEADING TO THE VILLAGE.

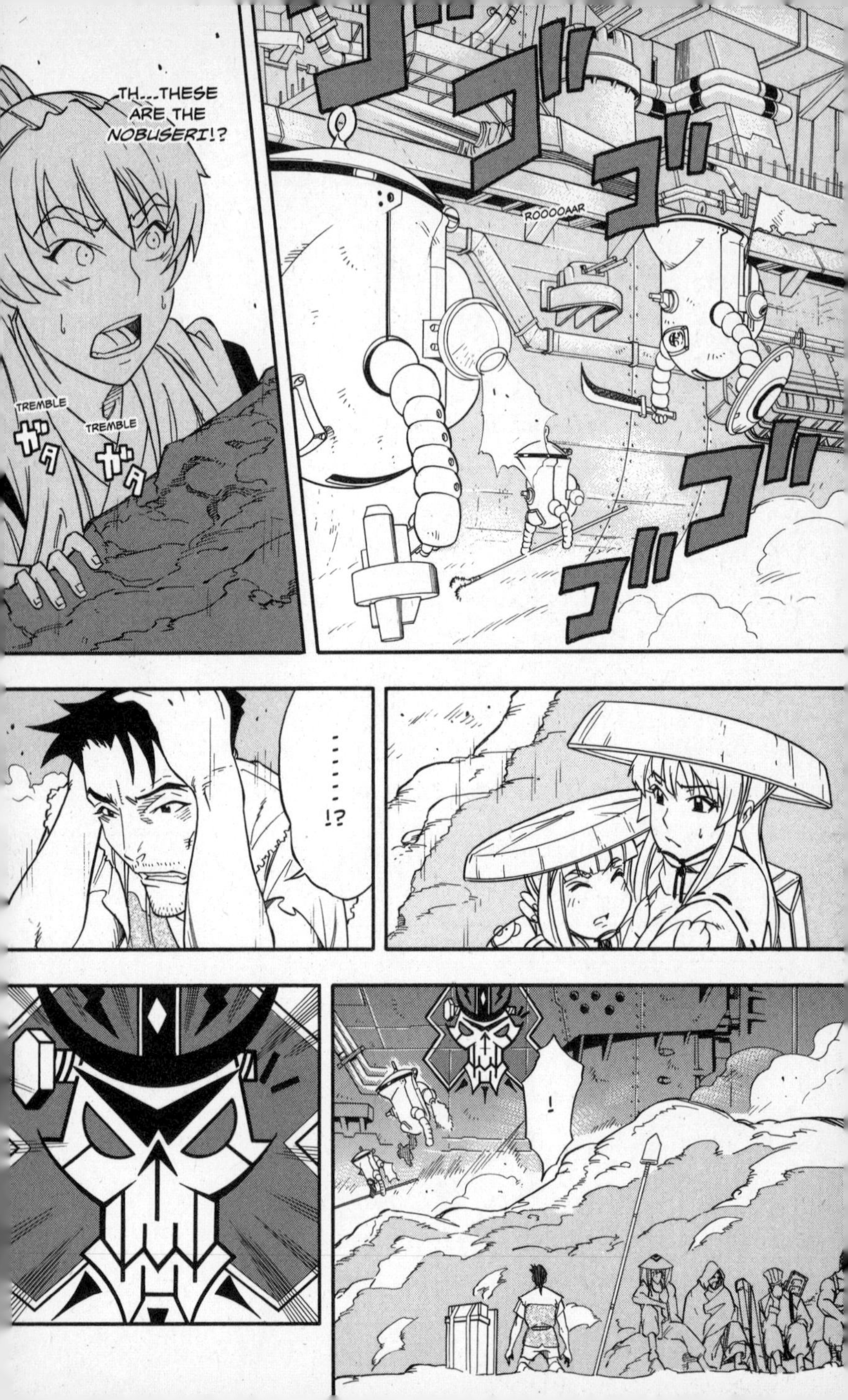
ゴゴゴ
ROOOOAAR
ゴゴゴ
TH...THESE ARE THE NOBUSERI!?
TREMBLE
ガタ
TREMBLE
ガタ
......!?
!

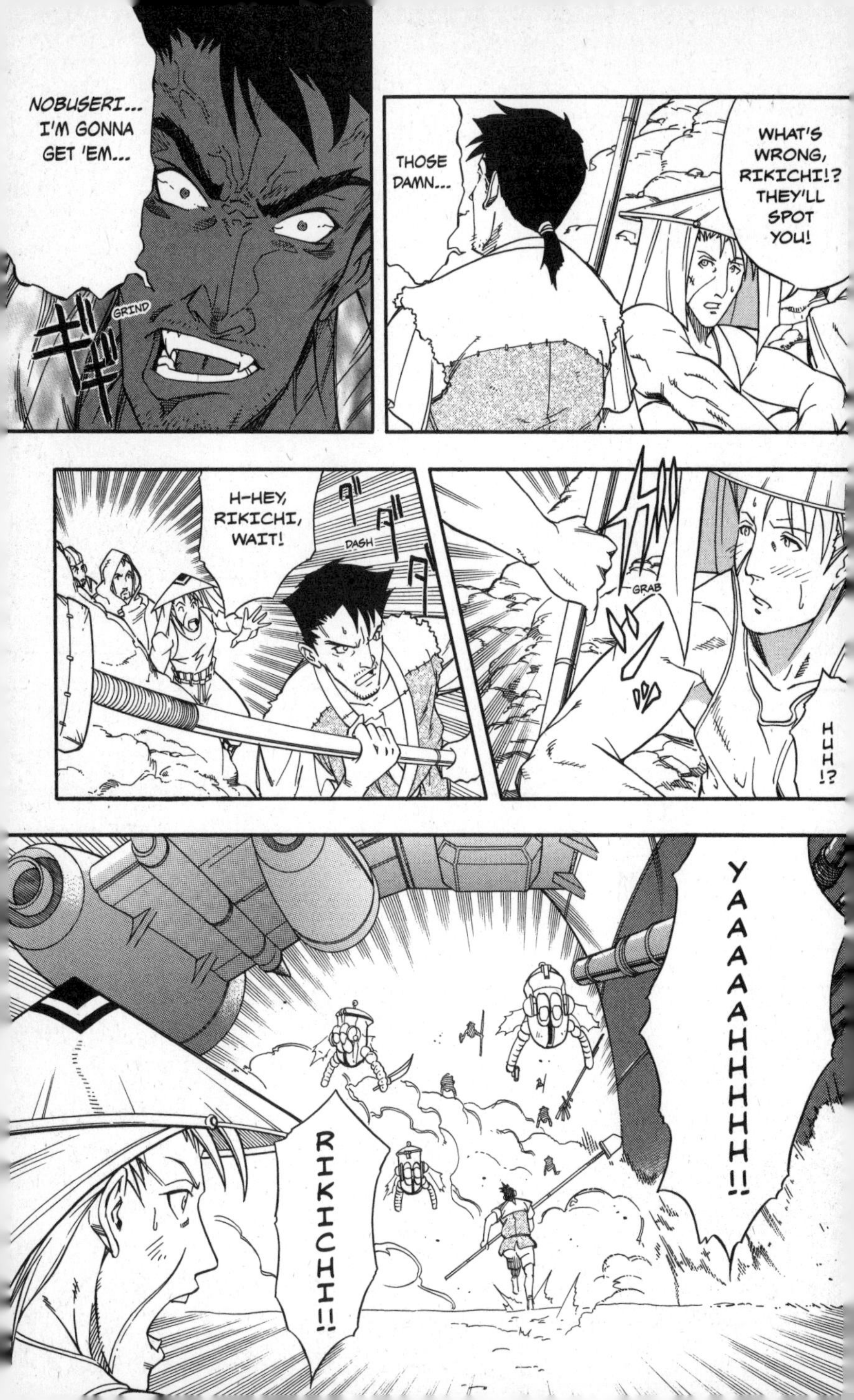
WHAT'S WRONG, RIKICHI!? THEY'LL SPOT YOU!
THOSE DAMN...
NOBUSERI... I'M GONNA GET 'EM...
GRIND
GRAB
HUH!?
H-HEY, RIKICHI, WAIT!
DASH
YAAAAAHHHHH!!
RIKICHI!!

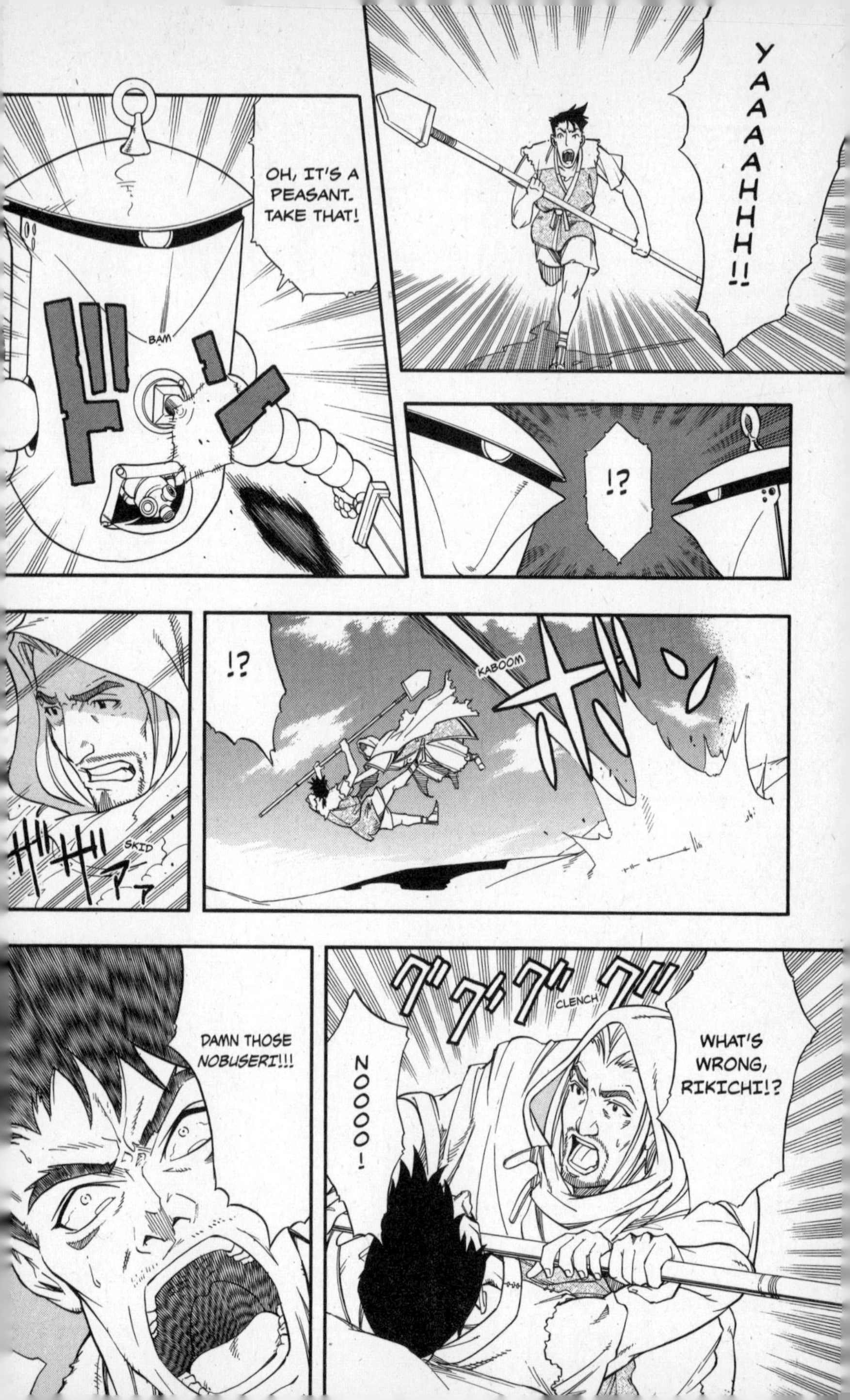
YAAAAHHH!!
!?
OH, IT'S A PEASANT. TAKE THAT!
BAM
KABOOM
!?
SKID
CLENCH
WHAT'S WRONG, RIKICHI!?
NOOOO!
DAMN THOSE NOBUSERI!!!

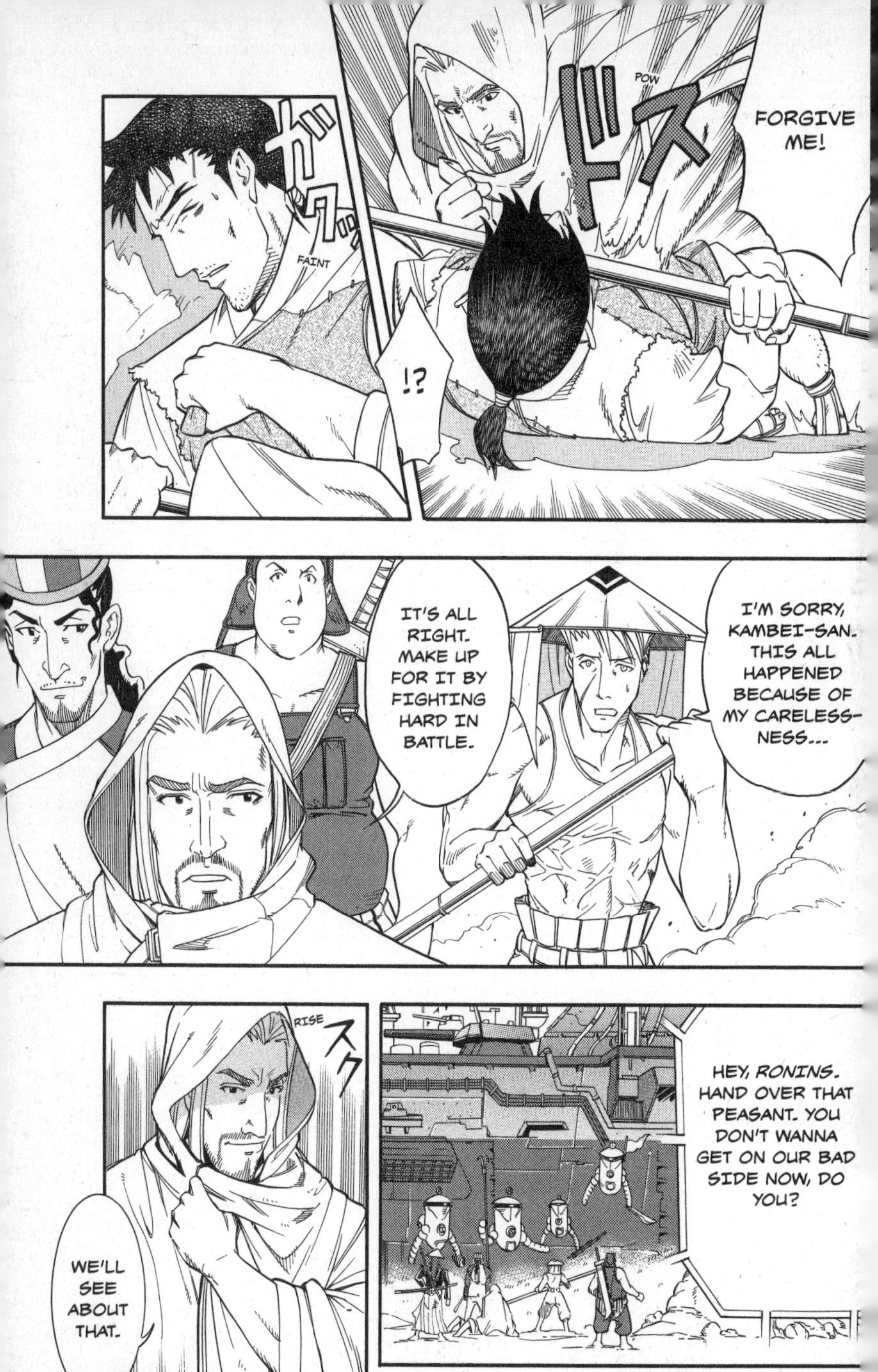
FORGIVE ME!
POW
!?
FAINT
I'M SORRY, KAMBEI-SAN. THIS ALL HAPPENED BECAUSE OF MY CARELESS-NESS...
IT'S ALL RIGHT. MAKE UP FOR IT BY FIGHTING HARD IN BATTLE.
HEY, *RONINS*. HAND OVER THAT PEASANT. YOU DON'T WANNA GET ON OUR BAD SIDE NOW, DO YOU?
RISE
WE'LL SEE ABOUT THAT.

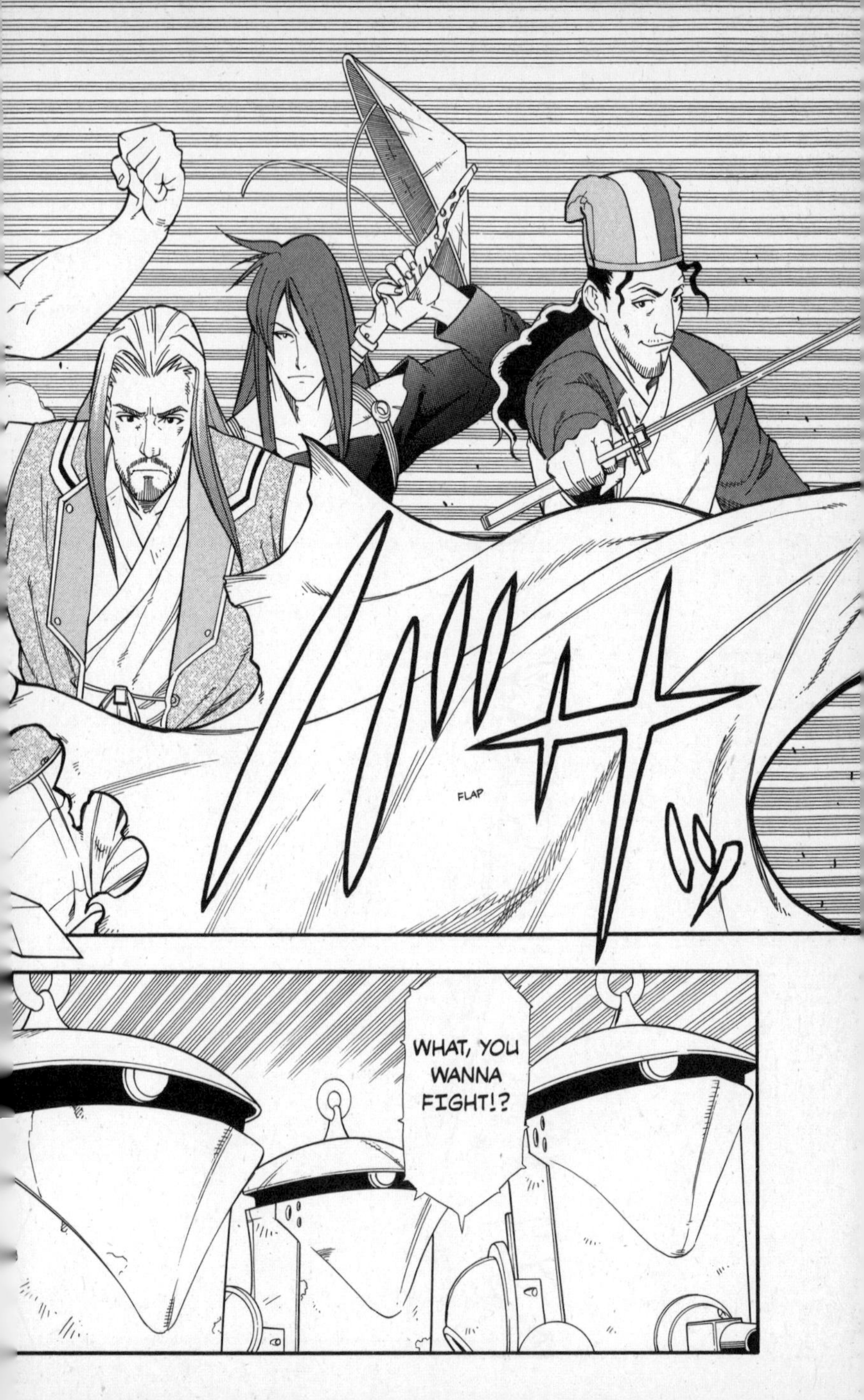
FLAP
WHAT, YOU WANNA FIGHT!?

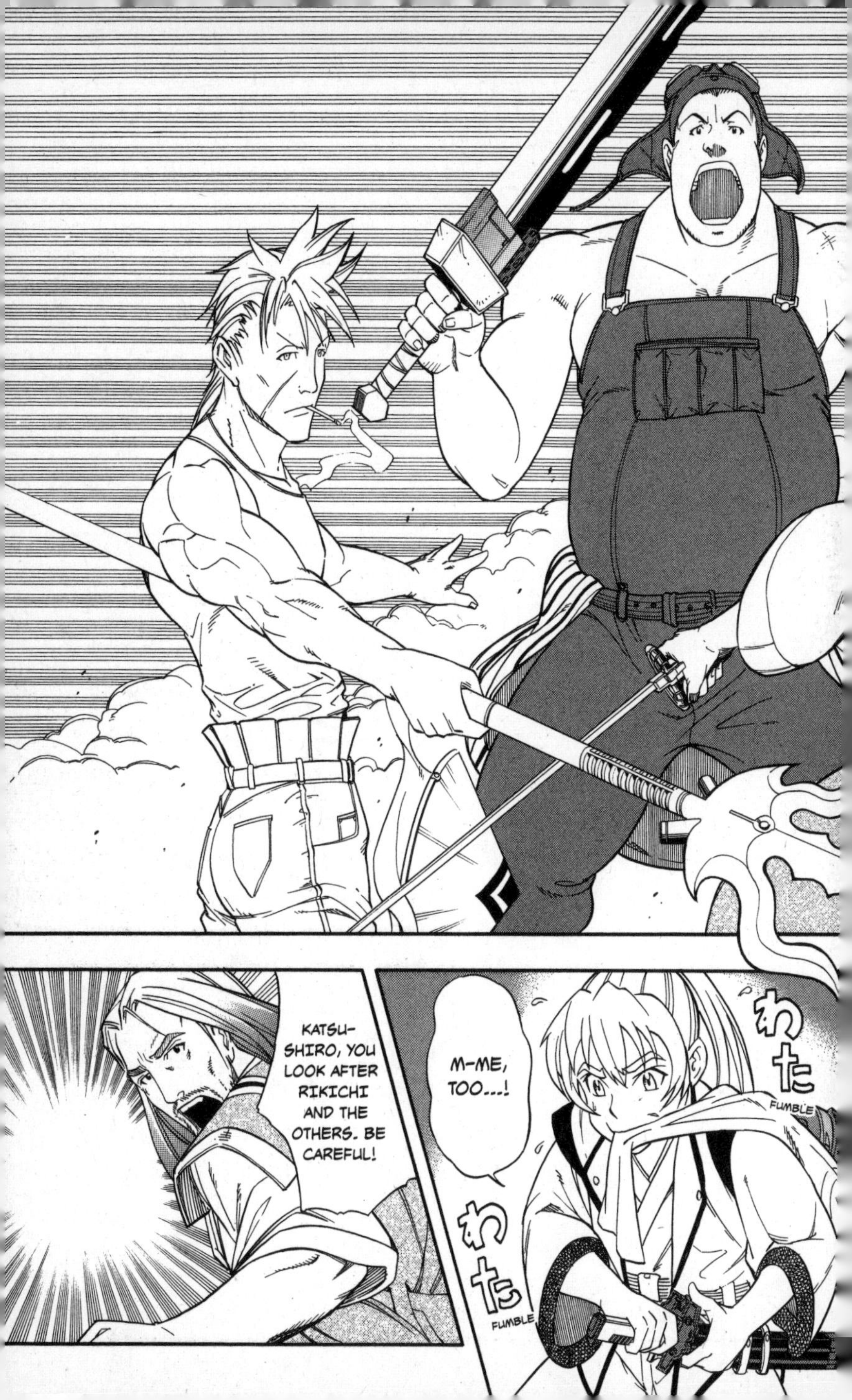
わた
FUMBLE
M-ME, TOO...!
わた
FUMBLE
KATSU-SHIRO, YOU LOOK AFTER RIKICHI AND THE OTHERS. BE CAREFUL!

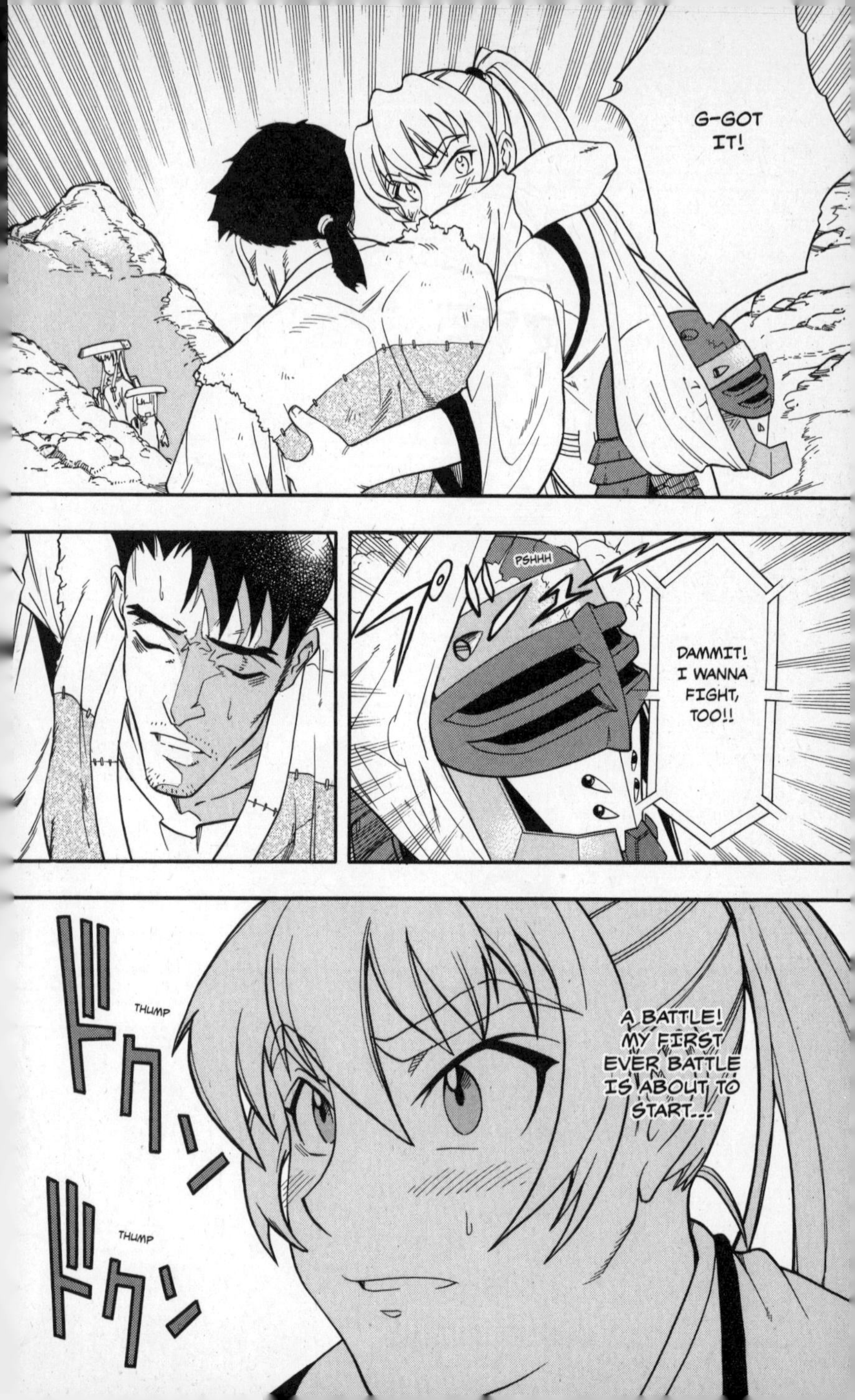
G-GOT IT!
PSHHH
DAMMIT! I WANNA FIGHT, TOO!!
A BATTLE! MY FIRST EVER BATTLE IS ABOUT TO START...
THUMP
THUMP

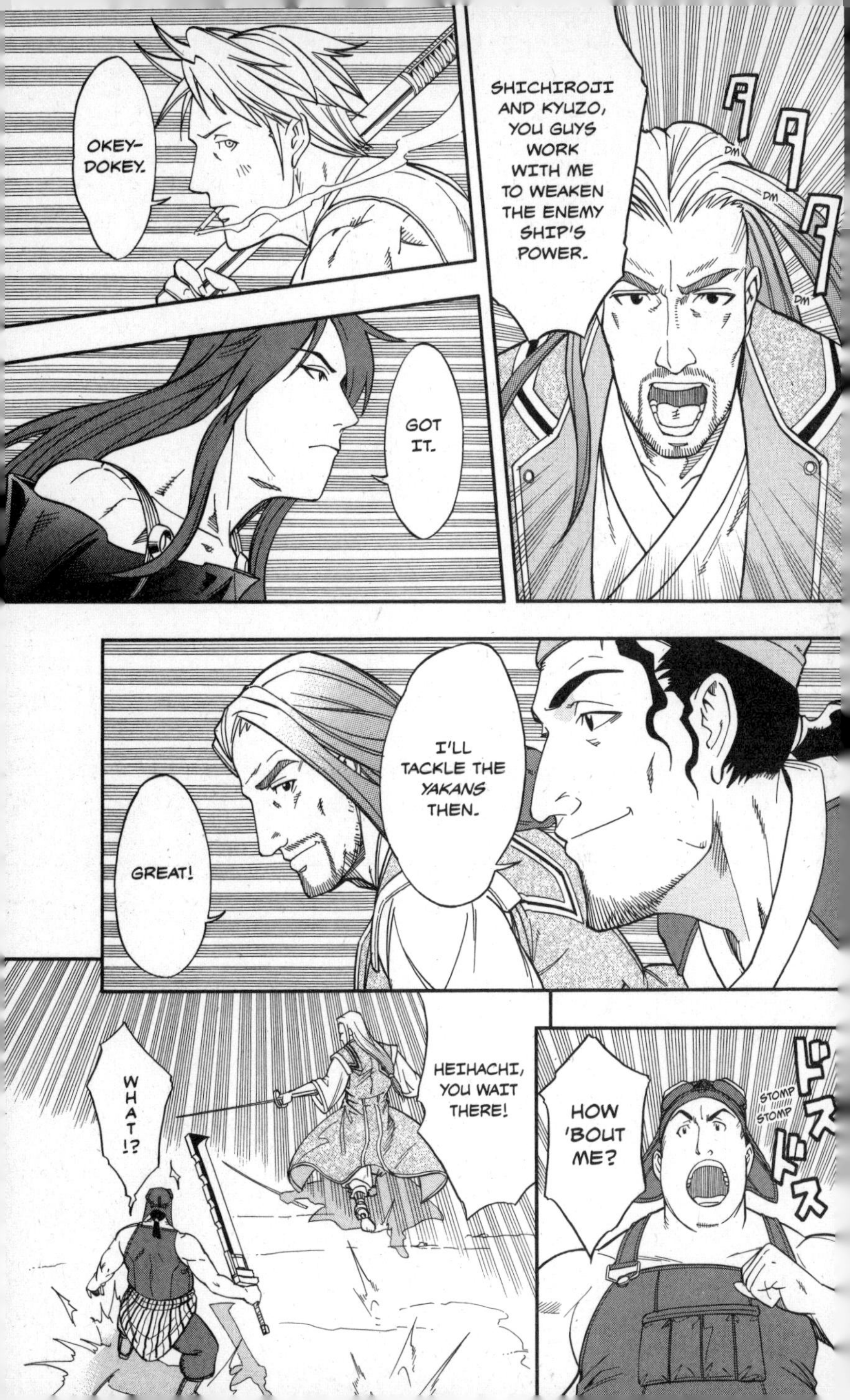
SHICHIROJI AND KYUZO, YOU GUYS WORK WITH ME TO WEAKEN THE ENEMY SHIP'S POWER.
タタタ
DM DM DM
OKEY-DOKEY.
GOT IT.
I'LL TACKLE THE *YAKANS* THEN.
GREAT!
HOW 'BOUT ME?
ドスドス
STOMP STOMP
HEIHACHI, YOU WAIT THERE!
WHAT!?

OH! UH, GOT IT!

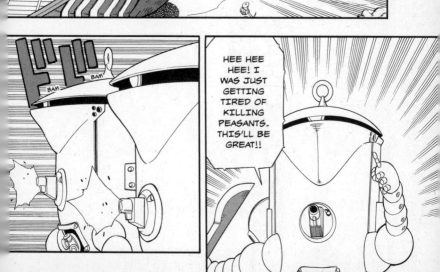

HEE HEE HEE! I WAS JUST GETTING TIRED OF KILLING PEASANTS. THIS'LL BE GREAT!!

BAM BAM

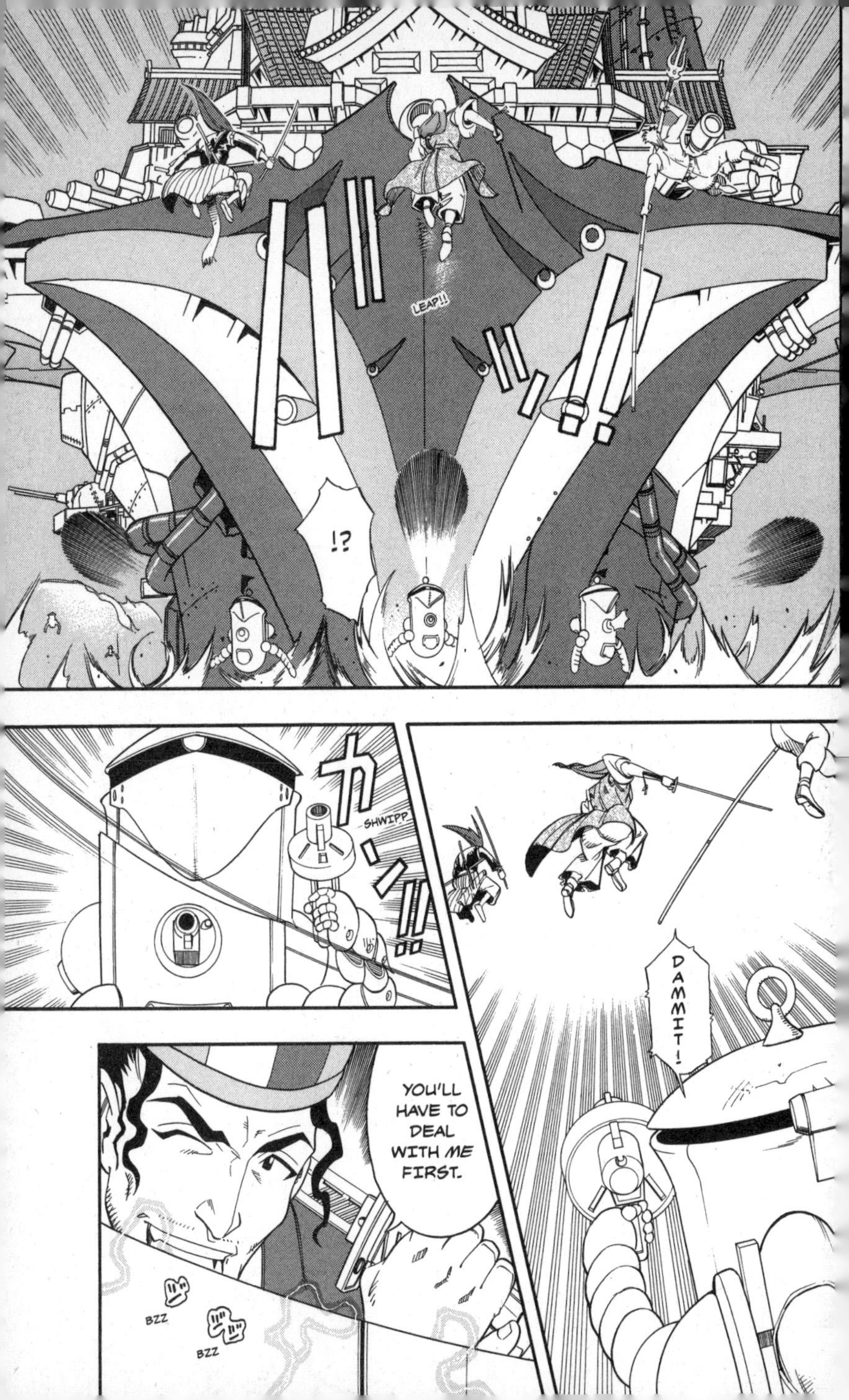
LEAP!!
!?
DAMMIT!!
SHWIPP
YOU'LL HAVE TO DEAL WITH ME FIRST.
BZZ
BZZ

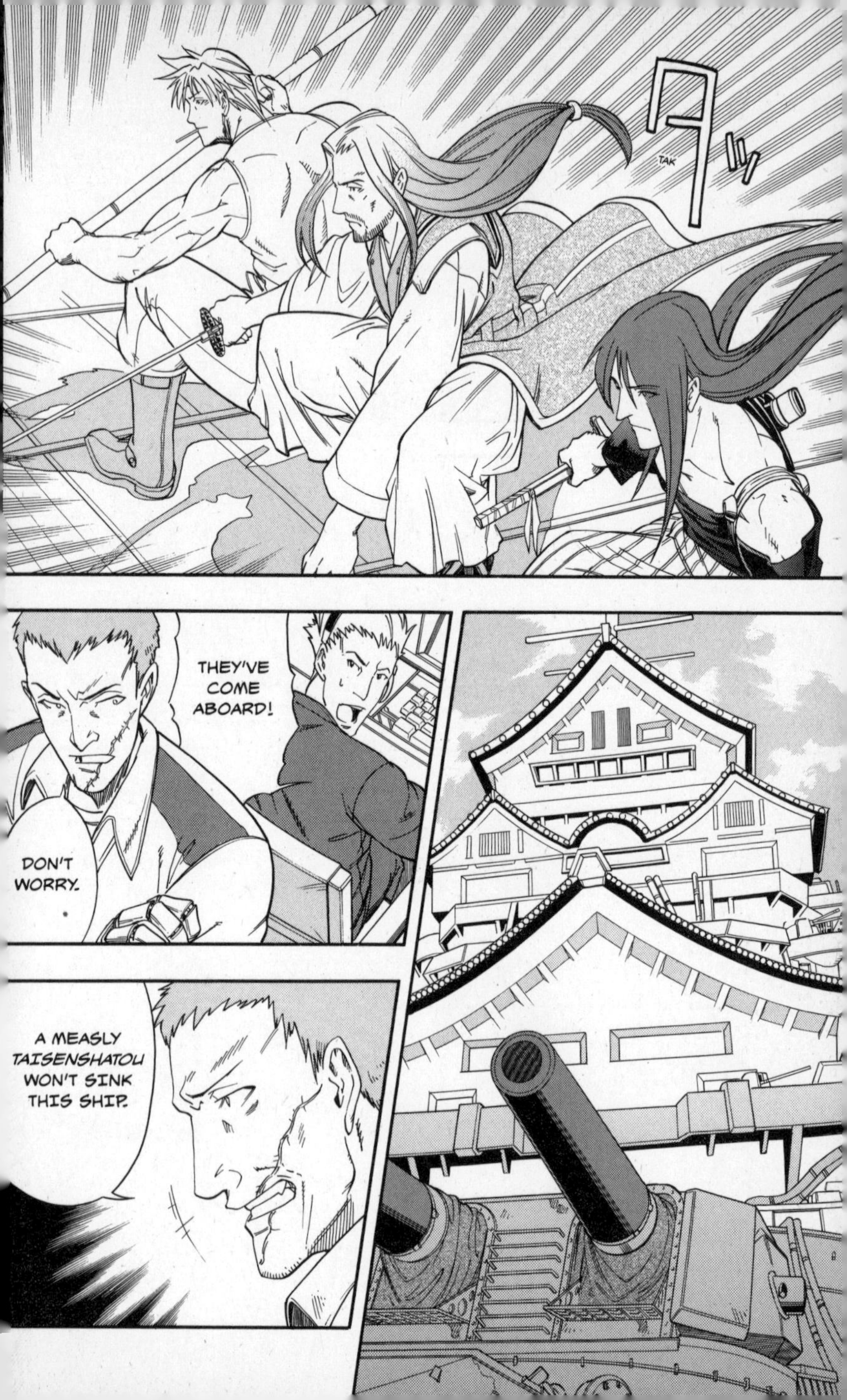
タッ
TAK
THEY'VE COME ABOARD!
DON'T WORRY.
A MEASLY TAISENSHATOU WON'T SINK THIS SHIP.

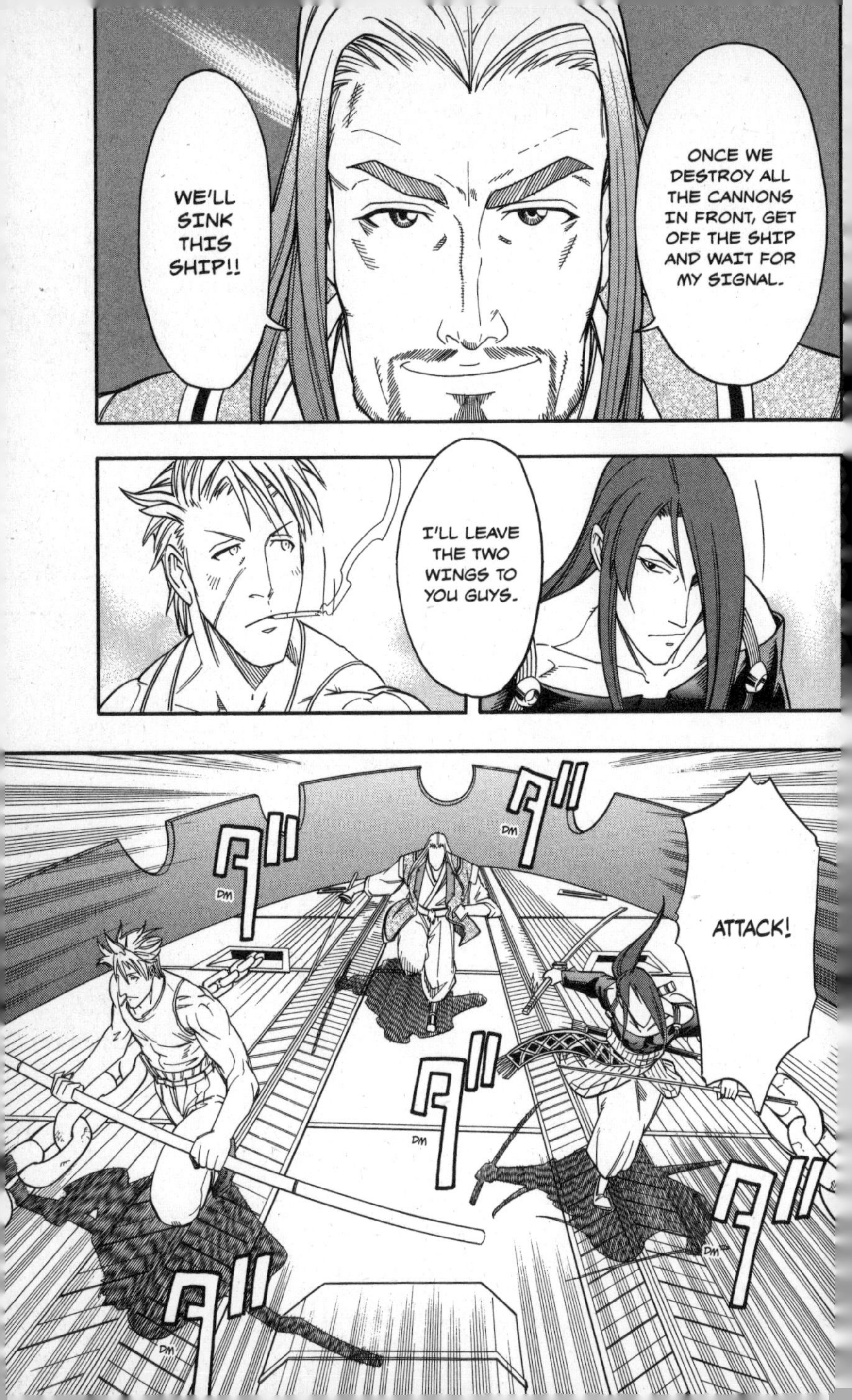
ONCE WE DESTROY ALL THE CANNONS IN FRONT, GET OFF THE SHIP AND WAIT FOR MY SIGNAL.
WE'LL SINK THIS SHIP!!
I'LL LEAVE THE TWO WINGS TO YOU GUYS.
DM
ATTACK!
DM
DM
DM
DM

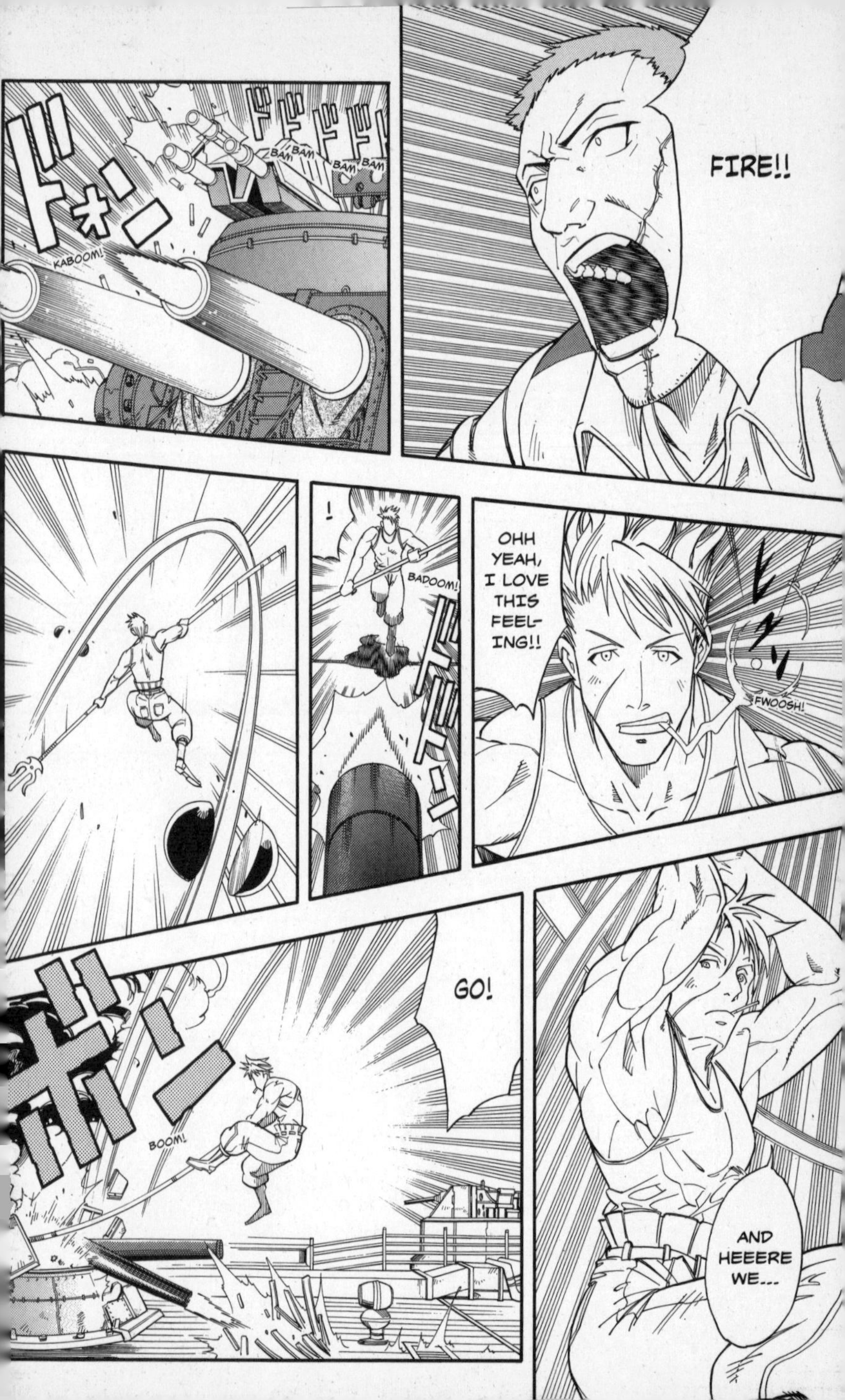
FIRE!!
BAM
BAM
BAM
BAM
KABOOM!
OHH YEAH, I LOVE THIS FEEL-ING!!
FWOOSH!
!
BADOOM!
AND HEEERE WE...
GO!
BOOM!

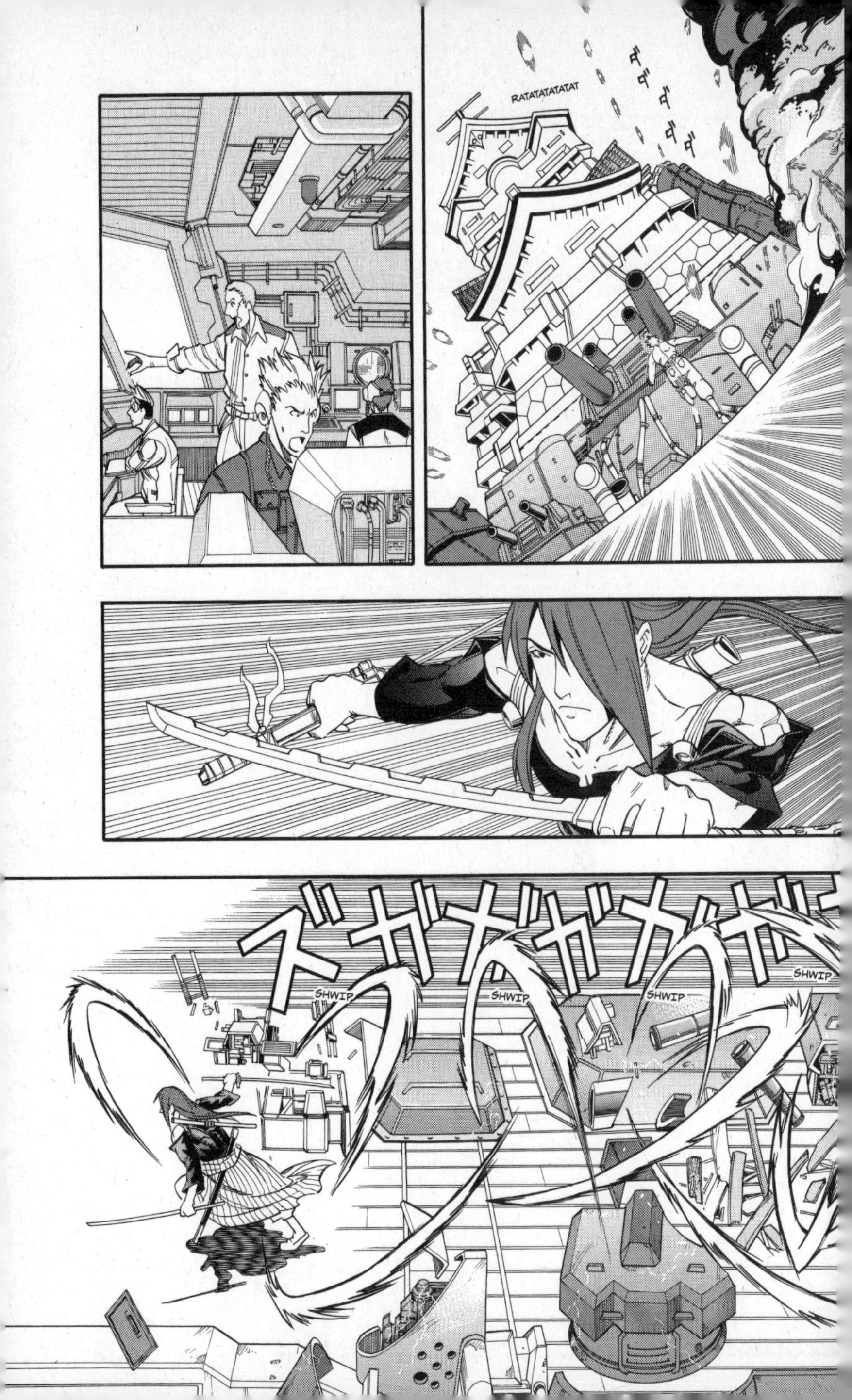
RATATATATATAT
ダダダダダ
SHWIP
ズガガガガガ
SHWIP
SHWIP
SHWIP

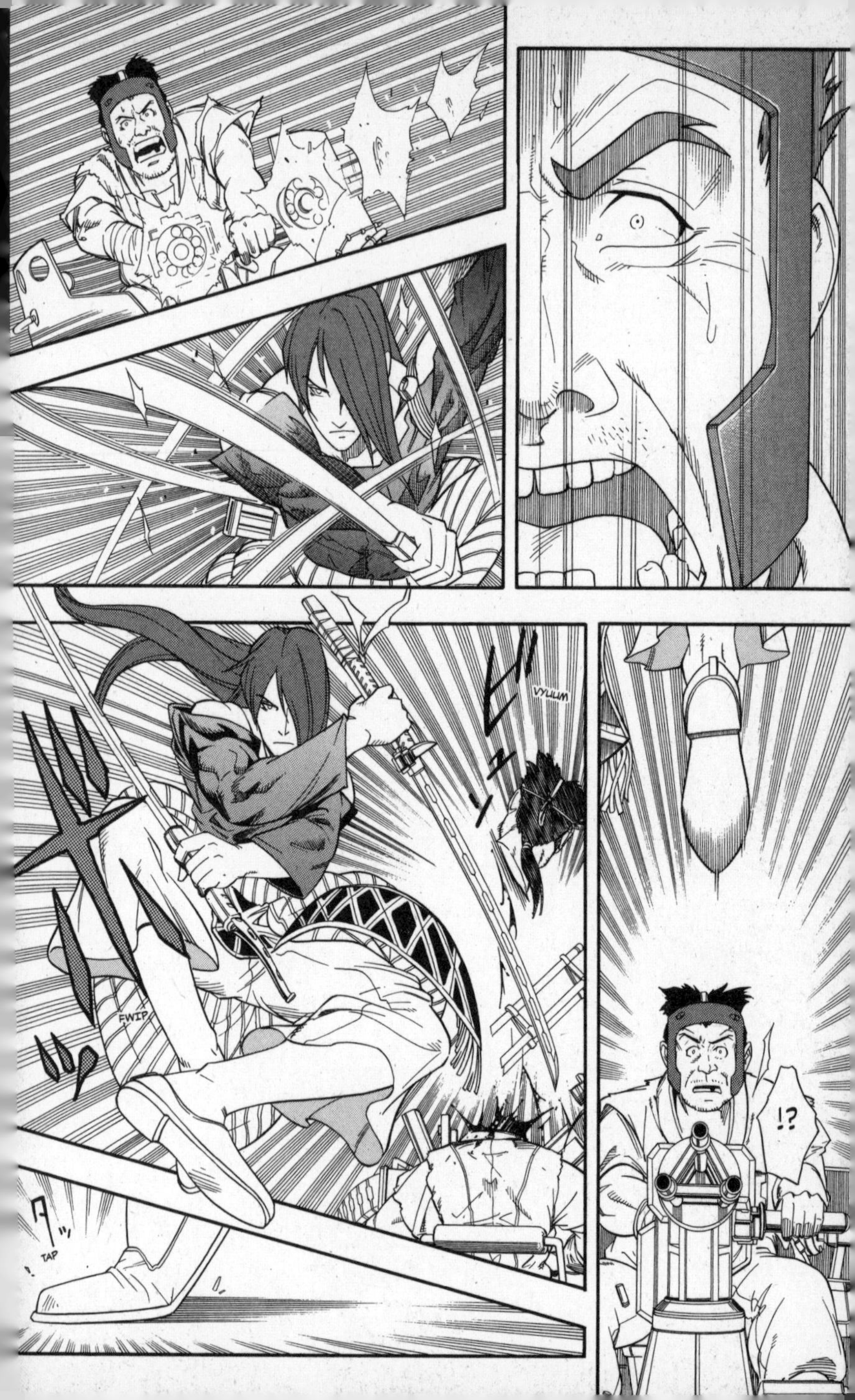
!?
VYUUM
FWIP
TAP

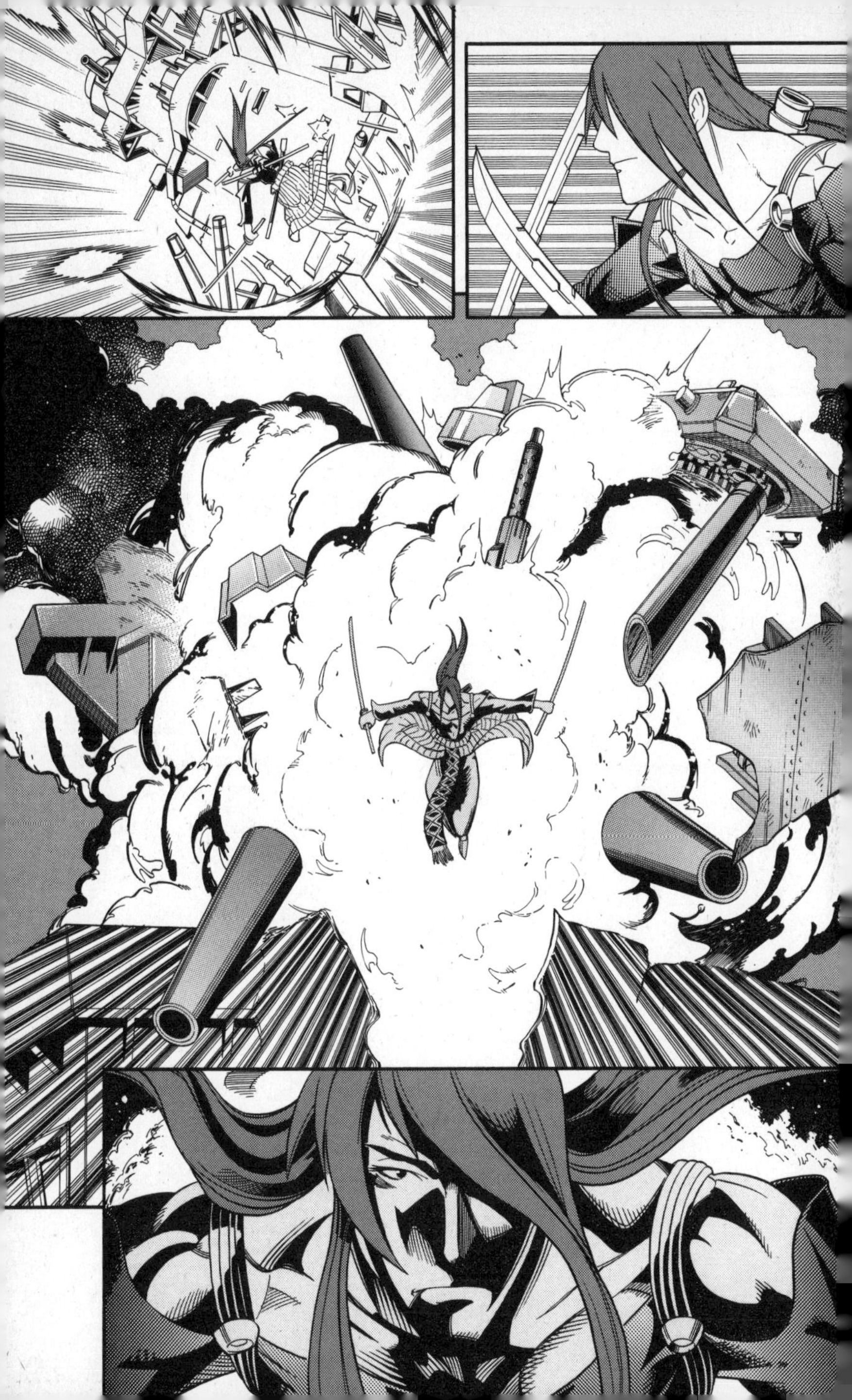

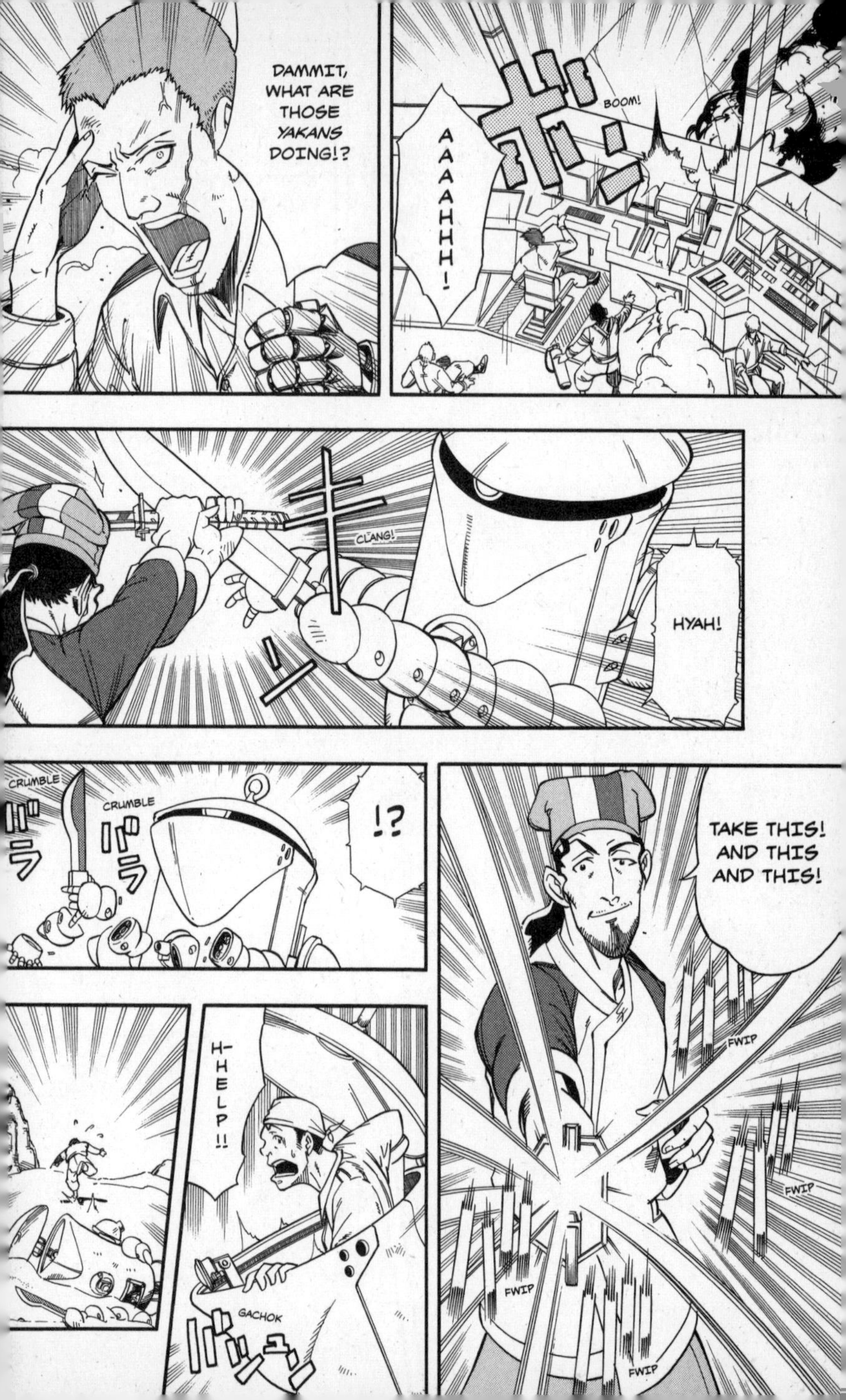
BOOM!
AAAAAHHH!
DAMMIT, WHAT ARE THOSE YAKANS DOING!?
CLANG!
HYAH!
TAKE THIS! AND THIS AND THIS!
FWIP
FWIP
FWIP
FWIP
!?
CRUMBLE
CRUMBLE
H-HELP!!
GACHOK

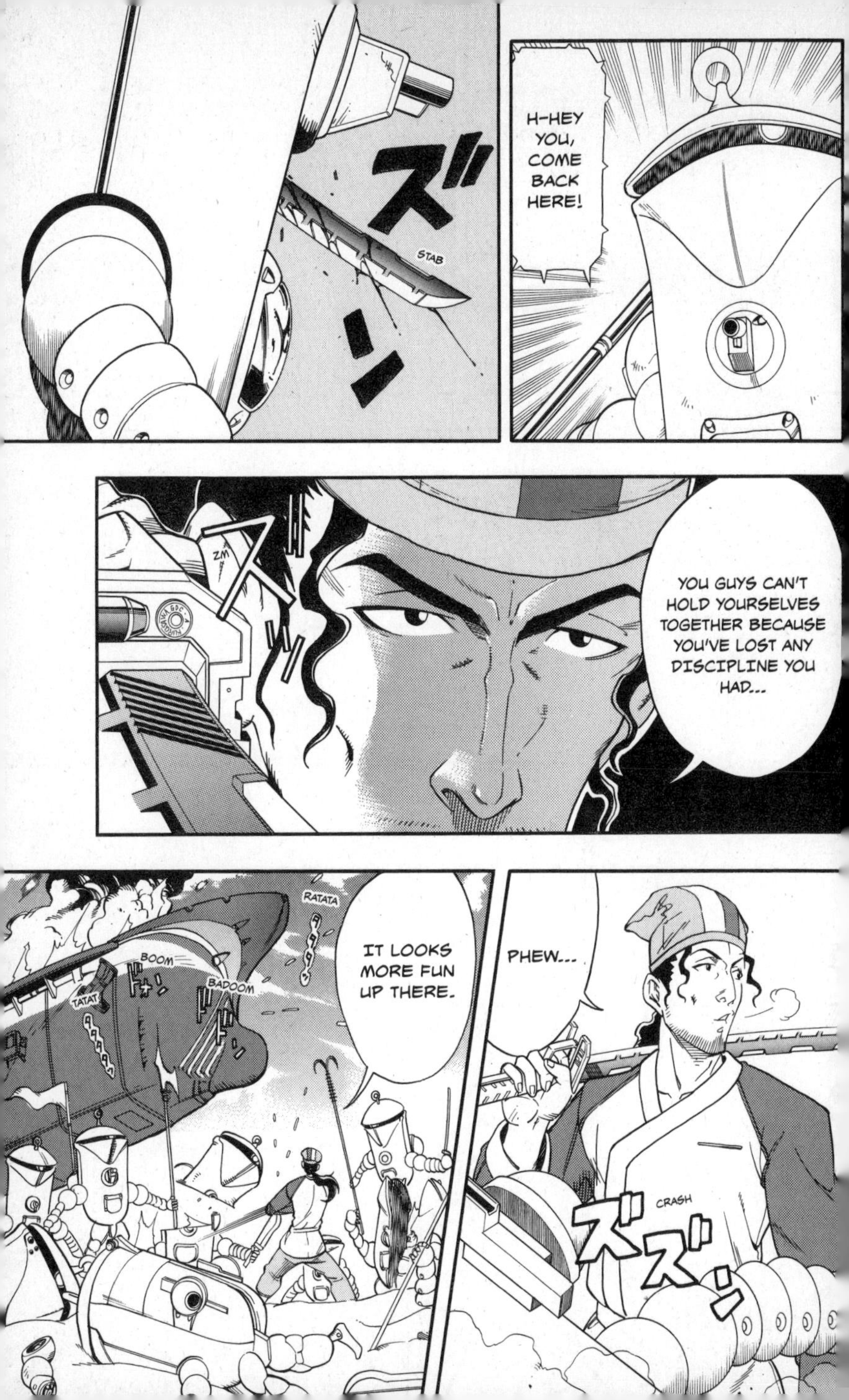
H-HEY YOU, COME BACK HERE!
STAB
ZM
YOU GUYS CAN'T HOLD YOURSELVES TOGETHER BECAUSE YOU'VE LOST ANY DISCIPLINE YOU HAD...
PHEW...
CRASH
IT LOOKS MORE FUN UP THERE.
RATATA
BOOM
BADOOM
TATAT

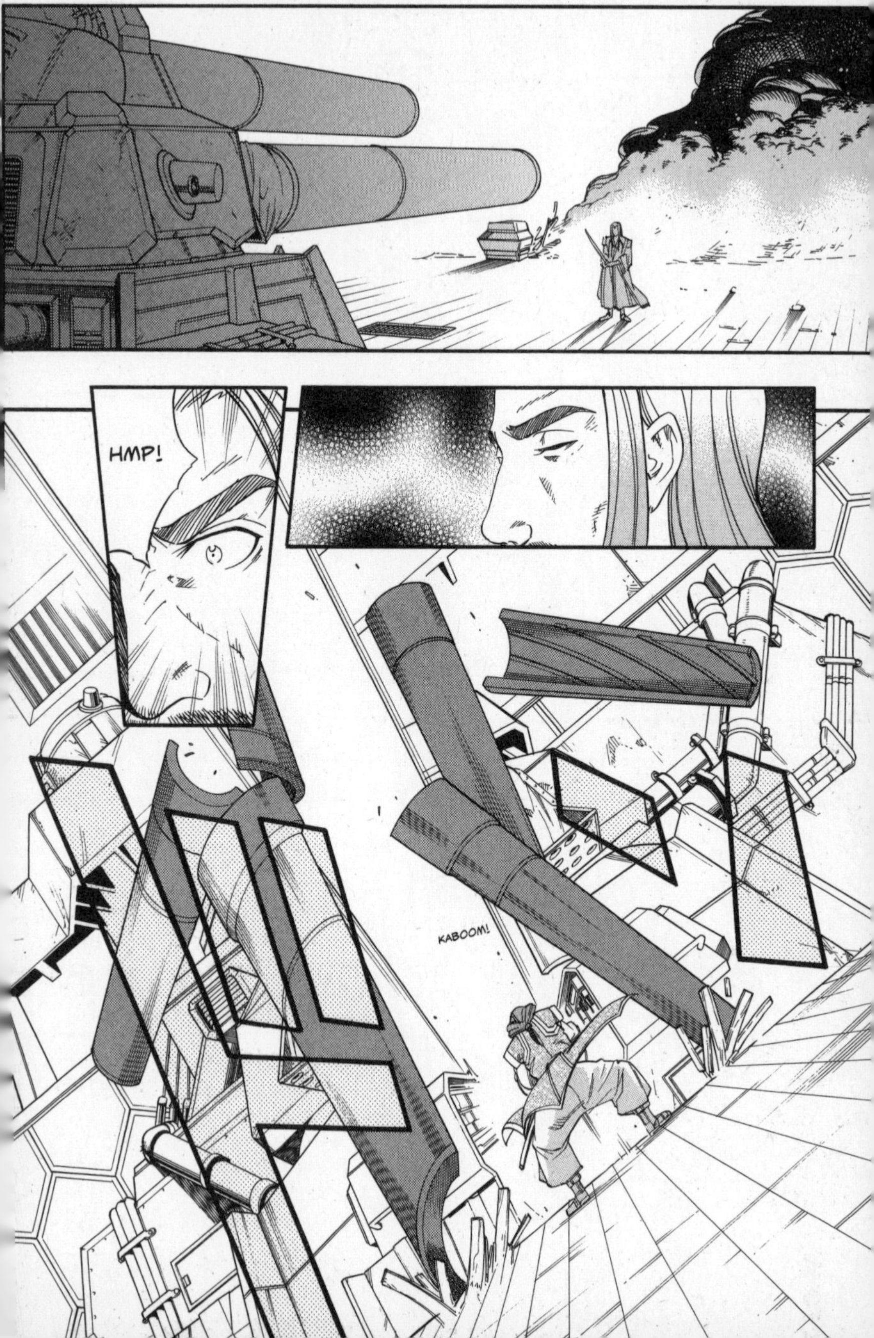
HMP!
KABOOM!

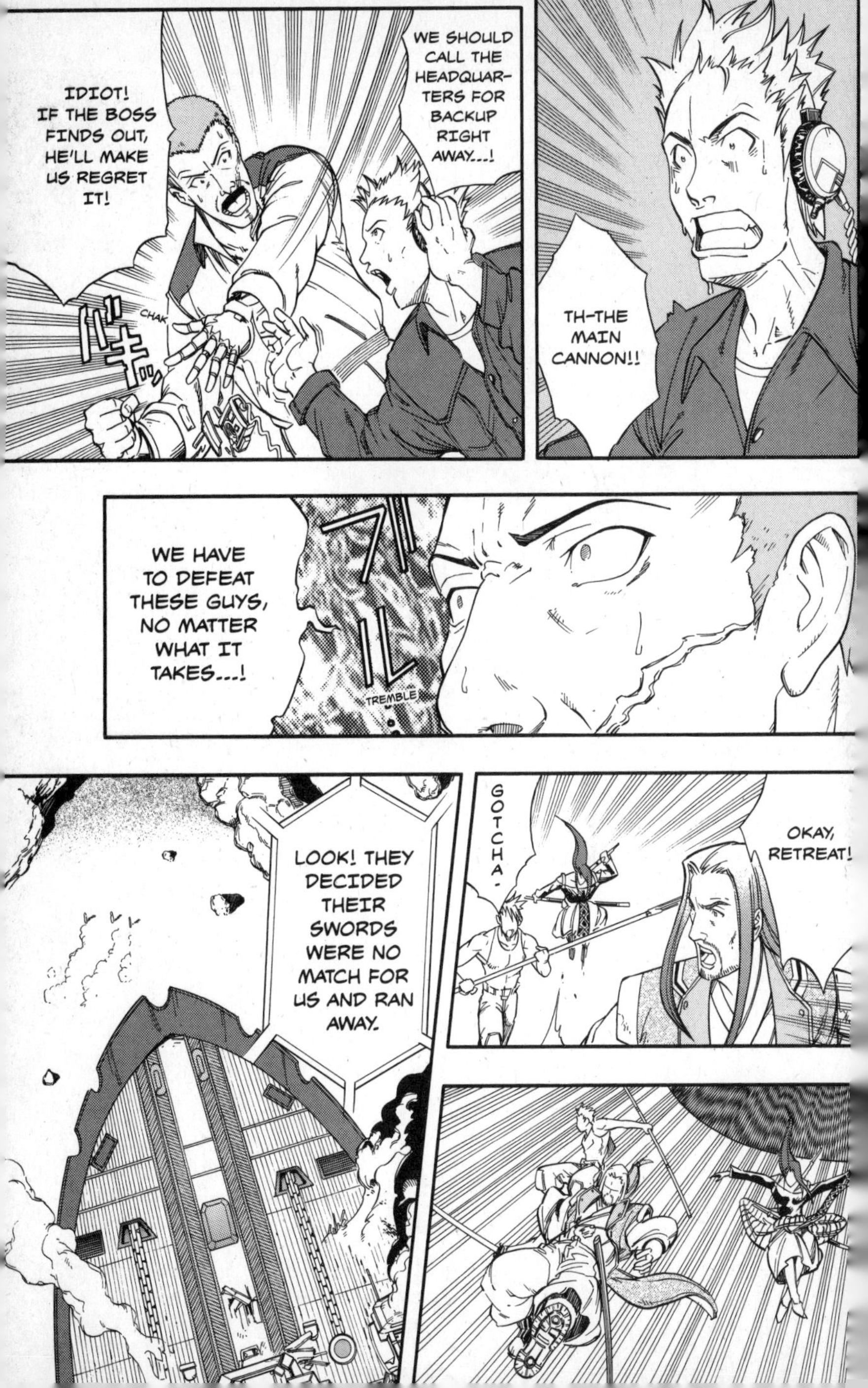
TH-THE MAIN CANNON!!
WE SHOULD CALL THE HEADQUARTERS FOR BACKUP RIGHT AWAY...!
IDIOT! IF THE BOSS FINDS OUT, HE'LL MAKE US REGRET IT!
CHAK
WE HAVE TO DEFEAT THESE GUYS, NO MATTER WHAT IT TAKES...!
TREMBLE
OKAY, RETREAT!
GOTCHA.
LOOK! THEY DECIDED THEIR SWORDS WERE NO MATCH FOR US AND RAN AWAY.

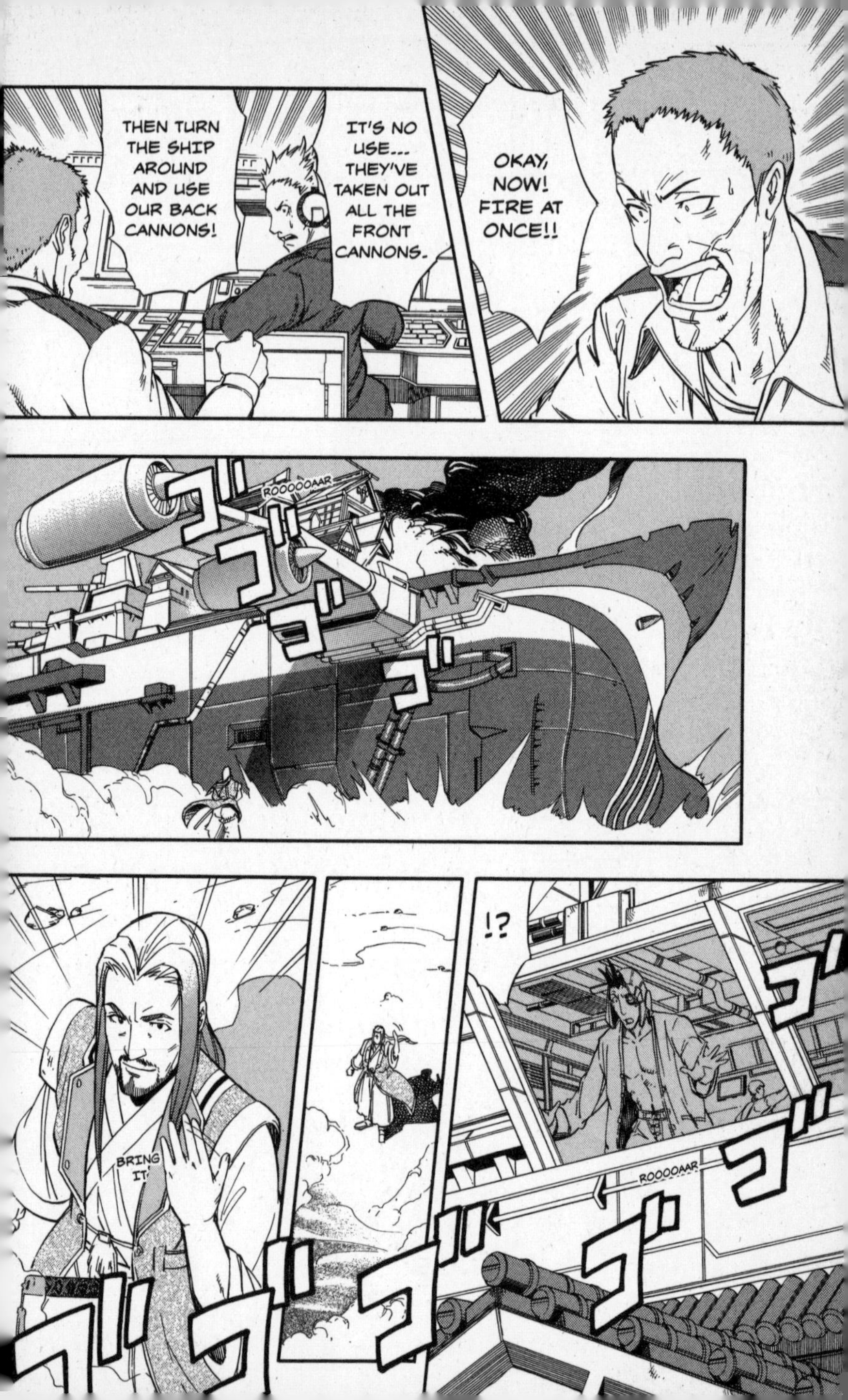
OKAY, NOW! FIRE AT ONCE!!
IT'S NO USE... THEY'VE TAKEN OUT ALL THE FRONT CANNONS.
THEN TURN THE SHIP AROUND AND USE OUR BACK CANNONS!
ROOOOOAAR
ゴゴゴゴゴ
!?
ゴゴゴ
ROOOOAAR
ゴゴゴゴゴ
BRING IT.

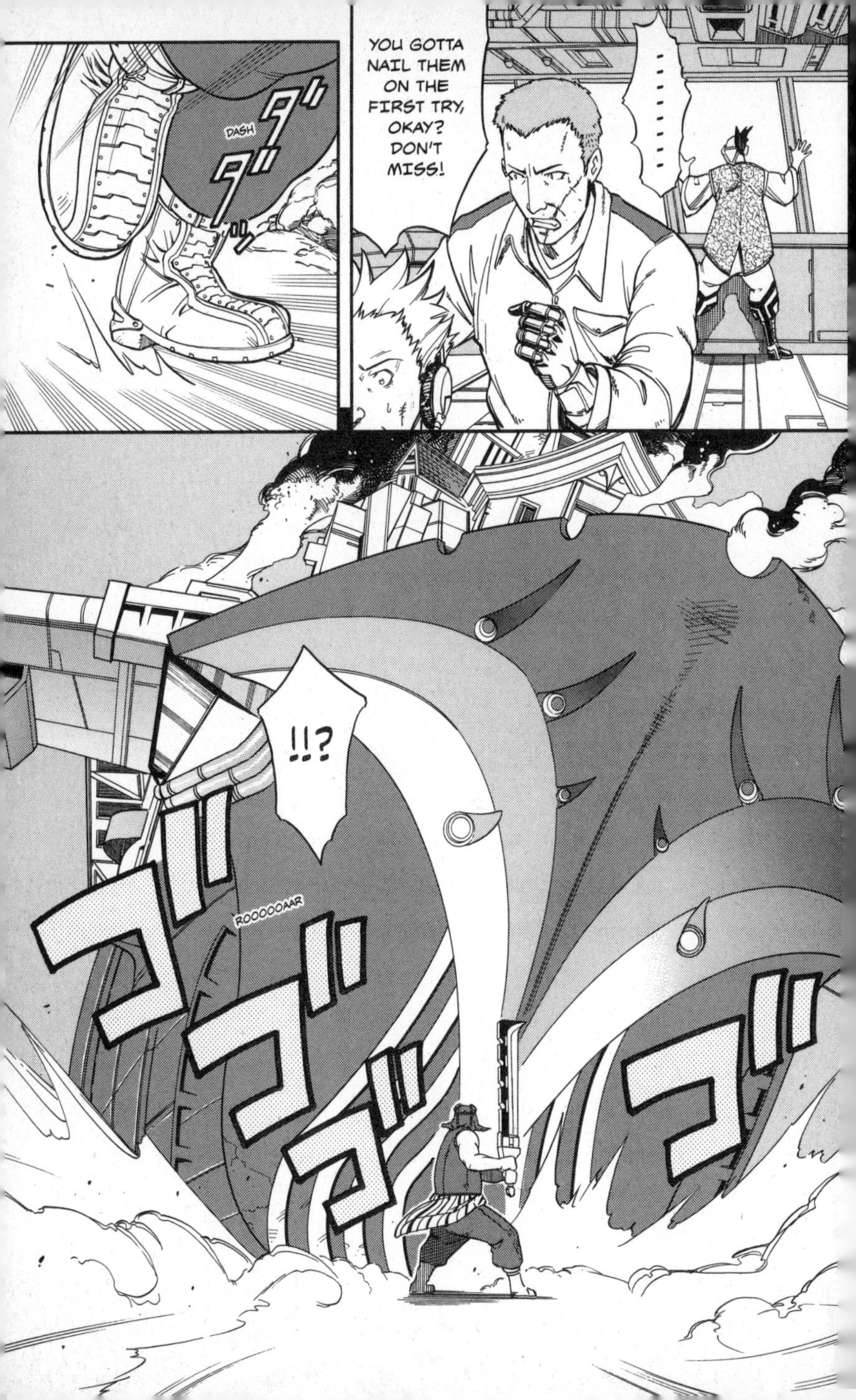
YOU GOTTA NAIL THEM ON THE FIRST TRY, OKAY? DON'T MISS!
DASH
!!?
ROOOOOAAR

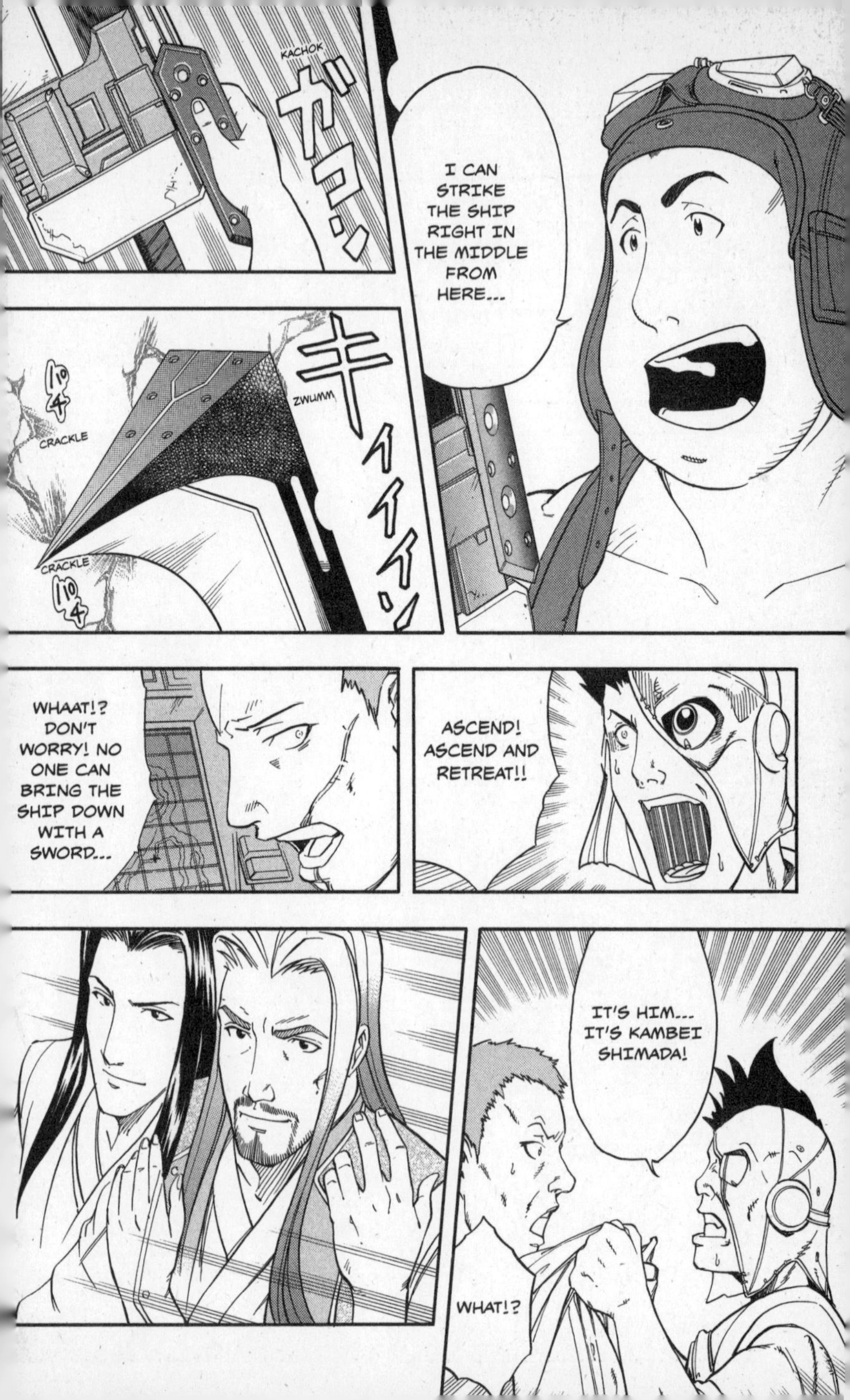
I CAN STRIKE THE SHIP RIGHT IN THE MIDDLE FROM HERE...
KACHOK
ZWUMM
CRACKLE
CRACKLE
ASCEND! ASCEND AND RETREAT!!
WHAAT!? DON'T WORRY! NO ONE CAN BRING THE SHIP DOWN WITH A SWORD...
IT'S HIM... IT'S KAMBEI SHIMADA!
WHAT!?

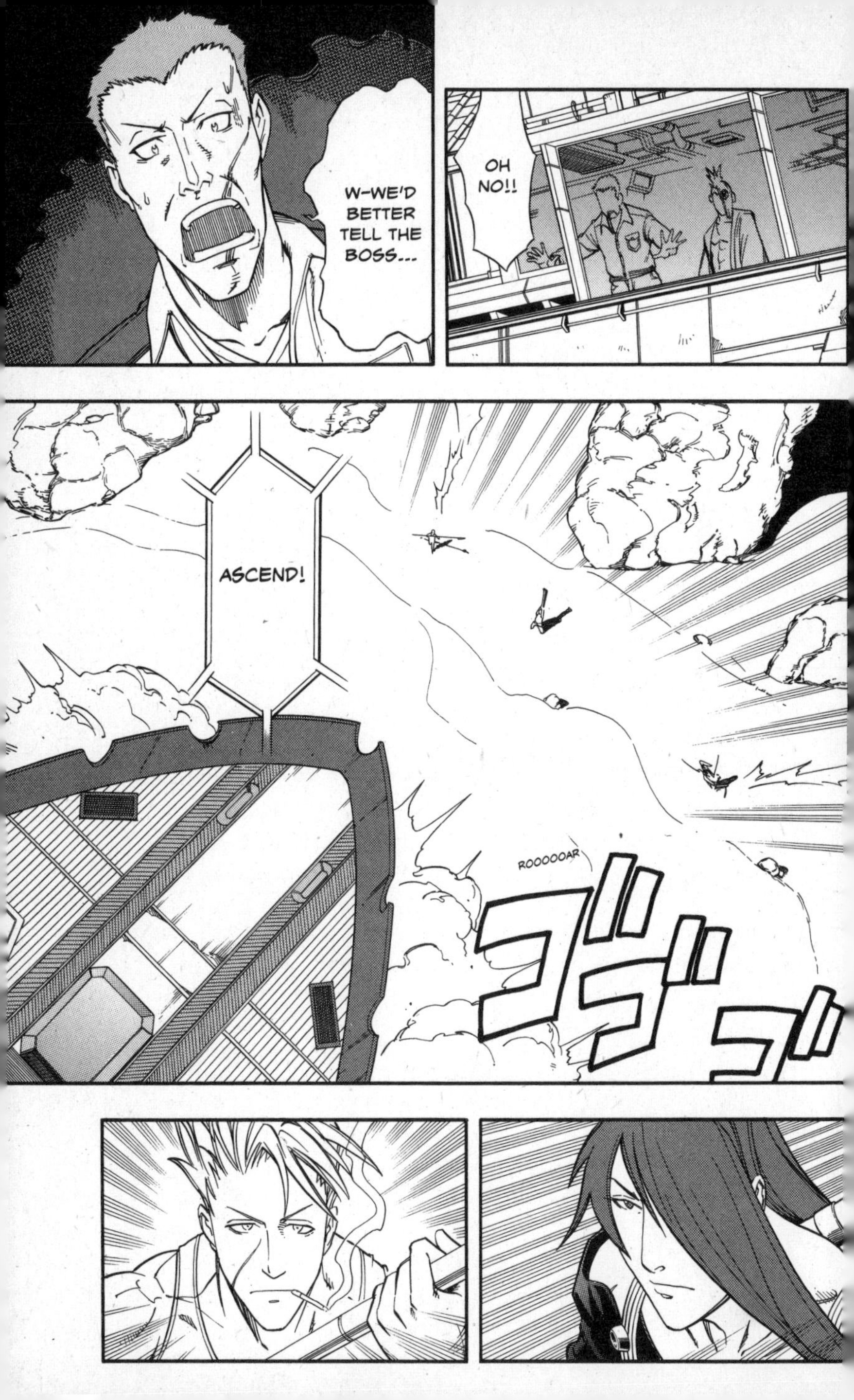

OH NO!!
W-WE'D BETTER TELL THE BOSS...
ASCEND!
ROOOOOAR
ゴゴゴ

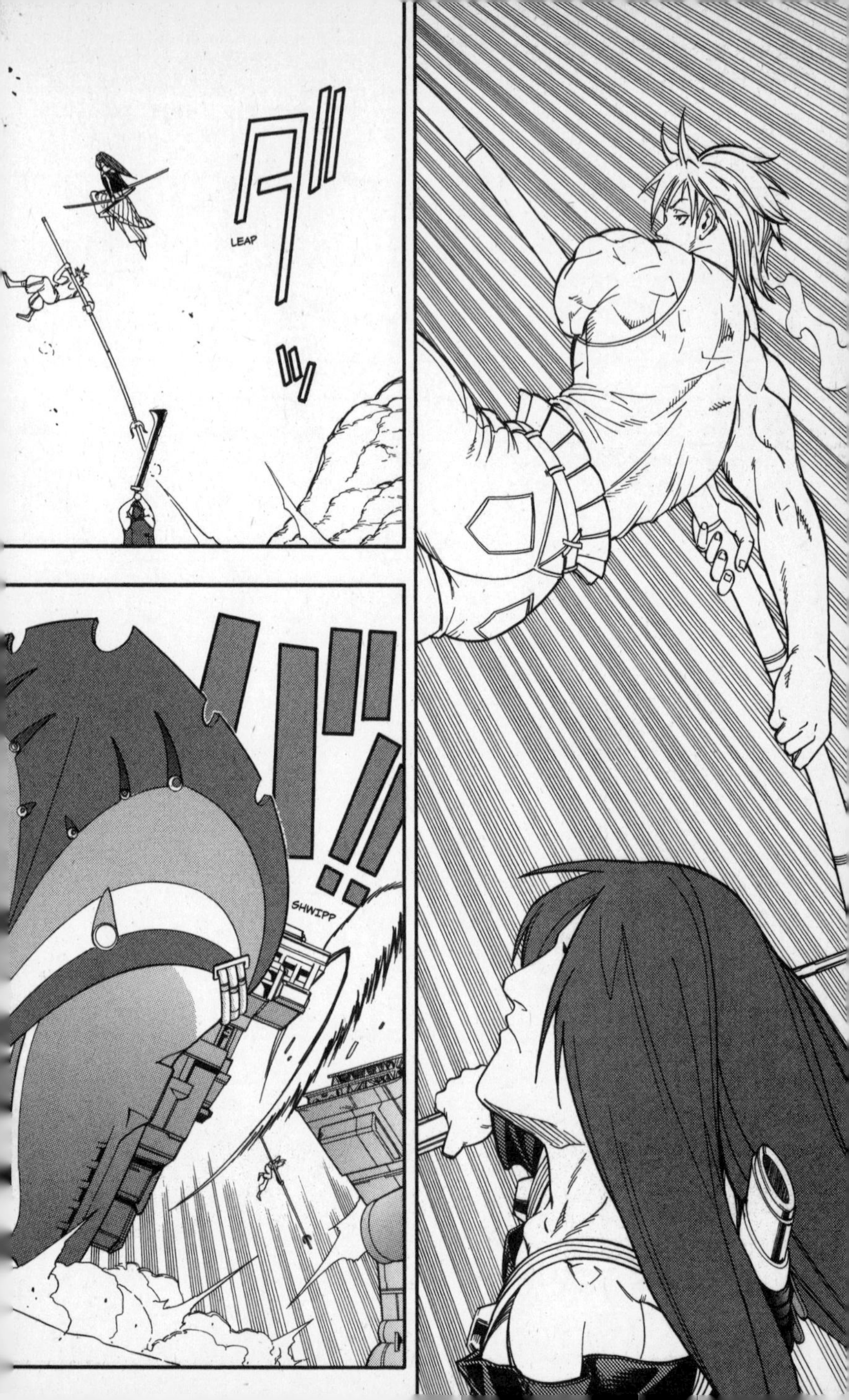
LEAP
SHWIPP

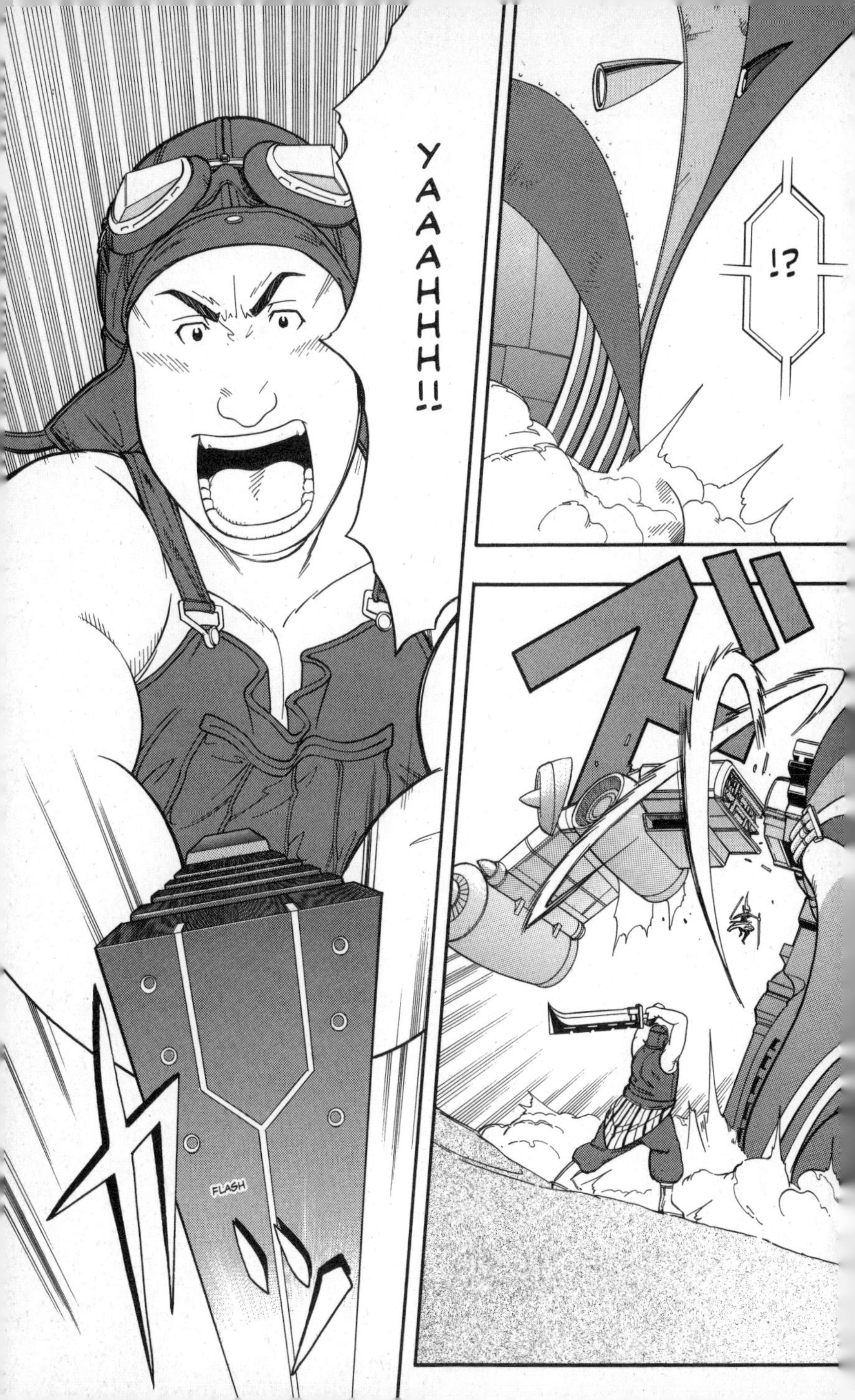
!?
ズ
YAAAAHHH!!
FLASH

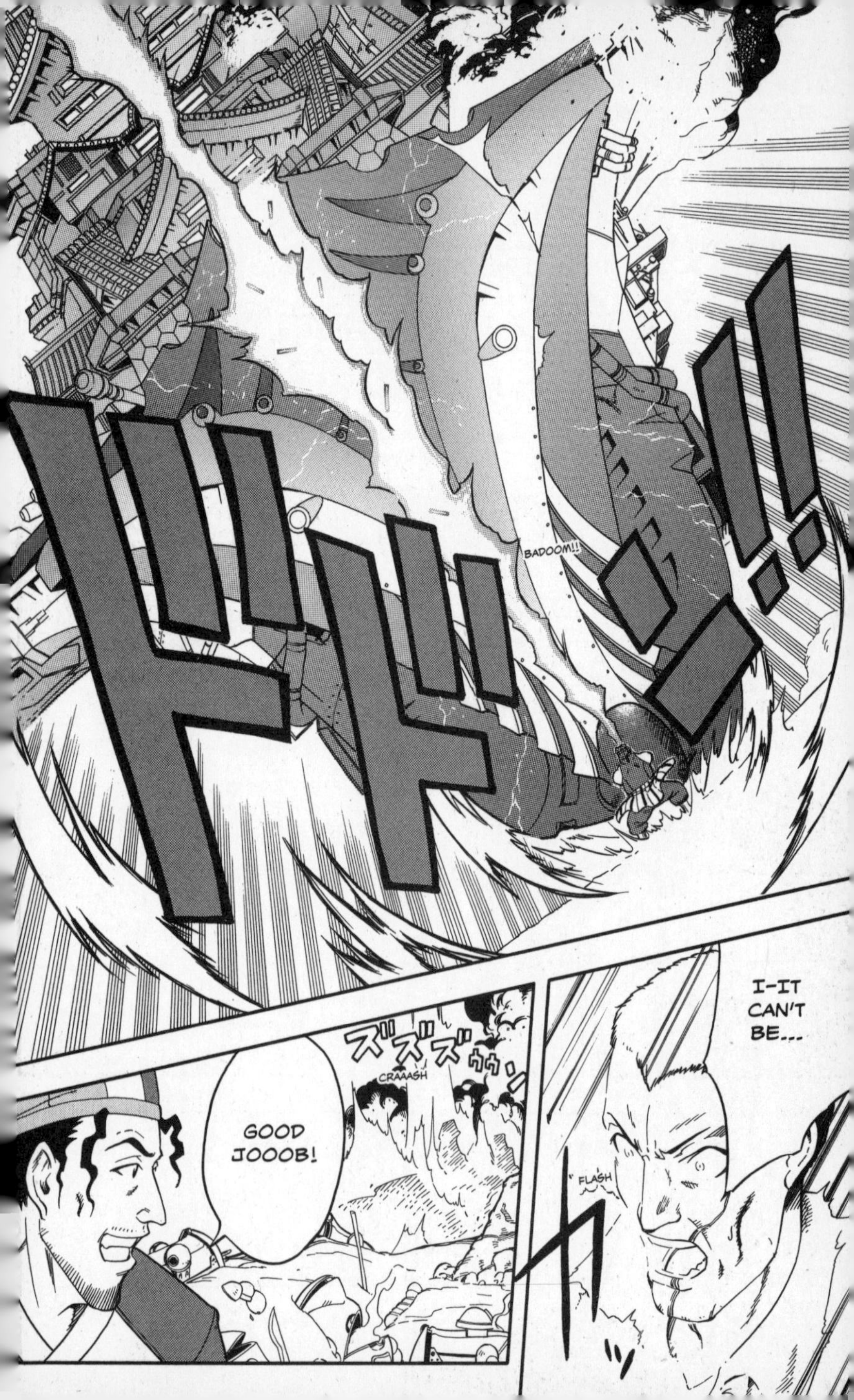
BADOOM!!
I-IT CAN'T BE...
FLASH
ズズズゥゥ
CRAAASH
GOOD JOOOB!

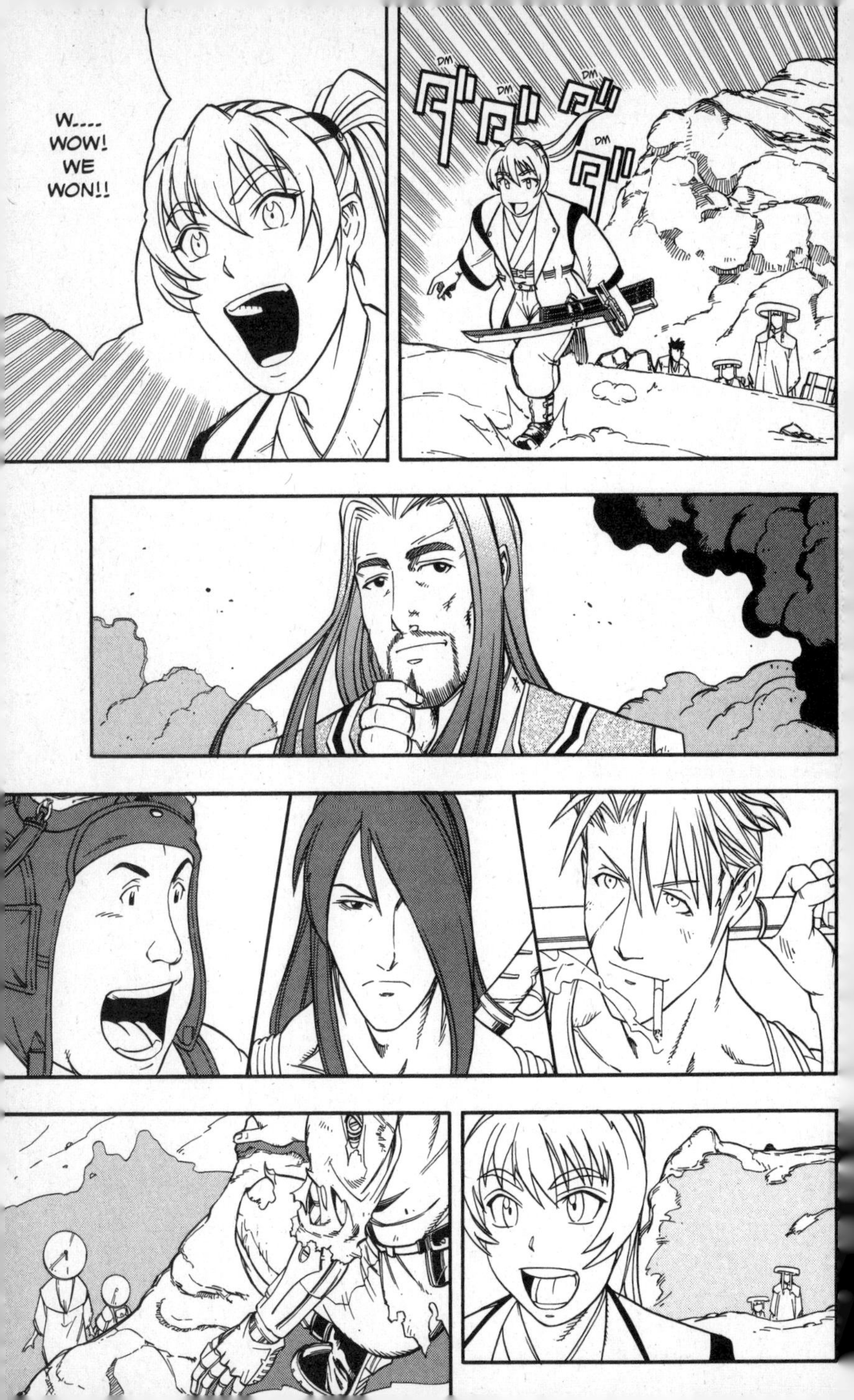
DM
DM
DM
DM
W.... WOW! WE WON!!

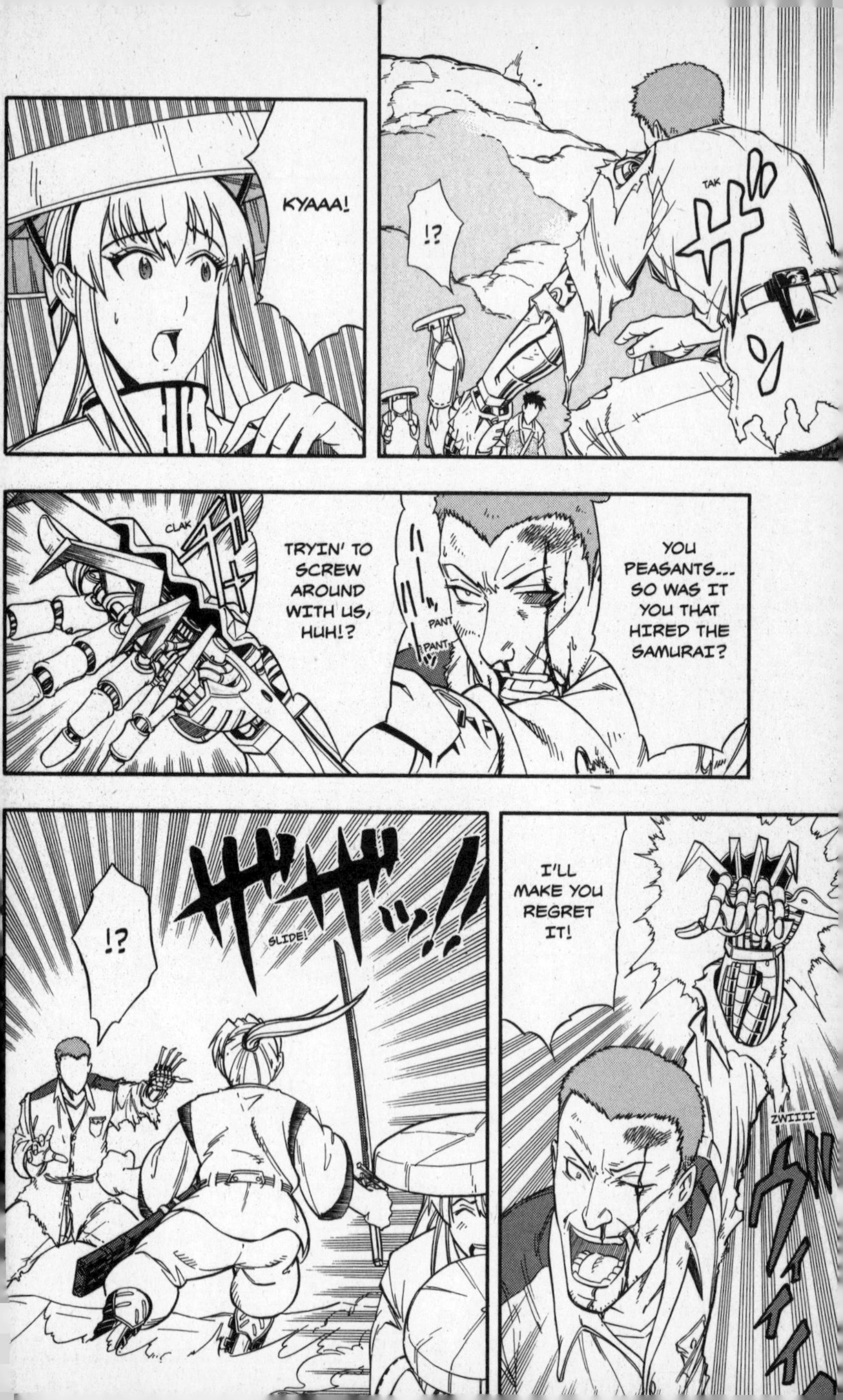
!?
TAK
KYAAA!
YOU PEASANTS... SO WAS IT YOU THAT HIRED THE SAMURAI?
TRYIN' TO SCREW AROUND WITH US, HUH!?
PANT
PANT
CLAK
I'LL MAKE YOU REGRET IT!
ZWIIII
SLIDE!
!?

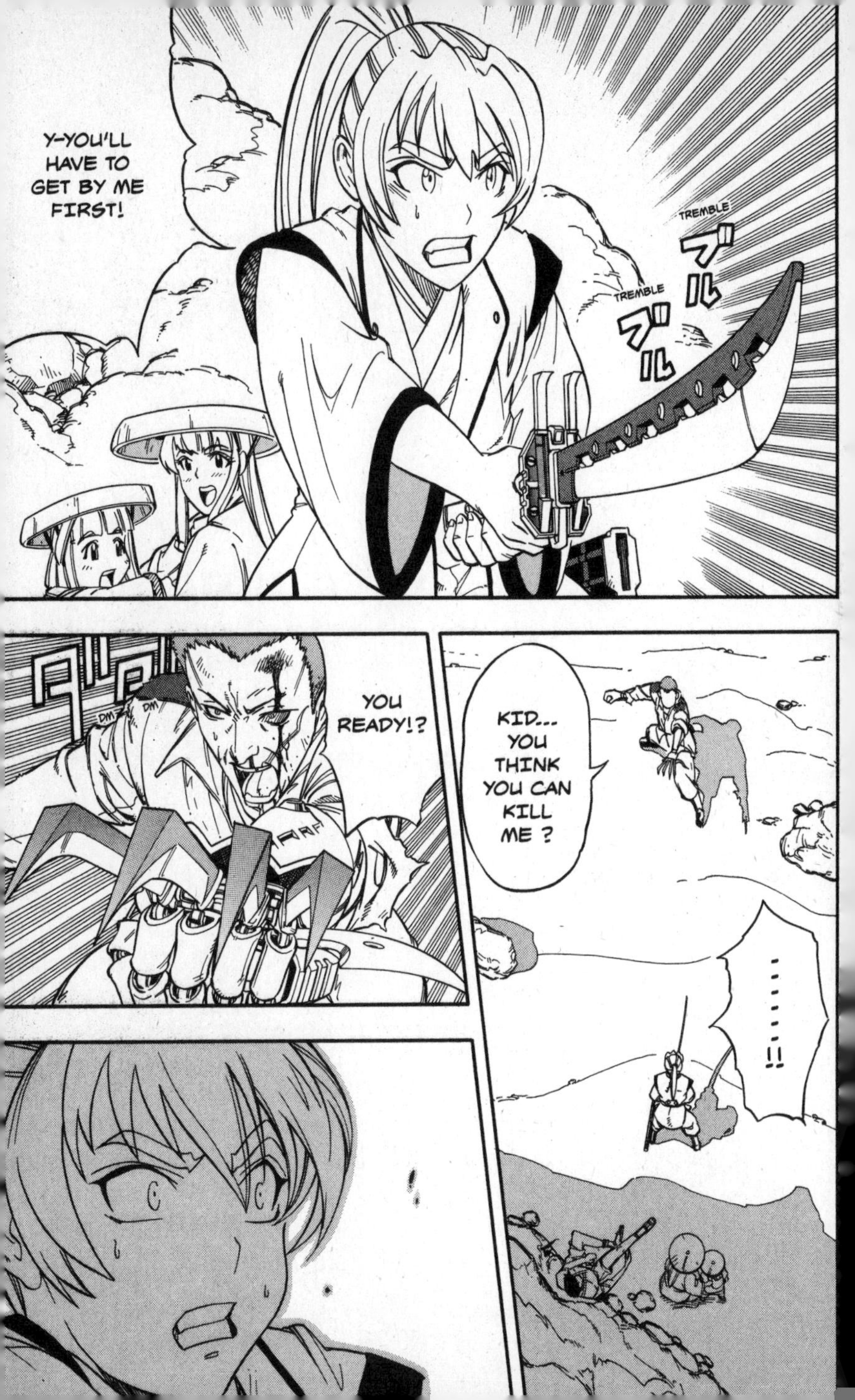
Y-YOU'LL HAVE TO GET BY ME FIRST!
TREMBLE
ブル
TREMBLE
ブル
KID... YOU THINK YOU CAN KILL ME ?
......!!
DM
DM
YOU READY!?

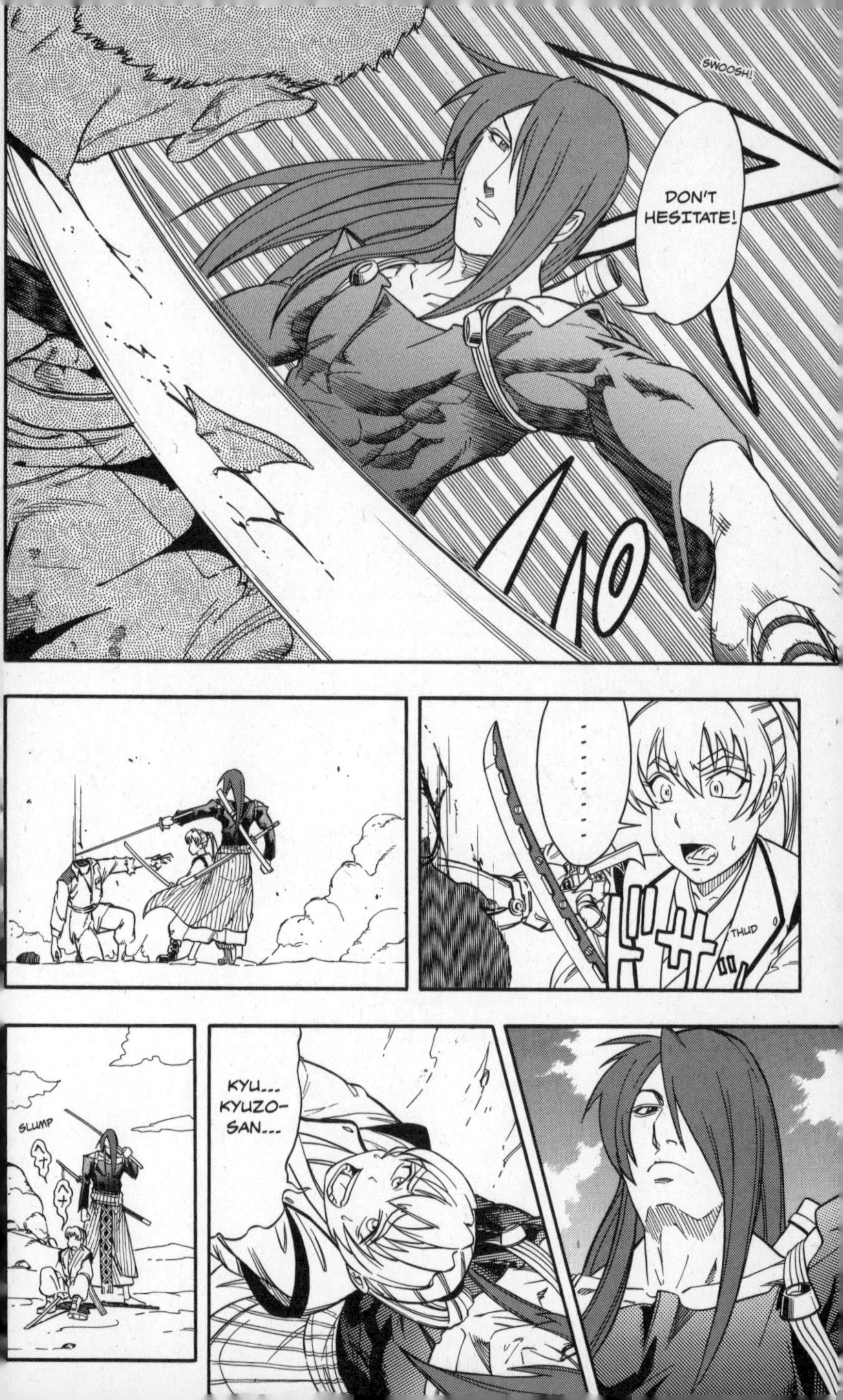
SWOOSH!
DON'T HESITATE!
......
THUD
KYU... KYUZO-SAN...
SLUMP

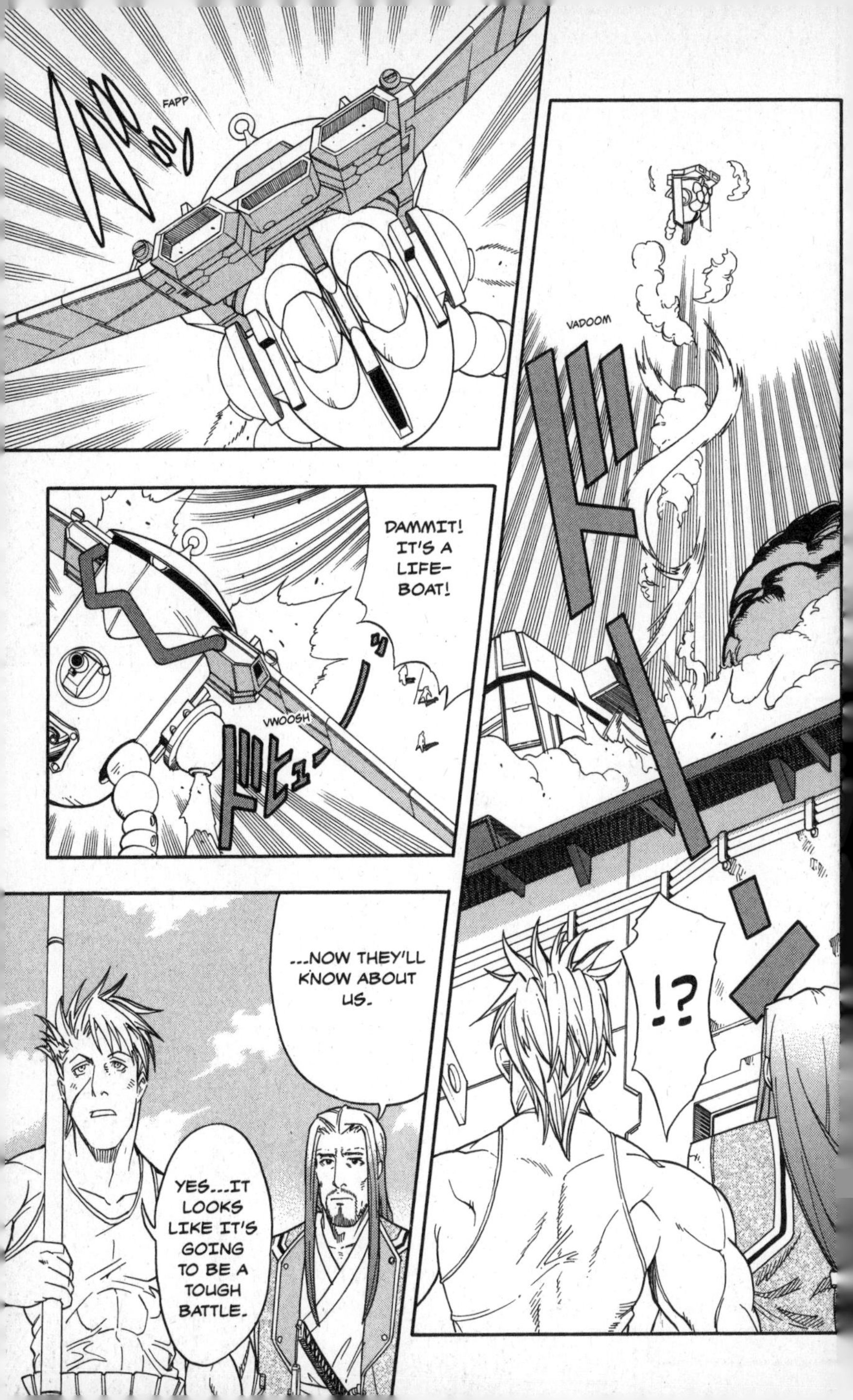
VADOOM
!?
FAPP
DAMMIT! IT'S A LIFE-BOAT!
VWOOSH
...NOW THEY'LL KNOW ABOUT US.
YES...IT LOOKS LIKE IT'S GOING TO BE A TOUGH BATTLE.

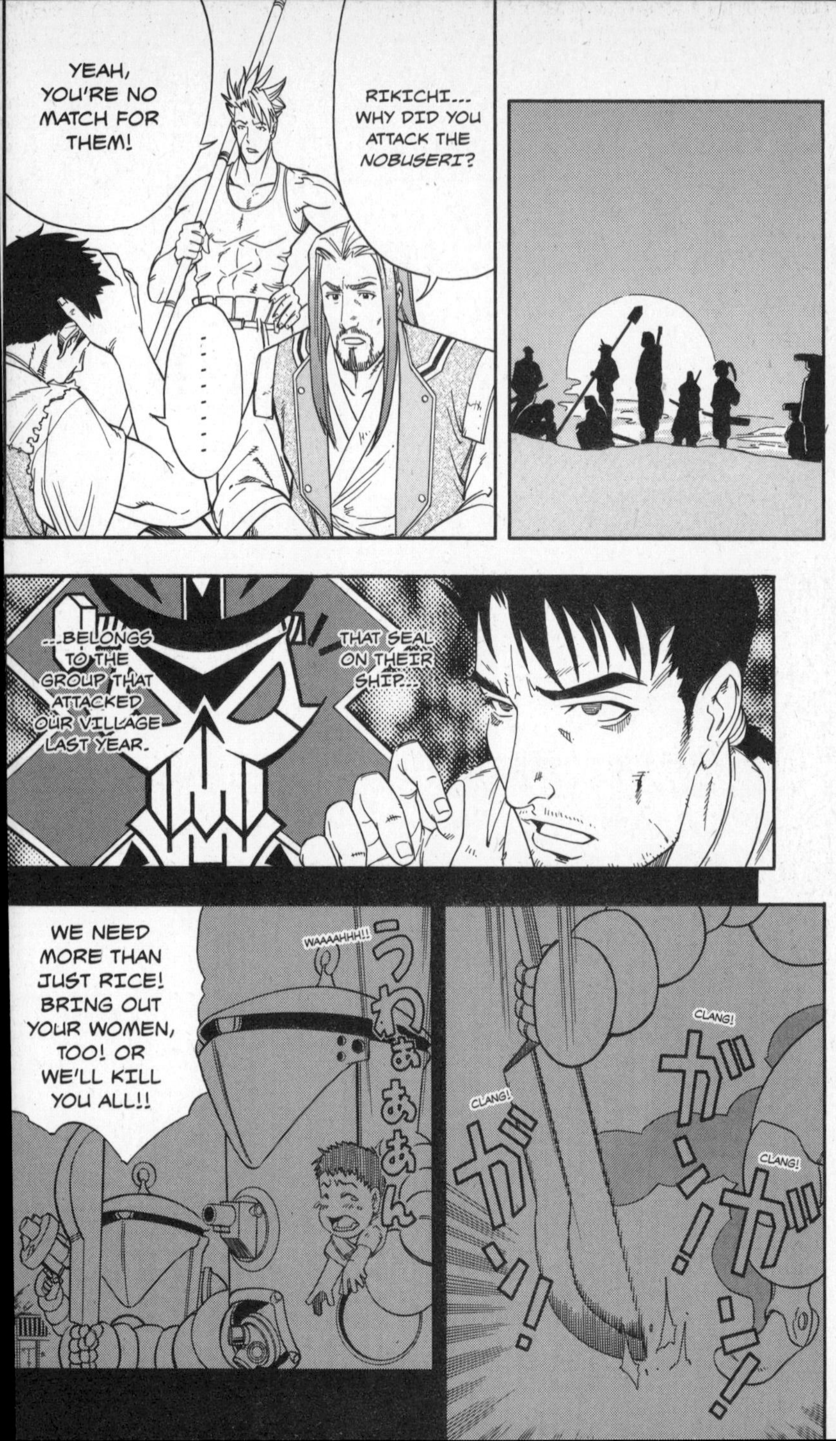
RIKICHI... WHY DID YOU ATTACK THE *NOBUSERI*?
YEAH, YOU'RE NO MATCH FOR THEM!
......
THAT SEAL ON THEIR SHIP...
...BELONGS TO THE GROUP THAT ATTACKED OUR VILLAGE LAST YEAR.
CLANG!
CLANG!
CLANG!
WAAAAHHH!!
うわぁああん
WE NEED MORE THAN JUST RICE! BRING OUT YOUR WOMEN, TOO! OR WE'LL KILL YOU ALL!!

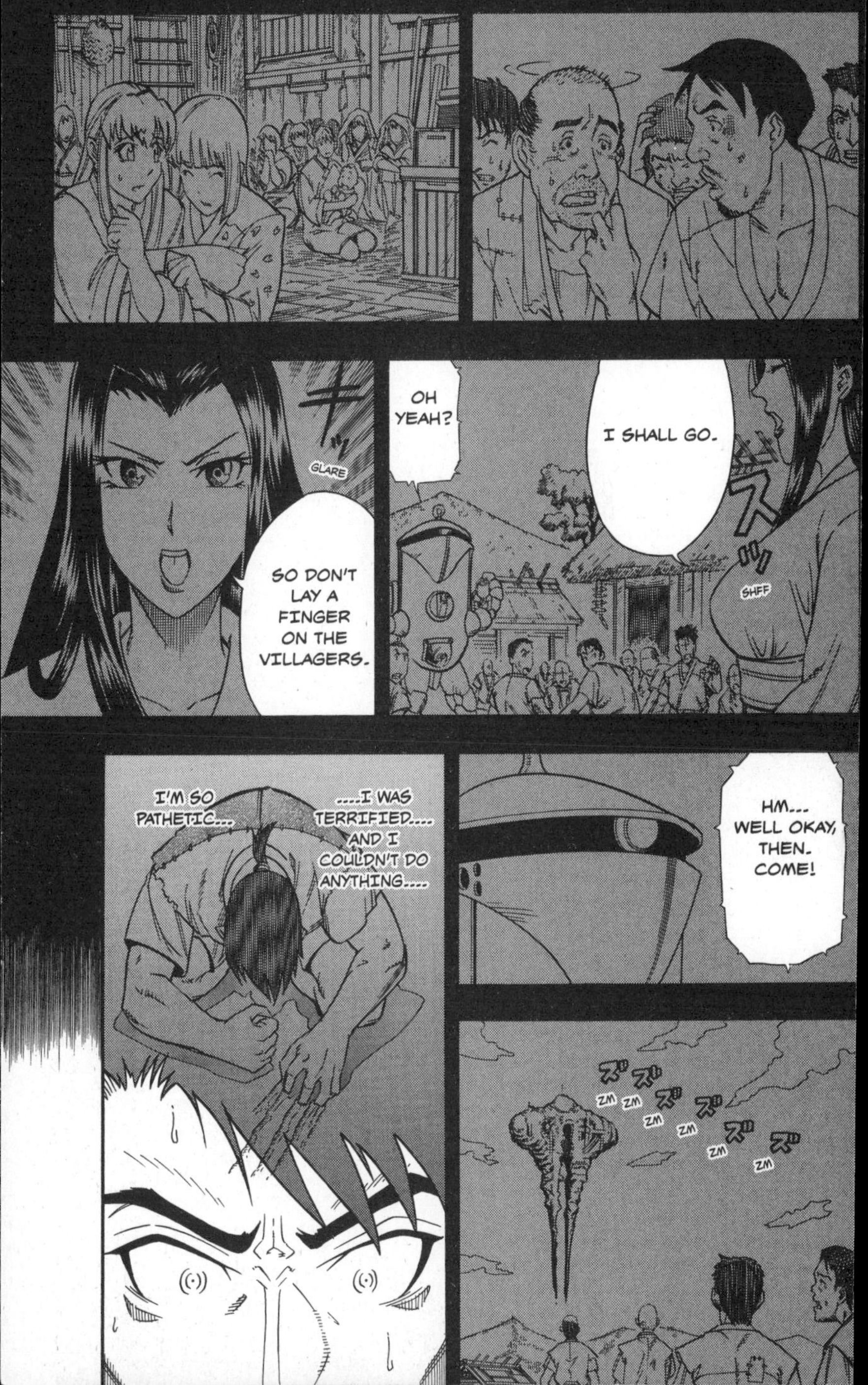
I SHALL GO.
SHFF
OH YEAH?
GLARE
SO DON'T LAY A FINGER ON THE VILLAGERS.
HM... WELL OKAY, THEN. COME!
ZM ZM ZM ZM ZM ZM
....I WAS TERRIFIED.... AND I COULDN'T DO ANYTHING....
I'M SO PATHETIC...

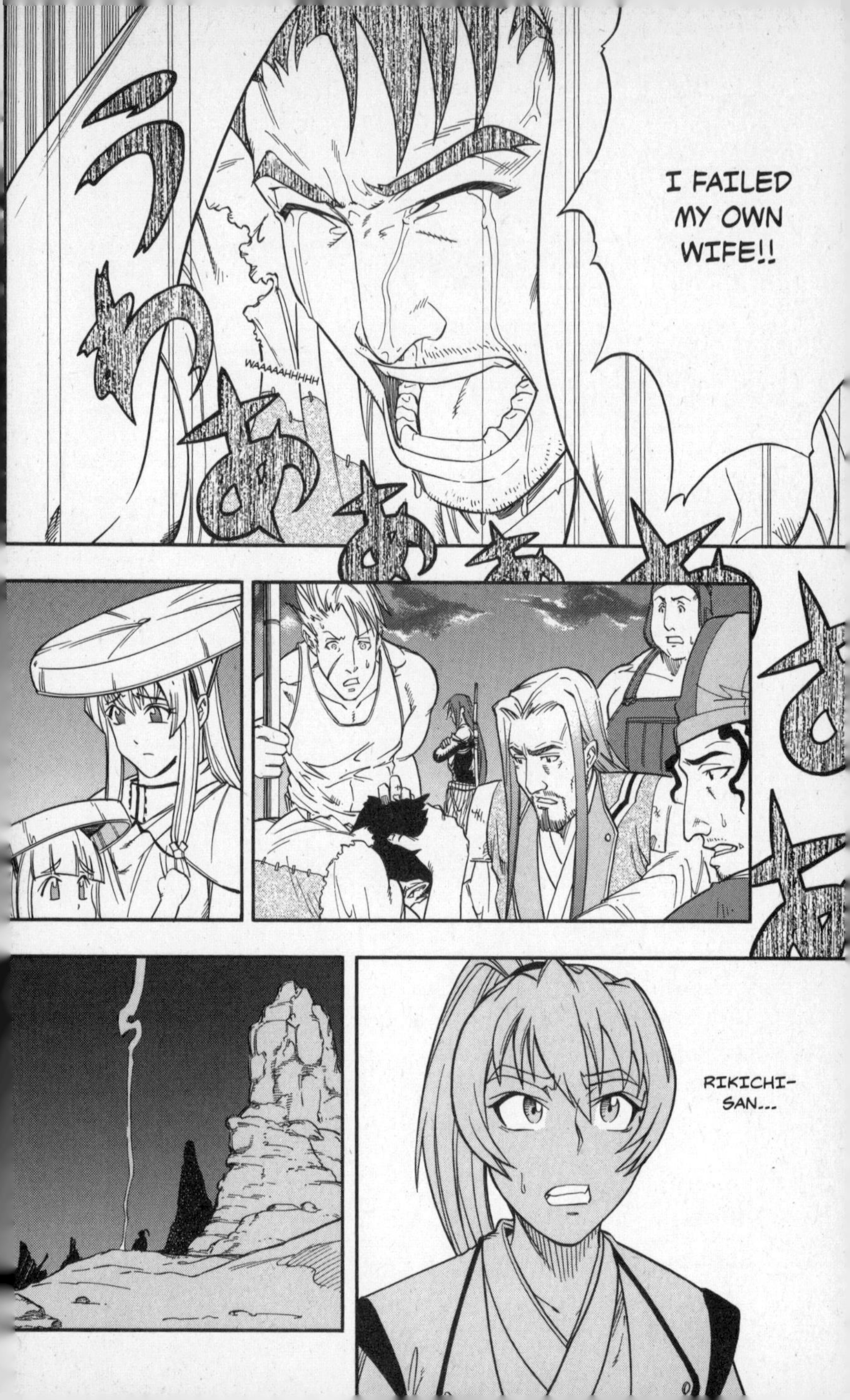
I FAILED MY OWN WIFE!!
WAAAAAHHHHH
RIKICHI-SAN...

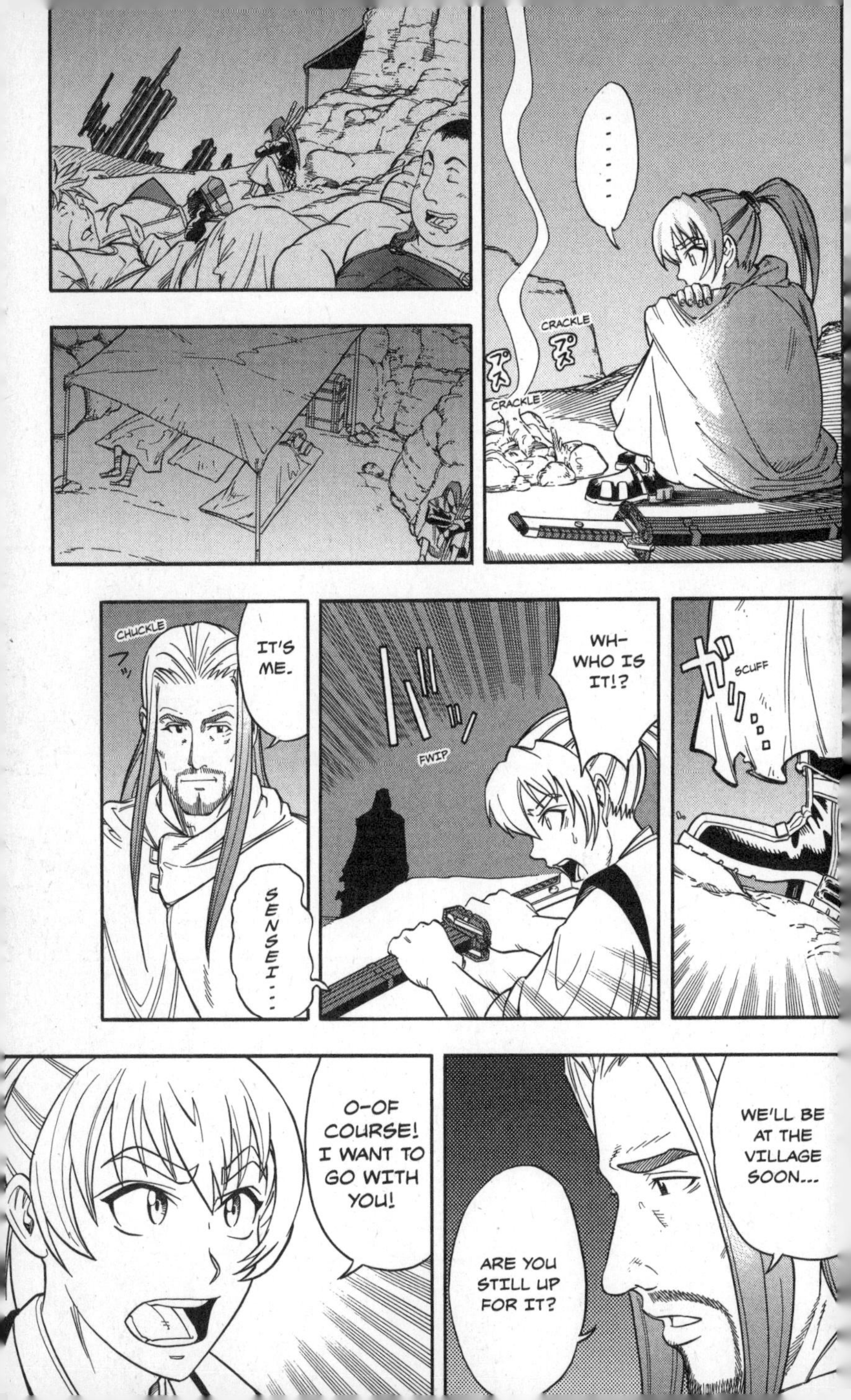
......
CRACKLE
プス
CRACKLE
プス
SCUFF
WH- WHO IS IT!?
FWIP
IT'S ME.
CHUCKLE
SENSEI...
WE'LL BE AT THE VILLAGE SOON...
ARE YOU STILL UP FOR IT?
O-OF COURSE! I WANT TO GO WITH YOU!

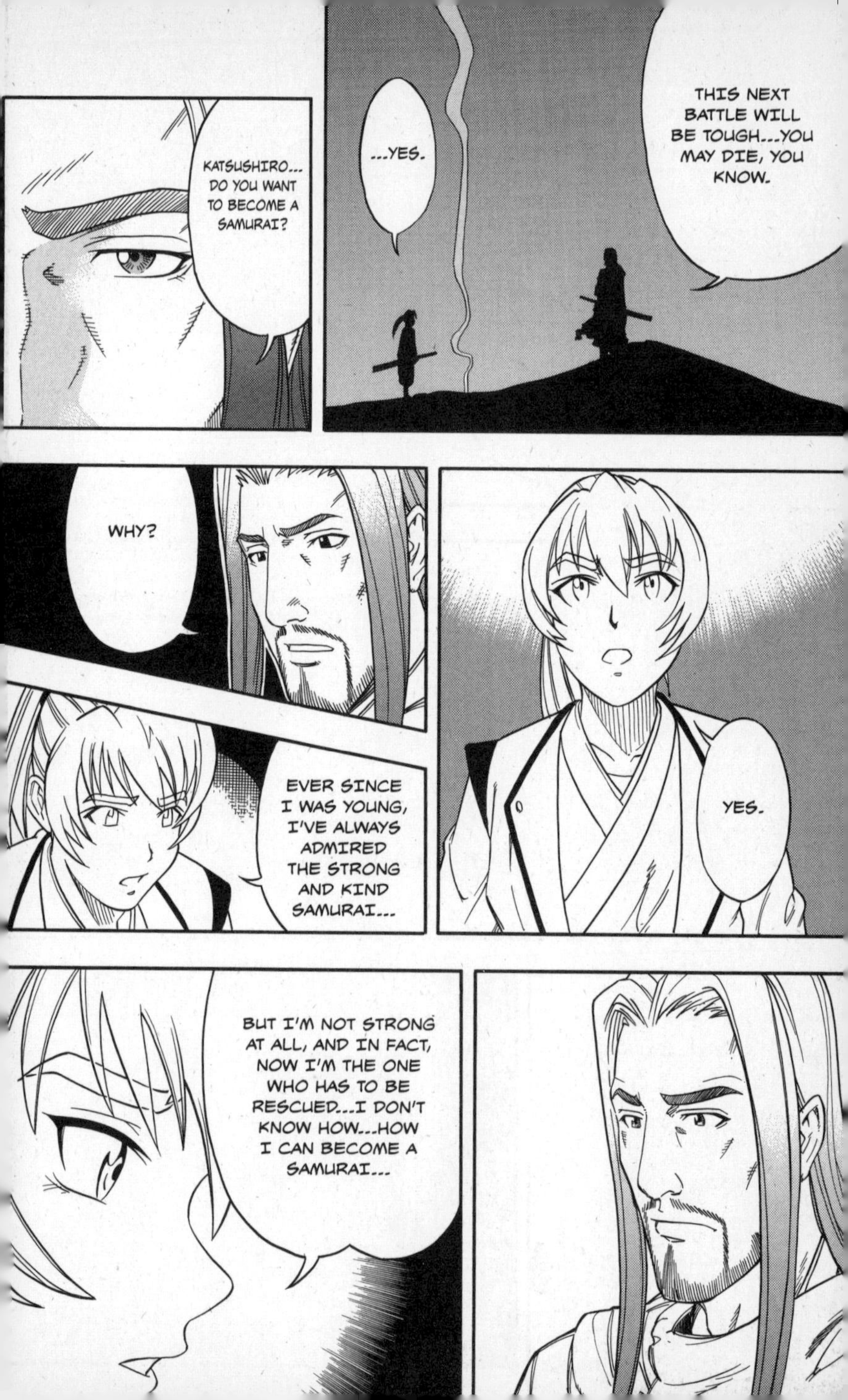
THIS NEXT BATTLE WILL BE TOUGH...YOU MAY DIE, YOU KNOW.
...YES.
KATSUSHIRO... DO YOU WANT TO BECOME A SAMURAI?
YES.
WHY?
EVER SINCE I WAS YOUNG, I'VE ALWAYS ADMIRED THE STRONG AND KIND SAMURAI...
BUT I'M NOT STRONG AT ALL, AND IN FACT, NOW I'M THE ONE WHO HAS TO BE RESCUED...I DON'T KNOW HOW...HOW I CAN BECOME A SAMURAI...

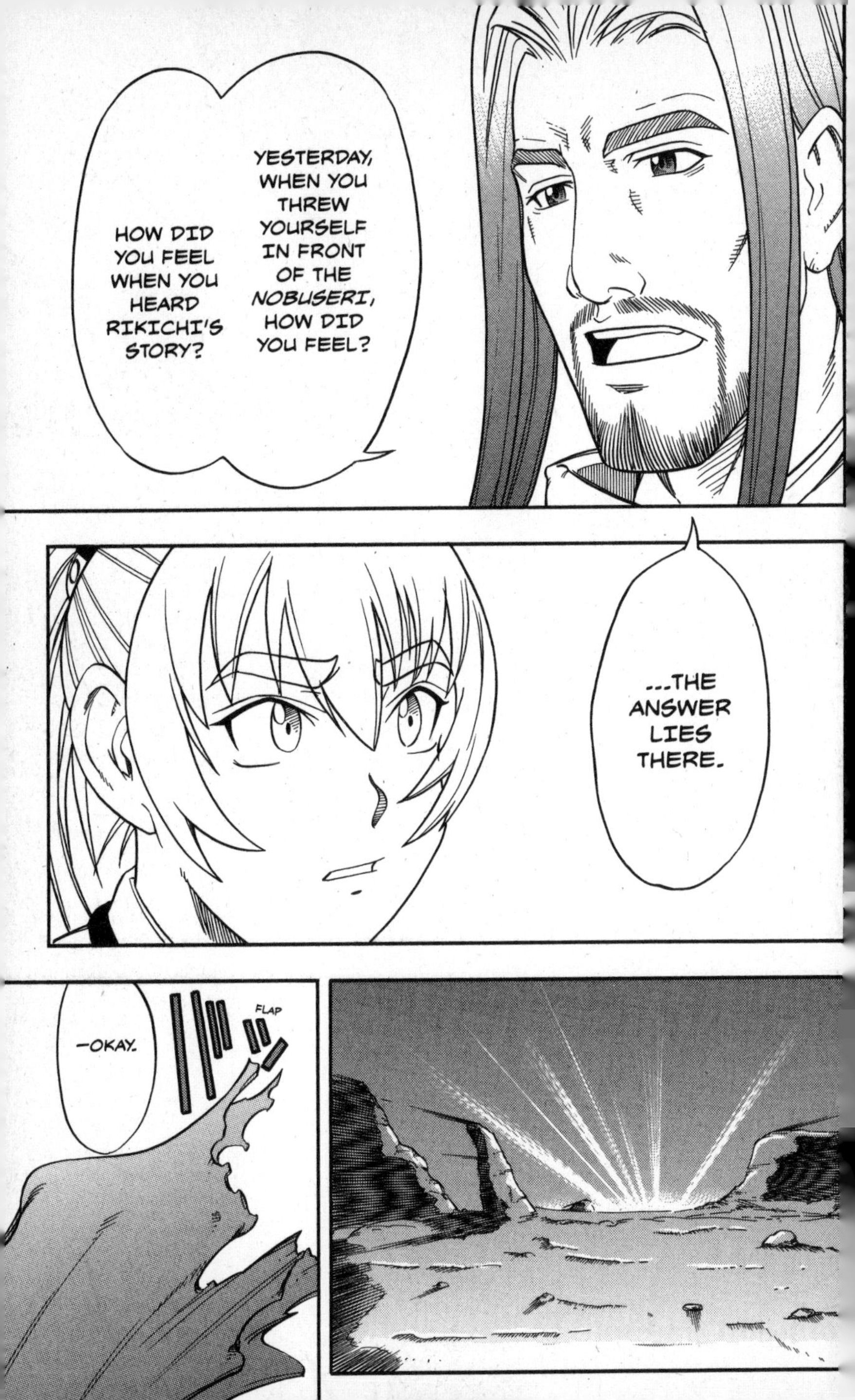
YESTERDAY, WHEN YOU THREW YOURSELF IN FRONT OF THE *NOBUSERI*, HOW DID YOU FEEL?
HOW DID YOU FEEL WHEN YOU HEARD RIKICHI'S STORY?
...THE ANSWER LIES THERE.
FLAP
—OKAY.

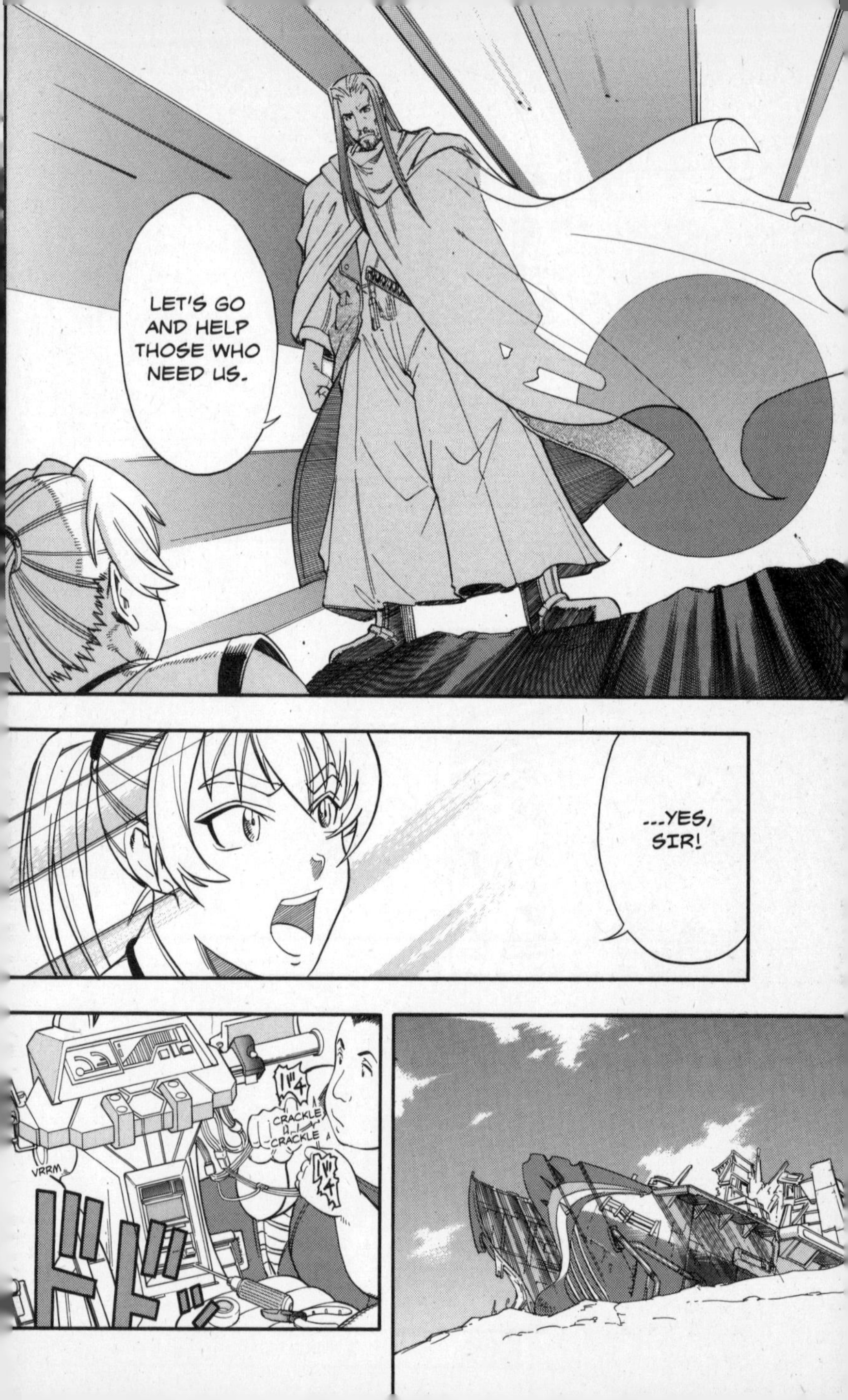
LET'S GO AND HELP THOSE WHO NEED US.
...YES, SIR!
CRACKLE
CRACKLE
VRRM

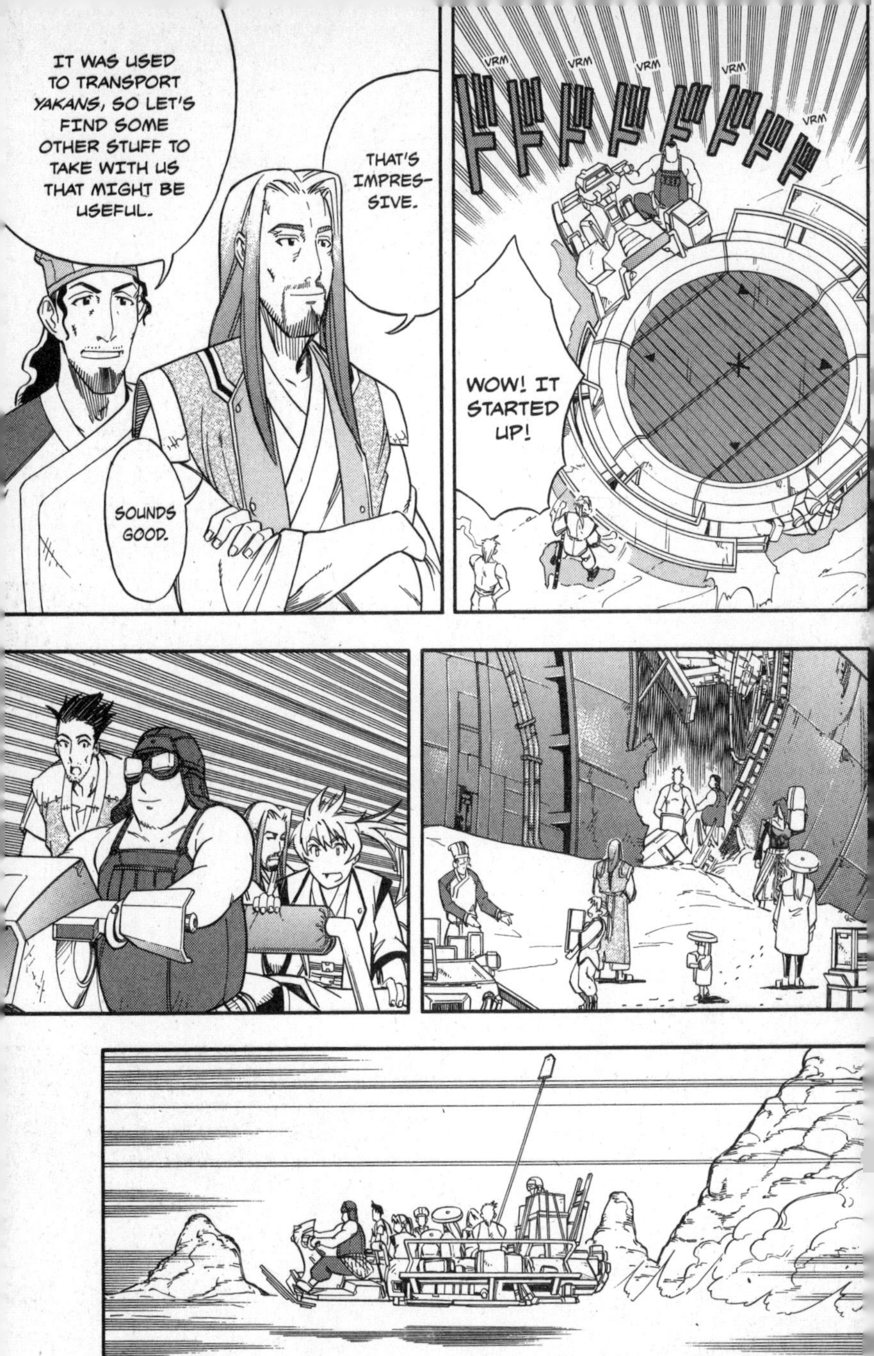
VRM
VRM
VRM
VRM
VRM
WOW! IT STARTED UP!
THAT'S IMPRES-SIVE.
IT WAS USED TO TRANSPORT YAKANS, SO LET'S FIND SOME OTHER STUFF TO TAKE WITH US THAT MIGHT BE USEFUL.
SOUNDS GOOD.

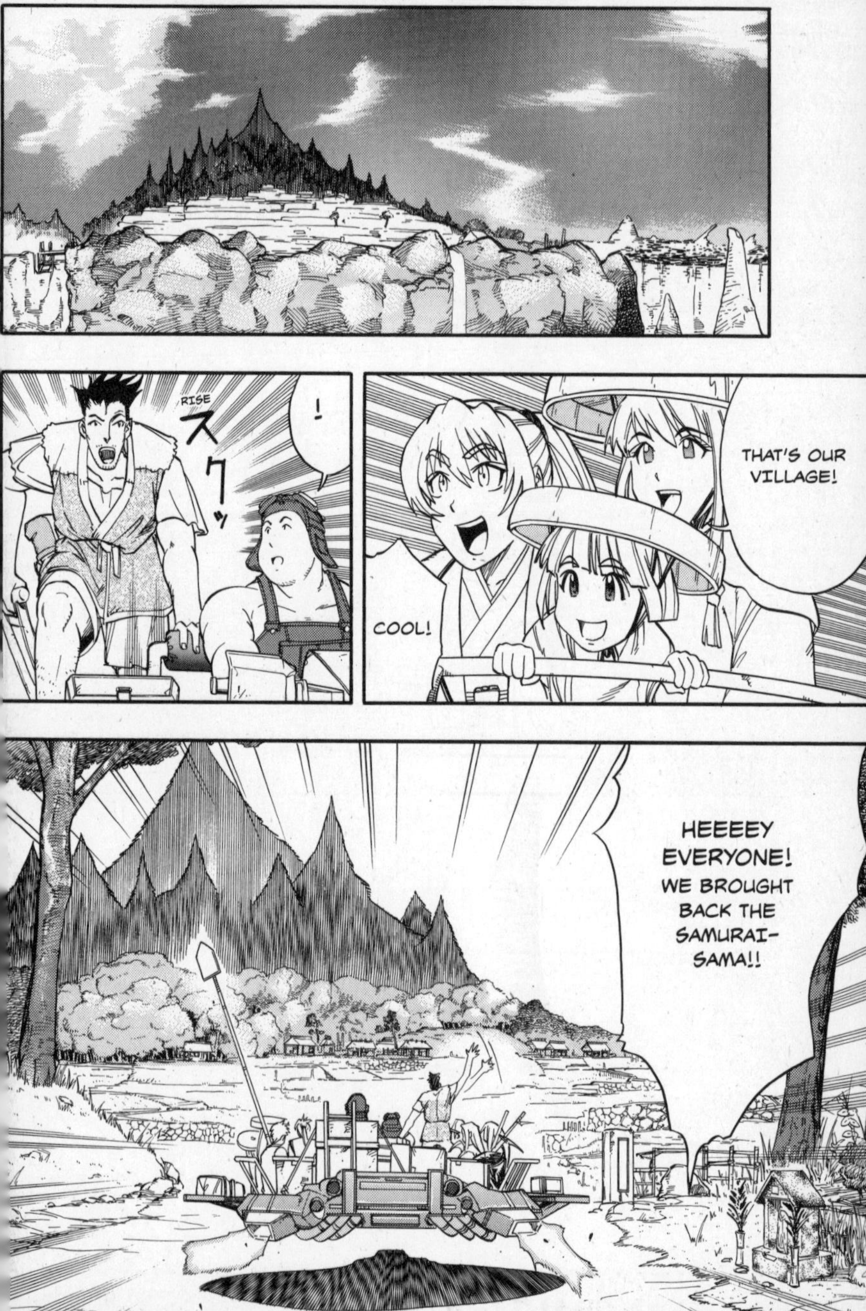
THAT'S OUR VILLAGE!
COOL!
!
RISE
スクッ
HEEEEY EVERYONE! WE BROUGHT BACK THE SAMURAI-SAMA!!

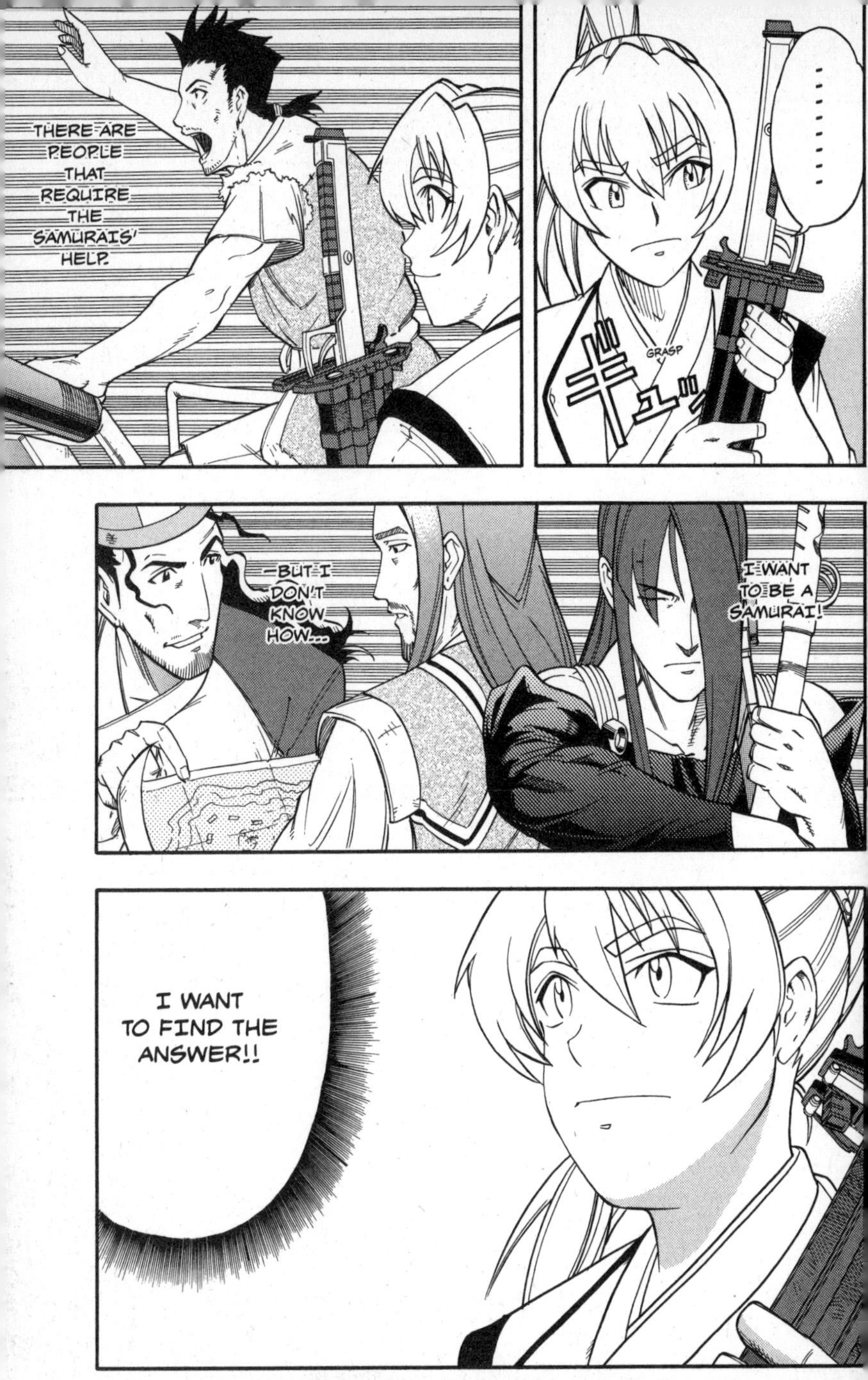
......
GRASP
ギュッ
THERE ARE PEOPLE THAT REQUIRE THE SAMURAIS' HELP.
I WANT TO BE A SAMURAI!
—BUT I DON'T KNOW HOW...
I WANT TO FIND THE ANSWER!!

SAMURAI 7 to be continued in volume 2

TRANSLATION NOTES

Japanese is a tricky language for most Westerners, and translation is often more an art than a science. For your edification and reading pleasure, here are notes on some of the places where we could have gone in a different direction, or where a Japanese cultural reference is used.

Based on the film *The Seven Samurai*, book cover & page 1

This manga is based on a 1954 Japanese film entitled *The Seven Samurai* or *Shichinin no Samurai*, which was co-written, edited, and directed by Akira Kurosawa and described as one of the greatest and most influential films ever made. Although the manga incorporates several futuristic elements, the plot still follows that of the original film fairly closely, and you will recognize several of the characters' names, that have been taken from the film.

***Kanzashi*, page 20**

A *kanzashi* is a hair ornament that is used in traditional Japanese hairstyles. Katsushiro is complimenting the girl's hair ornament to try to flirt with her.

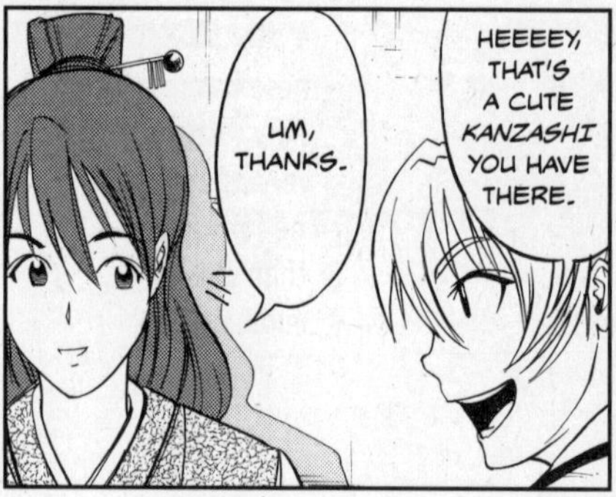
HEEEEY, THAT'S A CUTE KANZASHI YOU HAVE THERE.
UM, THANKS.

***Ronin*, page 21**

Ronin refers to "masterless samurai," in other words, poor samurai who have no work. During the war period, these people had plenty of work as samurai serving the *daimyo*, or the military lords. However, after the war ended, the samurai, who had lost the war and were now poor and jobless, became *ronin* and were looked down upon.

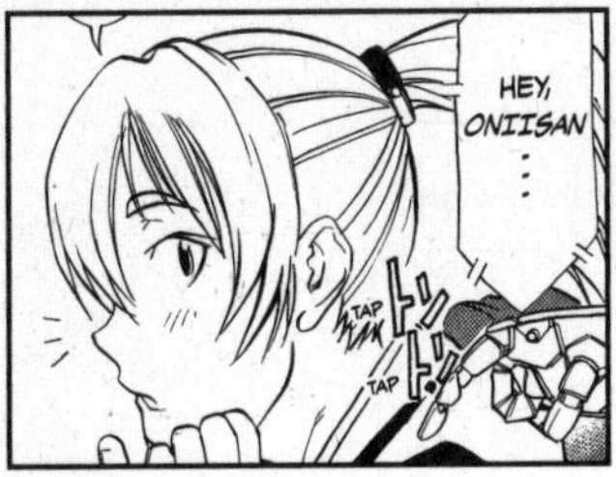
HEY, ONIISAN
...
TAP
TAP

Oniisan, page 23

Oniisan means older brother, and is the more formal version of *oniichan*, which is usually what younger siblings call their older brothers. However, the term is also used by people to refer to a young man.

Kichinyado, page 25

A *Kichinyado* refers to a very cheap inn for travelers that was seen along the roads before the Edo period (1603–1867) in Japan. Travelers had to cook for themselves, and often even had to provide their own bedding. The word is made up of "*kichin*," which means "the cost for wood," and "*yado*," which means accommodation, as the price for a night was often equivalent to the cost of the wood which the travelers used as fuel to cook with.

Kyaa, page 27

Kyaa is a girlish shriek, and you may see this being used in Japanese manga, anime, and films by girls and women from time to time.

Katushiro-sama, page 30/ Rikichi-san, page 33/ Kambei-dono, page 121

As you may know, Japanese has many honorifics, which are attached to the end of a person's name to show respect to that person. The most common honorific is *-san* which you'll hear very often when you listen to Japanese people talking to one another. *-Sama* is the formal version of *-san* and is used to address people who are higher in rank than oneself. *-Dono* roughly means master or lord, and its use is archaic or old-fashioned. It shows slightly more respect than *-sama*.

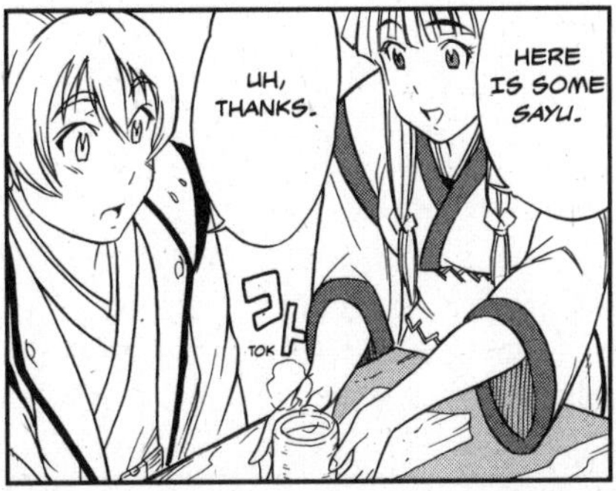
HERE IS SOME SAYU.
UH, THANKS.
TOK

Sayu, page 32

Sayu is basically hot water for drinking purposes, served as an alternative to tea, which was expensive.

Mikumari-sama, page 33

Kirara is a *mikumari,* or water maiden. She has a special crystal on a necklace that allows her to detect the flow of water underground. The villagers call her *Mikumari-sama,* with *-sama* as the honorific suffix, as a sign of respect.

***Jisama*, page 40**

Jisama is a provincial dialect for *Jiisama* or *Ojiisama,* which is a formal way of referring to your grandfather or a respected elderly man.

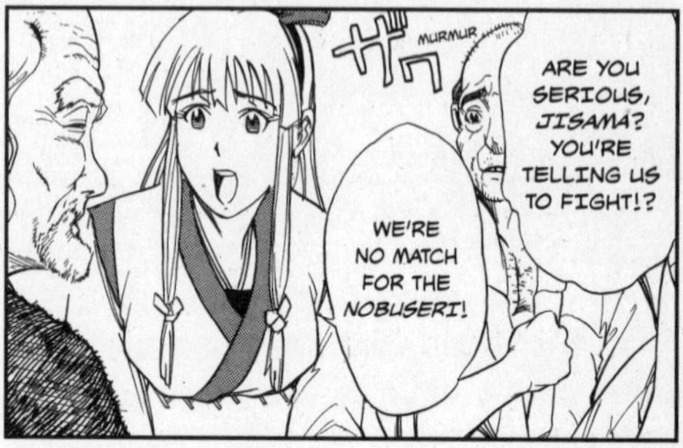
MURMUR
ARE YOU SERIOUS, JISAMA? YOU'RE TELLING US TO FIGHT!?
WE'RE NO MATCH FOR THE NOBUSERI!

"Sheaves of rice will bow their heads," page 43

When the rice is ripe, the rice plant will bow its head, signaling that it is ready for harvest. Jisama warns Kirara and Rikichi to bring back the samurai before the sheaves of rice bow their heads, because he knows that the *nobuseri* will be back when the rice is ripe.

***Neesama*, page 46**

Neesama (or *Oneesama*) is the formal version of *Oneesan*, which means older sister.

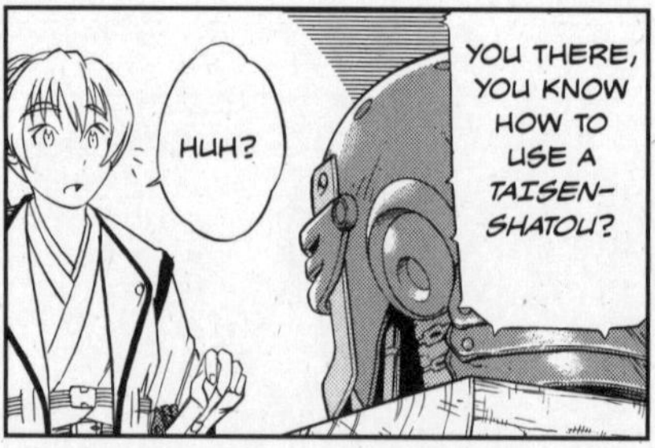
YOU THERE, YOU KNOW HOW TO USE A TAISEN-SHATOU?
HUH?

***Taisenshatou*, page 52**

The name given to this sword, *Taisenshatou*, literally means "sword that fights against tanks (*sensha*)."

Katsunoji, page 57

Katsunoji is a nickname that Kikuchiyo gives Katsushiro.

"Even a chance acquaintance is decreed by destiny...," page 62

This is a Japanese saying ("*Sode furiau mo tashou no en*") that says that if you are walking down the street and your sleeve happens to brush against a stranger's sleeve, even this is due to fate as decided in your previous life.

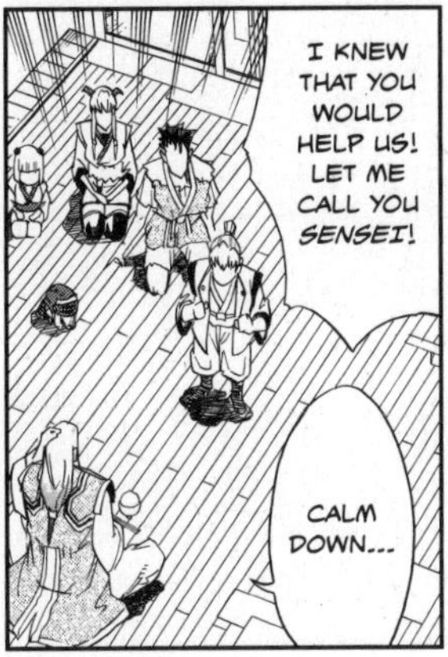
I KNEW THAT YOU WOULD HELP US! LET ME CALL YOU SENSEI!
CALM DOWN...

Sensei, page 102

You may have heard the term *sensei* used in Japanese films and manga to refer to people such as teachers and doctors. *Sensei* is used to show respect for a person who has attained mastery in an art form or some other skill. Katsushiro asks Kambei if he can call him *sensei* because he respects him and sees him as his master.

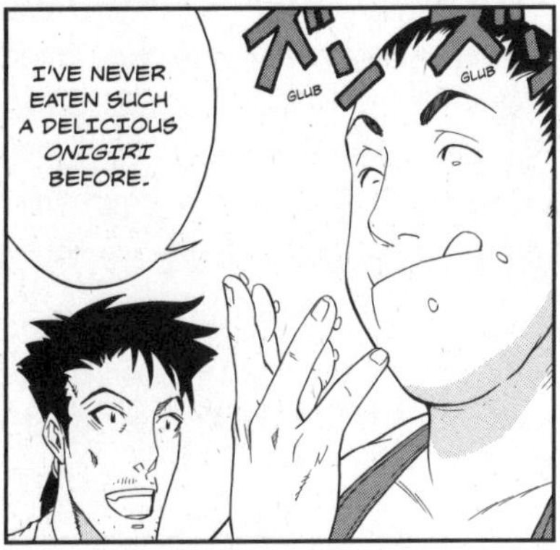
GLUB
GLUB
I'VE NEVER EATEN SUCH A DELICIOUS ONIGIRI BEFORE.

***Onigiri*, page 118**

Onigiri is a rice ball, often formed into a triangle or an oval shape and wrapped with *nori* (dried seaweed). It can be filled with ingredients, such as pickles or salmon, or eaten plain.

***Tenkuurappazan!!*, page 120**

Tenkuurappazan is the name that Katsushiro gives his ultimate move; literally, it means "Sword blade falling from the heavens."

***Ryo*, page 129**

Ryo was a monetary unit used in the Edo period (1603–1867) in Japan. It is difficult to say exactly how much 1 *ryo* would be worth in today's currency, but it has been estimated to be around 60,000 yen (or $600). Using this estimate, the reward for 100 *ryo* offered by Katsushiro's father would be around 6,000,000 yen (or $60,000), which is a huge sum of money.

Yobimizu, page 134

Yobimizu literally means "water that calls," referring to water such as that used to prime a pump and therefore produce more water. When Gorobei said that perhaps Katsushiro was the *yobimizu*, he was saying that perhaps Katsushiro was the force that attracted the samurai to them.

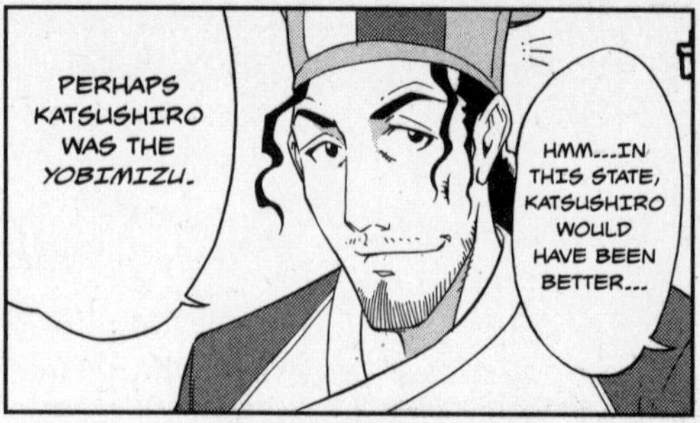
HMM...IN THIS STATE, KATSUSHIRO WOULD HAVE BEEN BETTER...
PERHAPS KATSUSHIRO WAS THE YOBIMIZU.

"Mango, ice cream, orange, egg," page 154/ _shiritori_, page 155

Here, the characters are playing a Japanese word game called *shiritori*, which literally means "taking the bottom." In this game, the players are required to say a word that begins with the last *kana* (syllable) of the previous word. The player who says a word ending in the *kana* "N" loses the game, as there is no word that begins with that letter, and thus the game cannot continue. There are optional and advanced rules that can be used, such as only playing with words of a certain genre (such as food) or using the last two *kana* of a word.

10 _ri_, page 154

A *ri* is a measure of distance used in China and ancient Japan. The distance of one *ri* differs in China and in Japan. In Japan, one *ri* is equivalent to about 4 km, so when Rikichi says that there are about 10 *ri* to go, this refers to a distance of about 40 km.

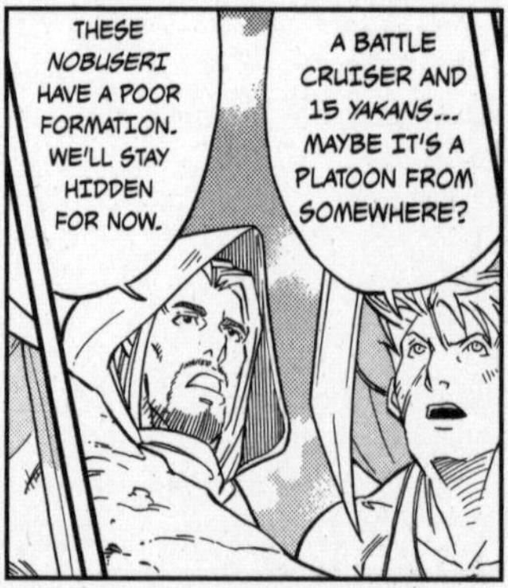
A BATTLE CRUISER AND 15 YAKANS... MAYBE IT'S A PLATOON FROM SOMEWHERE?
THESE NOBUSERI HAVE A POOR FORMATION. WE'LL STAY HIDDEN FOR NOW.

Yakan, page 157

Yakan literally means a kettle in Japanese, and the *Yakans* in the story are probably given this name because they resemble kettles in appearance.

PREVIEW OF VOLUME 2

We're pleased to present you a preview from volume 2. Please check our website (www.delreymanga.com) to see when this volume will be available in English. For now you'll have to make do with Japanese!

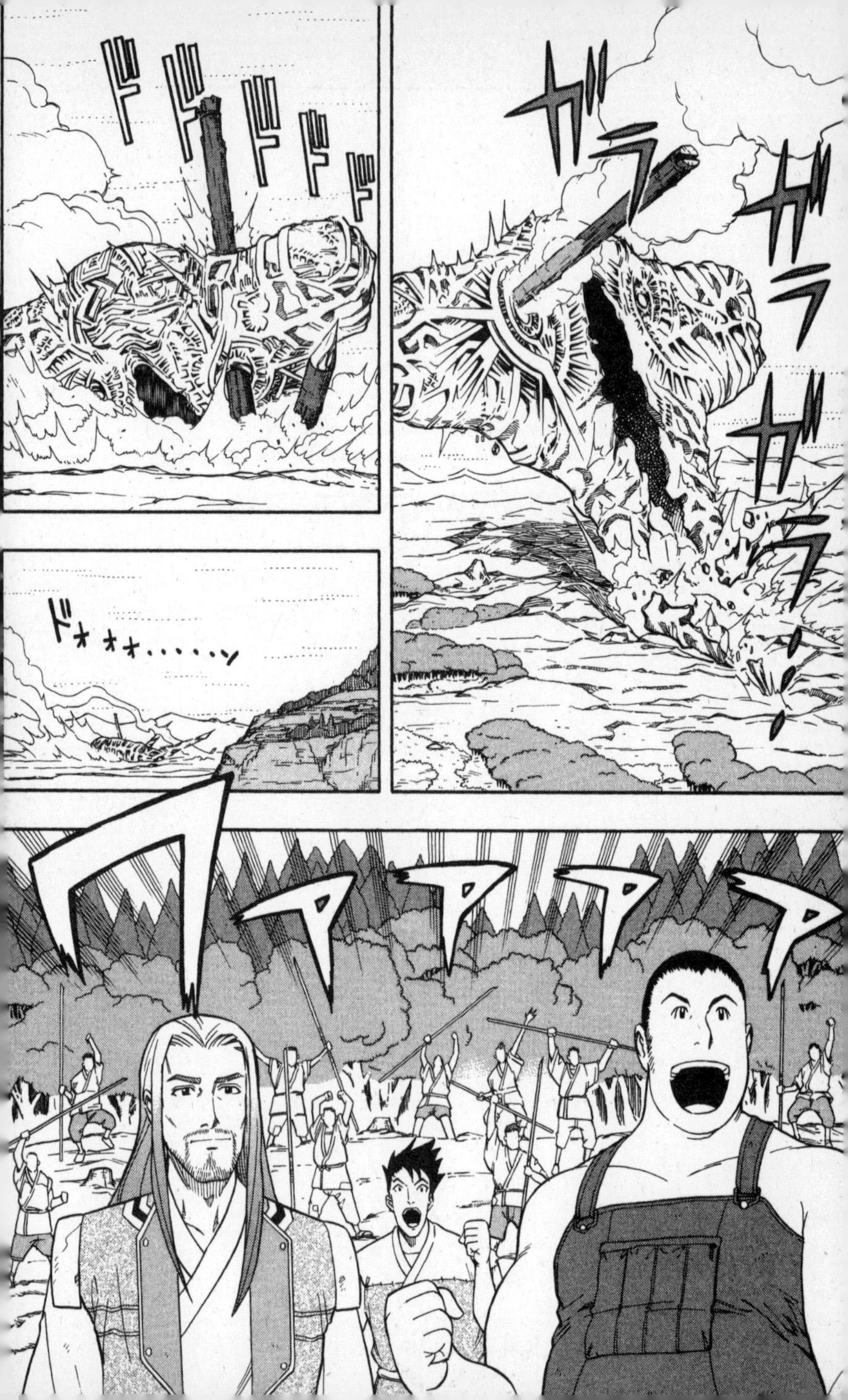
ガラ
ガラガラーッ
ドドドドドド
ドォォ……ッ
ワアアアア

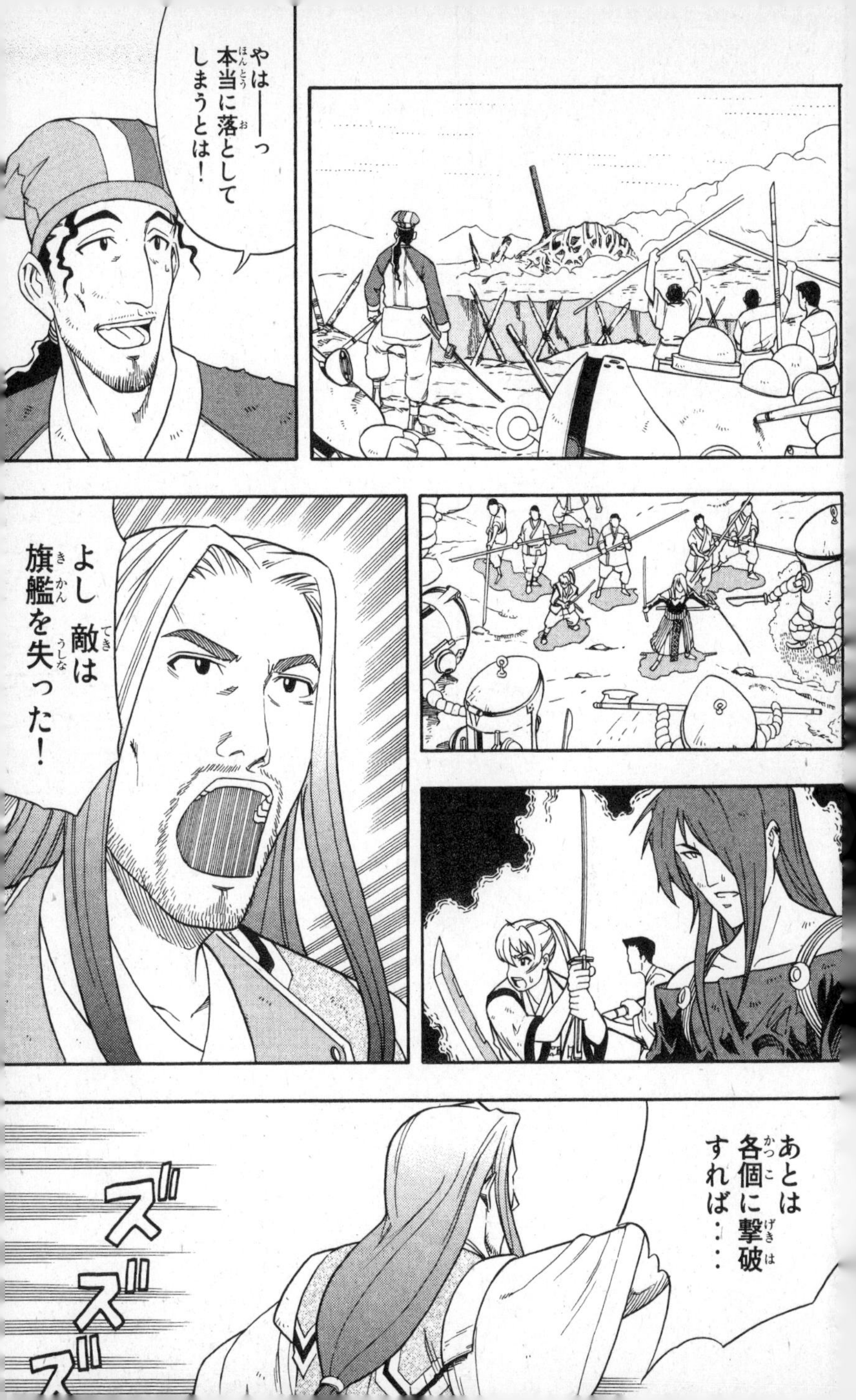
やは――っ本当に落としてしまうとは！
よし 敵は旗艦を失った！
あとは各個に撃破すれば・・・
ズズズ

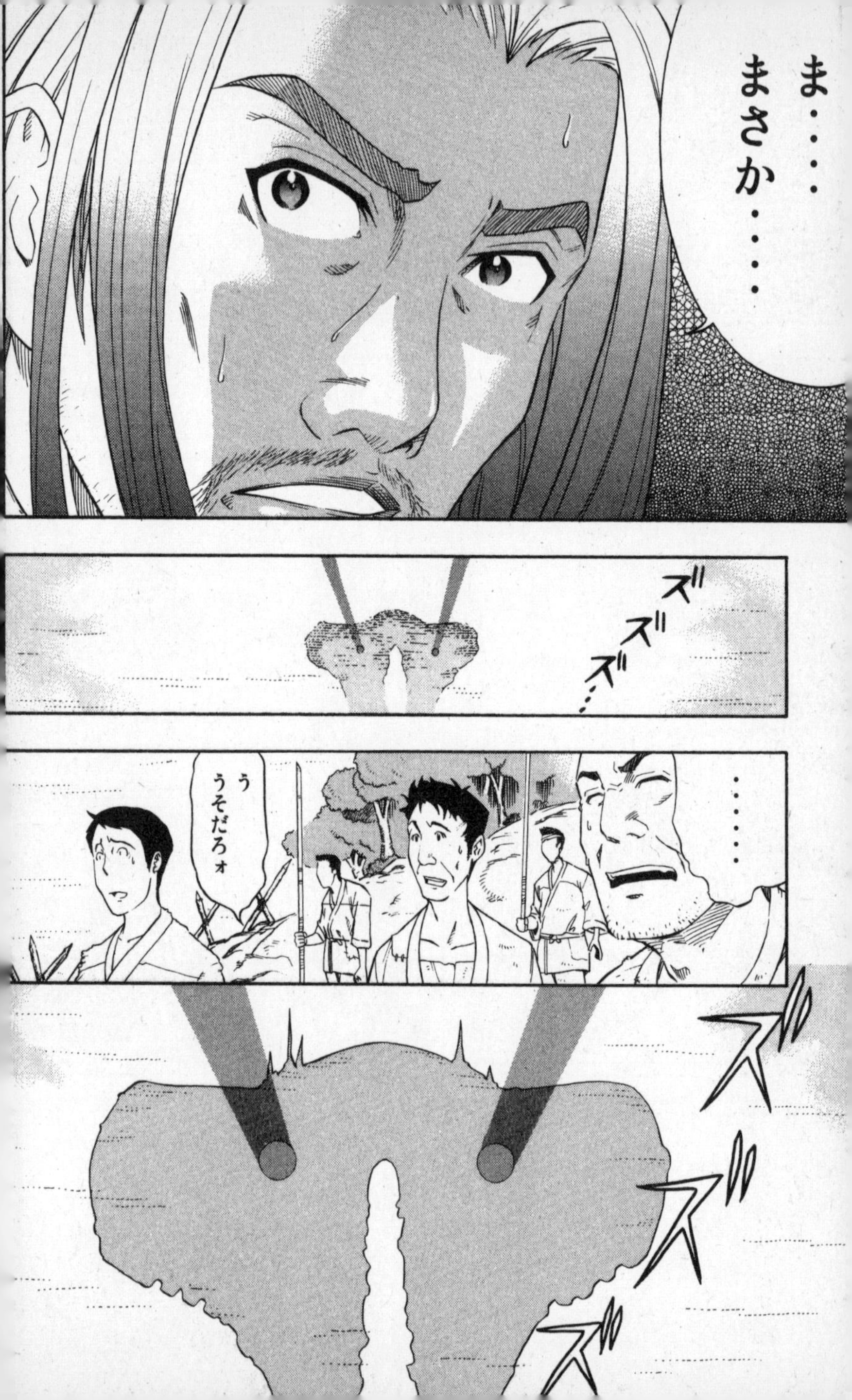

ま・・・
まさか・・・・
ズズズ・・・
・・・・・・
う
うそだろォ
ズズズズ

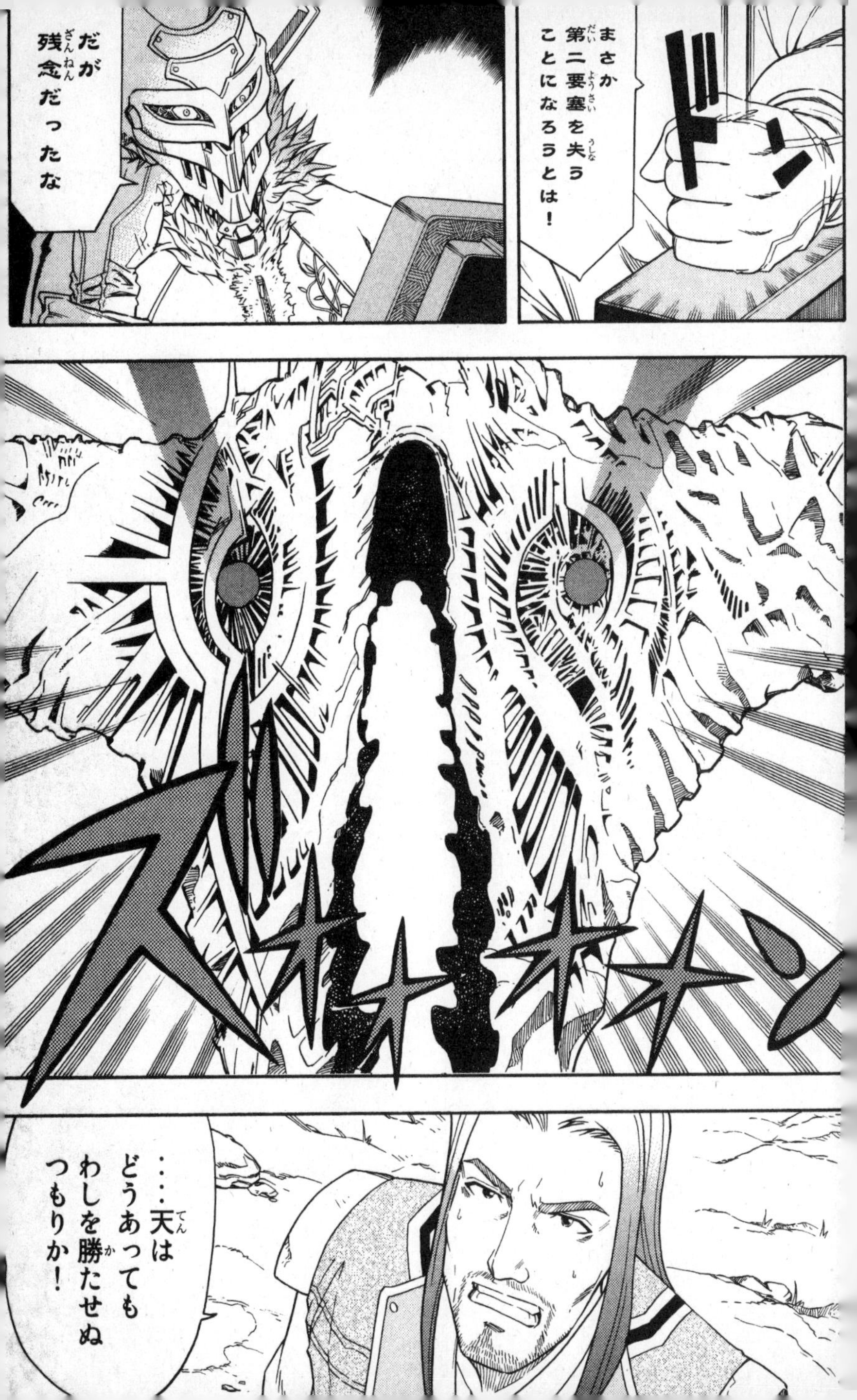
まさか第二要塞を失うことになろうとは!
ドン
だが残念だったな
・・・天はどうあってもわしを勝たせぬつもりか!

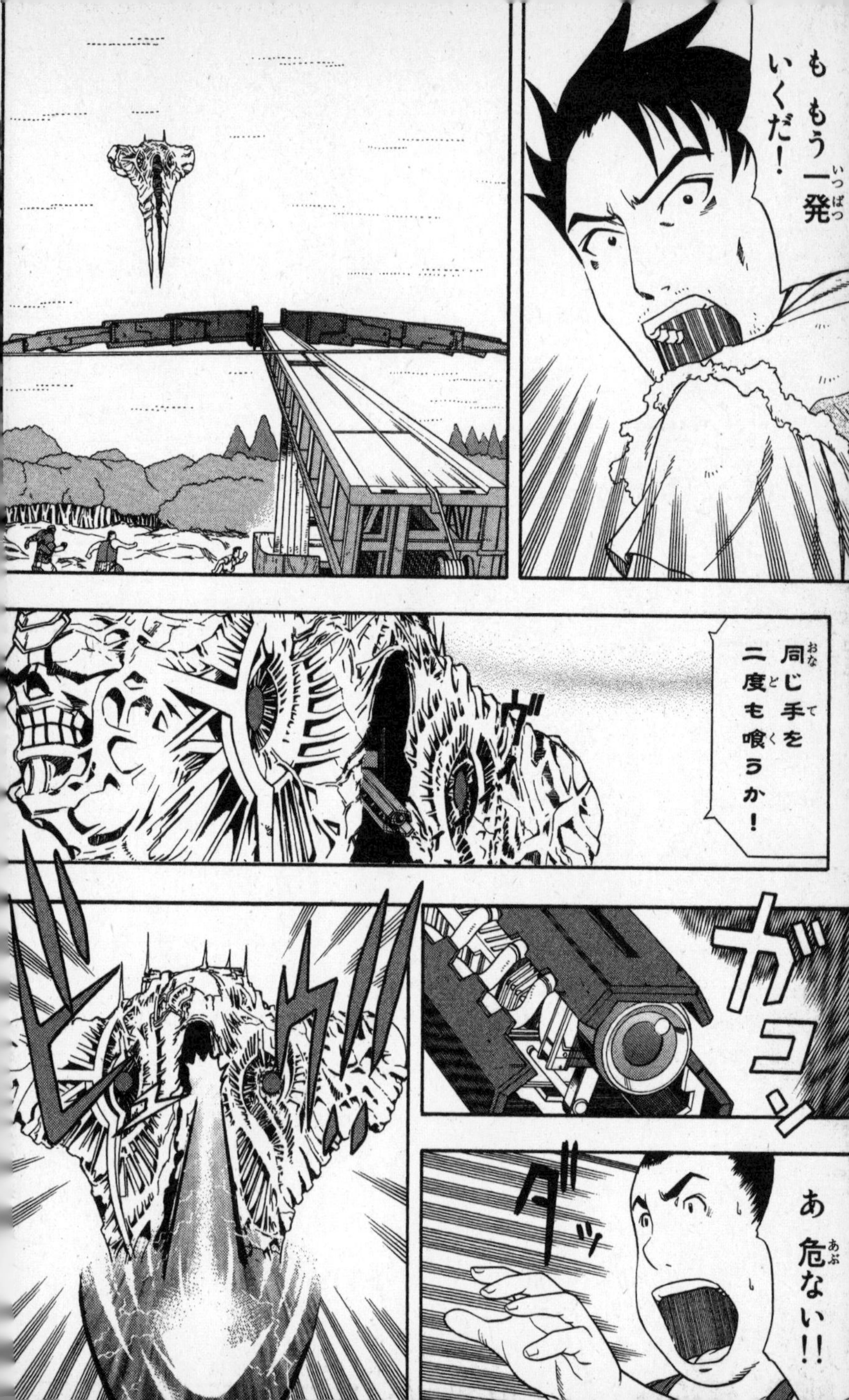
も もう一発いくだ!
同じ手を二度も喰うか!
ヴ
ガコン
ダッ
あ 危ない!!

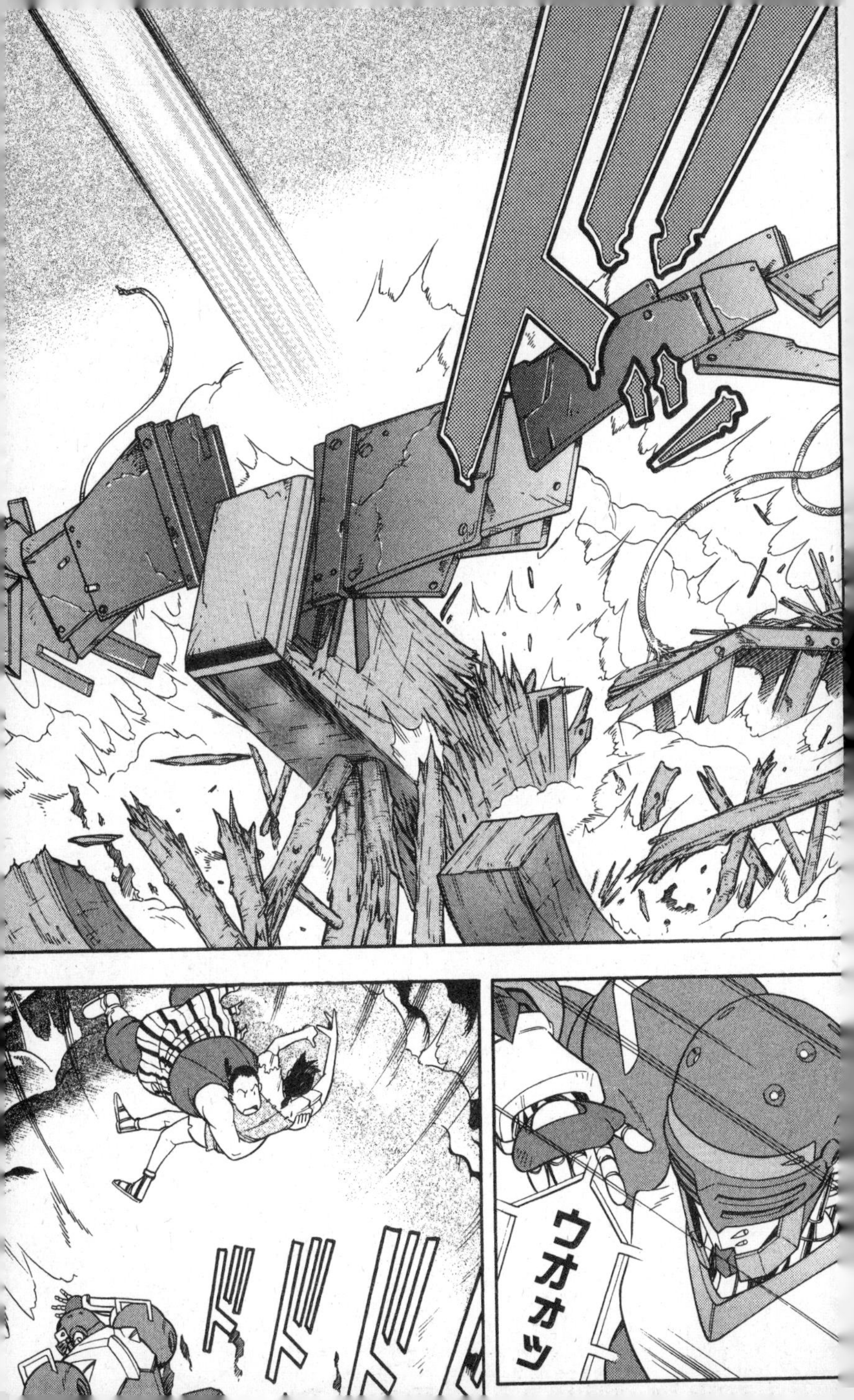
ウオオッ
ドドド

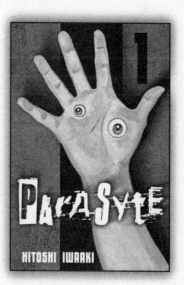

Le Chevalier d'Eon

STORY BY TOU UBUKATA
MANGA BY KIRIKO YUMEJI

DARKNESS FALLS ON PARIS

A mysterious cult is sacrificing beautiful young women to a demonic force that threatens the entire country. Only one man can save Paris from chaos and terror, the king's top secret agent: The Chevalier d'Eon.

- **Available on DVD from ADV Films.**

Le Chevalier d'Eon I
Story by TOU UBUKATA
Manga by KIRIKO YUMEJI

Special extras in each volume! Read them all!

VISIT WWW.DELREYMANGA.COM TO:
- Read sample pages
- View release date calendars for upcoming volumes
- Sign up for Del Rey's free manga e-newsletter
- Find out the latest about new Del Rey Manga series

RATING OT AGES 16+

DEL REY MANGA デルレイ
The Otaku's Choice™

Psycho Busters

MANGA BY AKINARI NAO
STORY BY YUYA AOKI

PSYCHIC TEENS ON THE RUN!

Out of the blue, a beautiful girl asks Kakeru to run away with her. This could be any boy's dream come true, but there's something strange afoot.

It turns out that this girl is on the run from a shadowy government organization intent on using her psychic abilities for its own nefarious ends. But why does she need Kakeru's help? Could it be that he has secret powers, too?

• Story by Yuya Aoki, creator of *Get Backers*

Special extras in each volume! Read them all!

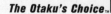

TO STOP!

[STOP!]

You are going the wrong way!

Manga is a completely different type of reading experience.

To start at the *beginning,* go to the *end*!

That's right! Authentic manga is read the traditional Japanese way—from right to left, exactly the *opposite* of how American books are read. It's easy to follow: Just go to the other end of the book, and read each page—and each panel—from right side to left side, starting at the top right. Now you're experiencing manga as it was meant to be.